I0307569

Praise for *Brothers from Afar: Rabbinic Approaches to Apostasy and Reversion in Medieval Europe*

"Drawing on previously unknown manuscript sources and the vast literature of Jewish law, *Brothers from Afar* offers readers a pathbreaking reassessment of the much-debated subject of apostasy. In this work of superb scholarship, Ephraim Kanarfogel reveals the inner workings of medieval Jewish public policy and the wider implications for Jewish-Christian relations in the Middle Ages and beyond."

—Jay R. Berkovitz, distinguished professor (emeritus) of Judaic and Near Eastern Studies, University of Massachusetts Amherst

"Who was a Jew in the Middle Ages? *Brothers from Afar* illuminates the complexities at the intersection of Jewish law and medieval Jewish identity, conversion and gender, Ashkenaz and Sepharad. Kanarfogel's penetrating scholarship contributes an important new chapter to the historical development of halakhah."

—Elisheva Carlebach, Salo Wittmayer Baron Professor of Jewish History, Culture, and Society, Columbia University

"An erudite and richly documented study of how medieval European rabbis required reverting apostate Jews to undergo a range of rites of passage to return to the fold. It revises the approach of the late Jacob Katz, who claimed that this process occurred only in early modern times. Precisely because of their social proximity to Christians, medieval Jews needed boundary markers to reassure themselves that returning apostates could be trusted again. A masterful contribution to the social contexts of Jewish legal history that dazzles on every page."

—Ivan G. Marcus, Frederick P. Rose Professor of Jewish History, Yale University

"This learned study is essential reading for those interested in the history of Jewish apostasy and reversion to Judaism. Its meticulous analysis of manuscript evidence fundamentally reorients understandings of the attitudes of medieval rabbinic authorities toward apostasy, opening new avenues for research in medieval Jewish-Christian relations."

—Paola Tartakoff, professor of history and
Jewish studies at Rutgers University

"Through extraordinary industriousness, Kanarfogel has unearthed a gold mine of material buried in medieval Hebrew manuscripts that sheds a whole new light on the place of repentant apostates in medieval Jewish societies and Jewish consciousness over the course of five centuries."

—Edward Fram, Solly Yellin Chair of Lithuanian and Eastern
European Jewry, Ben-Gurion University of the Negev

BROTHERS *from* AFAR

BROTHERS *from* AFAR

Rabbinic Approaches to Apostasy and Reversion in Medieval Europe

EPHRAIM KANARFOGEL

Wayne State University Press
Detroit

ISBN 978-0-8143-4028-8 (hardback); ISBN 978-0-8143-4029-5 (ebook)

Library of Congress Control Number: 2020944302

Wayne State University Press
Leonard N. Simons Building
4809 Woodward Avenue
Detroit, Michigan 48201-1309

Visit us online at wsupress.wayne.edu

לז״נ

אבי מורי ואמי מורתי ע״ה

ומרת הינדא לאה ע״ה בת ר׳ מנחם מענדל הי״ו

CONTENTS

Preface and Acknowledgments ix

1. Assessing the Ashkenazic Context 1
2. Establishing Boundaries: Immersion, Repentance, Verification 27
3. The Effectiveness of Marriage and Participation in *Ḥaliẓah* 67
4. Economic Issues and the Implications for Other Areas of Jewish Law: Money-Lending at Interest 103
5. Between Jews and Christians: Doctrinal and Societal Changes 137
6. Reverting Apostates in Christian Spain: Sources and Strategies 165
7. The Responsa and Rulings of Israel Isserlein and His Contemporaries 195

Conclusion 213

Appendix: Rabbinic Scholars in Europe during the High Middle Ages 221

Index of Manuscript References 223

Index of Subjects and Names 227

PREFACE AND ACKNOWLEDGMENTS

The genesis of this book goes back to an invitation to speak at a conference held in 2005 at the Center for Jewish History in New York City, on the larger theme of Jewish-Christian relations in the medieval and early modern periods. In discussing possible paper topics with one of the conveners, my friend and colleague Professor Elisheva Carlebach of Columbia University, I mentioned that I had recently come across a published passage attributed to the German Tosafist Simḥah of Speyer (d. c. 1230), in which he suggests that reverting apostates must undergo a ritual immersion at the time of their return.

This struck me as rather unusual, in light of the strongly held and well-known thesis of my *doctorvater*, the late Professor Jacob Katz of the Hebrew University of Jerusalem. Professor Katz maintained (in *Exclusiveness and Tolerance*, which first appeared in 1961, and in other publications from around the same time) that those who apostatized and later returned to the Jewish community during the medieval period in northern Europe were encouraged by rabbinic authorities, following Rashi's adaptation of the talmudic phrase, *ʾaf ʿal pi she-ḥata Yisraʾel hu* (a Jew, even if has sinned grievously, remains a Jew), to once again take their places within the community without the need for any special ceremony or act that signified or verified the genuineness of their reversion. Moreover, while reading through medieval Jewish manuscripts for completely different topics, I had come across additional evidence which suggested that northern French Tosafists from the mid-thirteenth century also mandated this immersion, and I succeeded in locating some earlier material as well.

The published version of that paper, "Returning to the Jewish Community in Medieval Ashkenaz: History and Halakhah," appeared in 2007. From that point on, I began to gather all kinds of additional sources, mainly in manuscript but also from published texts, which seemed to support what I had initially argued, even as these materials led me in a number of new directions as well.

Another central aspect of Rashi's approach is that apostates to Christianity who had not returned to the Jewish community were still to be treated by the community as Jews. Money could not be lent to them at interest, bills of divorce that apostate husbands gave their Jewish wives were seen as fully effective, and so on, even as certain aspects of socialization were perforce discouraged. Here too, however, I came across Tosafist texts that challenged these guidelines in significant ways.

An article on these issues appeared in 2012 (in a volume that was co-edited by Professor Carlebach), and the die was cast. Although there are elements from both of these articles in the present book, the thinking and the specifics behind the larger investigation have been significantly expanded and at times modified along conceptual, geographic, and chronological lines. Professor Katz was a sensitive yet demanding *doctorvater*, who always had us carefully question our fundamental research assumptions. I asked myself why, given his tremendous gifts as a scholar, he had gone in one direction in researching these issues and I was now going in quite another. Time and time again, I came back to the same conclusion. The manuscript texts, which are barely reflected in most instances within the published texts, and the rereading of the published materials in light of what is found in manuscript, make all the difference. I firmly believe that my conclusions are correct, although the reader will be the judge.

This book is not a complete treatment of the presence of apostates (or reverting apostates) in medieval Europe by any means. Although individual apostates and their particular situations will be noted and discussed, at times in detail, this book looks at how rabbinic figures considered apostasy and reversion as phenomena about which they needed to make halakhic and even meta-halakhic rulings and judgments, and how these views developed and changed. In many ways, this is a book about the history of *halakhah* as it relates to apostasy and reversion. As was their wont, leading rabbinic scholars and halakhists tended to look beyond the confines of the specific cases and behaviors before them, to provide guidance and leadership for the Jewish community as a whole.

This book will also not offer a systematic survey of every issue involving apostasy that attracted rabbinic rulings or discussion. It is focused on the larger components and trends that underlie rabbinic thought (and practice) in these matters, as they emerge from a myriad of details. For those who may already be wondering, reversion is defined in this study simply as "to return to a previous practice or belief"—in this instance, Judaism. A more detailed outline of the chapters of the book will be provided in the course of chapter 1.

Managing all the details that are contained in the rich rabbinic texts and other types of medieval Jewish (and Christian) literature treated by this study, and identifying and defining the larger patterns that emerge, have been exhilarating and at times daunting tasks. Given what amounts to a fairly wide historical and geographic scope, across a range of topical foci, I asked a number of distinguished colleagues to read and comment on my work, and they graciously acceded to my request: Professors David Berger, Edward Fram, David Malkiel, Ivan Marcus, Marc Saperstein, and Moshe Sokolow, and Rabbi Abraham Lieberman. Needless to say, I alone am responsible for any errors that remain; but also needless to say, these experts have saved me from many errors, and have improved the final product immensely. To all of them go my deepest thanks.

I am privileged and truly blessed to serve as the E. Billi Ivry University Professor of Jewish History, Literature and Law at Yeshiva University. As always, I tried out some of my findings and arguments on my graduate students at Yeshiva's Bernard Revel Graduate School of Jewish Studies and on my honors students at Stern College for Women. And as always, both groups made a number of helpful comments about what seemed to work (and what did not), causing me to make several important changes and adjustments in the presentation of my arguments and materials.

Many thanks to Rabbi Dr. Ari Berman, president of Yeshiva University (and a fellow medievalist), for his unflagging support and interest in my work, and to Dr. Selma Botman, our current provost (and a distinguished modernist), for the same; and to Dr. Mort Lowengrub, who bestowed upon me a series of very meaningful academic appointments and honors over his nearly two decades as provost, which have made my scholarly achievements possible. Deans Karen Bacon and David Berger, good friends and colleagues both, have always done their utmost to ensure that my research and writing could be accomplished productively, and that our students in Jewish Studies, graduate and undergraduate, would have everything they needed. The staffs of the Mendel Gottesman Library at Yeshiva University in New York and the National Library of Israel in Jerusalem (and especially the Institute for Microfilmed Hebrew Manuscripts), both of which I consider my "home" libraries, have outdone themselves in providing me with necessary (and often hard to get) literary materials of all types.

My frequent research travels to Israel are always enhanced by colleagues from the Hebrew University of Jerusalem, Bar-Ilan University, and Ben-Gurion University of the Negev. They have been of great assistance over these many years in scholarship and friendship. I sorely miss several Israeli mentors: Professor Israel Ta-Shma z"l, Rav Reuven Aberman z"l, Mr. Victor Geller z"l, and Rav Binyamin Tabory z"l. Nonetheless, the meaningful friendships that I have made with my Israeli academic colleagues sustain me not only during the research trips to Israel, but as I work in the States as well. And my dear friend and colleague at Yeshiva, Professor Jeffrey Gurock, always helps to keep me grounded. I also want to mention Dr. Charles Raffel z"l, who read and commented (and advised) on much of my published work over many years. Finally, Kathy Wildfong and her talented staff at Wayne State University Press, with special thanks to Kristin Harpster, have done their usual excellent job in producing this volume, and Mindy Brown has once again provided her top-notch editorial skills.

The most important and effective personal and emotional sustenance comes of course from our family. As all the children and grandchildren know well, another new book is just the thing that Abba (and Zaide) looks for in order to deeply thank his family and to note his great pride in them. Unfortunately, we have suffered some powerful losses. My father z"l passed away seven years ago, just as my last book was in galleys, and my mother a"h passed away as this book was being completed. While I know that she and my father are looking on together and "shepping nachas" as only they can, my sister Susan and I, along with the entire family, miss them both tremendously.

A cataclysmic event for our family that I never would have expected to write about is the passing of our beloved daughter-in-law, Dr. Hindi Krinsky Kanarfogel a"h. Hindi was a truly amazing wife, mother, and daughter, an accomplished scholar, and a superb and revered teacher, and a fun (and really interesting) person. There are no words to say, except הנסתרות לה׳ אלקינו. All I can do here is dedicate this book to the memories of my parents and Hindi. May the entire family know no further sorrow.

Not wanting to end on this sad and somber note, I now move to the members of our family, *bli 'ayin ha-ra*, all of whom are expecting to see their names mentioned. Tova and Yossi Milgrom and the fellas, Yehudah Barak, Zecharyah Alon, Yonatan Boaz, Avraham Eliezer (aka Adam), and Eliyahu Gavriel, have been joined by the princess, Talia Sara (Layla Hannah). Dovid continues to do a remarkable job with the "trips," Eliana Koa, Yehudis Shira, and Shlomo Ezra, and with Raizel Dorit and Avraham Eliezer (aka Abie). Not to be outdone, Moshe and Sharoni have the "twin towers," Shoshana Raizel (Re-Re) and Chaya Dina (Dessi). Giving us good production from the bottom of the order, Atara and Dov Ehrman recently celebrated the bris of the newest "big guy," Calev Itai, and Chaya and Adin Rayman have the regal Avigayil (Gali). And Temima will be entering medical school iy"H. I am very proud of all of you, and I thank you all for letting me play with my blocks . . . I mean my books.

These acknowledgments end as they always do, with Devorah, because that is where everything begins. After forty-three years together b"H (even though she's only 29), "we're still having fun, and you're still the one," עמו״ש.

E. K.

ערב שביעי של פסח תש״פ

1

ASSESSING THE ASHKENAZIC CONTEXT

IN HIS PIONEERING STUDY of Rashi's posture toward a Jew who had apostatized (a *meshummad*) either willingly or under duress, Jacob Katz argues that Rashi's interpretive shift of the talmudic principle "[*Yisra'el*] *'af 'al pi she-ḥata Yisra'el hu*" ("A Jew, even though he has sinned [grievously], remains a Jew"), from a broad aggadic formulation to one that has halakhic valence for the individual apostate, had a decisive impact on subsequent halakhic policy in medieval Ashkenaz. According to Katz, this talmudic principle, as it was applied by Rashi, became the dominant policy with respect to the status of the apostate in medieval Ashkenazic society.

Jews who succumbed under duress and were forcibly converted to Christianity during times of persecution, or had converted so that their lives would be spared, or had willfully abandoned Judaism could return (or revert) to the Jewish community at any time. Moreover, a returning apostate could once again participate in prayer services and in other aspects of religious and communal life without any additional requirements or representations beyond a personal commitment to repent and to be a loyal and law-abiding member of the Jewish religious community once again. Indeed, Katz asserts that Rashi's underlying intent was to delineate that conversion to Christianity via the baptismal font did not diminish in any way the apostate's ability to return, swiftly and completely, to full participation in Jewish life.[1]

1 J. Katz, "Af 'al pi she-ḥata Yisra'el hu," *Tarbiz* 27 (1958): 203–17 [= idem, *Halakhah ve-Qabbalah* (Jerusalem, 1986), 255–69].

Thus Rashi rules that it is forbidden to take interest from a *meshummad*, except in extreme situations where the apostate had resorted to trickery to hurt the Jewish lender. Similarly, Rashi ruled (as his predecessor Rabbenu Gershom of Mainz did, and against what appears to be the regnant geonic view) that a *kohen* who had accepted Christianity but later recanted and returned to the Jewish community could resume pronouncing the priestly blessing. In addition, Rashi held that an apostate must in every instance (where he is the only brother available), and regardless of when he had apostatized, perform *ḥaliẓah* to free his deceased brother's childless wife from the potential marital bond (*ziqah*) between them, since he is still considered to be a Jew.[2]

During the time an apostate lived outside the Jewish community as a Christian, the members of the Jewish community in good standing were not to consider an apostate (or relate to him) in either personal or economic matters as a non-Jew, although limitations were placed on certain forms of fraternization, such as partaking from the food of an apostate. Thus, in addition to the prohibition against lending to an apostate (or borrowing from him) at interest,

2 See J. Katz, *Exclusiveness and Tolerance* (Oxford, 1961), 67–81 [= *Bein Yehudim le-Goyim* (Jerusalem, 1960), 75–84]; and *Teshuvot Rashi*, ed. I. Elfenbein (New York, 1943), #170. R. Natronai Gaon ruled that a *kohen* who reverts cannot resume pronouncing the priestly blessing or receiving the first *'aliyyah* to the Torah (and in these respects is to be treated as a "blemished" *kohen*, a *ba'al mum*), although he can receive and partake of the *ḥallah* gift. See *Teshuvot R. Natronai b. Hila'i Gaon*, ed. R. Brody (Jerusalem, 1994), 140–43 (sec. 35); and see also *Oẓar ha-Geonim*, ed. B. M. Levin, vol. 10 [*Gittin*] (Jerusalem, 1941), 132–33 (secs. 325–29). In the case of a *kohen* who had willingly apostatized and become a Christian priest, Rabbenu Gershom b. Judah of Mainz held that he was not permitted to recite the priestly blessing after his return. See Avraham Grossman, *Emunot ve-De'ot be-'Olamo shel Rashi* (Alon Shvut, 2008), 301–2; idem, *Ḥakhmei Ashkenaz ha-Rishonim* (Jerusalem, 1981), 122–26, 155 (n. 181), 224–25; idem, *Ḥakhmei Ẓarefat ha-Rishonim* (Jerusalem, 1995), 152–53; Edward Fram, "Perception and Reception of Repentant Apostates in Medieval Ashkenaz and Premodern Poland," *AJS Review* 21 (1996): 301, n. 8; and Micha Perry, *Massoret ve-Shinui* (Tel Aviv, 2011), 158–74. A concern of the more stringent view is whether the possibility for a reverting apostate to return to his special rights and privileges as a *kohen* is of the same moment as the ability of a non-*kohen* to be returned to the more basic dimensions of Jewish practice and status; see the section on pronouncing the priestly blessing in this volume, chapter 4.

the apostate's betrothal of a Jewish woman (assuming her acquiescence) was fully effective. At the same time, once an apostate made the decision to return to the practice of Judaism and to the Jewish community, and his commitment to repent became known, other Jews were permitted to "consume his bread and drink his wine." There was no need for a waiting or probation period to confirm that his return was undertaken in good faith.[3]

Rashi's rulings in instances such as these were not always novel,[4] but he had two overarching aims in offering them. First, he wished to dispel the notion that apostasy to Christianity constituted an irrevocable dislocation of the individual from Judaism and the Jewish community. Baptism did not vitiate the individual's halakhic status as a Jew, even in instances where the apostate had accepted Christianity willingly. Second, Rashi understood that Jewish converts to Christianity during this period often vacillated in their new religious commitment. In accordance with the status of the *mumar* in talmudic parlance—whose rejection of Judaism or Jewish law was perhaps only partial or temporary, and whose return to observance was deemed possible if not imminent—Rashi, and those leading halakhists in Ashkenaz during the twelfth and thirteenth centuries who embraced his view, wished to encourage and ease the way for the apostate's return.[5]

---

3 See *Teshuvot Rashi*, ed. Elfenbein, #168–171, 173, 175.

4 See, e.g., E. Fram, "Perception and Reception," 300–304; and Simcha Emanuel, "Teshuvot ha-Geonim ha-Qeẓarot," in *'Atarah le-Ḥayyim: Meḥqarim be-Sifrut ha-Talmudit veha-Rabbanit Likhvod Professor Ḥaim Zalman Dimitrovsky*, ed. D. Boyarin et al. (Jerusalem, 2000), 447–49.

5 On the near interchangeability of the terms *meshummad* and *mumar*, in later rabbinic literature if not within the Talmud itself, see J. Katz, *Exclusiveness and Tolerance*, 68 (n. 6) [= *Bein Yehudim le-Goyim*, 76 (n. 8)]; idem, *Halakhah ve-Qabbalah*, 262; my "Rabbinic Attitudes toward Nonobservance in the Medieval Period," in *Jewish Tradition and the Non-traditional Jew*, ed. J. Schacter (Montvale, NJ, 1992), 6 (and the literature cited in n. 7); Elisheva Carlebach, *Divided Souls* (New Haven, CT, 2001), 12, 24–25; David Malkiel, "Jews and Apostates in Medieval Europe: Boundaries Real and Imagined," *Past and Present* 194 (2007): 10; Uriel Simonsohn, "Halting between Two Opinions: Conversion and Apostasy in Early Islam," *Medieval Encounters* 19 (2013): 354–55; A. M. Gray, "R. Eliezer of Metz's Twelfth-Century Exclusion from Charity of the Jewish *Avaryan be-Mezid* ('Deliberate Transgressor')," in *Approaches to Poverty in Medieval Europe*, ed. S. Farmer

Katz contends, however, that at least some members of Ashkenazic society intuitively felt that one who had undergone baptism but now sought to return to the Jewish community should not be automatically readmitted. Thus, despite the smooth and immediate process of return advocated by Rashi and other rabbinic figures, Katz concludes that "the popular view did not, however . . . accept the view that baptism did not affect the Jew's character *qua* Jew. Indeed, advocates of this view felt that the repentant apostate must undergo a ceremony of purification in the ritual bath in the same way as a proselyte, a practice that was not in vogue during the geonic period."[6] Katz maintains that this popular practice was occasionally reflected and even referred to in Ashkenazic rabbinic literature of the thirteenth century, by sources and authorities such as *Sefer Ḥasidim* and Meir of Rothenburg (d. 1293).[7]

(Turnhout, 2016), 72–73; Avraham Reiner, "Mumar Okhel Nevelot le-Te'avon Pasul: Mashehu 'al Nosaḥ u-Perush Bidei Rashi," in *Lo Yasur Shevet mi-Yehudah: Hanhagah, Rabbanut u-Qehillah be-Toledot Yisra'el*, ed. Yosef Hacker and Y. Harel (Jerusalem, 2011), 219–28; and cf. David Berger, "Jacob Katz on Jews and Christians in the Middle Ages," in *The Pride of Jacob: Essays on Jacob Katz and His Work*, ed. J. M. Harris (Cambridge, MA, 2002), 54–55.

6 See Katz, *Exclusiveness and Tolerance*, 73 [= *Bein Yehudim le-Goyim*, 80]; and cf. E. Fram, "Perception and Reception," 301. Immersion was not required for returning apostates during the geonic period. See *Teshuvot R. Natronai*, ed. Brody, 469 (sec. 315), and n. 6 (for the similar rulings of R. Amram and R. Paltoi in this matter). See also ms. Bodl. 678, fol 195r; *Oẓar ha-Ge'onim*, ed. Lewin, vol. 7 [*Yevamot*] (Jerusalem, 1936), 111–13 (secs. 258–62); Moshe Yagur, "Zehut Datit u-Gevulot Qehillatiyyim be-Ḥevrat ha-Genizah (Me'ot ha-10–13): Gerim, 'Avadim, Mumarim" (PhD diss., Hebrew University, 2017), 193–200, 205–12; and this volume, chapter 2, n. 4. On the uses of *mikva'ot* in medieval Europe, see, e.g., Joseph Shatzmiller, "Les bains juifs aux XIIe et XIII siècles," *Medievales* 43 (2002): 83–90; Judith Baskin, "Male Piety, Female Bodies: Men, Women and Ritual Immersion in Medieval Ashkenaz," *Jewish Law Association Studies* 17 (2007): 11–30; and Neta Bodner, "She-yir'eh ha-Adam et 'aẓmo aḥarei ha-tevilah ke-'ilu nivra be-'otah hasha'ah: 'al Tevilat Gevarim, Kelim u-Kelal ha-Ẓibbur ba-Mikva'ot be-Germanyah Bimei ha-Benayim," *Ḥiddushim be-Ḥeqer Toledot Yehudei Germanyah u-Merkaz Eiropah* 21 (2009): 47–83.

7 Katz, *Exclusiveness and Tolerance*, 73 (n. 3), also refers to *Nimmuqei Yosef*, a late-fourteenth-century Spanish commentary on *Hilkhot ha-Rif* composed by Yosef Ḥaviva. See this volume, chapter 2, n. 50.

Katz's characterization of the origins and status of ritual immersion for the returning apostate was utilized by historians who encountered other kinds of evidence for an immersion ceremony in medieval Europe. Yosef Yerushalmi, in his study of the Church inquisition in France at the time of Bernard Gui (c. 1320),[8] presents information on Jewish practices that Bernard obtained from the confessions of Jewish converts to Christianity who had subsequently lapsed (which may also have included those who lived at some point in Germany). In reporting "on the manner in which apostates were received back into the Jewish community," Bernard transmits a description from those he had interrogated about the rituals employed to re-judaize them. The returning apostate was stripped of his garments and bathed in warm water. The Jews would energetically rub sand over his entire body but especially on his forehead, chest, and arms, which were the places that received the anointments of the chrism during baptism. The nails of his hands and feet would be cut until they bled, and his head was shaved. He was then immersed three times in the waters of a flowing stream, and a blessing over this immersion was recited.[9]

Yerushalmi searched for Jewish legal sources that mandated or could otherwise confirm these practices. He found no such requirement in "the standard medieval codes," although he does point to the small number of rabbinic passages from the medieval period that seem to have acknowledged the practices noted by Katz.[10] At the same time, however, Yerushalmi found that quite a few of the leading sixteenth- and seventeenth-century halakhists in Eastern Europe referred to and embraced the requirement that a returning apostate undergo immersion; these included Moses Isserles (Ramo, d. 1572), Solomon Luria (Maharshal, d. 1573), Yo'el Sirkes (*Baḥ*, d. 1640), and Shabbetai b. Meir ha-Kohen (*Shakh*, d. 1663). Yerushalmi concludes that, "from the sources available to us, we cannot prove with finality that the re-judaizing rite as

8 Y. H. Yerushalmi, "The Inquisition and the Jews of France in the Time of Bernard Gui," *Harvard Theological Review* 63 (1970): 317–76.

9 See Yerushalmi, "The Inquisition and the Jews of France," 363–67; Jeremy Cohen, *The Friars and the Jews* (Ithaca, NY, 1982), 93–96; and Ram Ben-Shalom, *Yehudei Provence: Renaissance be-Ẓel ha-Kenesiyyah* (Raanana, 2017), 245–55.

10 See this chapter, n. 6.

described by Bernard Gui is authentic. We can assert, however, that most of the elements appear highly plausible. The custom of requiring a ritual bath of the penitent apostate definitely existed."[11]

As did Katz, Yerushalmi regards this act of "un-baptism" (as some have referred to it, since this act might also have been considered a way to symbolically undo or reverse what had occurred at the baptismal font) as a popular custom that perhaps had a measure of rabbinic approbation during the medieval period, rather than as the more formal halakhic requirement that it seems to have become by the early modern period. Similarly, William Chester Jordan has succinctly characterized the situation in northern France during the twelfth and thirteenth centuries as follows: "Whatever elitist rabbinic views might have been [especially since a ritual of un-baptism implied that the Christian ceremony of baptism was efficacious], an 'un-baptizing' ritual was being practiced."[12]

Writing a decade after Yerushalmi, Joseph Shatzmiller returned to the question of whether an apostate from Judaism who had decided to abandon Christianity and return to Judaism was required to undergo immersion. Shatzmiller notes that two responsa found among those issued by an older contemporary of Bernard Gui, Solomon b. Abraham ibn Adret of Barcelona (Rashba, d. c. 1310), rule, in accordance with the geonic view, that such an immersion ceremony or ritual was not required, although according to these

---

11 See Yerushalmi, "The Inquisition and the Jews of France," 371–74; and Batsheva Albert, *Mishpato shel Barukh: Ha-Protocol ha-Rishon shel Shefitat Anus Bifnei ha-Inqvizizyah [1320]* (Ramat Gan, 1974), 99–102. Similar details appear in confessions obtained by the inquisitor Jacques Fournier, a contemporary of Bernard Gui in southern France (and the future Pope Benedict XII). See Albert, *Mishpato shel Barukh*, 9–10, 42–46; J. Cohen, *The Friars and the Jews*, 78–79; Shlomo Simonsohn, *The Apostolic See and the Jews: History* (Toronto, 1991), 352–53; Anna Foa, *The Jews of Europe After the Black Death* (Berkeley, CA, 2000), 96; Paola Tartakoff, "Testing Boundaries: Jewish Conversion and Cultural Fluidity in Medieval Europe, c. 1200–1391," *Speculum* 90 (2015): 757–58; idem, *Conversion, Circumcision, and Ritual Murder in Medieval Europe* (Philadelphia, 2020), 117–21; and R. Ben-Shalom, *Yehudei Provence*, 255–56, 262–64.

12 W. C. Jordan, *The French Monarchy and the Jews* (Philadelphia, 1989), 140–41. See also E. Fram, "Perception and Reception," 311–12.

geonic sources, public admission of guilt along with words of admonition—and even lashes—might well be indicated.[13]

Shatzmiller also highlights a passage from the talmudic commentary to tractate *Yevamot* composed by Rashba's student, Yom Tov b. Abraham Ishvilli (Ritva, d. c. 1325). Ritva asserts that while there is no requirement according to the letter of Torah law to undergo immersion, there is a rabbinic requirement to do so: "*ve-'af 'al pi khen, hu tovel mi-derabbanan mishum ma'alah*," which Shatzmiller understands as "for the sake of perfection." After citing an additional inquisitorial account of such an immersion, Shatzmiller concludes that the formulations associated with Rashba which dismiss the need for immersion are legal prescriptions that do not necessarily reflect what was actually being done in Spain in his day as a matter of practice. Indeed, even if this immersion was being imposed "for the sake of perfection" (as his younger contemporary Ritva put it), Rashba regards this rite as inappropriate, since it implies recognition of the efficacy of the Christian sacrament of baptism. By stating unequivocally that no such immersion was required or should be performed in practice, Rashba, who was also an effective communal leader of long standing, sought to stress that no recognition of baptism should be implied in any way, against what might well have been the current practice.[14]

In accordance with the studies of Yerushalmi and Shatzmiller, Elisheva Carlebach concludes that, despite the vigorous efforts of Meir of Rothenburg in the late thirteenth century—following those of Rabbenu Gershom and Rashi—to sustain and nurture the Jewish status of repentant apostates, "Jewish folk beliefs and traditions concerning the efficacy of baptism endured. Returning apostates or forced converts were required to undergo various purification rites in order to rejoin the Jewish community." The persistence of these rituals reinforces the notion that Jews in medieval Ashkenaz felt the

13 The geonic position that required lashes is also cited in *Shibbolei ha-Leqet le-R. Ẓidqiyyah b. Avraham ha-Rofeh mi-Romi*, part 2, ed. S. Ḥasida (Jerusalem, 1988), 198 (sec. 147).

14 See J. Shatzmiller, "Converts and Judaizers in the Early Fourteenth Century," *Harvard Theological Review* 74 (1981): 63–77; and R. Ben Shalom, *Yehudei Provence*, 255–56.

need to counteract in a demonstrative way the baptism that an apostate to Christianity underwent, despite the fact that Jewish law did not recognize it. Among the responsa cited by Carlebach to demonstrate how these ritual forms of counter-baptism survived over time is one penned by the fifteenth-century Austrian authority Israel Isserlein.[15]

The question asked of Isserlein was whether an apostate who had come forward to be "purified" (i.e., to return to the Jewish community) on the intermediate days of a festival (*ḥol ha-mo'ed*) could be shaved (given that shaving was typically proscribed during this period) in order to be immersed "and thereby [re-]enter the true faith." In his response Isserlein permits this to be done, noting that "without this shaving and subsequent immersion, the penitent cannot be included in a quorum or any holy matter [*ve-khol davar shebi-qedushah*]. Although [the absence of] this [immersion] surely does not prevent him from doing so according to the letter of the law [*ve-'af 'al gav de-vaddai 'eino me'akkev*], the custom of our forefathers is akin to the law of the Torah [*minhag 'avoteinu Torah hi]*."[16] In considering the historical implications of this responsum, Edward Fram has called attention to the fact that, rather than trying to eliminate this "folk custom," Isserlein adduces significant additional support for it from an interpretation offered by Rashi in his Torah commentary (to Nu. 8:7), in the name of Moses *ha-Darshan* of Narbonne.[17]

All the studies noted to this point presume that ritual immersion for a returning apostate was not initially instituted or mandated by Ashkenazic halakhists during the high Middle Ages. Such immersions are barely mentioned in published medieval rabbinic texts, nor were they highlighted by Ashkenazic rabbinic authorities at this time. This is in accordance with the halakhic posture of Rashi, that the re-judaization of an apostate who wished to return to the Jewish community should remain unencumbered. Rather, these rituals emerged as a kind of folk custom or popular tradition, one that rabbinic

---

15 See E. Carlebach, *Divided Souls*, 28–29.

16 See Israel Isserlein, *Terumat ha-Deshen*, ed. S. Abittan (Jerusalem, 1991), *Responsa*, no. 86.

17 See E. Fram, "Perception and Reception," 318; and see this volume, chapter 7.

authorities slowly began to countenance and then embrace only by the late Middle Ages, and to a greater extent as the early modern period unfolds.[18]

Indeed, at least two twelfth-century Tosafists appear to support Rashi's approach. The early German Tosafist Isaac b. Asher (Riba) *ha-Levi* of Speyer (d. 1133) maintains unequivocally that "ritual immersion can never be required of a [born] Jew who has already been circumcised, even according to rabbinic law."[19] Moreover, Isaac b. Abraham (Riẓba, d. 1209), a student of Ri of Dampierre (d. c. 1190), rules that an apostate who had repented does not have to appear before a *beit din* (tribunal) of three, either to verify his sincerity or so that the *beit din* can formally supervise his re-inclusion within the community,

> since it can easily be ascertained that he has returned to his Creator. . . . And even according to those who might be more stringent in this matter, his wine is no longer considered to be that of an idolater once

18 Cf. E. Carlebach, "Early Modern Ashkenaz in the Writings of Jacob Katz," in *The Pride of Jacob*, ed. Harris, 77. It should be noted that Rashi never explicitly discusses the question of whether immersion is required. See, however, ms. Bodl. 566 (#19437), fols. 59v–60r, for a passage that reflects formulations by Rashi (and Rabbenu Gershom). The taking of interest from an apostate is proscribed, as Rashi held (including the one slight allowance that he made; see this volume, chapter 4, nn. 3, 25); and an apostate's bill of divorce (*get*), *ḥaliẓah*, and *qiddushin* are deemed to be fully valid and effective, all of which are essential for Rashi. The passage concludes with the statement that an apostate (like a convert to Judaism who strayed and now seeks to return) is not required to immerse (*meshummad ve-ḥazar 'o ger she-ḥazar le-suro ve-ḥazru bi-teshuvah, 'ein ẓarikh tevilah*). It is then followed by another formulation, akin to that of Rashi, that a penitent *kohen* can resume giving the priestly blessing. Avraham Grossman, *Ḥakhmei Ashkenaz ha-Rishonim* (Jerusalem, 1981), 460, notes that the copyist of the collection of rulings in which this passage appears reports that he copied these rulings (in brief) from the writings of students and colleagues of Rabbenu Tam (including his student, Ḥayyim b. Ḥanan'el *Kohen*, and his brother Rashbam). In addition, a responsum by Rabbenu Tam's nephew and leading student, Ri of Dampierre, regarding a penitent apostate, is found in close proximity (on fols. 60v–61r). See also S. Emanuel, *Teshuvot Maharam mi-Rothenburg va-Ḥaverav* (Jerusalem, 2012), 489–90.

19 See the standard *Tosafot* to *Pesaḥim* 92a, s.v. *'aval 'arel Yisra'el*; and *Tosafot ha-Rashba mi-Rabbenu Shimshon b. Avraham mi-Sens 'al Massekhet Pesaḥim*, ed. M. Y. From (Jerusalem, 1956), 221. On Riba *ha-Levi*'s role as an early Tosafist, see I. Ta-Shma, *Ha-Sifrut ha-Parshanit la-Talmud*, vol. 1 (Jerusalem, 1999), 66–70.

> he [again] practices the Jewish faith even if he did not immerse himself [*ve-'afilu lo taval*], or even if he lent money at interest to a Jew and has not yet returned the interest. . . . An apostate who has repented is considered to be a penitent [*ba'al teshuvah*] in every respect. He is a bit similar [*ve-domeh qeẓat*] to a *ger* [convert] but must only return to his Creator and correct his misdeeds [*raq she-yesh lo lashuv 'el bor'o ule-taqqen 'avatato*].[20]

This suggestive formulation of Riẓba is parallel to a passage found in *Sefer Ḥasidim*, the bulk of which was composed in Germany by 1225:

> An apostate who has returned to living as a Jew [*lihyot Yehudi*], and accepted upon himself to repent [*ve-kibbel 'alav la'asot teshuvah*] according to the directives of the rabbinic sages [*ka'asher yoruhu ha-ḥakhamim*], from the time that he has accepted to do this [*harei mi-sha'ah she-kibbel*] other Jews may drink wine with him and he may be included in a quorum, provided that he does as all other Jews do.

20 See E. E. Urbach, *Ba'alei ha-Tosafot* (Jerusalem, 1980), 1:268–69, citing Moses of Zurich, *Semaq mi-Ẓurikh*, ed. Y. Har-Shoshanim, vol. 2 (Jerusalem, 1977), 49 (*miẓvah* 156); *Shitah Mequbbeẓet li-Bekhorot* 31a (citing *Tosafot ḥiẓoniyyot*); *Teshuvot ha-Rashba ha-Meyuḥasot la-Ramban*, #180; S. Emanuel, *Teshuvot Maharam mi-Rothenburg va-Ḥaverav*, 487 (n. 2); and Simcha Goldin, *Ha-Yiḥud veha-Yaḥad* (Tel Aviv, 1997), 94–95. Note the later position of Isaac b. Joseph of Corbeil (d. 1280), author of *Sefer Miẓvot Qatan* (taken from his no longer extant *Tosafot* to tractate *Yevamot* and cited in the same section of *Semaq mi-Ẓurikh*), that a penitent apostate (who is characterized as a *Yisra'el ba'al teshuvah*) does not need to be given a document testifying that he has properly repented (as was often done for a convert to Judaism, to certify that he had undergone a bona fide conversion process) because the former apostate was a Jew from birth who is now once again conducting himself in accordance with Jewish law. See also Emanuel, *Shivrei Luḥot* (Jerusalem, 2006), 199 (n. 57), and this volume, chapter 2, n. 8; and cf. my "Rabbinic Figures in Castilian Kabbalistic Pseudepigraphy: R. Yehudah he-Ḥasid and R. Elḥanan of Corbeil," *Journal of Jewish Thought and Philosophy* 3 (1993): 88–99. Bernard Gui, however, learned from the lapsed Christians he interrogated (see, e.g., P. Tartakoff, "Testing Boundaries," 760) that those apostates who reverted to Judaism needed to have a certificate of re-judaization, although this too may have been a reflection of additional requirements that were demanded on the popular (non-rabbinic) level.

For on the festivals, an *'am ha-'areẓ* is trusted with respect to ritual impurity.[21]

In his annotations to *Sefer Ḥasidim*, Reuven Margoliot suggests that *Sefer Ḥasidim* was aware of the popular practice that included the immersion of a former apostate, and that this passage in *Sefer Ḥasidim* means to convey that no such ritual act is required.[22] *Sefer Ḥasidim* finds support for this position in a talmudic passage (*Ḥagigah* 26a), according to which an *'am ha-'areẓ* present in Jerusalem during a festival period may be entrusted to come in contact with *terumah* and other consecrated foods and utensils, even though he had not formally accepted responsibility for maintaining these higher standards and observances before a panel of three *ḥaverim* (who are fully qualified in this regard), as was typically required according to the talmudic discussion in

21 *Sefer Ḥasidim* (Parma), ed. Y. Wistinetzki (Jerusalem, 1924), sec. 209 [= *Sefer Ḥasidim* (Bologna), ed. R. Margoliot (Jerusalem, 1973), sec. 203]; and see also *Sefer Ḥasidim* (Parma) [hereafter referred to as *SḤP*], sec. 208. Cf. the gloss by Moses Isserles (Ramo) to *Shulḥan 'Arukh, Ḥoshen Mishpat*, 34:22 (based on *Teshuvot Mahariq*, #85). On the dating of *Sefer Ḥasidim*, see Haym Soloveitchik, "Le-Ta'arikh Ḥibburo shel *Sefer Ḥasidim*," in *Tarbut ve-Ḥevrah be-Toledot Yisra'el Bimei ha-Benayim*, ed. R. Bonfil et al. (Jerusalem, 1989), 383–88. To be sure, however, not all apostates considering reversion were encouraged or welcomed to the same extent, according to *Sefer Ḥasidim*. A passage in *SḤP*, 75 (sec. 201), describes the scholars and communal leaders in one locale who were aware that an apostate wished to revert. Their role, however, was not to oversee his reversion. Rather, it was to aid and allow him to effectively escape (to an unidentified locale where he could then revert) without attracting the curiosity of the Christian authorities. To accomplish this he was permitted to continue to carry a cross so that he could appear as a Christian as he made his escape. He would thereby misdirect the authorities, who would now not be able to accuse the local Jewish community of aiding in his reversion. In another passage (*SḤP*, 73, sec.183), the Pietist sage seeks to discourage parents from offering their apostate son a sum of money for him to revert, since it appears the son's true intentions (which were evident in some respects even while he was still part of the Jewish community) were to convince others to apostatize. See also *SḤP*, 75 (sec. 200); E. Fram, "Perception and Reception," 305–7; D. Malkiel, "Jews and Apostates in Medieval Europe," 26–28; and cf. P. Tartakoff, "Testing Boundaries," 754–56.

22 See this chapter, n. 6; and see R. Margoliot's *Meqor Ḥesed* commentary to *Sefer Ḥasidim* (Bologna), 192–93, sec. 203 (n. 1).

tractate *Bekhorot* (31a). The Talmud in *Ḥagigah* adduces, from a verse in the Book of Judges, that *'ammei ha-'areẓ* who are in close quarters with the ritually careful *ḥaverim* during the festival, and who appear to be fully committed to proper observance of ritual purity at that time, can immediately acquire the status of a *ḥaver* for this purpose,[23] although, to be sure, the beginning of this section in *Sefer Ḥasidim* indicates that a returning apostate was also expected to take on an unspecified penitential regimen over the course of time, according to the sages' instructions.

It should also be noted that although Riẓba appears to agree with *Sefer Ḥasidim* about the permissible status of the wine touched by an apostate who had repented and reaccepted a commitment to Jewish religious practice, he nonetheless refers to the act of immersion as an appropriate one, even if it is not an absolute requirement for the returning apostate (as it was for the *ger*, a convert to Judaism). This would seem to be the meaning of Riẓba's nuanced formulation that a reverting apostate is "a bit similar [*ve-domeh qeẓat*] to a convert."

Riẓba's brother, the distinguished Tosafist (and successor of Ri), Samson b. Abraham of Sens (Rash *mi-Shanẓ* [d. 1214 in Israel]), agrees that immersion is not required for the returning apostate. However, as we shall see in the next chapter, Samson of Sens, unlike Riẓba, suggests that the returning apostate must reaccept his commitment to Judaism in a more formal way, similar to the requirement placed on a convert to Judaism, who had to accept the observance of *miẓvot* in the presence of a *beit din*. R. Samson was apparently more concerned about the need to verify the sincerity of the returning apostate and to ascertain that his return was not merely opportunistic or deceitful.[24]

Moreover, we shall encounter in the next chapter a series of manuscript passages (along with some published texts) which indicate that a number of Tosafists and other leading Ashkenazic rabbinic authorities from this same period and beyond (in both northern France and Germany), including Ri of

---

23 Cf. *Tosafot ha-Rosh 'al Massekhet Ḥagigah*, ed. A. Shoshana (Jerusalem, 2002), 251.

24 See this volume, chapter 2, n. 20, for the view of Rash *mi-Shanẓ*. Cf. U. Simonsohn, "Halting between Two Opinions," 342, 350, 362–67.

Dampierre, Eli'ezer b. Joel *ha-Levi* (Rabiah, d. c. 1225), Simḥah b. Samuel of Speyer (d. c. 1230), Eleazar b. Judah of Worms (d. c. 1230), and "the brothers of Evreux" (Moses and Samuel b. Shne'ur, d. c. 1250, or perhaps their direct student, Rabbenu Pereẓ b. Elijah of Corbeil, d. 1297), recognized and embraced the need for ritual immersion by an apostate who wished to return to the community, and in some cases imposed additional requirements as well. Although these Tosafists and Ashkenazic rabbinic figures did not consider ritual immersion to be an obligation mandated by Torah law for a reverting apostate (as it was for a convert to Judaism), they supported this practice to an increasingly noticeable extent. They certainly did not consider it simply a matter of popular custom or folk tradition, even if it had originated in that way at some earlier point.[25]

The Ashkenazic authorities who embraced this practice of immersion for a returning apostate advanced a number of different reasons for this requirement: as a visceral means of reminding the returning apostate of what his (renewed) religious and communal responsibilities are, and as a means of binding him to those responsibilities; as an act of penance or penitence on the part of the returnee; as a means of ritual separation from the spiritual and physical corruption of idolatry that accrues even when simply living with and among idolaters; or as a tangible sign of the change in the apostate's personal status as he or she returns to full membership in the Jewish community.

In any case, these authorities posited the existence of a larger gap between Jewish and Christian societies that had to be traversed by the returning apostate (for which the act of immersion was necessary) than did Rashi or those Tosafists who continued to maintain that no immersion was needed. At stake here perhaps was the extent to which those Ashkenazic rabbinic authorities could continue to maintain that baptism had made no impact (from the societal, if not the halakhic, perspective) on the apostate. Those who required a form of ritual immersion were suggesting that it had become necessary for the returning apostate to undergo an act that would

25 See this volume, chapter 2.

mark the sincerity of his recommitment, or at least signify a rejection of where he had been.[26]

To be sure, Katz's thesis concerning the impact of Rashi's larger approach to reversion on subsequent generations in medieval Ashkenaz remains intact in one significant aspect. None of the Tosafists just listed disagree with the essential premise of the principle that *'af 'al pi she-ḥata Yisra'el hu* as Rashi applied it. An apostate is still considered to be of the Jewish faith, and at least in theory, apostates should be encouraged to return to the Jewish community and the full observance of Jewish law and practices.[27] Nonetheless, these and other manuscript passages suggest that there was a wider range of Ashkenazic rabbinic views concerning apostasy to Christianity, including with regard to how the apostates were to be treated according to Jewish law, and what needed to be accepted or demonstrated during the reversion process.

Katz acknowledges that there was some variation concerning the permissibility of lending money at interest to apostates among the Tosafists of northern France. However, since the prohibition on taking interest is limited by the Torah (Deut. 23:21) to one who is identified as "your brother" (*'aḥikha*), Katz concludes that those relatively few Tosafists who allowed interest to be taken were not necessarily deviating from Rashi's overall approach toward apostates, even as Rashi did not allow interest to be taken from them.[28] As we shall see, however (in chapters 3 and 4), when the Tosafist positions regarding money-lending and an apostate's ability (or inability) to inherit are analyzed and placed alongside the range of Tosafist views in other matters related to apostasy, it becomes increasingly difficult to explain these differences in halakhic matters and economic policy in the more compartmentalized way

---

26 This is similar to the way Shatzmiller (this chapter, n. 14) explains the differing views of Rashba and Ritva (in Spain, c. 1300) on whether ritual immersion was required for a returning apostate.

27 As demonstrated by E. Fram, "Perception and Reception," 319–39, this aspect as well changes significantly in Poland beginning in the seventeenth century, when the issue of *rodef* is raised, reflecting a strong concern that the return of apostates could damage the larger Jewish community in the eyes of the Christian authorities.

28 See Katz, *Exclusiveness and Tolerance*, 71–73 [= *Bein Yehudim le-Goyim*, 79–80].

favored by Katz. We shall see that additional talmudic formulations were invoked which negated the need to sustain individuals who had willfully and completely abandoned their commitment to Judaism and its observances, and that a number of the Tosafists involved in these discussions were advocating a response to apostasy that diverged in significant ways from that of Rashi.

We shall also see that another striking position that stood firmly against the view of Rashi—holding that *ḥaliẓah* did not have to be performed in cases where the brother of the deceased husband was an apostate (and was the only surviving or otherwise available brother to perform this ceremony)—had a number of adherents among the Tosafists. A geonic ruling maintained that if the brother of the husband had been an apostate at the time of the marriage, *ḥaliẓah* need not be administered by the deceased husband's brother, because the woman had married her husband only on the basis of an acknowledged (if not fully explicit) precondition that she would not be at the mercy of his apostate brother should the husband die and the couple be childless. However, when the brother apostatized only after the wedding had taken place, the geonic view asserts that the wife was required to receive *ḥaliẓah* from this brother in order to be permitted to marry another.

Rashi strongly disagreed with the geonic leniency (of which he was aware). He required *ḥaliẓah* even when the brother was an apostate at the time of the wedding, since that brother is still considered to be a Jew and is thus fully capable of performing *ḥaliẓah* according to Jewish law.[29] Moreover, as noted by Katz in his initial study on Rashi's development and use of the principle *'af 'al pi she-ḥata Yisra'el hu*, Meir of Rothenburg indicates that he had been prepared to present a strong proof for the geonic view, based on a passage toward the end of tractate *Bava Qamma* (110b–111a). This talmudic passage suggests the possibility that a woman effectively stipulates at the time of her marriage that she will not allow herself to be subject in any way to a subsequent levirate *ziqah* (i.e., the tie that binds the woman to her husband's brother[s], which prevents her from marrying an outsider and requires an act of *ḥaliẓah* to be released) that involves a brother with pronounced physical

29 See ibid., 70–71 [= *Bein Yehudim le-Goyim*, 78–79].

blemishes. Maharam concludes, however, that despite this proof he could not bring himself to disagree with the approach of Rashi in practice, and he therefore rules that the apostate must perform *ḥaliẓah* in all such circumstances, irrespective of when the brother became an apostate.[30]

Katz also notes the opinion of a late-twelfth-century rabbinic figure, Abraham (*ha-gadol*) of Regensburg (as cited by Israel Isserlein in his *Terumat ha-Deshen*), that a woman whose brother-in-law apostatized does not ever have to receive *ḥaliẓah* from him in order to remarry, irrespective of when the apostasy took place, and even if he is the only surviving brother. R. Abraham arrived at this ruling because the widow cannot possibly be married to this brother through *yibbum* (levirate marriage)—and thus according to talmudic law is not required to undergo *ḥaliẓah* either—since living with an apostate is an exceedingly grave sin which this woman cannot be required to commit. Indeed, transposing the principle of Jewish law that allowed Pinḥas to directly and publicly kill both Zimri ben Salu and his non-Jewish consort (Kozbi, the daughter of Ẓur) without need for a formal trial or any other *beit din* procedure or intervention, Abraham of Regensburg maintains that, if the widow were to attempt to live with the deceased husband's brother, "zealots would be allowed even to kill her [*qanna'im pog'im bah*]" to prevent this act and union from occurring.

Although Katz dismisses R. Abraham's view as a "lone voice" that did not have other rabbinic adherents or "sociological support,"[31] we shall see

---

30 See J. Katz, *Halakhah ve-Qabbalah*, 266 (n. 60), citing *Sefer Mordekhai 'al Massekhet Yevamot*, sec. 30; and *Sha'arei Teshuvot Maharam b. Barukh*, ed. M. A. Bloch (Berlin, 1891), 280 (#130). See also *Teshuvot Maimuniyyot le-hilkhot 'ishut*, #29.

31 See Katz, *Exclusiveness and Tolerance*, 267. Katz notes that Isaac *Or Zarua'* (and his son, Ḥayyim) supported the geonic leniency in this matter (ibid., 266, n. 58), but he does not trace the full extent and scope of the leniencies they considered. See this volume, chapter 3, n. 34. The same holds true for Gerald Blidstein, "Who Is Not a Jew?—The Medieval Discussion," *Israel Law Review* 11 (1976): 378–82, although Blidstein does note the objections Isaiah di Trani sent to Isaac *Or Zarua'*. Both Katz and Blidstein ("Who Is Not a Jew?" 374–77) present the unusual view of the late-twelfth-century Provençal halakhist Isaac b. Abba Mari of Marseilles (*Sefer ha-'Ittur* [repr. Jerusalem, 1970], *qiddushin ha-ḥeleq ha-sheni*, fols. 77d–78a), that the *qiddushin* of an inveterate Sabbath violator and apostate were of doubtful

that there were in fact other German Tosafists at this very same time, during the late twelfth and early thirteenth centuries, who independently ruled as R. Abraham did, even as they expressed their position in somewhat different terms. Thus the position of Abraham of Regensburg cannot be dismissed as marginal or unsupported. Once again this becomes especially evident when placed alongside other Tosafist views in both northern France and Germany that were more stringent than Rashi's position in terms of the halakhic status of the apostate and his ability to participate in various religious acts and contexts.

Based primarily on manuscript evidence that has remained largely untapped, we shall see that, in all the areas described, the extent of the debate between Tosafist halakhists over apostasy and reversion in medieval Ashkenaz was much more vigorous than Katz imagined. Indeed, Rashi himself adopts a stricter position with regard to a returning apostate in an area of transgression that Katz does not treat. In a responsum reproduced by *Sefer Mordekhai* in Rashi's name, Rashi is cited as ruling that a female apostate by choice, who willingly consorted during her apostasy with a non-Jew, is unable to remain with her Jewish husband if she subsequently returns to Judaism, while a woman who had been coerced to convert to Christianity (and was then sexually violated against her will) is permitted to return to her husband at the point that she is able to return to the Jewish community.

This responsum is attributed to Rashi in a gloss to *Sefer Mordekhai* citing *Sefer ha-Pardes*. Although the responsum is not found in the extant versions of *Sefer ha-Pardes*, or in the manuscripts on which these editions are based (which contain extensive amounts of Ashkenazic material but reflect an Italian milieu of the late twelfth century), it is possible that this responsum originated in an Ashkenazic version of *Sefer ha-Pardes* that is referred to on occasion but is no longer extant.[32] In any case, this responsum maintains that a woman

---

validity (which is recorded as an alternate opinion in *Arba'ah Turim, Even ha-'Ezer*, sec. 44). Blidstein ("Who Is Not a Jew?" 374–77) also notes the similar view entertained by Simḥah of Speyer. See ms. Bodl. 820, fol. 26r–v; and this volume, chapter 3, n. 50.

32 See *Haggahot Mordekhai 'al Massekhet Ketubbot*, sec. 286; ms. Vercelli C1, fol. 96r (in a marginal gloss at the bottom of the page); *Sefer ha-Pardes le-Rashi*, ed.

who willingly had relations with a non-Jew is unequivocally prohibited to her husband. Support for this ruling comes from the remark of Esther (*Megillat Esther* 4:16, *ve-ka'asher 'avadti 'avadti*), which is understood by the Talmud in tractate *Megillah* 15a to mean (as noted by Rashi in his commentary on the biblical verse), "I will be lost not only to my father's house, but to you as well." Because Esther continued to have relations with Aḥashverosh after revealing her familial origins to him, she was now considered to be his willing consort (*niv'alti be-raẓon*), and was therefore prohibited to her husband, Mordekhai. Rashi's responsum stipulates that a female apostate who willingly had relations with a non-Jew is similarly prohibited to her Jewish husband even if they were not caught *in flagrante* by witnesses, since it can be assumed that, in cases of willful apostasy, neither men nor women retain any inhibition with regard to sexual relations: "For there is no apostasy at this time in the name of idolatry, whether undertaken by a man or by a woman, during which their inhibition against committing [all other types of] sins remains intact." The original Hebrew passage reads: "*de-'ein hamarut ha-'idna bein de-'ish bein de-'ishah leshem 'avodat kokhavim ve-yeẓer de-'aveirah 'adayin qayyam.*"

The responsum notes that some attempted to challenge this approach, but that there was no substantive textual support for such a challenge. The formulation of this responsum does suggest, however, that if it were possible to demonstrate or to otherwise maintain that a female apostate had been converted by force or under duress (or that sexual relations with a non-Jew had occurred against her will), she would be able to return to her Jewish husband.

Rashi does not typically distinguish between a willing apostate and one who had been coerced in terms of encouraging their return to Judaism. Thus,

---

H. J. Ehrenreich (Jerusalem, 1960), editor's introduction, 17–18; and Pinchas Roth, "Sefer ha-Pardes: Le-Darkhei Hivvaẓruto shel Yalqut Hilkhati Bimei ha-Benayim" (Master's thesis, Hebrew University, 2008), 77, 125–27. This responsum is not included by Israel Elfenbein in his edition of *Teshuvot Rashi* (New York, 1942). The responsum concludes with a prooftext from tractate *Yevamot*, *pereq kohen gadol*, whose origin remains unclear. Cf. G. Blidstein, "The Personal Status of Apostate and Ransomed Women in Medieval Jewish Law" [Hebrew], *Shenaton ha-Mishpat ha-'Ivri* 3–4 (1976–77): 56–59. Blidstein also cites a responsum of R. Hai Gaon which holds a similar view.

for example, he does not take this distinction into account when allowing an apostate who was a *kohen* to resume offering the priestly blessing after his repentance and return. In this instance, however, Rashi supports this significant limitation with regard to a female apostate returning to her husband.[33] Indeed, the same approach is evident in another responsum whose attribution to Rashi is certain, about the need to deliver a *get* to a woman who had been an apostate for a goodly amount of time (*yamim rabbim*) but who had decided after that period (*le-'aḥar yamim*) to return of her own free volition to the practice of Judaism (*shavah mi-da'atah ve-linhog be-darkhei Yisra'el*). In this instance as well, Rashi's conclusion is that the period of her willful apostasy prohibits her irrevocably to her husband (*ne'esrah 'al ba'alah*).[34]

33 See D. Malkiel, "Jews and Apostates in Medieval Europe," 11–14, 19–22, 31. With regard to (immediately) permitting the wine of those who reverted, Rashi distinguishes between willing and forced converts in theory, but concludes that the permitted status of their wine is in practice the same. On Rashi's support for the return and proper treatment of both willful apostates and those who converted under duress, see also Avraham Grossman, *Ḥakhmei Ẓarefat ha-Rishonim*, 153–56; and cf. David Malkiel, *Reconstructing Ashkenaz* (Stanford, CA, 2009), 131–34; and Paola Tartakoff, "Testing Boundaries," 734–35 (n. 20). Rashi distinguishes between two types of testimony from reverting apostates who witnessed pertinent matters during their apostasy: testimony provided by a former apostate who had been forcibly converted but who privately continued to observe what he could as a Jew (which is admissible testimony), and by an apostate who had converted willingly and behaved wantonly during his apostasy but later fully reverted (whose testimony is unacceptable). See I. A. Agus, *Teshuvot Ba'alei ha-Tosafot* (New York, 1954), 51–52 (sec. 9). Here too Rashi distinguishes between forced and willing converts only with respect to their status while they were both still in a state of apostasy. They are considered the same, however, regarding Jewish legal issues and situations that arose after their reversions. Cf. this volume, chapter 4, n. 52.

34 See *Teshuvot Rashi*, ed. Elfenbein, 96 (sec. 73) and 94, 226 (sec. 202); and Isaac b. Moses of Vienna, *Sefer Or Zarua'*, pt. 1, sec. 706, ed. Machon Yerushalayim (Jerusalem, 2010), 595. In his talmudic commentary to *Megillah* 15a, s.v. *'avadti*, Rashi paraphrases *Yevamot* 56b: "The wife of a Jew who has been raped is permitted to her husband, while willful sexual activity [*ube-raẓon*] prohibits her to her husband." Cf. Aharon Ahrend, *Perush Rashi le-Massekhet Megillah* (Jerusalem, 2008), 185. At the same time, Rashi (*Teshuvot*, ed. Elfenbein, 191–93, sec. 171) considers two individuals who were forced to convert to Christianity (*'anusim*) and subsequently married each other to be fully sincere (and moral) Jews (*libbam la-shamayim*), which meant that a *get* was required to dissolve their marriage. See Blidstein, "The

To be sure, willfully engaging in sexual relations with a non-Jew is a strong act of rebellion against Judaism, especially given the fact that the women in these circumstances had converted voluntarily. Nonetheless, Rashi's stringency in this matter is noteworthy, especially given that his grandson Jacob b. Meir Tam (d. 1171) ruled that a Jewess who had apostatized and subsequently become intimate with a non-Jewish paramour was permitted to remain with him if she returned to the Jewish community and he subsequently converted to Judaism. The halakhic underpinning of Rabbenu Tam's ruling, which was contested by his senior student Isaac b. Mordekhai (Ribam) of Bohemia (and apparently by his successor in northern France, Ri of Dampierre, as well), is that relations with a non-Jew are not considered to be a disqualifying act of adultery according to Jewish law.

Indeed, several Tosafist formulations suggest that, according to Rabbenu Tam, the female apostate who returned was also permitted to remain (instead) with her first (Jewish) husband if he did not divorce her, since her relations with the non-Jew did not constitute an adulterous assignation that prohibited her return to her husband. In support of this approach, a rather brief manuscript passage cited in the name of Meir of Rothenburg suggests that Rabbenu Tam went so far as to permit a Jewess who had relations with a non-Jew outside of her marriage (even not within the context of apostasy) to return to her husband, since this sexual relationship was not considered by the *halakhah* to be an adulterous one, while Isaac of Dampierre, according to this passage, firmly disagrees with this allowance.[35]

Later Tosafist sources permitted the woman (according to their formulation of Rabbenu Tam's ruling) to return only to her former paramour if he converted to Judaism. She could not, however, remain with her Jewish husband, who was required to divorce her because of her sinful act.[36] Although the issue

---

Personal Status of Apostate and Ransomed Women in Medieval Jewish Law," 62.

35 See *Tosafot Yeshanim Yoma* 82a, s.v. *ḥuẓ*; *Tosafot Ketubot* 3b, s.v. *ve-lidrosh*; *Tosafot Sanhedrin* 74b, s.v. *ve-ha*; *Teshuvot Maharam mi-Rothenburg va-Ḥaverav*, ed. Emanuel, 439 (sec. 142).

36 See my "Meshumadot Nesu'ot she-Ḥazru: Heteran li-Bnei Zugan ha-Yehudi veha-Nokhri lefi Meqorot Ẓefon Ẓarefat ve-Ashkenaz ve-Ashkenaz Bimei ha-Benayim,"

at hand was whether this Jewish woman had willfully committed adultery, allowing her to remain even with her paramour is quite significant, in light of her adulterous act. As such, Rabbenu Tam's ruling, which at least permits the woman to remain with her former paramour if he converted, has been aptly characterized by Ephraim Urbach as a suggestive leniency on his part, which was clearly intended to smooth the return of penitent former apostates.[37] Jacob Katz, however, addresses neither the relative stringency of Rashi in this area nor the leniency of Rabbenu Tam. Indeed, he does not appear to have discussed the status of female apostates who had engaged in sexual relations with non-Jews during their apostasy at all.[38]

The next three chapters of this book will address the methodological and textual challenges and other lacunae in the areas and issues of apostasy and reversion that have been raised and briefly identified here. They will present a comprehensive picture of these matters based on the published rabbinic literature of medieval Europe and on the many rich sources still found in manuscript.[39] Much light will also be shed on the motivations, strategies, and challenges of the apostates, especially those who were ultimately able to return. As we shall see throughout, a number of Rashi's students and successors known as the Tosafists did not so readily concur with aspects of Rashi's approach to the cases and larger issues that needed to be addressed.

Although apostates were still considered to be Jews because of the principle of *'af 'al pi she-ḥata Yisra'el hu*, two related questions nonetheless had to be addressed: What kind of a Jew is an apostate, and presuming that she or

---

in *Halakhah u-Mishpat: Sefer ha-Zikkaron li-Menaḥem Elon*, ed. A. Edrei et al. (Jerusalem, 2018), 593–606; and the present volume, chapter 5. As noted there, German Tosafists appear to have followed Ribam's approach in this matter.

37 See E. E. Urbach, *Ba'alei ha-Tosafot*, 1:82; and see also Shalom Albeck, "Yaḥaso shel Rabbenu Tam li-Be'ayot Zemanno," *Zion* 19 (1954): 139.

38 See Katz, *Exclusiveness and Tolerance*, 67–76 [= idem, *Bein Yehudim le-Goyim*, 75–83]; and idem, *Halakhah ve-Qabbalah*, 255–69.

39 As will be noted in each instance, a number of the manuscript passages to be analyzed and discussed have been published (with brief comments) by Simcha Emanuel in his *Shivrei Luḥot: Sefarim Avudim shel Ba'alei ha-Tosafot* (Jerusalem, 2007); and in *Teshuvot Maharam mi-Rothenburg va-Ḥaverav* (Jerusalem, 2013).

he is unable to act as a righteous Jew while in a state of apostasy, what acts of contrition or remorse are required by Jewish law or custom on his or her return? As Katz notes, Rashi refers to an apostate (in different places) as a *Yisra'el ḥashud* (a Jew who was suspect), a *Yisra'el meshummad*, and even a *Yisra'el rasha* (a wicked Jew).[40] The apostate's status as a *Yisra'el ḥashud* meant that as long as he did not return to the community, his wine (among other foods) was not considered fit for Jewish consumption, and he was not considered capable of providing any testimony concerning ritual matters (or to perform any of these matters for others). However, once an apostate decided to return, and resumed his participation in the rituals and life of the community as before, all was forgiven, according to Rashi, without the need for any type of probation period or other demonstration of his renewed fealty to Jewish law.[41]

On the basis of several talmudic *sugyot* and their implications, a number of Tosafists maintained that, even though an apostate was still a Jew in the absolute sense, as Rashi held, an apostate was not to be accorded the same religious status as other Jews, since he was indeed considered to be a Jew who is suspect (*ḥashud*) due to his systematic abandonment of Jewish rituals and his acceptance of baptism and other Christian rites. This meant that the Jewish community could not treat an apostate like a member in good standing in a variety of contexts, in ways that differed from both the theoretical and practical positions advocated by Rashi.[42]

---

40 See Katz, *Halakhah ve-Qabbalah*, 261.

41 See A. Grossman, *Emunot ve-De'ot be-'Olamo shel Rashi*, 303–6. In his talmudic commentary (to *'Avodah Zarah* 26b, s.v. *minin*, and *Ḥullin* 13b, s.v. *min*), Rashi defines an incorrigible heretic as someone who is strongly committed to and directly involved with idolatrous worship. Cf. *Teshuvot Rashi*, ed. Elfenbein, 195–96 (sec. 174); and A. Reiner, "Mumar Okhel Nevelot le-Te'avon Pasul—Mashehu 'al Nosaḥ u-Perusho Bidei Rashi," (this chapter, n. 5).

42 Thus, for example, with respect to money-lending, Tosafist sources go well beyond noting that an apostate was not considered to be a "brother" (from whom interest could not be taken). They cite talmudic sources (*'Avodah Zarah* 26b, *Gittin* 46b–47a) indicating that a Jew who systematically violates Jewish law (even when he has an easy choice to observe it) is akin to a heretic, and he should not be supported or sustained. See, e.g., the northern French Tosafist sources (and figures) cited by the *Beit Yosef* at the beginning of *Arba'ah Turim, Yoreh De'ah*, sec. 159;

Moreover, even at a point where an apostate chose to revert to the Jewish community, there were talmudic requirements that suggest it was necessary to verify in some concrete way that the apostate's return was genuine. Tosafists in both northern France and Germany were concerned about this problem, and put forward a series of solutions and methods to accomplish this—none of which had been recommended or even countenanced by Rashi.[43] To be sure, the Tosafists occasionally make reference to earlier geonic views in these matters, and we shall consider these sources from the east as they become relevant.

These various Tosafist requirements and adjustments increased with the passage of time and beg the question as to whether they were based solely on the halakhic sources and considerations that are adduced or alluded to or whether temporal considerations also stood in some way behind these developments in rabbinic policy. Katz maintains that Rashi's all-encompassing approach, which allowed for the smooth return of apostates to the Jewish community and also attempted to lessen their alienation from the community as long as they were still outside it, was occasioned in no small measure by the events surrounding the First Crusade, during which many Jews were forcibly converted to Christianity quite suddenly (and after which King Henry IV allowed these forced converts to return to Judaism, against the stated Church policy).[44]

It would seem that for a number of the Tosafists as well (who addressed a continuing stream of actual cases, and were not putting forward only broader halakhic theories), changes over time, from the late twelfth century and

---

and cf. J. Katz, *Bein Yehudim le-Goyim*, 79 (n. 20); A. M. Gray, "R. Eliezer of Metz's Twelfth-Century Exclusion from Charity of the Jewish *Avaryan be-Mezid*," 67–89; and this volume, chapter 7, n. 38. At the same time, the question also arises as to how a returning apostate can extricate himself from his past misdeeds, since the Talmud (*Sanhedrin* 25a) requires the return of any ill-gotten gains before a *rasha* can be fully returned to his status as a law-abiding Jew; see this volume, chapter 2, n. 18.

43 See this volume, chapter 2, nn. 19–20, for the concerns of Isaac b. Abraham (Riẓba) of Dampierre and his brother, Samson b. Abraham (Rash) of Sens.

44 See J. Katz, *Exclusiveness and Tolerance*, 68 [= *Bein Yehudim le-Goyim*, 76.]; E. Fram, "Perception and Reception," 302–3; Jeremy Cohen, *Sanctifying the Name of God* (Philadelphia, 2004), 4–5.

beyond, in the relationship and positioning of the Jewish and Christian communities in both doctrinal and perceptual terms, played a role in the different approaches they advanced with regard to reverting apostates.[45] These changes will be discussed in chapter 5, along with additional halakhic patterns in related matters that the Tosafists addressed, which have the same chronological contours. The last two chapters (6 and 7) will focus on how a range of approaches toward penitent apostates that had developed in northern France and Germany during the twelfth and thirteenth centuries was adopted by rabbinic authorities in Spain during the late thirteenth century and beyond as the instances of apostasy increased there. They will also trace the role these earlier Ashkenazic views played in the renewed discussion and treatment of apostasy in late medieval Ashkenaz, prior to the rise of the centers in Eastern Europe during the early modern period.

All this means that the relatively easy path by which Rashi and others allowed reverting apostates to return to the Jewish community had become more arduous and challenging well before the beginning of the early modern period. Moving beyond his monochromatic assessment of the medieval period, Katz held that a major change in Jewish attitudes toward Jewish-Christian relations occurred with the beginning of that period. By this time, according to Katz, the apprehension and tension that Jews in northern Europe felt regarding Christianity had largely disappeared. Doctrinal differences between Judaism and Christianity were no longer put forward as signs of the mutual awareness of the diversity that existed. Rather, Judaism became a more closed system of thought, which was largely indifferent to religious developments and teachings within Christianity.

In Katz's view these changes greatly affected the way the Jewish community related to and dealt with apostates from Judaism and converts to Judaism. Solomon Luria, among others, took a strong stand against accepting converts, suggesting that the Jewish community ought to be focused solely on retaining its own followers; the halakhic literature of this period more broadly has little

45 Cf. Fram, "Perception and Reception," 302 (n. 12); and S. Goldin, *Ha-Yiḥud veha-Yaḥad*, 87–88.

practical discussion of the laws of conversion. The widening gulf between Judaism and Christianity also brought changes in the rabbinic attitudes toward apostates. Although apostasy to Christianity continued, authorities such as R. Yo'el Sirkes believed that those who apostatized did so solely to freely and publicly partake in prohibited acts and pleasures, as a matter of complete self-interest.[46] If an apostate sought to return to Judaism, his motives and commitment had to be thoroughly questioned and examined, and his return to the Jewish community was to be seen almost as an act of conversion.

Katz maintains that strategies to keep apostates at a distance were developed for the first time only during the fifteenth century. Thus, for example, rabbinic authorities at that time ruled that an apostate brother was not required to perform *ḥaliẓah* to release the childless wife of his dead brother, and they inserted an explicit condition to this effect into the marriage contract.[47] Because the gulf between the apostate from Judaism and the Jewish community was now much wider than it had been, bringing an apostate back into the community was also more difficult. As opposed to passages in *Sefer Ḥasidim* (and other contemporaneous medieval texts) which suggest that an apostate often remained relatively close to the Jewish community in social and other contexts, Katz's work maintains that the apostate was now regarded, for all intents and purposes, as lost to Judaism. He was to be feared because he might inform against the Jewish community; there was also contempt for what he had done and for the motives of his conversion to Christianity. Thus efforts to return him to the Jewish fold are barely mentioned in the early modern period.[48]

---

46 See his *Bayit Ḥadash* (*BaḤ*) commentary to *Arba'ah Turim, Yoreh De'ah*, sec. 268 (end).

47 This procedure was countenanced by Israel Isserlein, as reported by Israel Bruna. See *She'elot u-Teshuvot R. Israel Bruna*, ed. M. Hershler (Jerusalem, 1960), #184; and as noted also by both Moses Isserles in his *Darkhei Mosheh* (n. 5), and Joel Sirkes in his Baḥ commentary (ad loc.) to *Arba'ah Turim, Even ha-'Ezer*, sec 157 (even as the *Beit Yosef*, loc cit., questions this approach because there are no talmudic texts that support it). See this volume, chapter 7, n. 24.

48 See Katz, *Exclusiveness and Tolerance*, 143–50 [= *Bein Yehudim le-Goyim*, 145–52].

The sharp division posited by Katz between the medieval and early modern periods, according to which the more restrictive or stringent views in these matters do not emerge until the latter period, is difficult to sustain on the basis of the many and varied sources that are now available.[49] The rabbinic elite of medieval Ashkenaz appear to have held views in these matters that were much more nuanced and variegated, from the late twelfth century and beyond. Indeed, a number of these Ashkenazic rulings (and values) subsequently reached other centers of Jewish life (most notably within Spain) well before the modern period begins. It is to a full discussion of these views and their impact that we now turn.

49 By the same token, German Jews who had apostatized nonetheless continued to revert in Amsterdam during the mid-seventeenth century and beyond. See E. Carlebach, "'Ich will dich nach Holland schicken': Amsterdam and the Reversion to Judaism of German-Jewish Converts," in *Secret Conversions to Judaism in Early Modern Europe*, ed. M. Mulsow and R. Popkin (Leiden, 2004), 54–59; and this chapter, n. 18. Cf. E. Fram (this chapter, n. 27).

2

ESTABLISHING BOUNDARIES

Immersion, Repentance, Verification

The purpose of immersion for a returning apostate is discussed by the leading northern French Tosafist of the late twelfth century, Isaac b. Samuel (Ri) of Dampierre, a great-grandson of Rashi and the nephew and main successor of Rabbenu Tam. Although Ri's formulation is not found in any *Tosafot* texts or collections, it is attested in a ruling of his recorded in three variant manuscript passages, in each instance with a different level of detail and nuance about the situation that gave rise to Ri's response.

The question put to Ri, as recorded in a *teshuvah be-qozer* (a brief responsum or perhaps a digest that is, nonetheless, the longest version of Ri's ruling) found within a manuscript collection of responsa,[1] concerns a former apostate who had arrived in a new locale and community following his return to Judaism. This was often the way an apostate rejoined the Jewish community, since the chances of detection and retribution by Christian authorities were significantly heightened if the reversion took place where the apostate had lived as a Christian.[2]

---

1 See ms. Bodleian (Neubauer) 566, fols. 60v–61r, published in *Teshuvot Maharam va-Ḥaverav*, ed. S. Emanuel (Jerusalem, 2013), 1:489–90 (#188). See also *Teshuvot R. Yiẓḥaq ben Shmu'el of Dampierre*, ed. P. Roth and A. R. Reiner (Jerusalem, 2020), 80–82 (sec. 53). I thank the editors for sharing their treatment of this responsum with me as the volume was in preparation.

2 See, e.g., *Teshuvot Rashi*, ed. I. Elfenbein (New York, 1942), 188–89 (secs. 168–69); Solomon Grayzel, *The Church and the Jews in the XIIIth Century*, vol. 2 (New York, 1989), 14, 36, 157–58; Joseph Shatzmiller, "Jewish Converts to Christianity in

As Ri's responsum describes, the former apostate now appears to be conducting himself according to the Jewish faith, but the extent and sincerity of his repentance has not been formally verified since he had not reaccepted his commitment to the commandments before a tribunal of three (*lo be-qabbalah bifnei sheloshah*)—nor does it seem that he was required to do so—and there is also no evidence that he had immersed in a *mikveh*. The specific halakhic question Ri was called on to answer deals with the status of a Jew's wine that had been touched by this reverting apostate. If the erstwhile apostate had not repented and returned sincerely, his ongoing status as an apostate would ostensibly render this wine unfit for consumption by Jews.[3]

Ri responds that he is inclined to permit the wine of the Jewish owner because the customary immersion by a reverting apostate (*tevilah zo she-nahagu*) is for the purpose of achieving spiritual cleansing and purity (*neqiyyut ve-tahorah*), and is not intended to signify or to certify (as it was in a

---

Medieval Europe, 1200–1500," in *Cross-Cultural Convergence in the Crusade Period*, ed. M. Goodich et al. (New York, 1995), 315–16; Shlomo Simonsohn, *The Apostolic See and the Jews: History* (Toronto, 1991), 1:262–63; Edward Fram, "Perception and Reception of Repentant Apostates in Medieval Ashkenaz and Premodern Poland," *AJS Review* 21 (1996): 311–13; Bernard Rosenzweig, "Apostasy in the Late Middle Ages in Ashkenazic Jewry," *Dine Israel* 10–11 (1981–83), 71–72; David Malkiel, "Jews and Apostates in Medieval Europe—Boundaries Real and Imagined," *Past and Present* 194 (2007): 21–22; Uriel Simonsohn, "The Legal Bonds and Social Ties of Jewish Apostates and Their Spouses According to Gaonic Responsa," *Jewish Quarterly Review* 105 (2015): 417–18; Paola Tartakoff, *Between Christian and Jew: Conversion and Inquisition in the Crown of Aragon, 1250–1391* (Philadelphia, 2012), 92–93; idem, "Testing Boundaries: Jewish Conversion and Cultural Fluidity in Medieval Europe, c. 1200–1391," *Speculum* 90 (2015): 758–59; idem, *Conversion, Circumcision, and Ritual Murder in Medieval Europe* (Philadelphia, 2020), 101–2; this chapter, n. 4; and this volume, chapter 4, n. 60. There is also the issue of whether the reverting apostate might have felt uncomfortable returning to the same Jewish community from which he or she had apostatized.

3 The question begins: אחד שנשתמד ובא למדינה אחרת ונהג עצמו כדת יהודית ולא נודעה תשובתו לא בקבלה בפני שלשה ולא בטבילה ונגע ביין של ישראל. On the collection in ms. Bodl. 566, see S. Emanuel, *Shivrei Luḥot* (Jerusalem, 2006), 179–80, 297 (n. 350); and see this volume, chapter 1, n. 18. On the unrepentant apostate as a *yehudi ḥashud* (whose wine was prohibited for Jewish consumption), see Rashi's responsum, cited in this volume, chapter 1, n. 41.

case of *gerut*, conversion to Judaism) that the former apostate has now fully reaccepted his obligations as a Jew. Immersion for a returning apostate is considered a meritorious act (*miẓvah*) but not an absolute obligation (*ḥovah*), as it is in the case of a non-Jew who converts to Judaism. Moreover, Ri points to a geonic ruling that even a convert to Judaism who slides back to his prior (non-Jewish) observances (*ger she-ḥazar le-suro*) is not required to undergo immersion when he returns to the practice of Judaism and, thus, neither is a returning apostate.[4]

Although an *'am ha-'areẓ* who wishes to be elevated to the status of a *ḥaver*—a full-fledged member of the circle of those who were punctilious about ritual purity and related matters during the Mishnaic and talmudic periods—is required to submit to a formal acceptance (*qabbalah*) of these obligations before a tribunal of three (as per *Bekhorot* 30b), Ri maintains that this requirement need not be imposed in the case of a returning apostate. The *'am ha-'areẓ* has to be trusted to properly observe the purity requirements. That cannot be established without a firm commitment by the aspiring *ḥaver*, which must be explicitly expressed before a tribunal of *ḥaverim*.

The former apostate's trustworthiness with respect to performing religious acts such as ritual slaughter has not been formally established in this instance; indeed, the ability to once again perform *sheḥitah* might well require a formal *qabbalah* to verify that the former apostate is able to perform the act properly, with the proper intention. Nonetheless, Ri held that to consider a former apostate's touch as still rendering wine non-kosher once he again appears to be practicing and living as a Jew is not required, even without a more formal verification process. Indeed, on the basis of two parallel *sugyot* (*'Avodah Zarah* 7a and *Bekhorot* 31a), Ri felt that this is so even though the repentant apostate

4 See *Oẓar ha-Geonim*, ed. B. M. Levine, vol. 7 (Jerusalem, 1936), 111–12 (secs. 259–60, to *Yevamot* 47b). However, Ri (unlike his student Samson of Sens) does not mention that there are geonic formulations (one of which begins, ששאלתם משומד שאמר רוצה אני לחזור שלא באותה המדינה שפשע מנגדינן ליה וצריך טבילה או דילמא מהימנינן ליה ולא צריך טבילה) which recommend that lashes should be administered to a returning apostate, and that he should make a public confession. See also *Teshuvot R. Natronai Gaon*, ed. Brody, 396 (n. 4); and this chapter, n. 19.

in the question being presented had apostatized and then returned to Jewish practice on a prior occasion, and his current (Jewish) behavior in private has not otherwise been verified.[5] The seemingly porous nature of the boundaries between the Jewish and Christian communities implicit in Ri's formulation, and the suggestion that at least some apostates apparently moved back and forth between these communities with relative ease (for pecuniary or other purposes), are attested by a number of other rabbinic texts from northern France in this period and beyond, as we shall have occasion to discuss further at the end of this chapter.[6]

---

5 See ms. Bodl. 566: דעתי נוטה להתיר כי טבילה זו שנהגו אינה אלא משום נקיות וטהרה כדכת׳ וזרקתי עליכם מים טהורי׳ וכו׳, מצוה ולא חובה. ובתשובו׳ הגאו׳ כדברי, דאפי׳ גר שחזר ונשתמד אין צריך טבילה כשישוב. ואי מחמ׳/משום חסרון קבלה, דאפי׳ עם הארץ צריך שלשה כשבא לקבל דברי חבירות כדאית׳ בפר׳ [עד כמה], נר׳ בעיני דהיינו שלא להאמינו, דישראל חשוד מקרי ונאמ׳ שאינו מקפיד על מגע גוי ומנבל שחיטה לתיבאון. אבל להחזיקו משומד לנסך יין לא כיון דנוהג כדת יהודית, דלא גרע ממשמר שבתו בשוק. ואע״ג דכבר פעם אחרת נשתמד ושב וחזר לקלקולו ולא ידעינן אי שב בצינעא או דוקא בפרהיסיא אין מקבלים אותו לר׳ יהוד׳ לפי׳ ר״ת, דהכי מוכח שמעתתא ובמס׳ דמאי, הא פסקינן בפר׳ ק׳ דע״ז ובשלהי עד כמה הלכה כאותו הזוג דבין כך ובין כך מקבלין אותו משום דכת׳ שובו בנים שובבים. ואע״ג דאפי׳ הכי קבלה צריך, היינו למיחש ולאו לאחזוקי כדפי׳. Ri points to a talmudic *sugya* (*'Eruvin* 69a–b) which asserts that if a *mumar* appears to observe the Sabbath publicly, he is considered sufficiently observant to allow for his participation in an *'eruv*, even if it is not certain that he observes the Sabbath in private. See also *Sefer Mizvot Gadol le-R. Mosheh mi-Coucy, hilkhot 'eruvin* (*'asin mi-derabban*, 1) (Venice, 1547), fol. 244b: תניא ישראל משומד המשמר שבתו בשוק הרי הוא כישראל ומבטל רשות. However, a *mumar* who publicly desecrates the Sabbath is treated like a non-Jew with respect to the *'eruv*. As noted by Ri, the parallel *sugyot* in *'Avodah Zarah* 7a and *Bekhorot* 30b–31a also deal with the question of public versus private observance; see also the *Tosafot* of Ri's son, *Tosafot R. Elḥanan 'al Massekhet 'Avodah Zarah*, ed. A. Y. Kreuzer (Jerusalem, 2003), 42–43, s.v. *ve-kulan she-ḥazru* (citing Ri), which are similar to *Tosafot Bekhorot* 31a, s.v. *ve-kulan* (and *Tosafot 'Avodah Zarah*, loc. cit). On the expression (and valence) of *mizvah ve-lo ḥovah* in medieval Ashkenazic rabbinic literature, see *Teshuvot Maharam defus Prague*, ed. M. A. Bloch (Budapest, 1895), #259, sec. 2. Although this responsum is loosely associated with a bloc of responsa produced by someone named R. Isaac, it cannot be attributed with any certainty to Ri; see S. Emanuel, "Teshuvot shel ha-Maharam mi-Rothenburg she-Einam shel ha-Maharam," *Shenaton ha-Mishpat ha-'Ivri* 21 (1998–2000): 161 (n. 54). On the (similar) connotation of these terms within talmudic literature (when juxtaposed), see *Yevamot* 65b, *Ketubot* 49b, *Ḥullin* 105a.

6 See Simcha Emanuel, *Shivrei Luḥot* (Jerusalem, 2006), 207 (n. 87); P. Tartakoff, "Testing Boundaries," 734–36; and this chapter, nn. 62–64. Cf. Oded Zinger, "One

Ri puts forward an additional explanation for the difference between a returning apostate and the *'am ha-'arez* who seeks to become a *ḥaver*. An *'am ha-'arez* who seeks to elevate his status to that of a *ḥaver* (*le-haḥmir be-divrei ḥaverut*) must make a formal acceptance before an appropriate tribunal so that he can now be deemed qualified to hold this new and more demanding status. On the other hand, although the penitent apostate had denied the essence of the Almighty (*kafar be-'iqqar*), now that he has recanted he can easily return to his Creator (and to his prior level of observance) by regretting his bad deeds, since he is returning to a status he occupied previously; a formal acceptance akin to what is demanded of the *'am ha-'arez* is therefore not required (*sagi be-lo qabbalah*). Ri further supports his contention that an apostate's (spiritual) return to the belief in and practice of Judaism is relatively easy and unencumbered with a suggestive observation about the venal motivations that in his view lead to one's becoming an apostate, especially as a means of escaping poverty: "For most of those [who apostatize] do so because of self-indulgence [or pleasure; *ki rubbam le-te'avon*], or due to the pressure of poverty [*doḥaq 'oni*] or because of [the monies lost and the debts incurred while] playing dice. They regret their actions immediately but are afraid of the non-Jews, and so they go to a different place and return there."[7]

Hour He Is a Christian and the Next He Is a Muslim: A Family Dispute from the Cairo Geniza," *Al-Mazaq: Journal of the Medieval Mediterranean* 10 (2018): 7–9.

7 To be sure, motivations for conversion to Christianity run the gamut from genuine conviction to pragmatic interests, and even despair. See, e.g., Jacob Katz, *Exclusiveness and Tolerance* (Oxford, 1961), 75–77 [= *Bein Yehudim le-Goyim* (Jerusalem, 1960), 83–85]; David Berger, "Jacob Katz on Jews and Christians in the Middle Ages," in *The Pride of Jacob: Essays on Jacob Katz and His Work*, ed. J. M. Harris (Cambridge, MA, 2002), 52–54; J. C. Schmitt, *The Conversion of Herman the Jew* (Philadelphia, 2003), 4–9, 19–20; Chaviva Levin, "Jewish Conversion to Christianity in Medieval Northern Europe: Encountered and Imagined, 1100–1300" (PhD diss., New York University, 2006), 103–112, 240–42; P. Tartakoff, "Testing Boundaries," 743–44; and idem, *Conversion, Circumcision, and Ritual Murder*, 100–101. For additional examples of the venal and self-indulgent (among other less ideological) reasons behind apostasy to Christianity in medieval Ashkenaz of the kinds noted by Ri, see *Sefer Ḥasidim* (Parma), ed. J. Wistinetzki (Frankfurt, 1924), 455 (sec. 1876); ibid., 76, sec. 210 [= *Sefer Ḥasidim* (Bologna), ed. R. Margoliot (Jerusalem, 1957), 193 (sec. 204)]; D. Malkiel, "Jews and Apostates in Medieval Europe,"

Moreover, Ri notes that the reverting apostate in question felt genuine remorse while still in a state of apostasy and had asked Ri for a written document that would serve to ease his return by allaying the concerns of the Jewish community. Although Ri denied this request, he again asserts that the apostate's level of repentance as seen when he returns to the Jewish community is of sufficient moment that any Jewish wine he touches from that point forward should be considered kosher and permissible for Jewish consumption. Finally, Ri notes that a convert to Judaism is required to indicate his acceptance of the precepts before a tribunal of three judges because the conversion process is associated by the Torah with a form of judgment (*mishpat*, in Nu. 15–16, Deut. 1:16), which mandates the involvement of a duly constituted Jewish court. The process of reversion, however, is not associated with the requirement of *mishpat* and therefore does not need acceptance before a formal (judicial) tribunal.[8]

7–8, 28–34; Tartakoff, "Testing Boundaries," 737–42; and cf. Moshe Yagur, "Zehut Datit u-Gevulot Qehillatiyyim be-Ḥevrat ha-Genizah (Me'ot ha-10–13): Gerim, 'Avadim, Mumarim" (PhD diss., Hebrew University, 2017), 143–57; and this volume, chapter 1, n. 7. New converts to Christianity were often promised (and sometimes received) economic and other forms of assistance. See S. Grayzel, *The Church and the Jews in the XIIIth Century*, vol. 1 (New York, 1966), 18–21; Tartakoff, "Testing Boundaries," 743, 747, 751; idem, *Between Christian and Jew: Conversion and Inquisition in the Crown of Aragon, 1250–1391* (Philadelphia, 2012), 83–95, 93–94; Rebecca Rist, *Popes and Jews* (Oxford, 2016), 208–13; S. Simonsohn, *The Apostolic See and the Jews*, 52–57, 79, 98–99, 275; D. Malkiel, "Jews and Apostates in Medieval Europe"; Bernard Rosenzweig, "Apostasy in the Late Middle Ages in Germany and Austria," *Dine Israel* 10–11 (1981–83): 54–55; and cf. Elisheva Carlebach, *Divided Souls* (New Haven, CT, 1991), 24. Nonetheless, Ri still felt that immersion as a means of expiation was appropriate (and a *mizvah*), since there was plenty of opportunity for sinful behavior while in a state of apostasy, irrespective of the intention(s) with which the apostasy was undertaken.

8 See ms. Bodl. 566: אי נמי עם הארץ דקמי הכי ישר׳ הוא ולהחמיר בדברי חברות צריך קבלה, אבל משומד שכפר בעיקר ונמלך, דדבר קל לשוב וחזר לבוראו וניחם על הרעה וסגי בלא קבלה. כי רובם לתיאבון או על ידי דוחק עוני ושחוק בקוביא עושין. ומתחרטין מיד אלא יריאים מפני הגוים והולכים למדינה אחרת ושבים. ואע״ג דגר שנחשד בדברי תורה צריך קבלה כדמוכח בההיא דע״ז ודבכורות קימ׳ נמי אגר כדמש׳ במסכת דמאי, נראה בעיני דשאני גר ובדבר קל וחומר לאסורין כדאמ׳ גיורא עד עשר׳ דרי לא תבז׳ ארמאה באפיה, הילכך צריך קבלה. ועוד כי מעשיו מקולקלין כדאמר׳ קשים גרים לישראל כספחת. ועוד זה בעודו משומד מתחרט ובקש ממני לעשות כתב וישוב, ולא רציתי. לכך תשובתו תשובה אפי׳ מעשיו מקולקלין לשתות יין נסך ולא מקרי עובד ע״ז ומחלל שבת בפרהסיא. ועוד נר׳ לי דכל קבלה דברי חברות בשלשה עשו כגר דצריך ג׳ דמשפט כתי׳ ביה. והתם אין צריך ג׳ אלא לכתחלה משום יושבי קרנות דקיימ׳ לן שנים שדנו

Although the wine touched by this reverting apostate after he returned to the Jewish community is permitted according to Ri (and need not be discarded), it is equally clear from this version of his responsum that Ri fully endorses the practice of immersion for a returning apostate, as was apparently customary. He refers to immersion as a *mizvah*, a meritorious act and precept that should be done, indicating that immersion serves to cleanse and expiate the former apostate on a spiritual level and perhaps also functions as a form of un-baptism, although Ri does not explicitly say this. At the same time, however, Ri does not require the returning apostate to make a formal reacceptance of his Jewish obligations before a tribunal of three on any level, although he implies that there are some rabbinic authorities who did. The technical point of Jewish law Ri addresses is the status of wine that a returning apostate touches after he had rejoined the Jewish community in its observances (which was *sine qua non*) but before he was able to immerse himself. In resolving this situation, Ri marshals several talmudic sources to rule that the wine is permitted. It should be noted that Ri's full name, Isaac ben R. Samuel, appears in this manuscript at the end of his responsum.

דיניהם דין. ואין לי להאריך בזה. ושלי, יצחק בר' שמואל. Cf. *Teshuvot R. Yiẓḥaq ben Shmu'el of Dampierre*, ed. Roth and Reiner, 82 (n. 24). Ri distinguishes similarly between a convert to Judaism who appears not to have accepted certain aspects of Jewish law (and is thus required to make a *qabbalah* before a *beit din* to have these suspicions removed) and the reverting apostate who is not required to make any *qabbalah* at all. On the need for a court of three judges for conversion to Judaism (and its biblical source), see *Yevamot* 46b and *Tosafot*, s.v. *mishpat ketiv beh*. See also this volume, chapter 1, n. 20, where Isaac b. Joseph of Corbeil is cited by *Semaq mi-Ẓurikh* (2:49; see also this chapter, n. 34, and the manuscript variants cited there) as ruling that a written document of return is not required because the former apostate himself asserts that he is a Jew (as he always was) and conducts himself religiously as a Jew (כיון שהוא אומר/מודה [ב]עצמו שהוא יהודי ונוהג עצמו כ[דת] ישראל; see esp. ms.Bodl. 879, fol. 95v; and ms. Paris 381, fol. 46v). Cf. *Tosafot Yevamot* 47a, s.v. *be-muḥzaq* (= *Sefer ha-Yashar*, sec. 336); and see also *Tosafot R. Shimshon mi-Shanẓ 'al Massekhet Pesaḥim* (3b), ed. M. Y. From (Jerusalem, 1956), 7, s.v. *ve-'ana*, for Rabbenu Tam's ruling that an otherwise unknown person who asserts that he is a Jew (or a convert to Judaism) can be believed without further verification. It would seem, however, from Isaac of Corbeil's formulation, there were some societal expectations with regard to an apostate who had reverted.

By comparing the reverting apostate to both a *ger* and an *'am ha-'arez* who was seeking to be elevated to the status of a *ḥaver*, Ri suggests that in the case of the reverting apostate as well, it would have been reasonable to think that a public act of verification was required, not because Torah law mandates such an act or because the former apostate needs to demonstrate his dedication as a symbolic matter or as an element of repentance, but because the Jewish community needs to be able to ascertain his true intentions. However, Ri's ruling maintains that since the reverting apostate is not changing his religious status (or the level of his required observance) to one that is new for him (which is the case for both a *ger* and a newly minted *ḥaver*) but is instead returning to where he had once been in terms of both the level of his observance and his membership in the Jewish community, no formal act is required. Nonetheless, it would appear that, for Ri, the ritual immersion he recommends as a *mizvah* for the reverting apostate not only grants the former apostate needed expiation but also serves as a kind of indicator or symbol for the returning apostate himself—and for the community—signifying the seriousness of his recommitment.

Before we move on to compare this responsum of Ri with similar passages from his student Riẓba and the German Tosafist Simḥah of Speyer—to note more precisely the differences between them with respect to the role of immersion in the *mikveh*—we must analyze the other manuscript versions of Ri's formulation. A second version found within an especially rich manuscript collection of marginal glosses to *Sefer Mordekhai* (ms. Vercelli C1) records the case of an apostate who appeared in the community of Troyes, suggesting that he had lived elsewhere during his apostasy and had then relocated to Troyes at the time of his reversion.[9] There, two Jews questioned the reverting apostate

9 See ms. Vercelli (Bishop's Seminary) C1, fol. 292a, in a marginal gloss (= *Teshuvot Maharam*, ed. Emanuel, 487, n. 2; and *Teshuvot R. Yiẓḥaq ben Shmu'el of Dampierre*, ed. Roth and Reiner, 80, n. 3): מעשה במשומד אחד שבא בטרוייש ושאלו לו ב׳ יהודי׳ אם עשה תשובה וא׳ הן. ונכנס בבית שירא ליאו׳ ועש׳ עצמו שמש והוצי׳ מכל היינו׳[ת]. ו[נ]שאל לר״י על היינות והכשיה, דל״ד לעם הארץ דצריך ג׳ אנשים, דבשלמ׳ הת׳ מחזיק עצמו בחבר ולא סגי בלא ג׳, אבל האי משומד יודע הו׳ שכל זמן שאי׳ טובל ומקבל עליו דברי חברו׳ הוא מוחזק כגוי. לכך לא צרי׳ לקבל לפניה׳ דבקל יש לנו לומ׳ ששב אל בוראו כיון שנוהג עצמו בדת יהדו׳. עיין בבכורות ס״פ עד כמה שם פי׳ באורך ועיי״ש.

about the sincerity of his repentance, which he directly affirmed. Subsequently, the penitent former apostate became a servant (*shamash*) in a Jewish household (of the Sirleon family), which brought him into contact with their wine. According to this version as well, the halakhic question put to Ri concerned the status of that wine.

Ri responds that the wine is certainly kosher. Only with respect to the designation of a (newly careful) *'am ha-'arez̤* as a fully qualified *ḥaver* (who is now permitted to handle ritually pure foods) does the Talmud require a religious tribunal of three to confirm or ratify this change in status.[10] In the case of the former apostate, however:

> He knows that as long as he has not immersed himself and accepted upon himself the yoke of full observance [*she-kol zeman she-'eino toveil u-meqabbel 'alav divrei ḥaverut*], his religious status is still to be considered as that of a non-Jew [*muḥzaq ke-goy*]. Thus, it is not necessary to have [a tribunal of] three before whom he must accept [Judaism once again], since it is easy for us to verify that he has returned to his Creator [*debe-qal yesh lanu lomar she-shav 'el bor'o*], for he now conducts himself in accordance with the Jewish religion [*kevan she-noheg 'az̤mo be-dat yehudit*].[11]

10 At the end of this passage, Ri refers to his discussion of this matter in tractate *Bekhorot*. See *Tosafot Bekhorot* 31a, s.v. *ve-kulan she-hazru*, and *Shitat ha-Qadmonim 'al Massekhet 'Avodah Zarah*, ed. M. J. Blau (New York, 1969), 45 (*A.Z.* 7a); and *Tosafot R. Elḥanan*, ed. Kreuzer, loc. cit (this chapter, n. 5). E. E. Urbach, *Ba'alei ha-Tosafot*, 2:667–69, maintains that Samson of Sens was a redactor of the standard *Tosafot* to *Bekhorot*, on the basis of Ri's teachings. R. Samson often cites Ri by name, although *Tosafot Shanz̤ 'al Massekhet Bekhorot*, ed. Y. D. Ilan (Bnei Brak, 1997), 61–62, does not contain this section.

11 The glosses to the Vercelli C1 manuscript record other rulings in the name of Ri, and all of them appear to connote Isaac b. Samuel of Dampierre. See fol. 226v for Ri's uncertainty as to whether young children as well must drink the four cups of wine at the Seder, also recorded in Ri's name in the *Tosafot* (*Rabbenu Perez̤*) contained in the *Sefer Mordekhai* to *'Arvei Pesaḥim* (108b), ed. Y. Horowitz (Jerusalem 2008), 180–181 (and see the editor's introduction, 14–15); fol. 376r, for a ruling by Ri that houses rented from non-Jews do not require a *mezuzah*, which is recorded in the *Tosafot* of his son, Elḥanan (in the name of his father and teacher) to

This version of Ri's ruling, which is shorter on certain details than the passage in the Bodleian manuscript discussed earlier but more illuminating in other respects, confirms the issues that were central to Ri regarding the question before him. In this version the apostate who had returned was asked by others about his sincerity, and he maintains that he is fully sincere. If he were a convert to Judaism, his own statement of sincerity before two individuals who were not connected with a bona fide rabbinic court that had been convened for this purpose would be meaningless. But in this instance, since the apostate is attempting to return to his earlier practices and status, this declaration to other people apparently holds some meaning.

In this version Ri openly suggests that the reverting apostate needs to do something to convince or assuage the members of the Jewish community regarding his sincerity, and that this is accomplished by the former apostate's immersion in the *mikveh*, along with his demonstrated recommitment to full Jewish observance. Although the Almighty knows what is in the reverting apostate's heart, he has been a *Yisra'el ḥashud* to this point, so the community

---

'Avodah Zarah 21a, s.v. *ha-'amar* (ed. Kreuzer, 116–17); and *Tosafot 'Avodah Zarah* 21a, s.v. *af* (end). See also fol. 144r for a gloss that records a question put to Ri about a problem with salting meat. This question actually came before Rabbenu Tam; see *Mordekhai* to *Ḥullin*, sec. 702. However, Ri was the narrator of the episode. He questioned his teacher's ruling, and then explains additional aspects according to his teacher's interpretation; the *Mordekhai* passage ends with the marking תוס׳. A second gloss appears on fol. 144r, in the name of Ri, about a different kind of problem incurred while salting; cf. *Mordekhai* to *Hullin* [98a], sec. 680, and *Sefer Or Zarua'*, pt. 1, sec. 453, ed. Machon Yerushalayim, 391–93. For another instance of a gloss in this manuscript where Ri appears to "take over" a responsum of his teacher Rabbenu Tam, see fol. 372r (*hilkhot sefer Torah*). See also fol. 354v, for a responsum by Ri (*ve-heshiv Ri*) concerning the validity of a bill of divorce (= *Haggahot Mordekhai to Gittin*, sec. 466). A gloss on fol. 102v (inserted into the body of the *Mordekhai* text in the right-side column) records a responsum by Ri about a note of debt. A gloss on fol. 365r (on the top right-hand side of the folio) records a responsum by Ri's student, Isaac b. Abraham (Riẓba) of Dampierre: ונשאל לריב״א על אשר כתב הר״ר שמחה במחזור ויטרי שלו בשם רש״י שאין נדה צריכה לפתוח פה בשעת טבילה. ונראה איסור גמור הוא וצריכה לפתוח פה . . . והשיב מה ששאלת אם צריכה לפתוח פה בשעת טבילה וכן הוא בעיניך שהיא צריכה . . . אך משם איו ראיה לפרש״י . . . וראיה לדברי [שלא צריכה] וכו׳ . . . ושלו׳ יצחק בן אברהם. On the use of the acronym ריב״א to refer to Riẓba of Dampierre, see Urbach, *Ba'alei ha-Tosafot*, 1:261.

needs to have evidence demonstrating that he wishes to be accepted once again as a member in good standing. Even though the wine he touched is kosher, Ri holds that, without immersion, the former apostate would still be considered a non-Jew (*muḥzaq ke-goy*) by the regular members of the community, even though there is no indication that the immersion has to be undertaken in the presence of any witnesses or rabbinic body. For Isaac of Dampierre (who is referred to in this passage only as Ri), ritual immersion in this version of his ruling is seen as a means of indicating and ensuring the compliance of the penitent with the requirements of Judaism, in addition to his accepting full observance once again, if not as a means of "undoing" his baptism. It certainly serves to alert the penitent to his renewed status and responsibilities.[12]

Just prior to this passage, another marginal gloss in this same *Sefer Mordekhai* manuscript records that Ri was asked about a convert to Judaism who had (improperly) undergone circumcision at night, in front of a tribunal of three that was also not properly constituted. In this case, Ri (who is identified fully at the end of the passage as Isaac b. Samuel) rules that most of the conversion procedures had to be redone due to the requirement that a (new) convert must be initiated into Judaism by a properly constituted judicial body.[13] The

12 Urbach, *Ba'alei ha-Tosafot*, 268–69, fails to note this (subtle) difference between the ruling of Ri and the similar ruling permitting the wine made by his student, Riẓba of Dampierre (this chapter, n. 18), who does not see a need for the immersion. *Sefer Yosef ha-Maqqane*, ed. J. Rosenthal (Jerusalem, 1970), 79, records an anecdote that involved Yosef b. Isaac *Bekhor Shor* of Orleans (who, like Ri, was a talmudic student of Rabbenu Tam) and an apostate who was so thoroughly convinced or mortified by R. Yosef's refutation of his claims with respect to Isaiah 53 that "he immediately tore his garments, rolled in the dust, and returned [to the Jewish community] in repentance." Cf. M. A. Signer, "God's Love for Israel: Apologetic and Hermeneutical Strategies in Twelfth-Century Biblical Exegesis," in *Jews and Christians in Twelfth-Century Europe*, ed. M. A. Signer and J. Van Engen (Notre Dame, IN, 2001), 124–25. If one assumes the anecdote has some basis in fact, the omission of halakhic details (such as ritual immersion) in a polemical text such as this would not be surprising. Moreover, these actions appear to have represented an initial, public demonstration of repentance by the apostate, which could easily have been followed later by immersion.

13 Ms. Vercelli, 291v: מעשה בא לפני ר״י בגר אחד שנמול בלילה בפני ג וגם השלשה לא היו כשרים זה לזה כי שניים מהם נשואין ב׳ אחיות. והשיב ר״י כיון שנמול בלילה לא עלתה לו מילה ליכנס בברית

formal differences between this case and that of the former apostate in Troyes are clear, but so is the basic expectation or requirement for a returning apostate to undergo immersion on his own, as he resumes full Jewish observance under the watchful eyes of the members of the community.

It is instructive to briefly compare this version of Ri's responsum on the returning apostate who touched the wine of a Jew with a responsum by Rashi about whether the wine of an apostate who had returned could now be consumed by other Jews, or whether it was necessary to wait until the former apostate had maintained his repentance for a lengthy period (*'ad she-'amdu bi-teshuvatan yamim rabbim*) so that it would be well known and clear to all (*ve-tihyeh teshuvatan mefursemet u-geluyah*). Rashi unequivocally permits other Jews to consume this wine immediately (whether the apostates in question had initially converted willingly or against their will), without requiring any act of return or acceptance or verification (or purification), neither immersion nor a tribunal: "As soon as they accept upon themselves to return to fear our God [*le-yir'at Ẓurenu*], their wine is kosher [as are they; *harei hen be-kashrutan*]."[14] The reacceptance of Jewish observance by the former apostate is considered valid and immediately effective even though it is self-initiated and it is not being formally monitored by anyone else. Rashi, however, is not trying to save the wine of another Jew from disqualification, as Ri was. Rather, Rashi permitted other Jews to drink this wine *a priori*, even if it had been handled by the former apostate. It is not clear that Ri would have allowed this, although Ri

על ידה מ"ד אטבילה שאינה אלא ביום משו' דמשפט כת' ביה . . . יתכן בעיני דצריך לחזור ולהטיף ממנו דם ברית ויזהר מכאן ואילך לעשות מילה וטבילה ביום. Ri also discusses whether three proper judges are needed only for the acceptance of the commandments or also to witness the immersion and circumcision. His conclusion is that, a priori, it is best to have three present at all times. This responsum is signed, ושלו' יצחק בן שמואל. See also ms. Jerusalem (Heichal Shlomo) Goldschmidt 45 ג (= Jerusalem NLI $4^0$6695; #38531), fol. 153v; and my "Approaches to Conversion in Medieval European Rabbinic Literature," in *Conversion, Intermarriage, and Jewish Identity*, ed. A. Mintz and M. Stern (New York, 2015), 221–23.

14 See *Teshuvot Rashi*, ed. Elfenbein, #168; Avraham Grossman, *Ḥakhmei Ẓarefat ha-Rishonim* (Jerusalem, 1995), 153–54; and Avraham Grossman, *Rashi* (Jerusalem, 2006), 257–58. Note the variant reading in *Teshvuot Rashi*, ed. Elfenbein, 189 (n. 19): *mishe-qiblu 'al 'aẓman lashuv*.

in effect agrees with Rashi that no public procedure or lengthy waiting period is necessary to verify the sincerity of the apostate's return, even in a case where the apostasy had been undertaken willingly. However, for Ri immersion was nonetheless incumbent upon the penitent, as a private act that serves to seal his return to the Jewish community. For Rashi this practice does not appear to have been required at all.[15]

The third version of Ri's ruling (found in the latest of the three manuscripts involved, which was written in a Spanish hand) is a summary paraphrase of the first, longer ruling in the Bodleian manuscript described earlier. It contains fewer details of the apostate's larger story than contained in either of the first two versions, but it does serve to confirm aspects in the Vercelli manuscript version, and it adds one potentially significant piece of reasoning that is not found at all in the first manuscript version.[16]

Ri's argument is that immersion is not an absolute talmudic requirement for a penitent sinner. However, as the relevant Talmudic *sugyot* (*Bekhorot* 31a and *'Avodah Zarah* 7a) indicate, a penitent sinner can be readmitted as a full

---

15 Urbach, *Ba'alei ha-Tosafot*, 1:244–45, maintains that Ri took a more lenient stance toward a returning apostate and was a model in this regard for his student Riẓba (who held that immersion was not required; see this chapter, n. 18). Urbach bases his assessment of Ri's approach primarily on the responsum about drinking the wine of a penitent apostate (in the previous note), which modern scholarship has attributed to Rashi. Urbach cites this responsum from *Shibbolei ha-Leqet*, part 2, ed. S. Ḥasida (Jerusalem, 1988), 21 (sec. 5), which begins with the phrase *sha'alu 'et rebbe* (as it does in Elfenbein's edition of *Teshuvot Rashi*). It is unclear why Urbach believed that Ri was the teacher and authority who responded to this question; the more demanding responsum of Ri, found in ms. Bodl. 566 and ms. Vercelli C1, was apparently unknown to Urbach.

16 See ms. Leipzig (University Library) 1119 (#74146, fifteenth–sixteenth century, a *liqqut be-halakhah* in a Spanish hand, with material from different areas and regions), fol. 16v (= *Teshuvot R. Yiẓḥaq ben Shmu'el mi-Dampierre*, ed. Roth and Reiner, 80, n. 2). This passage appears right after a piece from *Sefer ha-Yashar le-Rabbenu Tam*, and before a ruling in the name of Riba: מעשה ביהודי אחד שאמ׳ לחברו לך למרתף והבא יין והלך והביא יין והלך והביא ואחר כך נמצא משומד. ופסק רבי׳ יצחק הזקן ז״ל דלא מצינו טבילה בתלמוד לבעל תשובה, אלא לקבל עליו דברי חברות. וכיון דאמ׳ לו יהודי אתה ואמ׳ לו הן, היינו קבלת דברי חברות. וכן מוכח ההיא דסנהדרין בפרק זה בורר (סנהדרין כה ע״ב) מאימתי חזרתן משישברו פספיסיהם, והאי נמי מדקאמ׳ יהודי אני היינו שבור ע״כ. For the possible impact of Spanish halakhic developments on this formulation, see this volume, chapter 6, n. 24.

member of the observant community if he has accepted its requirements (= *le-qabbel 'alav ḥaverut*). This is akin to the *'am ha-'areẓ* who seeks to become a *ḥaver*, where a more formal *qabbalah* is explicitly required to grant the former *'am ha-'areẓ* this new level of expertise. However in this particular case, a Jew had challenged the reverting apostate about whether he had sincerely and fully repented, and he answered in the affirmative; this is tantamount to his accepting *ḥaverut*. Moreover, the Talmud instructs (*Sanhedrin* 25a–b), regarding the reacceptance of a former gambler as a reliable witness, that this is accomplished when he destroys his gambling cards (and other implements) and will not play with them even when money is not involved—thus demonstrating that he has been broken of his prior bad habits and negative status. In the case of the former apostate, when he says that he is once again a fully committed and practicing Jew, he has broken, in effect, his prior status as an apostate.

In this version of Ri's ruling, the verbal reacceptance of his Judaism in front of others appears to be more substantive than immersion in the *mikveh* (which is not indicated by the Talmud) as a means of demonstrating sincere repentance and change. Nonetheless, a formal *qabbalah* before a duly constituted tribunal (such as the one an *'am ha-'areẓ* must undergo to become a *ḥaver*), which would obviously serve to verify his qualifications even more extensively, was not endorsed by Ri for the reverting apostate, although we will shortly see that there were other Tosafists who sought to make this a requirement in such instances as well.[17]

We can now proceed to examine the responsum about a similar case composed by Ri's student, Riẓba. Although the discussion of this case clearly shows that it was about a separate situation (and was not merely a reassessment of the same case Ri had addressed), the fact that there are only slight differences in the details and circumstances of these accounts suggests that reversion to Judaism following apostasy was not a rare occurrence at this time, despite the grave concerns (and threatened punishments) expressed by the Church and Christian rulers with regard to such reversions. Riẓba's responsum maintains that neither *qabbalah* nor *tevilah* (acceptance before a tribunal of three or

17 Cf. this volume, chapter 1, at n. 24.

immersion) are required *a priori* to permit the wine a penitent apostate had touched, since he is now acting in accordance with Jewish religious practices (*kevan she-noheg be-dat yehudit*). He has completely abandoned their abominations (*kevan she-hinniaḥ kol tarfutam*) and has returned to his Creator.

Riẓba accepted the self-admission of the former apostate in the case before him because, in addition, he had given Riẓba his wallet to hold for safekeeping during the Sabbath (*hifqid kiso be-Shabbat*). This shows that the former apostate was prepared to observe the Sabbath once again, at least publicly, which serves for Riẓba as at least a partial verification of his intent. Although this act was not so meaningful in the eyes of Riẓba's brother, Samson of Sens, as we shall see shortly, Riẓba suggests (employing terms used by Ri as well) that, because we can see that the former apostate has returned to his Creator, the wine he touches at this point is permissible for other Jews to drink. Riẓba adds that this is true "even for those who are more stringent [in terms of what a returning apostate is required to do] . . . since he conducts himself according to the Jewish religion [*be-dat yehudit*], and even if he did not immerse himself."

Riẓba, unlike Ri, was not convinced about the usefulness of immersion, and in this regard Riẓba's position is indeed closer to that of Rashi's. Riẓba is aware that some advocated this additional requirement, but immersion does not speak to the sincerity issue, which was what most concerned him. However, in the specific case that came before him, Riẓba was most impressed that the penitent apostate left his wallet with him for the Sabbath; this accords with the ruling in *'Eruvin* 69b (*shomer Shabbato ba-shuk*) that one who does so is treated as a Jew with respect to the placing of an *'eruv*, a *sugya* that Ri also referred to in the lengthiest version of his ruling as a solid theoretical benchmark. Although this does not constitute a formal declaration before a rabbinic tribunal, it was deemed sufficient by Riẓba to establish the sincerity of the penitent in this case, as he repented and returned from his apostasy on his own.

Indeed, Riẓba adds in conclusion that, although the Talmud maintains (*Sanhedrin* 25b) that a person who was heavily involved in lending (to Jews) at interest or in gambling cannot reverse his status of untrustworthiness until his various ill-gotten monetary gains are returned, in this instance—in which the person involved had apostatized but has now returned—he is considered a *ba'al teshuvah* in all respects and is somewhat similar to a convert (*ve-domeh qeẓat la-ger*). As long as he returns to his Creator and endeavors to return any ill-gotten gains accrued during his apostasy (*le-taqqen 'avtato asher 'ivvet*), his status as a penitent is not vitiated, even if he still has outstanding ill-gotten monetary gains in his possession that have not yet been fully restored to their rightful owners.[18]

This kind of personal acceptance or repentance (*beino le-vein 'aẓmo*) is explicitly deemed by the Talmud (*Yevamot* 47a) to be insufficient with respect to conversion to Judaism. However, according to Riẓba, it appears to be acceptable for a reverting apostate if it is linked with a public indication of his seriousness and sincerity. Ri did not require even this much verification, but both he and Riẓba were concerned with several dimensions that had not been sufficiently addressed by earlier Ashkenazic rabbinic authorities and literature: What acts or representations are necessary to establish an acceptable level of sincerity? To what extent is a return to the Jewish community and its observances sufficient by itself? Are additional acts of contrition or commitment required? And what is the role of immersion in a *mikveh*?

Indeed, these same issues underlie an exchange between Riẓba and his brother, Samson of Sens, as well. R. Samson had been asked to express his own view in the case that came before Riẓba. Against the ruling of Riẓba, who permitted the wine without any further proof of the apostate's sincerity or commitment—other than the fact that he had given up Christian practices and returned to a community, and was now practicing Judaism again as reflected by his public observances—Rash *mi-Shanẓ* maintains that a repentant apostate is required to make a formal acceptance or recommitment before a tribunal of

18 See *Sefer Or Zarua'*, pt. 1, sec. 448 (end, ed. Machon Yerushalayim, fol. 387a); the passage from *Tosafot Ḥiẓoniyyot* recorded in the *Shitah Mequbbeẓet 'al Massekhet Bekhorot* (31a), ed. Y. D. Ilan (Bnei Brak, 1992), 149; *Semaq mi-Ẓurikh*, ed. Y. Har-Shoshanim, vol. 2 (Jerusalem, 1977), 49 (*miẓvah* 156); *Teshuvot ha-Rashba ha-Meyuḥassot la-Ramban*, sec. 180; and *Teshuvot Maharam va-Ḥaverav*, ed. S. Emanuel, 487, n. 2. In *Shibbolei ha-Leqet* (this chapter, n. 15), Riẓba's view is recorded in the name of R. Isaac (without his father's name or a full acronym).

three (*qabbalah*), in the same way the Talmud requires an *'am ha-'arez̤* who wishes to become a *ḥaver* to make such an acceptance (*Bekhorot* 30b).

In accordance with a ruling by R. Z̤emaḥ Gaon (late ninth century), R. Samson does not require or see great value in immersion, since it is only a private act. But R. Z̤emaḥ did require, in addition to lashes, that the apostate stand up before the congregation and confess what he had done and what sinful actions he had been unable to resist. Once the reverting apostate does that, everyone will know that he has repented, and others are once again permitted to eat and drink with him. Rash *mi-Shanz̤* asks (perhaps in part to negate Riz̤ba's contention that the apostate had returned to a level of Sabbath observance) how wine touched by this apostate may be permitted without this kind of public acceptance, "when he arrives [still] without a *talit*, like a non-Jew?"[19]

An individual who has apostatized and moved completely away from Torah observance needs to present a demonstrably sincere and verifiable level of acceptance:

> Can we indeed rely on the fact that he says that he has immersed privately, with no one to witness it [*ve-khi nismokh 'al mah she-hu 'omer she-tavalti beni u-ven 'az̤mi akh lo hayah sham adam*]? Perhaps he is saying this only so that some Jews will now give him charity. If he was truly sincere [*libbo la-shamayim*], would he not come before religious people [*ḥaverim*] to be accepted through his repentance? Since he has not done this, his thoughts [about return] can be detected through his actions [or lack thereof], which indicate that his heart is not yet in his return [*she-'ein be-libbo 'adayin*].[20]

19 The precise import of this imagery is unclear. Perhaps it is meant to undercut Riz̤ba's observation that the former apostate had given him his wallet for safekeeping prior to the Sabbath as a sign of his newfound religious commitment. See *Teshuvot Maharam va-Ḥaverav*, ed. Emanuel, 488, n.6; and cf. *Teshuvot Maharam*, ed. Prague, #186.

20 See *Teshuvot Maharam va-Ḥaverav*, ed. Emanuel, 487–88 (based on ms. Bodl. 844, fols. 82d–83a, sec. 206, which is a much-expanded version of Samson of Sens's response as found *Sefer Or Zarua'*, pt. 1, sec. 448): אנת אחי אן היא חכמתך וסכלנותיך, וכי דבריך הלכה למשה מסיני להתיר יין בלא ראיה. ופעם הראשון אשר שאלוני חביריי היושבי׳ עמי אמרי הא

Although there is no explicit discussion by Samson of Sens about the motives that led to apostasy in this case, he raises the possibility that the apostate's purported return to Jewish observance is a ploy on his part to now receive charity from Jews, which is also perhaps a response to his teacher, Ri of Dampierre. The apostate may well have had deeper dissatisfactions with Judaism, but if in fact he left the community to collect alms or to receive other support, as Ri had suggested, why should it not be assumed that he is now returning to the Jewish community (especially if it is a different one, located in a different place) for the same reason? Immersion or other forms of penance done in private will not accomplish the necessary level of verification for R. Samson to ensure that the apostate is not seeking to return for opportunistic reasons.

To this point we have seen that Ri of Dampierre considered immersion for a returning apostate to be a meritorious act (a *miẓvah*) as a means of expiation, and perhaps as a means of binding the former apostate to his recommitment to the Jewish community as well. At the same time, however, Ri's students, Rash *mi-Shanẓ* and Riẓba, while aware that some recommended or even required immersion, did not see much value in this act for returning apostates, albeit for rather different reasons; nor did *Sefer Ḥasidim* or any

---

אמרי׳ בפ׳ עד כמה [בכורות דף ל ע״ב] הבא לקבל דברי חבירות צריך שיקבל בפני שלשה חבירי׳ ק״ו זה המשומד לכל התורה כולה שצריך קבלה. אע״פ שאין צריך טבילה כמו שכת׳ רב צמח גאון, הלא הוא עצמו כת׳ (=אוצה״ג ליבמות, סוף סי׳ רנט) אע״ג דמקבל מלקות צריך שיעמוד בפרהסיא בפני הצבור ויתוודה על מה שעשה ועל מעשי׳ שבאו לידו ולאחר שיעשה שידוע לכל שעשה תשובה, מותר לאכול ולשתות עמו, עכ״ל רב צמח גאון. והיאך נמלכת להתיר מגעו של זה המשומד שבא בל[א] טלית כגוי. ועוד אמרי׳ בפ׳ השולח (דף מו ע״ב—מז ע״א) ההוא גברא דזבין נפשי׳ ללודאי וכו׳ . . . וזה שנשתמד לכל התורה ולא נודע תשובתו . . . וכי נסמוך על מה שהוא אומ׳ שטבלתי ביני ובין עצמי אך לא היה שם אדם. וגם שמא היה אומ׳ אלא כדי שיתנו לו צדקה. ואם היה לבו לשמים וכי לא היה בא אצל חכמים לקבלו בתשובה. מדלא עשה, מחשבתו ניכרת מתוך מעשיו שאין בלבו עדיין. Samson of Sens places heavy emphasis on the talmudic requirement for restitution and verification by a tribunal of Torah scholars when serious sins and misdeeds have been committed. Similarly, according to the *Or Zarua‘* passage, R. Samson notes the case recorded in *Sanhedrin* 25a, of a butcher who had sold non-kosher meat (and prohibited fat) who was required not only to personally repent but also to positively demonstrate (in the presence of others) that his lust for any profits gained through prohibited acts had in fact abated. Cf. Urbach, *Ba‘alei ha-Tosafot*, 265; and *Shibbolei ha-Leqet* (this chapter, n. 15).

penitential writings associated with Rash and Riẓba's contemporary, Judah *he-Ḥasid* (d. 1217).[21]

However, a number of rabbinic texts and manuscripts record a ruling by the German Tosafist and halakhist Simḥah b. Samuel of Speyer that all penitents (*ba'alei teshuvah*) are required to undergo *tevilah* as an obligatory ritual.[22] R. Simḥah bases his position on a case found in *Avot de-R. Natan* concerning a young woman held captive by gentiles. During the period of her captivity, she ate from their non-kosher food. Partaking of non-kosher food and drink does not create or engender ritual impurity of the body that must be nullified or removed according to statute; yet upon her release, immersion was required to purify her from these sinful acts or perhaps from her state of sinfulness.[23] Simḥah of Speyer was not concerned about verification per se. Like Ri he considered the immersion to be an act of purification. But for R. Simḥah, this was an obligation that had to be undertaken and not simply a meritorious act. Both Simḥah of Speyer and Ri display pronounced pietistic tendencies,[24] although their positions in this matter are expressed in halakhic terms.

---

21 Although no penitential tracts associated with Judah *he-Ḥasid* refer to immersion for a returning apostate, one such text does contain a penitential regimen for someone who "worshipped idolatry," ostensibly connoting apostasy to Christianity. See ms. Paris 1408 (#24886), fols. 137v–139r (*seder ha-teshuvah le-'oved 'avodah zarah lefi R. Yehudah he-Ḥasid*). The prescribed regimen includes acts of self-abnegation and denial that are to be undertaken through the first year after the sinful behaviors ceased. Cf. this volume, chapter 1, n. 23; this chapter, n. 43 (regarding Eleazar of Worms); and Emese Kozme, "Sidrei Teshuvah li-Meshummad she-Ḥazar la-Yahadut be-Austriah ube-Germanyah ba-Me'ah ha-Ḥamesh 'Esreh," *'Alei Sefer* 24–25 (2015): 201–4.

22 See Simcha Emanuel, *Shivrei Luḥot*, 160 (*she-kol ha-ḥozer bi-teshuvah ẓerikhin tevilah*). As Emanuel notes, one of the manuscript texts (ms. Vatican 183, fol. 186r) identifies R. Simḥah's (no longer extant) halakhic tome, *Seder 'Olam*, as the literary source of this ruling. Cf. ms. Bodl. 1210, fol. 83v (*katav Rabbenu Simḥah b"R. Shmu'el*); ms. Bodl. 784, fol. 99v; and J. Elbaum, *Teshuvat ha-Lev ve-Qabbalat Yissurim* (Jerusalem, 1993), 225–26.

23 See *Teshuvot Maharam va-Ḥaverav*, ed. Emanuel, 435 (sec. 139) [= Y. Z. Kahana, "She'elot u-Teshuvot R. Yiẓḥaq Or Zarua' u-Maharam b. Barukh," *Sinai* 24 (1949): 312 (sec. 109)]: שכל אותם הימי' שהיתה שרוייה בגוים היתה אוכלת משלהם ושותה משלהם ועכשיו בטהרה אלא לחזור בתשוב' . . . [מעבירה] הטבילוה כדי שתטהר.

24 See my *"Peering through the Lattices": Mystical, Magical, and Pietistic Dimensions in the Tosafist Period* (Detroit, MI, 2000), 43–44, 57–58; and this chapter, n. 33.

Nonetheless, R. Simḥah's student, Isaac b. Moses *Or Zarua'* (d. c. 1255; who also studied with Judah Sirleon of Paris, a student of Ri), adds that, although immersion is required (*ve-khen qibbalti mi-mori ha-rav Rabbenu Simḥah she-kol ba'alei teshuvah ẓerikhin tevilah*), its absence or delay does not withhold or compromise the penitent sinner's state of repentance (*'einah me-'akkevet et ha-teshuvah*). Rather, as soon as a person who has transgressed a sin of any magnitude (willingly or unwillingly) decides to repent, he or she is immediately considered to be fully righteous. However, one must make himself uncomfortable (*le-ẓa'er et 'aẓmo*) and afflict his body (*le-sagef 'et gufo*) to achieve expiation (*kapparah*), and this is the role of the ritual immersion prescribed by R. Simḥah.[25] Indeed, Isaac *Or Zarua'*'s son, Ḥayyim Eli'ezer, and the Italian halakhist Zedekiah b. Abraham *ha-Rofe* (d. c. 1260) base the Ashkenazic custom requiring Jewish males to immerse themselves on the eve of Rosh Hashanah and before Yom Kippur on R. Simḥah's ruling.[26]

A manuscript version of R. Simḥah's ruling which contains additional information was published by Efraim Kupfer nearly fifty years ago.[27] A Jewish woman who had been "submerged" (*nitme'ah*, with an *'ayin*, signifying apostasy) among non-Jews had given birth to two sons as a non-Jew (*yaldah be-goyut*). She then returned to Jewish practice and life together with her young

25 See *Sefer Or Zarua'*, pt. 1, sec. 112, ed. Machon Yerushalayim, fols. 105–6. Isaac *Or Zarua'* resided for a time in R. Simḥah's home in Speyer. See *Sefer Or Zarua'*, pt. 4, *pisqei 'avodah zarah*, sec. 271, ed. Machon Yerushalayim, fol. 667; Urbach, *Ba'alei ha-Tosafot*, 1:413–14; and cf. my *Jewish Education and Society in the High Middle Ages* (Detroit, MI, 1992), 66–67. For a complete list of Isaac *Or Zarua*'s teachers, in both Germany and northern France, see Uzi Fuchs, "Iyyunim be-Sefer Or Zarua' le-R. Yiẓḥaq me-Vienna" (Master's thesis, Hebrew University, 1993), 11–32.

26 See *Pisqei Halakhah shel R. Ḥayyim Or Zarua'* (*Derashot Maharaḥ*), ed. Y. S. Lange (Jerusalem, 1993), 153; *Shibbolei ha-Leqet*, ed. S. Buber (Vilna, 1887), 266 (sec. 283; in this version, a blessing over the immersion is also required). Cf. *'Arugat ha-Bosem le-R. Avraham b. 'Azri'el*, ed. E. E. Urbach, vol. 2 (Jerusalem, 1942), 110.

27 See *Teshuvot u-Pesaqim*, ed. E. Kupfer (Jerusalem, 1973), 290–91 (sec. 171). The manuscript from which Kupfer published this volume, Bodl. 692, is a significant repository of material from R. Simḥah's lost *Seder 'Olam*. See Kupfer's introduction, 11–12; and cf. G. Blidstein, "Who Is Not a Jew?—The Medieval Discussion," *Israel Law Review* 11 (1976): 160.

sons, who were immersed in the *mikveh* prior to their circumcisions. These immersions, however, were not considered part of a halakhically mandated conversion process, since the mother was Jewish and therefore so were her children. Thus, these immersions did not require the presence of three rabbinic scholars sitting as a Jewish court, and they took place after the circumcisions. Nonetheless, immersion was considered necessary, as in the case in *Avot de-R. Natan* noted earlier, where the young woman had been immersed after her experiences in captivity. However, these boys would not have rendered any wine they touched as *yayn nesekh* prior to their immersion, for even an adult who had been an apostate does not taint wine for Jewish consumption from the moment he renounces his actions and begins his return. A Jew who announces that he has sinned but wishes to return is still a Jew, "and he can immerse himself privately [*ve-tovel beino le-vein ʿaẓmo*]."

At this point the text cites R. Bonfant (a sobriquet for the German halakhist Samuel b. Abraham *ha-Levi* of Worms, d. c. 1275), in the name of his teacher *SaR* (ש״ר = R̲abbenu S̲imḥah),[28] to explain that the purpose of the immersion is to purify the penitent from sin. Although non-Jewish food did not defile the body of the young captive woman more than other things (*yoter mi-she'ar devarim*), these penitents who returned to Judaism with their mother had to undergo immersion as she did so that they would be purified from sin, repent,

28 Kupfer also includes several rulings by Samuel of Worms in his *Teshuvot u-Pesaqim*, 129–32 (a ruling issued jointly by R. Samuel and his teacher, R. Simḥah); 218–20 (*seder ḥaliẓah me-nimmuqei R. Shmu'el ha-Levi*), 282–89; and see the index, 343. See also I. A. Agus, *Teshuvot Ba'alei ha-Tosafot* (New York, 1954), 206–15; S. Emanuel, "Teshuvot Maharam mi-Rothenburg she-'Einan shel Maharam," *Shenaton ha-Mishpat ha-'Ivri* 21 (1998–2000): 173–76; and idem, *Shivrei Luḥot*, 181–83. For R. Samuel's contributions to Ashkenazic *piyyut*, see my *The Intellectual History and Rabbinic Culture of Medieval Ashkenaz* (Detroit, MI, 2013), 423–30. On R. Bonfant's close tutorial relationship with R. Simḥah, see I. Ta-Shma, *Kneset Meḥqarim*, vol. 1 (Jerusalem, 2004), 161–62. On the name "Bonfant," cf. S. Schwarzfuchs, *Yehudei Ẓarefat Bimei ha-Benayim* (Tel Aviv, 2001), 319, n. 27. R. Samuel's son was the German *dayyan* and *payyetan* Yaqar *ha-Levi* of Cologne. See Kupfer's introduction to *Teshuvot u-Pesaqim*, 12–13, and 122–23, 264, 287; Ta-Shma, *Kneset Meḥqarim*, 1:168–74; and my "Religious Leadership During the Tosafist Period: Between the Academy and the Rabbinic Court," in *Jewish Religious Leadership*, ed. J. Wertheimer (New York, 2004), vol. 1, 277–79, 292.

and return in purity. This passage continues by noting that a *sugya* in tractate *Pesaḥim* (92a) may also have mandated immersion for a penitent.[29] Moreover, a partial proof (*qeẓat yesh re'ayah*) is seen in the case of Queen Esther, who immersed herself upon returning from Aḥashverosh to live once again with Mordekhai. Just as Esther's immersion rid her of the impurity imparted by the wicked king (*mishum zuhamato shel 'oto rasha*), so too must penitent apostates (*ba'alei teshuvah*) also immerse themselves to eliminate the residue transmitted by the impurity of idolatry (*mipnei zihum tum'at 'avodah zarah*).[30] Further support may be derived from a passage in the Jerusalem Talmud that mandates immersion whenever one passes from a state of impurity to a state of holiness. It is for this reason, according to the *Talmud Yerushalmi*, that a utensil purchased by a Jew from a non-Jew must be immersed prior to its use.[31]

Although it is unclear whether this entire passage was composed by R. Simḥah or his student Samuel *ha-Levi* of Worms, the inclusion of their material raises the possibility that the initial formulation of R. Simḥah's ruling—that immersion should be undertaken as part of the overall process of repentance—was expressed in the case of a Jewish apostate who had returned to the community, and was then broadened to include other sins.[32] The

29 Cf. this volume, chapter 1, n. 19.

30 On Esther's immersion in this way, see *Megillah* 13b, and see also *Tosafot*, ad loc., s.v. *ve-tovelet*.

31 Cf. Ephraim Shoham-Steiner, "An Almost Tangible Presence: Some Thoughts on Material Purity among Medieval European Jews," in *Discourses of Purity in Transcultural Perspective (300–1600)*, ed. M. Bley et al. (Leiden, 2015), 64–66. For R. Bonfant's lenient ruling regarding the status of the married Jewish women who were forcibly converted and held captive by Christians in connection with a pogrom in Frankfurt in 1241, see Rachel Furst, "Captivity, Conversion, and Communal Identity: Sexual Angst and Religious Crisis in Frankfurt, 1241," *Jewish History* 22 (2008): 206–11. Given the level of coercion involved, R. Bonfant sought to underplay the significance of baptism as defilement in formulating his ruling.

32 Cf. this chapter, n. 22. David Ibn Zimra (Radbaz), a leading sixteenth-century Sefardic authority, begins (and concludes) his responsum on the status of forced converts to Islam (*She'elot u-Teshuvot ha-Radvaz*, pt. 3, #858) by citing the view of Simḥah of Speyer that, while a *ba'al teshuvah* returning from any grave sin (including apostasy) should immerse himself (and thereby afflict himself), the absence of such an immersion does not inherently compromise or deny the substance of his

circumstances of apostasy reflect precisely the situation of the young woman who had been held captive, as described in *Avot de-R. Nathan*. Whether or not apostates to Christianity lived with non-Jews in sexual arrangements, they (like the young woman) had ample opportunity to sin, through the partaking of non-kosher food and other such acts in the course of daily life. Although the additional proof suggested on the basis of Esther's return to Mordekhai does bespeak a sexual context, the phrase *mipnei zihum tum'at 'avodah zarah* can also refer to other forbidden activities one would likely encounter while living in a non-Jewish setting without any Jewish guidance or protection.

For Simḥah of Speyer and his student R. Bonfant, the immersion of a returning apostate was a required act of penance and not simply an indicator of the apostate's return to the fold or of his commitment. Although this immersion was not technically required by Jewish law, it was mandated as a penitential act. R. Simḥah displays several affinities with the German Pietists, although the presence of various penitential acts (*tiqqunei teshuvah*) in the writings of a number of German Tosafists and rabbinic authorities from the late twelfth and early thirteenth centuries reflects the currency of these practices even outside the narrowly constructed circle of *Ḥasidei Ashkenaz*.[33] Moreover, the comparison to Esther perhaps suggests a form of un-baptism, which serves in this instance to remove the impurity of idolatry. In any case, for Simḥah of Speyer and for Samuel *ha-Levi* of Worms (as for Ri), ritual

repentance. The only other (named) position cited by Radbaz in this responsum is that of Riba *ha-Levi* of Speyer (see this volume, chapter 1, n. 19). Cf. this volume, chapter 6, n. 55.

33 On the affinities between R. Simḥah and the *Ḥasidei Ashkenaz*, see my "*Peering through the Lattices*," 102–11, 255–28. Among those Ashkenazic rabbinic scholars who preserved and applied R. Simḥah's ruling (this chapter, nn. 25–26), Isaac Or Zarua' and Abraham b. 'Azri'el were also direct students of the leading German Pietists Judah *he-Ḥasid* and Eleazar of Worms. For the influence of *Ḥasidei Ashkenaz* on *Shibbolei ha-Leqet*, see my "Mysticism and Asceticism in Italian Rabbinic Literature of the Thirteenth Century," *Kabbalah* 6 (2001): 135–49. On *tiqqunei teshuvah* in the writings and thought of the Tosafist Rabbenu Ephraim b. Isaac and his rabbinic colleagues in Regensburg, see my "R. Judah he-Ḥasid and the Rabbinic Scholars of Regensburg: Interactions, Influences, and Implications," *Jewish Quarterly Review* 96 (2006): 17–37.

immersion for a returning apostate was not merely a matter of popular custom or tradition.

A formulation attributed by the early fourteenth-century compendium *Semaq mi-Ẓurikh* to Simḥah of Speyer's contemporary, Eliezer b. Joel *ha-Levi* (Rabiah of Cologne, d. c. 1225, author of *Avi ha-'Ezri*), goes even further. According to Rabiah, an apostate who wishes to return must shave his head (*le-ha'avir 'al rosho ta'ar*) and immerse himself, as a convert does (*ka-ger*).[34] The apostate's immersion does not have to take place during the daytime (as does the immersion of a *ger* due to the requirement of *mishpat*; Jewish courts cannot meet at night), but the apostate's (re-)acceptance of Judaism (*ha-qabbalah*) must also be undertaken before a tribunal of three.[35]

---

34 See Moses of Zurich, *Semaq mi-Ẓurikh*, 2:49 (*miẓvah* 156). See also ms. Paris BN 381 (#4360), fol. 46v [sec. 152]; ms. Bodl. 879 (#21838), fol. 95v [sec. 157]; ms. Parma de Rossi 172 (#13898), fol. 73r; ms. Moscow 187 (#6866), fol. 59v; ms. Zurich Braginsky 115 (#4683), fol. 46v; ms. Berlin 37 (#1731), fol. 72v; ms. Paris 388 (#4367), fol. 40v; ms. Cambridge Add. 559–60 (#16848), fol. 8v; S. Goldin, *Ha-Yiḥud veha-Yaḥad* (Tel Aviv, 1997), 94–95; and my "Halakhah and Meẓi'ut (Realia) in Medieval Ashkenaz: Surveying the Parameters and Defining the Limits," *Jewish Law Annual* 14 (2003): 211–16. The requirement for a convert to shave (and to pare the nails on his hands and feet) prior to his immersion to ensure that there is no *ḥaẓiẓah* (but also as a preparation for this new beginning) appears in *Hilkhot ha-Rif le-Massekhet Shabbat*, fol. 55b (toward the end of chapter 19: וגייזי ליה ממזייה ושקליה ליה טופריה דידיה ודכרעיה). See also *Pisqei ha-Rosh le-Massekhet Shabbat*, 19:11; *Arba'ah Turim, Yoreh De'ah*, sec. 268 (and the *Beit Yosef*, ad loc., s.v. *ve-'ein marbin 'alav*). Cf. *Sefer Asufot* (whose author self-identifies as a student of Rabiah), ms. Montefiore 134, fols. 85b–86r [= *Zikhron Brit la-Rishonim*, ed. J. Glassberg (Berlin, 1892), 133–34]; and *Perushim u-Pesaqim le-R. Avigdor Katz*, this chapter, n. 38.

35 Although Moses of Zurich compiled his work in the early fourteenth century (and this passage is not found within the extant *Sefer Rabiah*), the authenticity of this passage and its attribution to Rabiah is accepted by Simcha Goldin, *Ha-Yiḥud veha-Yaḥad*, 200 (n. 46). Moreover, I have had occasion to show that another highly significant position of Rabiah (*Avi ha-'Ezri*) on Jewish martyrdom, which is also found only in *Semaq mi-Ẓurikh*, can be confirmed by its appearance (in somewhat tighter form) in several manuscripts of Abraham b. Ephraim's *Sefer Simmanei Taryag Miẓvot*, a northern French halakhic digest that was completed circa 1265 and is based on Moses of Coucy's *Sefer Miẓvot Gadol*. See my "Halakhah and *Meẓi'ut* (Realia) in Medieval Ashkenaz," 211–16. Indeed, the publication of Abraham b. Ephraim's work under the title *Qiẓẓur Sefer Miẓvot Gadol le-R. Avraham b. Ephraim*, ed. Y. Horowitz (Jerusalem, 2005), reveals that this work contains

Unlike Simḥah of Speyer (or Ri), Rabiah focuses on formalizing and verifying the return of the apostate in a rather public manner (similar to what the northern French Tosafist Samson of Sens had suggested, but with additional dimensions and demands), in a way that approaches the level of requirements for a convert to Judaism. Indeed, allowing the immersion to take place at night is the only difference Rabiah creates to distinguish between the procedures for the apostate and the convert.[36] A passage in the *Sifra* commentary attributed initially (but incorrectly) to Samson of Sens, which was actually composed by a German Tosafist contemporary of Simḥah of Speyer and Rabiah, also maintains that the accepted procedure for a penitent apostate is to shave his head and pare his nails prior to his immersion. In that passage, the reverting apostate is referred to as a convert (*ger*).[37]

---

a series of passages cited in the name of *Avi ha-'Ezri* (see, e.g., 29, 32, 69, 94, 102, 129, 178–80, 204, 225), some of which can be found in Rabiah's extant *Sefer Avi ha-'Ezri/Sefer Rabiah* and others which cannot but nonetheless appear to be authentic. (In one instance, on p. 206, a position attributed to Eli'ezer b. Joel *ha-Levi* by name is not found in his extant writings.) It should also be noted that most of Rabiah's commentary to tractate *Yevamot* (which, as the present study confirms, is a common locus in medieval rabbinic literature for discussion of the status of returning apostates) appears to have been part of Rabiah's second (and now lost) halakhic work, *Sefer Avi'asaf*; see S. Emanuel, *Shivrei Luḥot*, 86–100. The Rabiah passage in *Semaq mi-Ẓurikh* under discussion here, on the treatment of a returning apostate, is also found (essentially verbatim) in *Qiẓẓur Sefer Miẓvot Gadol*, 194, albeit as a directive put forward by an otherwise unidentified rabbinic source (*'omrim*). On the involvement of a rabbinic tribunal, cf. J. C. Schmitt, *The Conversion of Herman the Jew*, 218–22.

36 Interestingly, Rabiah characterizes the custom of men immersing before Yom Kippur as a broader act of piety or asceticism (*perishut*) and not as a *tiqqun teshuvah*, which is the way it is identified in the ruling associated with Simḥah of Speyer discussed earlier. See *Sefer Rabiah*, ed. V. Aptowitzer, vol. 2, 185; my "*Peering through the Lattices*," 45; and *Pisqei Rabbenu Yosef Talmid Rabbenu Shmu'el ha-Ro'eh mi-Bamberg*, in *Shitat ha-Qadmonim*, ed. M. J. Blau (New York, 1992), 372, sec. 271. Cf. Eleazar b. Judah of Worms, *Sefer Roqeaḥ* (Jerusalem, 1967), secs. 214, 218.

37 See the *Perush la-Sifra ha-Meyuḥas le-R. Shimshon mi-Shanẓ* (Jerusalem, 1959), *parashat Emor*, *parsheta* 14, n. 1, fol. 110b. Analysis of the other rabbinic names and figures cited has shown conclusively that the author of this commentary was not R. Samson (or any other French rabbinic figure) but rather a German contemporary of Rabiah who refers to David b. Qalonymus of Muenzberg as his teacher.

Another student of Simḥah of Speyer, Avigdor b. Elijah *Kohen Ẓedeq* (Katz) of Vienna (who lived well into the thirteenth century), assumes without question that a married couple who were both returning apostates must be immersed prior to their reacceptance into the community, and they must shave their hair prior to the immersion as a symbolic removal of all the impurities of idolatry. The matter before R. Avigdor for his consideration was only whether they also had to be separated for a period of three months (*havḥanah*), as was required of a female convert to Judaism. His response to that question is that, while typically a returning female apostate (like a convert) is required to separate to ascertain whether she was pregnant with the child of a non-Jewish father, the period of separation is not needed in this instance because it can be assumed that this married couple continued to live only with each other during their period of apostasy.[38]

We have just seen that a cluster of Tosafists and other German rabbinic figures, beginning with Rabiah, considered reverting apostates as akin to converts who were required to submit to an arduous reentry process, even as not all these German authorities agreed with Rabiah that a formal *qabbalah* before a rabbinic tribunal was also required. The reports received

---

R. David asked a halakhic question of Rabiah's father, Joel of Bonn, and also answered (and queried) Rabiah. See Urbach, *Ba'alei ha-Tosafot*, 1:366; S. Emanuel, "Biographical Data on R. Barukh b. Isaac" [Hebrew], *Tarbiz* 69 (2000): 436–37; Y. Sussman, "Rabad on Shekalim? A Bibliographical and Historical Riddle" [Hebrew], in *Me'ah She'arim: Studies in Medieval Jewish Spirituality in Memory of Isadore Twersky*, ed. E. Fleischer et al. (Jerusalem, 2001), 147–48 (n. 64).

38 See *Perushim u-Pesaqim le-Rabbenu Avigdor (Ẓarefati) mi-Ba'alei ha-Tosafot*, ed. Makhon Harerei Qedem (Jerusalem, 1996), 410–11. On the provenance and literary output of R. Avigdor Katz of Vienna, see my "*Peering through the Lattices*," 107–10, 225–27; my "Mysticism and Asceticism in Italian Rabbinic Literature of the Thirteenth Century," *Kabbalah* 6 (2001): 135–49; and S. Emanuel, *Shivrei Luḥot*, 175–81. R. Avigdor discusses this issue at the beginning of the portion of *Ki Teẓe*, in the context of the *yefat to'ar*. Samson of Sens also presumes that a married couple did not stray sexually if they had apostatized together. See *Haggahot Maimuniyyot*, *hilkhot 'issurei bi'ah* 18:2 [1]; and my "Meshummadot Nesu'ot she-Ḥazru: Heteran li-Bnei Zugan ha-Yehudi veha-Nokhri lefi Meqorot Ẓefon Ẓarefat ve-Ashkenaz Bimei ha-Benayim," in *Sefer Menaḥem Elon*, ed. A. Edrei et al. (Jerusalem, 2018), 599–600.

by Bernard Gui and other inquisitors during the fourteenth century (described earlier, in chapter 1) about the immersions required by the Jews for *relapsi* (apostates to Christianity who subsequently sought to revert to Judaism) proved they were not merely popular lay practices, and they were indeed quite demanding. We shall have the opportunity shortly to discuss additional evidence for these rabbinic practices which suggests that this phenomenon also became more widespread in northern France as the thirteenth century progressed.

The position of Eleazar b. Judah of Worms (d. c. 1230), a prominent German halakhist and a leading figure among the German Pietists (and a contemporary of both Simḥah of Speyer and Rabiah), requires clarification. In a text found in several rabbinic collections alongside the ruling of Riẓba discussed earlier, R. Eleazar is noted as being relatively lenient with a returning apostate, taking an approach similar to that of Riẓba.[39] According to this formulation, R. Eleazar does not require the returnee to take on any acts of physical suffering or self-abnegation, even though these kinds of physical *tiqqunei teshuvah* were typically prescribed by R. Eleazar for those who had sinned in various other ways.[40] R. Eleazar also does not make any reference to a need for ritual immersion. When the one returning "rejoins the exile of his brethren, and recites the *Shema* daily, and is careful once again with what is permitted and prohibited to every Jew, he is vouchsafed that he will not sin [grievously] again as a Jew, and we should not be so strict with him, by requiring him to undergo afflictions in order to achieve expiation."

39 See Urbach, *Ba'alei ha-Tosafot*, 1:407; *Shitah Mequbbeẓet 'al Massekhet Bekhorot*, ed. Bar-Ilan, 149; *Semaq mi-Ẓurikh*, 2:49; *Teshuvot ha-Ramban ha-Meyuḥasot la-Ramban*, #180; ms. Vercelli C1, fol. 291v (upper margin); and this chapter, nn. 18, 34 (וגם הר"ר אלעזר מוורמ"ש לא החמיר עליו לקבל ייסורין להתכפר כישראל שעשה עבירות חמורות ולא כפר בעיקר). Urbach suggests that Riẓba and Eleazar of Worms had been called upon to respond to the same situation. However, aside from the fact that their rulings are juxtaposed in these sources, no other evidence is offered to support this suggestion.

40 See, e.g., I. Marcus, "*Ḥasidei Ashkenaz* Private Penitentials: An Introduction and Descriptive Catalogue," in *Studies in Jewish Mysticism*, ed. J. Dan and F. Talmage (Cambridge, MA, 1982), 57–83.

However, in the laws of repentance found at the beginning of his halakhic work, *Sefer Roqeaḥ*, R. Eleazar writes "that as soon as the former apostate feels remorse and immerses himself in a *mikveh*, he [once again] has the status of a Jew."[41] According to R. Eleazar, the seriousness of this violation requires that the former apostate engage in a series of penitential activities over a period of years (*yit'abbel ve-yivkeh ve-yiẓta'er ve-yit'anneh kammah shanim*), and that these be performed each day (*be-khol yom va-yom yanmikh ruḥo ve-yitvaddeh shalosh pe'amim be-khol yom*). R. Eleazar also lists a series of specific penances that accord with the regimen found in his penitential treatises (which will be discussed in the next paragraph). Moreover, the former apostate also must repent and regret the pleasures he experienced during his apostasy, such as celebrating Christian holy days while desecrating the Sabbath, eating forbidden foods, and engaging in forbidden sexual relations, among other serious religious violations. He must lie on the ground and suffer many indignities. And if someone refers to him as a "evil *mumar*," he should remain silent.

In his penitential treatises as well, Eleazar of Worms explicitly mandates immersion, as well as a series of more arduous *tiqqunei teshuvah* for an apostate who wishes to return.[42] In the fullest version of these works, R. Eleazar presents the paradigm of Menasheh, son of Hezekiah, who denied the Almighty for some thirty-three years and yet was able to return the moment he repented fully in his heart and pledged to correct his actions. According to R. Eleazar, the returning apostate must similarly remove all signs of splendor or glory from his body and his being (*le-hasir mi-mennu kol malbushei tif'arto ve-lo yashit 'edyo 'alav*); he must feel remorse, and fast regularly over a period of several years. He should not eat meat or drink wine, and he should not bathe, except for just prior to the festivals. His head should be washed only once or twice a month, and so on. In addition, he should not sit together with clergymen and

41 See *Sefer Roqeaḥ*, ed. B. S. Schneerson (Jerusalem, 1967), 31, *hilkhot teshuvah*, sec. 24: הכופר בעיקר הרי עבר על כל התורה . . . ומיד כשמתחרט וטובל במקוה דינו כישראל.

42 On this apparent contradiction within texts by and about R. Eleazar, see Yedidyah Dinari, *Ḥakhmei Ashkenaz be-Shilhei Yemei ha-Benayim* (Jerusalem, 1984), 86 (n. 74), 91 (n. 101). Cf. Y. Elbaum, *Teshuvat ha-Lev ve-Qabbalat Yissurim*, 28, n. 22; Pinchas Vilman, *Ha-Teshuvah be-Sifrut ha-Shu"t* (Bnei Brak, 1995), 131.

priests, or in places where Christians are discussing the "impure idolatry." He must keep away from all idolaters and derive no pleasure from them, and he may not come near their homes or the courtyard of a church. From the moment he regrets what he has done and immerses himself, he is considered to be a Jew. He must return to his Creator, repent for all the sins he has committed, and regret the sinful pleasures he had enjoyed.[43]

Although the specific physical afflictions prescribed by R. Eleazar vary a bit within the different versions of his penitential treatises, the need for ritual immersion in all these works (and in *Sefer Roqeaḥ*) is unequivocal. That act, together with the former apostate's good intentions, reestablishes his presence within the Jewish community, which is then supported by the various penances he undertakes. Moreover, the passage attributed to R. Eleazar which downplays the need for *tiqqunei teshuvah* does not specifically mention *tevilah*, but positing the need for ritual immersion would not contradict anything else

43 See ms. Parma de Rossi 563, fols. 111c–d; and ms. Vatican 183/3, fols. 165v–166v. The lengthy regimen of penances (*seder ha-teshuvah*) for all sorts of sins found in ms. Vatican concludes on fol. 188v. It begins on fol. 162r with a penitential responsum ascribed to R. Judah *he-Ḥasid*. However, the long list of penitential instructions that follows corresponds to the style and intent of Eleazar's writings in this area. See I. Marcus, "*Ḥasidei Ashkenaz* Private Penitentials," 74, and cf. idem, "Ḥibburei ha-Teshuvah shel Ḥasidei Ashkenaz," in *Meḥqarim be-Qabbalah, be-Filosofiyah ube-Sifrut ha-Musar vehe-Hagut Mugashim le-Yeshayah Tishby*, ed. J. Dan and J. Hacker (Jerusalem, 1986), 369–79. See also Eleazar's *Sefer Roqeaḥ* (repr. Jerusalem, 1967), *Hilkhot Teshuvah*, 31, sec. 24 (and Marcus, "*Ḥasidei Ashkenaz* Private Penitentials," 62–63); *Sefer Kol Bo*, sec. 66 [*sefer niqra Moreh Ḥatta'im ve-niqra Sefer ha-Kapparot, ḥibbero ha-R. Eleazar mi-Germaiza*] (Tel Aviv, 1997), fol. 26a (and Marcus, "*Ḥasidei Ashkenaz* Private Penitentials," 69–70); and *Darkhei Teshuvah* (appended to *Teshvuot Maharam b. Barukh mi-Rothenburg* [Prague, 1608], ed. M. A. Bloch [Budapest, 1895], fol. 160c). Simḥah of Speyer's ruling that repentant sinners should immerse themselves (as derived from the case in *Avot de-R. Nathan* about the young woman had who returned from captivity) appears toward the end of Eleazar's *seder ha-teshuvah* in ms. Vatican 183, on fol. 186r; see this chapter, n. 22. R. Judah *he-Ḥasid*'s responsum in this manuscript (along with two others found in ms. Bodl. 682) was published by S. Spitzer, "She'elot u-Teshuvot Rabbenu Yehudah he-Ḥasid be-'Inyanei Teshuvah," in *Sefer ha-Zikkaron le-R. Shmu'el Barukh Verner*, ed. Y. Buksboim (Jerusalem, 1996), 199–205. Cf. Marcus, "Ḥibburei ha-Teshuvah," 380–82. See also Y. Y. Stal, *Teshuvot Rabbenu Eleazar ha-Roqeaḥ mi-Vermaiza* (Jerusalem, 2014), 40–58 (sec. 14, *teshuvah le-'ovdei 'avodah zarah*).

found in that passage. For Eleazar of Worms, as it was for Simḥah of Speyer, the immersion of the penitent can be understood as a painless yet necessary act of penance. It also reflects the more basic kind of commitment the reverting apostate must make (which was endorsed by Tosafists from Ri to Rabiah) to once again serve his Creator. In addition, the proximity of this requirement in R. Eleazar's regimen of penances to those which require avoiding contact with church officials, edifices, and ceremonies perhaps suggests that the immersion served as a kind of un-baptism as well. The different approaches offered by R. Eleazar concerning the more difficult penitential regimens were meant to be tailored to the needs and stability of a particular returning apostate, acknowledging the possibility they might prove to be too onerous for some.

The more stringent requirements enunciated by Rabiah—for immersion, extensive preparations, and a *qabbalah* before a rabbinic tribunal—made their way to northern France by the second half of the thirteenth century. *Qiẓẓur Semag* cites these requirements in the name of anonymous figures or sources (*ʾomrim*), but this passage appears to be taken verbatim from the Rabiah passage, as is the case for several other such passages from Rabiah that are cited by this work.[44]

In addition, the *Ḥizzequni* Torah commentary, compiled in northern France circa 1275 by Hezekiah b. Manoaḥ, assumes that similar kinds of preparations were required of returning apostates there. When the Levites were selected to replace the firstborn sons in the service of the Tabernacle (because the firstborn sons were complicit in the sin of the golden calf), the Levites required purification (Nu. 8:6–7). As part of this process, they were immersed in holy water, their clothing was washed, and they were required to shave their entire bodies (*ve-heʿeviru taʿar ʿal kol besaram*). *Ḥizzequni* cites Rashi's commentary, which records a comment made in the eleventh century by Moses *ha-Darshan* of Narbonne. The appointment of the Levites was meant to atone for the firstborn sons' sin of idolatry in worshipping the golden calf. Idolatry is characterized as the offering of sacrifices to the gods by spiritually dead officiants, *zivḥei metim*, as opposed to the worship service and the slaughter of

44 See Abraham b. Ephraim, *Qiẓẓur Sefer Miẓvot Gadol*, 194; and this chapter, n. 35.

animals to the Almighty in the Tabernacle and, later, in the Temple. A leper is referred to as dead by the Talmud (*Nedarim* 64b, *meẓora ḥashuv ke-met*), and so the Torah required the Levites to shave their entire bodies just as former lepers do when they seek purification. The Levites too are moving forward from the state of death associated with idolatry (and the sin of the golden calf in particular) to a renewed life in the service of God.

This passage in the *Ḥizzequni* commentary concludes: "And for that reason, penitents [who were apostates] are required to shave themselves." Textual variants of this commentary add that returning apostates are required to shave themselves and to immerse, which was also the case for both the lepers and the Levites. This suggests that such preparations were required of returning apostates in at least some locales in northern France as well.[45]

These findings take us well beyond the beginning of the thirteenth century.[46] We are now in a position to better understand the historical and halakhic

---

45 See ms. British Museum Or. 9931 (#6987), fol. 113v–114r (*mi-kan lamadnu tevilah ve-ta'ar le-ba'alei teshuvah*); ms. JTS 791 (#2402), fol. 123r (*le-kakh ẓarikh ba'al teshuvah tiglaḥat* [and see also ms. JTS 794, fol. 73r]); and my "Perush ha-Torah le-R. Mosheh mi-Coucy u-Parshanut ha-Miqra be-Ẓefon Ẓarefat ba-Me'ot ha-Yod Bet veha-Yod Gimmel," in *Hakhamim ve-Ḥidotam*, ed. A. Shinan and Y. Y. Yuval (Jerusalem, 2019), 376 (n. 4). On the provenance and nature of the *Ḥizzequni* commentary (which is heavily weighted in terms of northern French material, although it also includes comments by Judah the Pious on occasion, even as it does not identify its sources in a clear way), see Sara Japhet, "Perush ha-Ḥizzequni la-Torah: Li-Demuto shel ha-Ḥibbur ule-Mataratо," in *Sefer ha-Yovel le-Rav Mordekhai Breuer*, ed. M. Bar-Asher (Jerusalem, 1992), 1:91–111; and my *The Intellectual History*, 121–24, 207–8, 359. My thanks go to Prof. Bernard Septimus for initially bringing this comment to my attention. It also appears in the slightly later Tosafist Torah compilation, *Perushei R. Ḥayyim Palti'el 'al ha-Torah*, ed. Y. S. Lange (Jerusalem, 1981), 485, where the reference to reverting apostates is made quite explicit: פי' רש"י לפי שהיו אדוקין לע"ז והיא קרויה זבחי מתים לכך הזקיקם בתגלחת כמצורעים. ומיכאן לאותם שהמירו שהם צריכים לגלח ראשם כשרוצים לעשות תשובה. Cf. ms. Moscow 349 (#47697), fol. 110v, for a different approach to the immersion of the Levites.

46 Although there was something of a separation in terms of literary sources as well as the movement of students between the Tosafist centers in northern France and Germany during the forty-year period from 1175 to 1215, both centers have been amply represented in the discussion to this point. As in many other instances, the various positions begin to come together in the halakhic writings and thought of Meir of Rothenburg and his teachers. See my "From Germany to Northern France

underpinnings of a rather striking responsum penned in the second half of the thirteenth century by Meir of Rothenburg, concerning the testimony of a former apostate in the case of a missing husband. R. Meir writes that he was loath to accept the testimony of this individual, whom he describes as "one who had become an apostate [*mumar*] and then repented albeit not with a full heart [*shav ve-lo bekhol libbo*], but rather with deceit [*teshuvah shel remiyyah*]." At the end of his responsum, R. Meir again remarks that the testimony of this individual is unacceptable, "since this abominable one and others like him immerse themselves while holding a rodent in their hands [*tovlim ve-sherez̦ be-yadam*]. As is well known, they do not consider themselves to be Jews except in order to have other [Jews] give them food, and in order to steal and to fulfill their every desire."[47]

Maharam was undoubtedly referring to a rabbinically endorsed or required act of immersion when he says that the apostate in question was *tovel ve-sherez̦ be-yado*, irrespective of which reason for this immersion he might have favored. For R. Meir genuine repentance and immersion (*tevilah*) are both required. Having studied with Tosafists in northern France and Germany, in addition to having numerous affinities with the German Pietists and with Eleazar of Worms in particular, R. Meir had easy access to this evolving and by now strong trend in Ashkenazic rabbinic thinking.[48] Indeed, as noted earlier, one of Maharam's senior colleagues, Avigdor b. Elijah *Kohen Z̦edeq* (Katz) of Vienna, assumed without question that a married couple who were both returning apostates must be immersed prior to their reacceptance into the Jewish community.[49]

Moreover, there is a *Tosafot* text that originated in northern France in the mid- to late-thirteenth century which may also have informed the responsum

---

and Back Again: A Tale of Two Tosafist Centers," in *Regional Identities and Cultures of Medieval Jews*, ed. J. Castaño et al. (London, 2018), 149–71.

47 See *Teshuvot Maimuniyyot le-Nashim*, #10 [= *Haggahot Mordekhai le-Massekhet Ketubot*, sec. 306].

48 See Urbach, *Ba'alei ha-Tosafot*, 2:523–28, and my "*Peering through the Lattices*," 115–24, 234–38.

49 See this chapter, n. 38.

of Meir of Rothenburg. As noted briefly in the first chapter, Ritva (d. c. 1325), in a passage in his talmudic commentary to tractate *Yevamot* (which is reproduced by *Nimmuqei Yosef* later in the fourteenth century), cites the view that ritual immersion was required for a returning apostate according to rabbinic law or policy (*mi-derabbanan, mishum ma'alah*), from an Ashkenazic source he refers to as "*Tosafot 'aḥaronot*."[50] According to these *Tosafot 'aḥaronot*, immersion for an apostate is akin to the talmudic requirement that an *'eved kena'ani* has to undergo ritual immersion twice, once at the beginning of his servitude, when he is initiated into the Jewish faith (and the partial observance of *miẓvot*), and again at the point of his release, when he becomes a full-fledged member of the Jewish community.

Several *Tosafot* texts maintain that this second immersion of the *'eved kena'ani* is required (only) by rabbinic law, and both Ramban (Naḥmanides, d. 1270) and Rashba attribute this position to "the rabbis of northern France, *rabbotenu ha-Ẓarefatim*."[51] A *Tosafot* variant to *Yevamot* characterizes this rabbinic requirement as a means of distinguishing formally between the states of slavery and freedom (*le-hakkir bein 'avdut le-ḥerut*).[52] But none of these *Tosafot* passages refers to the case of a returning apostate.

---

50 See *Ḥiddushei ha-Ritva le-Massekhet Yevamot*, ed. A. Jofen (Jerusalem, 1988), 330–32 (*Yevamot* 47b); *Nimmuqei Yosef*, ad loc. (at the top of fol. 16b in the standard pagination of *Hilkhot ha-Rif*); and chapter 1, n. 14, in this volume.

51 See *Tosafot* and *Tosafot ha-Rosh* to *Yevamot* 47b, s.v. *sham ger ve-'eved (meshuḥrar) tovlim*, ed. Y. D. Bar-Ilan (Jerusalem, 2016), 464–65; *Ḥiddushei ha-Ramban* and *Ḥiddushei ha-Rashba* to the end of *Yevamot* 47b; and cf. *Tosafot Qiddushin* 62b, s.v. *'ela me-'attah*. Naḥmanides' own position is that this immersion is required according to Torah law (and is akin to the immersion of a *ger*). This possibility is implicit in some of the *Tosafot* texts as well. See, e.g., the discussion in *Ḥiddushei ha-Ritva 'al Massekhet Yevamot*, ed. Jofen, 332, n. 263, and 348–49, n. 294. On (circumcised) non-Jewish slaves owned by Jews in medieval Ashkenaz, see *R. Eleazar mi-Vermaiza—Derashah le-Pesaḥ*, ed. S. Emanuel (Jerusalem, 2006), 21 (and the literature cited in n. 74).

52 See *Tosafot Maharam ve-Rabbenu Perez 'al Massekhet Yevamot*, ed. H. Porush (Jerusalem, 1991), 129–130 (48a), s.v. *ki tanya ha-hi le-'inyan tevilah 'itmar*. This passage (and explanation) is not found, however, in a parallel collection, *Tosafot Yeshanim ha-Shalem 'al Massekhet Yevamot*, ed. A. Shoshana (Jerusalem, 1994), 283–86.

However, among the manuscript glosses to *Sefer Mordekhai* in ms. Vercelli C1 noted earlier, there is a passage marked *Tosafot Shitah* that explicitly extends the requirement of immersion to an apostate who had repented, for the same reason that immersion was required for an *'eved kena'ani* who had been freed. Although the refrain popularized by Rashi, *'af 'al pi she-ḥata Yisra'el hu*, is mentioned by this *Tosafot Shitah* passage as well, the passage asserts that a penitent apostate must undergo immersion *la'asot hekkera*, in order to make a distinction or demarcation.[53] This is the rabbinic requirement (and *Tosafot* source) for immersion referred to by Ritva and *Nimmuqei Yosef*, which they characterize as *mishum ma'alah*.[54] The former apostate is not going from a state of slavery to one of freedom, but he is returning to a different or higher status, as a fully recognized and religiously obligated member of the Jewish community. The comparison to an *'eved kena'ani* is thus particularly apt.

The term *Tosafot Shitah* in this text refers, in all likelihood, to a type or genre of *Tosafot* that were produced in the Tosafist *beit midrash* at Evreux (led by the brothers R. Moses, R. Samuel, and R. Isaac b. Shne'ur) during the mid-thirteenth century, or as part of the *Tosafot* of their direct student, Rabbenu Pereẓ b. Elijah of Corbeil (d. 1297).[55] According to this *Tosafot* passage, ritual

53 See ms. Vercelli C1, fol. 291v (in the left-side margin): ואחד עבד המשוחרר צריך טבילה. תי׳ אמאי זקוק טבילה שניה כשמשחררי׳ אותו. והלא אי׳ טעון לחזור ולהטיף ממנו דם ברית. וי״ל דההיא מדרבנן כדי לעשו׳ הכיר׳ בין עבו׳ לחירות דה״נ ישראל משומד אע״פ שחטא ישראל הוא ואפ״ה כששב צריך טבילה. וכן משמ׳ פ׳ השולח שלא בעי טבילה אלא מדרבנן דקאמ׳ הכותב שטר אירוסי׳ לשפחתו ואו׳ צאי בו והתקדשי בו יש בלשון הזה ל׳ שחרור והוי מקודש׳ אע״ג שלא טבלה. תוס׳ שיטה. Just prior to this (on fol. 290r), a passage from *Tosafot Shitah* suggests that a woman of means ought to appropriately compensate her brother-in-law for performing *ḥaliẓah*; cf. A. Grossman, *Ḥasidot u-Mordot* (Jerusalem, 2001), 159–63.

54 Ritva also notes the requirement, at least *a priori*, of a formal reacceptance of Jewish practices (*qabbalah*) as well. See this volume, chapter 6.

55 On *Tosafot/Shitat Evreux*, see Urbach, *Ba'alei ha-Tosafot*, 1:479–84, esp. 480, n. 11, and 484, n. 26* (the responsum of Maharam [ed. Prague] listed in 480, n. 11, should be corrected to #608 = *Mordekhai Shavu'ot*, sec. 771, and cf. S. Emanuel, "Teshuvot Maharam mi-Rothenburg she-'Einan shel Maharam," 181–84); I. Ta-Shma, *Ha-Sifrut ha-Parshanit la-Talmud*, vol. 2, 108–10; idem, *Kneset Meḥqarim*, vol. 2 (Jerusalem, 2004), 111–14; my *Jewish Education and Society in the High Middle Ages*, 74–76; my "Rabbinic Conceptions of Marriage and Matchmaking in Medieval Europe," in *Entangled Histories: Knowledge, Authority, and Jewish Culture in*

immersion for a reverting apostate serves as an indication or a sign for the penitent of his new status and for the community as well, rather than as a personal act of penance (as had been suggested by Simḥah of Speyer and others). This would seem to be a way of further formalizing what one version of Ri of Dampierre's treatment had assumed from the former apostate's personal perspective, that the immersion serves to sensitize the returning apostate to his renewed commitment to Jewish observance, although there is no indication that this immersion had to be undertaken more publicly, in front of a rabbinic tribunal. Indeed, there are *Tosafot* texts that hold that a freed Canaanite slave also does not have to undergo his immersion under the supervision of a *beit din* of three judges.[56]

---

the Thirteenth Century, ed. E. Baumgarten et al. (Philadelphia, 2017), 28–29 (and the literature cited in n. 28 on the provenance of *Tosafot Shitah*); and *Tosafot Yeshanim ha-Shalem 'al Massekhet Yevamot*, editor's introduction, 24–26. I am preparing a separate Hebrew study that presents an extensive list of citations from *Tosafot Shitah* associated with either the Tosafist study hall of Evreux or the *Tosafot* of Rabbenu Pereẓ. On Ritva's awareness and use of additional sources of northern French *Tosafot* (as compared to his Spanish predecessors, Ramban and Rashba), see my "Between Ashkenaz and Sefarad: Tosafist Teachings in the Talmudic Commentaries of Ritva," in *Between Rashi and Maimonides: Studies in Medieval Jewish Thought, Literature and Exegesis*, ed. E. Kanarfogel and M. Sokolow (New York, 2010), 249–73.

56 *Tosafot ha-Rosh* to *Yevamot* 47b (this chapter, n. 51, which does not discuss the case of a returning apostate), maintains that the *tevilah de-rabbanan* of a freed Canaanite slave does not have to be done in the presence of a rabbinic court, since he is technically able to give *qiddushin* from the moment he is freed. If a court of three was yet required to oversee his immersion, he would not be able to offer *qiddushin* at that point, according to talmudic law. See also Isaac of Corbeil, *Sefer Miẓvot Qatan* (Isaac was also a student of *Ḥakhmei Evreux*), sec. 159: "When [Canaanite] slaves are freed they require another immersion, but not in the presence of [a court of] three." This is ostensibly the position of the *Tosafot Shitah* as well, although Maimonides (*Mishneh Torah, hilkhot 'issurei bi'ah*, 13:12) and others ruled (see the comment of *Maggid Mishneh*, ad loc., and see also *Shulḥan Arukh, Yoreh De'ah*, 267:7) that the immersion of a freed slave also requires the presence of three. If the *Tosafot Shitah* passage follows this view (which is the less likely possibility to be sure), the passage would then be supporting the more far-reaching view attributed to Rabiah (as outlined earlier), that a form of public ratification is required. Cf. M. Yagur, "Zehut Datit u-Gevulot Qehillatiyyim be-Ḥevrat ha-Genizah," 72–80, 86–88, 136–37.

When Maharam of Rothenburg characterizes the shortcomings of the former apostate in question as one who was *tovel ve-sherez̤ be-yado*, he is not merely referring to a popular custom, as Jacob Katz had suggested. Rather, his ire is directed toward the flouting of a solemn rabbinic requirement by someone who had undergone the required ritual immersion without the corequisites of proper repentance and subsequent Jewish practice.[57] Meir of Rothenburg may have had direct access to the *Tosafot Shitah* passage (if not to the earlier Tosafist passages that required immersion, which have been noted to this point), given that Samuel of Evreux was a direct teacher of his when R. Samuel taught in Chateau-Thierry, and Maharam also had a close relationship with the slightly younger Rabbenu Perez̤ of Corbeil.[58]

How are we to understand the changing attitudes of Ashkenazic rabbinic authorities during the twelfth and thirteenth centuries with respect to the requirement of ritual immersion for an apostate who wished to return to the Jewish community, as reflected in the texts that have been presented here? This rite might have begun initially in Ashkenaz as a local custom, and it may also have been embellished along the way by popular practice. If so, the main goal or intent of the Tosafists was to provide formal legal grounding for this rite, as was their wont with regard to other bona fide Ashkenazic customs that preceded them.[59] On the other hand, it is possible that the practice of ritual immersion for a returning apostate was initiated and promoted by talmudists and halakhists who were members of the rabbinic elite. In either case, were these changes in the rabbinic view on the need for this immersion, which can be traced from the late twelfth century onward, solely the result of talmudic and other strictly halakhic considerations, or were there temporal factors that impacted the rabbinic view as well? We shall return to this question shortly, after a discussion of concomitant changes in the attitudes of Ashkenazic rabbinic authorities toward apostates who did not express interest in reverting.

57 Cf. *Maharam mi-Rothenburg: Teshuvot, Pesaqim u-Minhagim*, ed. Y. Z. Kahana, vol. 1 (Jerusalem, 1957), 157 (secs. 90–92); and this volume, chapter 1, n. 7.

58 See Urbach, *Ba'alei ha-Tosafot*, 2:528, 576–78.

59 See, e.g., my "Halakhah and Realia in Medieval Ashkenaz," *Jewish Law Annual* 14 (2003): 193–201.

However, a final observation about the nature of reversion to Judaism during this period in northern Europe is in order. At several points in this chapter, the Tosafist sources cited reflect what seems to be the relative ease with which Jews accepted Christianity and were then able to return to the Jewish community (in some cases on more than one occasion). This was sometimes linked with the ability of these religious "flip-floppers" to collect charity from both Christians and Jews. Ri of Dampierre dealt with one such figure in the late twelfth century,[60] as did Maharam of Rothenburg a century later,[61] and there are additional instances (in northern France) involving marriages between Jews who reverted to Judaism (after having lived as Christians, and with Christians) and their paramours, who then converted from Christianity to Judaism in situations that cannot all simply be coincidental.[62]

---

60 See this chapter, n. 7. In the early eleventh century, a Rhenish Jew willfully apostatized and studied to become a priest, but later reverted. See *Teshuvot Ba'alei ha-Tosafot*, ed. Agus, 45–46 (sec. 3), noted in Katz, *Exclusiveness and Tolerance*, 76 [= *Bein Yehudim le-Goyim*, 83]. The early twelfth-century cleric Guibert of Nogent tells the story of Count Jean of Soissons, who was accused of judaizing even as he publicly practiced Christianity. See J. M. Ziolkowski, "Put in a No-Man's Land: Guibert of Nogent's Accusations against a Judaizing and Jew-Supporting Christian," in *Jews and Christians in Twelfth-Century Europe*, ed. Signer and Van Engen, 113–22; *A Monk's Confession: The Memoirs of Guibert of Nogent*, trans. P. J. Archambaut (University Park, PA, 1996), 103–4, 111–13; and Jay Rubinstein, *Guibert of Nogent: Portrait of a Medieval Mind* (New York, 2002), 114–17.

61 See this chapter, n. 47.

62 See S. Emanuel, *Shivrei Luḥot*, 207 (n. 87); idem, *Teshuvot Maharam va-Ḥaverav*, 723 (#360); my "Meshummadot Nesu'ot she-Ḥazru: Heteran li-Bnei Zugan ha-Yehudi veha-Nokhri lefi Meqorot Ẓefon Ẓarefat ve-Ashkenaz Bimei ha-Benayim," 593–606; D. Malkiel, "Jews and Apostates in Medieval Europe," 18, 24–26; and this chapter, n. 6. See also this volume, chapter 3, n. 9, for the concern expressed by Simḥah of Speyer about an apostate who might revert in order to perform *ḥaliẓah* and thereby inherit from his brother, but would then apostatize once again; and *Maharam mi-Rothenburg: Teshuvot, Pesaqim u-Minhagim*, ed. Y. Z. Kahana, vol. 2 (Jerusalem, 1960), 108–9, sec. 119 (שאלו למהר״ם איש ואשה שקבלו חרם קהלות לישא זה את זה והמיר דתו האיש ושב לאח״כ בשתובה אם צריך להתיר לה חרם של הקהלות שקבלה עליה . . . והשיב הר״ם דלא בעיא התרה לחכם לאחר ששב דהא אי איתא קמן כל זמן שהיה מומר לא שבקינן לה לאינסובי דאין זו דעת המקום והקהלות להיות יחדיו . . . אבל הכא אפילו כשחזר בתשובה אינו צריך התרה . . . אבל אם לא הותרה עד ששב צריכה שאלה לחכם. ואין יכולים להתיר לה החרם כי אם בפניו או שלא בפניו ומדעתו וכו׳). Regarding the *ḥerem ha-qehillot* to which Maharam refers, see Louis

A Christian source dated April 1266 refers to the involvement of Eudes Rigaud, archbishop of Rouen, in the case of an apostate and heretic who was judged and condemned after he had converted from Judaism to Christianity, reverted back to Judaism, was then baptized again, but returned to the Jewish community—and now refused to be restored to the Catholic faith. Although he was admonished several times to do so, he refused, and was burned at the stake. It is noteworthy that, although his initial conversion to Christianity may well have been motivated by self-interest, the claim made by the Christian source is that this person's deep commitment to Judaism by the end of his life impelled him to die *'al qiddush ha-Shem*.[63]

Solomon ibn Adret of Barcelona (Rashba, d. c. 1310) records a ruling by his teacher Yonah b. Abraham of Gerona (d. 1263) concerning wine touched by an apostate from Judaism. Rabbenu Yonah had heard of the case from *Ḥakhmei Ẓarefat*, ostensibly during his student days in northern France, when he studied with the Tosafists Moses and Samuel b. Shne'ur of Evreux.[64] Rabbenu Yonah describes how this apostate would go from place to place, professing belief in Christianity in front of Christians in one locale while entering a Jewish home in another locale and asserting that he was a Jew. The rabbinic authorities remarked, "And we do not know if he is a Jew or not."

The ruling transmitted by Rabbenu Yonah is that if this person says he is a Jew when he enters a Jewish home (and appears to act like one), the wine he touches can be consumed by other Jews because his alleged declarations about being a Christian are considered to be untrue. He is making these claims only to address some frivolous need or desire (*hu 'oseh le-hana'at yiẓro ha-ra*), but he does not believe this in his heart. If, however, he also repeatedly violates

Finkelstein, *Jewish Self-Government in the Middle Ages* (New York, 1964), 140–41, 193, 206.

63 See Robert Chazan, *Medieval Jewry in Northern France* (Baltimore, MD, 1973), 147, citing *The Register of Eudes of Rouen*, ed. J. F. O'Sullivan (New York, 1964), 618.

64 See *She'elot u-Teshuvot ha-Rashba*, 7:179; *Beit Yosef, Yoreh De'ah*, sec. 119, s.v. *katav ha-Rashba*; *Darkhei Mosheh, Yoreh De'ah* 124:3 (end); and cf. Urbach, *Ba'alei ha-Tosafot*, 245. On Rabbenu Yonah and the brothers of Evreux, see my "*Peering through the Lattices*," 59–72.

the Sabbath or denies the words of the rabbis (or participates in Christian worship), he is considered a heretic.

Nonetheless, the episode Rabbenu Yonah heard about from his French teachers serves again to confirm that the boundary between the Jewish and Christian communities was a fairly porous one and was not so clearly delineated. Indeed, some ongoing apostates (who did not revert) maintained close ties with their friends, relatives, and communities.[65] As described earlier, Ri of Dampierre highlighted the venal causes of apostasy when dealing with a serial apostate. At the same time, however, the stain of apostasy was apparently becoming more intense within the Jewish community. Tosafists in both northern France and in Germany were not nearly as generous as Rashi had been in the positioning of apostates relative to the Jewish community, a tendency that will be further documented in the next two chapters for other areas of Jewish law and practice.

65 See D. Malkiel, *Reconstructing Ashkenaz* (Stanford, CA, 2009), 137–41; P. Tartakoff, "Testing Boundaries: Jewish Conversion and Cultural Fluidity in Medieval Europe," 732, 752. Cf. E. Carlebach, *Divided Souls*, 13–15; Chaviva Levin, "Jewish Conversion to Christianity in Medieval Northern Europe: Encountered and Imagined, 1100–1300" (PhD diss., New York University, 2006), 124–36; this volume, chapter 3, n. 56, and chapter 4, at n. 6. Cf. M. Yagur, "Zehut Datit u-Gevulot Qehillatiyyim be-Ḥevrat ha-Genizah," 176–93, 247–53.

3

THE EFFECTIVENESS OF MARRIAGE AND PARTICIPATION IN *ḤALIẒAH*

THIS CHAPTER DEALS WITH an aspect of Rashi's approach to the status of an apostate that was openly challenged by several German Tosafists during the late twelfth and early thirteenth centuries. As seen in the previous chapter, a number of Tosafists required the returning apostate to immerse as a means of expiation, if not for other reasons. According to Simḥah b. Samuel of Speyer, this immersion is derived from a passage in *Avot de-R. Nathan* that concerns a woman who lived among idolaters prior to her return to Jewish practice, and perhaps from Queen Esther's situation as well. Moreover, Rabiah of Cologne saw the apostate as even closer to a convert to Judaism (a *ger*) than did most contemporary Tosafists, as evidenced by the intense preparations for immersion that Rabiah required of the reverting apostate, along with the need for a formal (re-) acceptance of Jewish observance before a *beit din* tribunal of three to establish the sincerity of the apostate's intention to return.

The requirements laid out by Rabiah are not found in any French halakhic sources except for *Qiẓẓur Semag*, which cites the formulation of Rabiah anonymously, although the need for immersion itself was supported by both twelfth- and thirteenth-century French Tosafists. Other German Tosafist sources were less concerned about the extent to which the sincerity of the apostate's return could be verified but nonetheless sought to ensure that the reentry process itself was demanding. The requirement of cutting one's hair (and beard) prior to the immersion is found in a German Tosafist commentary to the *Sifra* and in a ruling of Avigdor Katz of Vienna. Such a practice is also referred to in the *Ḥizzequni* Torah commentary, which suggests the presence of this regimen in northern France as well. A number of German Tosafist writers, like Rabiah, viewed the apostate at his point of return to be like a convert to Judaism to a certain extent (*ka-ger*), although even the twelfth-century northern French Tosafist Riẓba characterizes the returning apostate as comparable (*domeh*) to a convert.[1]

The German Tosafist position to be discussed in this chapter relates to the precept of levirate marriage and the rite of *ḥaliẓah*, through which a childless widow is released from having to marry her deceased husband's brother. Although instances of *yibbum* and *ḥaliẓah* were more common in medieval Europe than they are today (undoubtedly owing to the lower average life expectancy during that era), the complex theoretical underpinnings of these requirements, which were even then not everyday occurrences, afforded the Tosafists a rich halakhic backdrop against which to fully develop and formulate their view, which in turn had important implications for additional dimensions of the status of an apostate, as we shall see.

The case in point concerns the need for an ongoing apostate (who had not reverted) to perform *ḥaliẓah* (which would allow his deceased brother's wife to marry another man), in a situation where no other brother was available or willing to nullify the *ziqah*, the halakhic tie that binds the wife to one of her husband's brothers until *ḥaliẓah* is performed.[2] Rashi's position in this matter

1 At issue here as well is the extent to which the sincerity of the reverting apostate's motives and commitment needs to be verified, to ensure that he or she was not being opportunistic or deceitful. See this volume, chapter 1, n. 24; and see also Simcha Goldin, *Ha-Yiḥud veha-Yaḥad* (Tel Aviv, 1997), 94–95.

2 *Yibbum* (through which a surviving brother is able to marry his brother's widow) by the apostate was obviously not an option, even though the apostate is referred to in many of the rabbinic texts cited in this chapter, by convention, as a *yavam*, just as the wife of the deceased brother with whom there is a *ziqah* is called a *yevamah* or a *shomeret yavam*. See also this chapter, n. 15. On the issue of whether *yibbum* or *ḥaliẓah* was generally preferred in medieval Ashkenaz, as well as the common practices in this regard, see J. Katz, *Halakhah ve-Qabbalah* (Jerusalem, 1986), 136–55; and A. Grossman, *Ḥasidot u-Mordot* (Jerusalem, 2001), 156–73. Parts of

is fully consistent with his larger view about apostates, and it is unequivocal: The apostate must perform *ḥaliẓah* in all circumstances, and his brother's wife cannot remarry until he does so.[3] As Jacob Katz explained Rashi's view, to exempt the woman from undergoing *ḥaliẓah*, and to allow her to remarry without this ceremony (as much as such an allowance might ease her plight, since it was unlikely that an apostate could or would cooperate in this matter), suggests that the brother who is an apostate does not have the same fundamental status as a Jew, a result Rashi could not countenance.[4]

Most subsequent Ashkenazic authorities appear to have supported the approach of Rashi, ruling that *ḥaliẓah* was required, at least to an extent. Katz was aware of a more lenient view proposed by Isaac b. Moses *Or Zarua'* of Vienna (d. c. 1255), who studied with a number of leading Tosafists in both northern France and Germany.[5] Isaac of Vienna's position was also followed by his son, Ḥayyim Eli'ezer, not only in his abridgment of his father's discursive legal work but also in a separate responsum.[6] Their view is based on several

the rabbinic correspondence about the case of a married *yavam* who refused to perform *ḥaliẓah* without compensation (which involved the Tosafists Netan'el of Chinon and Yeḥi'el of Paris) can be found in ms. Bodl. 672 (*QiẓẓurMordekhai le-R. Shmu'el Schlettstadt*, Ashkenaz, 1393; #20588), fol. 89r (in the margin), as noted in Grossman, "R. Netan'el me-Chinon: mi-Gedolei Ba'alei ha-Tosafot be-Ẓarefatba-Me'ah ha-Yod Gimmel," in *Meḥqerei Talmud*, vol. 3, ed. Y. Sussmann and D. Rosenthal (Jerusalem: Magnes Press, 2005), 175 (n. 6, on the basis of *Teshuvot Mahariq* and *Teshuvot Binyamin Ze'ev*).

3 See *Teshuvot Rashi*, ed. I. Elfenbein (New York, 1942), 193–94 (#173). Cf. *Ma'aseh ha-Geonim*, ed. Y. Freimann (Berlin 1910), 65 (sec. 69), which notes that Rabbenu Elyaqim *ha-Levi* (of Speyer), along with unnamed authorities in Mainz (circa 1100), required apostates to perform *ḥaliẓah* in all situations, although this passage suggests that the performance of *ḥaliẓah* was necessary mainly because the apostate might repent at some point in the future. Cf. this chapter, nn. 8, 29.

4 See J. Katz, *Halakhah ve-Qabbalah*, 265–66. See also the similar halakhic position taken by Rabbenu Gershom (without explicit recourse to the larger notion of *'af 'al pi she-ḥata Yisra'el hu*), in *Sefer Mordekhai 'al Massekhet Yevamot*, sec. 28 (= *Teshuvot Rabbenu Gershom*, ed. S. Eidelberg [New York, 1955], 118, #40): תשובת שאלה לר־ בינו גרשום. יבמה שנפלה לפני יבם משומד אינה נפטרה בלא חליצה שאם קידש, קדושיו קידושין וצריכה גט, לענין חליצה נמי צריך; and cf. this chapter, n. 36.

5 See E. E. Urbach, *Ba'alei ha-Tosafot* (Jerusalem, 1980), 1:436–39.

6 See this chapter, n. 43. On R. Ḥayyim's abridgment, see Urbach, ibid., 442–48. This

geonic responsa, which did not require an apostate to perform *ḥaliẓah* if he had already apostatized at the time of his brother's wedding.[7] Rashi had rejected the geonic approach as inconsistent, since these geonic sources ruled that *ḥaliẓah* need not be performed only if the brother had become an apostate before his brother's marriage took place. If the apostasy occurred after the marriage, however, these Geonim held that *ḥaliẓah* was required. In this case, the wife could not maintain that she had acquiesced to marry in the belief that she would not be subject to a *ziqah* involving this apostate.

A passage in *Maḥzor Vitry*, as cited in manuscript versions of *Sefer Mordekhai*, notes that Rashi offered support for his view based on the comparison to a *mamzer*, who is required to perform *ḥaliẓah* with his deceased brother's wife. If a *mamzer*, who is prohibited forever from marrying a (non-*mamzer*) Jewess, must perform *ḥaliẓah*, an apostate, who has the ability to repent (and thereby regain all the religious rights and privileges he previously had, including marriage to a Jewess without question), must certainly perform *ḥaliẓah* as well.[8]

---

work is variously referred to as *Or Zarua' Qatan/Qaẓar* or *Simmanei Or Zarua'*. See also *Pisqei Or Zarua' le-Rabbenu Ḥayyim b. Yiẓḥaq me-Vienna*, ed. M. J. Blau (New York, 1996), editor's introduction, 8–10.

7 See *Sefer Or Zarua'*, pt. 1, fols. 82a–b, *hilkhot yibbum ve-qiddushin*, sec. 605, ed. Machon Yerushalayim (Jerusalem, 2010), 1:494–96 (which also includes R. Ḥayyim's summary, and see this chapter, n. 40); *Haggahot Mordekhai le-Massekhet Yevamot*, sec. 107; and this chapter, n. 41. For the views of the Geonim in this matter, which for the most part did not accord with the approach favored by Rashi, see *Oẓar ha-Geonim*, ed. Lewin, vol. 7, 34–37 (secs. 76–88); ms. Bodl. 820, fols. 24r–v; *Teshuvot R. Natrona'i ben Hilla'i Gaon*, ed. R. Brody (Jerusalem, 1994), 468–69; and *Teshuvot Maharam mi-Rothenburg ve-Ḥaverav*, ed. S. Emaunel, 720 (sec. 357). See also Uriel Simonsohn, "The Legal Bonds and Social Ties of Jewish Apostates and Their Spouses According to Gaonic Responsa," *Jewish Quarterly Review* 105 (2015): 421–22, 434–36.

8 See ms. JTS Rab. 674 (#41419), fol. 125r (cited by Elfenbein, this chapter, n. 3); ms. Vercelli C1 (#30923), fol. 290v; ms. Toronto FR 5-011 (#9334; formerly ms. Sassoon 534); ms. Cambridge Add. 490 (#16784), fol. 74v (in the margin). See also the glosses of *Shiltei ha-Gibborim* to the (standard) *Sefer Mordekhai 'al Masshekhet Yevamot* [39b], sec. 30, n. 6; and *She'elot u-Teshuvot Mahariq* (Jerusalem, 1988), #85, fols. 164–66. The passage begins with the phrase *maẓati be-Maḥzor Vitry*, and continues with *shuv maẓati be-Maḥzor Vitry*. The latter part cites (anonymously)

A rabbinic court in Wurzburg (c. 1200) followed the view favored by Rashi, requiring one who had apostatized before his brother's marriage to perform *ḥaliẓah*. Nonetheless, an unnamed judge on that court implies that Simḥah of Speyer (who was one of Isaac b. Moses of Vienna's German Tosafist teachers) was apparently sympathetic, at least in theory, to the geonic view that *ḥaliẓah* is not required *de jure* in such a situation. This emerges from a case in Speyer that was heard by R. Simḥah and his brother, Eleazar of Strasbourg, in which a person who had apostatized prior to his brother's marriage was required to perform *ḥaliẓah*. As R. Eleazar explains, however, this requirement was imposed on the apostate brother in this particular case before the court, lest he claim that he had repented at the time of his brother's death. His alleged repentance would have allowed for the possibility of *yibbum* (and a marriage with the deceased brother's wife), through which this seemingly penitent brother would have then been able to inherit his deceased brother's assets. The concern of the rabbinic judges in this instance was that perhaps this brother would then return to his state of apostasy (*yaḥzor le-suro*), having acquired his brother's assets through *yibbum*. Once the brother is compelled to perform *ḥaliẓah*, however, there is no possibility for him to perform *yibbum*, and he cannot lay claim to the inheritance.

Thus *ḥaliẓah* was mandated in this case not because Simḥah of Speyer held that it was required as a matter of law (as Rashi did) but because of his concern that the surviving brother (who was currently an apostate) would take advantage of the situation.[9] Although Isaac *Or Zarua'* does not mention

the geonic view that *ḥaliẓah* is not required if the apostasy occurred prior to the marriage, but suggests (based on the reasoning presented) that in fact the opposite might well be true (that *ḥaliẓah* is not required only if the apostasy took place after the marriage), and concludes that further investigation is necessary (*ve-yesh livdoq ba-davar*). To this point, however, I have been unable to locate any of this discussion in the extant manuscripts of *Maḥzor Vitry* itself. Cf. D. S. Sassoon, *Ohel Dawid* (London, 1935), 174.

9 See *Teshuvot Maharam va-Ḥaverav*, ed. Emanuel 718 (sec. 355), from ms. Hamburg 45: וכן אירע פה בווירצפורק, שמשומד אחד חלץ ליבמתו, והוא נשתמד קודם קדושי המת. ואני הייתי אחד מן הדייני׳. וכן אירע בשפירא לפני הר׳ שמחה ואחיו הר׳ אלעזר מסטרספורק, ואמ׳ הר׳ אלעז׳ סברא שעל כן יש לו לחלוץ, שמא יאמר המשומ׳ רוצ׳ אני לחזור בתשוב׳ ולייבם אותה, והוא ישוב כדי שתתייבם לו ויזכה בממון של אחיו המת, ואחריכ׳ יחזור לסורו, לזה יש לחוש. אבל כשיחלוץ לה אין לחוש

his teacher R. Simḥah when discussing the need for an apostate to perform *ḥaliẓah*, it would seem that they were in agreement that it was possible to avoid *ḥaliẓah* in situations where the brother had apostatized prior to the marriage of his deceased brother, if no other circumstances warranted its being done.

The approach suggested by Isaac (and Ḥayyim) *Or Zarua'* on the basis of the lenient geonic position is rejected, however, in a responsum by Meir of Rothenburg (Maharam), who had studied briefly in his youth with Isaac *Or Zarua'* and was a teacher of R. Ḥayyim.[10] Maharam asserts that he had been prepared to present strong proof for the geonic view, based on a passage toward the end of tractate *Bava Qamma* (110b–111a) in which the Talmud considers the possibility that a woman effectively stipulates at the time of her marriage that she will not allow herself to be subject in any way to a subsequent levirate *ziqah* that involves a brother with pronounced bodily blemishes. Maharam concludes, however, that, despite this proof, he did not feel he could disagree with the approach of Rashi in practice, and he therefore rules that the apostate brother must perform *ḥaliẓah* in all such circumstances, irrespective of when he became an apostate.[11]

לדבר זה לארחב׳, וכן נראה. Cf. *Ma'aseh ha-Geonim*, this chapter, n. 3. Simḥah of Speyer generally allowed and even preferred *yibbum*. See Avraham Grossman, *Ḥasidot u-Mordot*, 163–65, although as Grossman notes, R. Simḥah made sure in other instances as well that this preference did not lead to any unfair advantage being taken by the surviving brother. As Emanuel indicates, this passage is recorded in ms. Hamburg 45 just after a copy of Rashi's responsum on the need for an apostate to perform *ḥaliẓah* in all instances.

10 See Urbach, *Ba'alei ha-Tosafot*, 2:523–25, 543; *Teshuvot Ba'alei ha-Tosafot*, ed. I. A. Agus (New York, 1954), 226; Noah Goldstein, "R. Ḥayyim Eli'ezer b. Isaac *Or Zarua'*—His Life and Work" (DHL diss., Yeshiva University, 1959), 18–19; and my *Jewish Education and Society in the High Middle Ages* (Detroit, MI, 2007), 18, 121–22 (n. 14).

11 See *Sefer Mordekhai 'al Massekhet Yevamot*, sec. 30; *Sha'arei Teshuvot Maharam b. Barukh*, ed. M. A. Bloch (Berlin, 1891), 280 (#130); *Maharam mi-Rothenburg: Teshuvot, Pesaqim u-Minhagim*, ed. Y. Z. Kahana, vol. 2 (Jerusalem, 1960), 108–9, sec. 119 (cited in chapter 2 of this volume, n. 62); *Teshuvot Maimuniyyot le-hilkhot 'ishut*, #29 (and cf. this chapter, n. 43, in the responsum of Ḥayyim *Or Zarua'*, where this talmudic possibility is accepted). Maharam was asked about a situation in which there were two brothers who could perform *ḥaliẓah*: an older one who

However, several manuscript passages (which are only partially reflected within published texts) demonstrate that two older Tosafist contemporaries of Isaac *Or Zarua'* in Germany ruled that an apostate is not required to perform *ḥaliẓah* for his deceased brother's wife in any situation, even when the apostasy occurred after his brother's marriage had taken place. Their position is that an apostate is not meant to perform *ḥaliẓah* because his status as a Jew has been compromised in a meaningful way by his apostasy; his status as a *Yisra'el rasha* is not merely a matter of rhetoric. By maintaining their view in all cases in which the brother had apostatized, these rabbinic figures avoided the charge of inconsistency that Rashi had leveled against the geonic position. We shall first identify these two earlier German Tosafist views, and then look again more closely at the material found in *Sefer Or Zarua'*.

A number of relatively early (and consistently reliable) manuscripts of *Sefer Mordekhai* to tractate *Yevamot* contain the following passage: "I have found written in the name of R. Abraham of Regensburg [in some texts the reference is to R. Abraham *ha-Gadol*] regarding a *yevamah* who falls to a *yavam* who is an apostate, that it is a wonderment that she requires *ḥaliẓah* from him." In some of the manuscript versions, R. Abraham states directly that she does not require *ḥaliẓah*: "This constitutes a forbidden sexual relationship [*in flagrante, ha-lo be-maqom 'ervah hu*], for which 'zealots are bidden to kill such a person in the act [*ve-qanna'im pog'im bo*]'. A woman who has sexual relations with a non-Jew [lit., an *'aramaei*] is subject to [the rule of] *qanna'im pog'in bah*."[12]

was an apostate and a younger one who lived in a faraway place (*bi-medinat ha-yam*). See *Sefer Mordekhai 'al Massekhet Yevamot*, sec. *30*; and *Teshvuot Maharam defus Prague*, ed. Bloch (Budapest, 1895) #491. The questioner wondered whether, in this instance, the older (and much nearer) brother could perform *ḥaliẓah* (if he were willing), in order to more easily allow the widow to remarry (*mipnei takkanat ha-'iggun*). R. Meir responds that, even in such a situation, it is preferable for the *yavam Yisra'el* to be utilized rather than the brother who is an apostate. The passage concludes with the instruction that *'azlinan hakha le-ḥumra ve-hakha le-ḥumra*, that an apostate is required to perform *ḥaliẓah* if he is the only brother. However, in cases where another brother exists, that brother should perform the *ḥaliẓah*, even in situations where this is not so easily accomplished.

12 מצאתי כתוב בשם ה"ר אברהם מרגנשבורק על יבמה שנפלה לפני יבם משומד שבזה איכא דברים בגו כי תימה דבעי' אפילו חליצה ממנו כי במקום ערוה הוא וקנאים פוגעים בו, כי גם [זו] הנבעלת לארמאי קנאים

For R. Abraham the point at which the apostate accepts Christian observances relative to his brother's marriage is irrelevant. The apostate is excluded from performing *ḥaliẓah* in all cases, inasmuch as he has the status of a non-Jew with whom the woman cannot live under any condition.

To be sure, Abraham of Regensburg is not a particularly well-known Tosafist figure, although there are historical (and literary) circumstances that may account for this. Abraham was the son of Moses Zaltman b. Joel, a member of the rabbinic court in Regensburg during the second half of the twelfth century along with two well-known German students of Rabbenu Tam—and important Tosafists in their own right—Rabbenu Ephraim b. Isaac and Isaac b. Mordekhai (Ribam). Moses b. Joel composed *Tosafot* to several tractates, but these have been lost for the most part. Indeed, his son R. Abraham also composed *Tosafot* (at least to tractate *Bava Batra*) that have been largely lost. However, more than ten remnants of these *Tosafot* are cited in manuscript versions of *Sefer Mordekhai* to *Bava Batra*.[13]

פוגעים בה. See ms. Budapest (National Museum) 2⁰1 (Ashkenaz, 1373), fol. 268a; ms. Vienna 72 (Ashkenaz, 1392), fol. 212b (and cf. Samuel Kahn, "R. Mordekhai b. Hillel ha-Ashkenazi," *Sinai* 14 [1944]: 316); ms. Cambridge Add. 490 (Ashkenaz, 1397), fol. 74b (in the margin); ms. Bodl. 667 (Ashkenaz, sixteenth century), fol. 122b; and ms. Vercelli C1 (Italy, 1453), fols. 290 a–b. See also the glosses of *Shiltei ha-Gibborim* to *Sefer Mordekhai 'al Massekhet Yevamot* (sec. 30, n. 6, end). Katz, *Halakhah ve-Qabbalah*, 267, was aware of R. Abraham's position only from its citation in the fifteenth-century *Terumat ha-Deshen* of Israel Isserlein (sec. 223), and he considers it to be a "lone voice, without any [broader] social support." Katz was also aware that *Haggahot Mordekhai, Yevamot*, sec. 107, maintains that *ḥaliẓah* by an apostate was not required in all cases, irrespective of when he became an apostate, but he was apparently unaware of the other relevant formulation by R. Abraham of Regensburg in this matter (see this chapter, n. 23). Cf. Gerald Blidstein, "Who Is Not a Jew?—The Medieval Discussion," *Israel Law Review* 11 (1976): 380; Bernard Rosensweig, "Apostasy in the Late Middle Ages in Ashkenazic Jewry," *Dine Israel* 10–11 (1981–83): 65; Ḥayyim Yosef David Azulai (*Ḥida*), *Birkei Yosef* (Vienna, 1859), pt. 3, *Even ha-'Ezer*, 4:14 (fols. 6b–c); and the formulation of Maharam of Rothenburg in chapter 2 of this volume, n. 62 (כל זמן שהיה מומר לא שבקינן לה לאינסובי דאין זו דעת המקום והקהלות להיות יחדיו).

13 See Urbach, *Ba'alei ha-Tosafot*, 1:207–8; my "Religious Leadership during the Tosafist Period: Between the Academy and the Rabbinic Court," in *Jewish Religious Leadership: Image and Reality*, ed. J. Wertheimer (New York, 2004), 1:271, 282

Abraham b. Moses was also a member of the rabbinical court in Regensburg. He served with Rabbenu Tam's student Isaac b. Jacob of Bohemia (known as Ri *ha-Lavan*) and subsequently with Barukh b. Isaac of Regensburg (not to be confused with Barukh b. Isaac [d. 1211], a French student of Ri of Dampierre and author of *Sefer ha-Terumah*), and with Judah *he-Ḥasid* (d. 1217; Judah had moved to Regensburg from Speyer c. 1195). Several court decisions and other rulings from this group of rabbinic judges in Regensburg are extant, including one recorded at some length in *Sefer Ḥasidim*,[14] and a *siddur* that belonged to R. Abraham is cited in connection with one of his prayer customs.[15] It should also be noted that in his youth Isaac *Or Zarua'* studied in Regensburg with both Judah *he-Ḥasid* and Abraham b. Moses, and he mentions their common practice concerning the fulfillment of the weekly requirement to review and recite the Torah portion twice, along with a single recitation of the Targum Onkelos (*shenayim miqra ve-'eḥad targum*).[16]

(n. 69), 301; and S. Emanuel, *Shivrei Luḥot* (Jerusalem, 2006), 83–86.

14 See *Sefer Ḥasidim* (Parma), ed. J. Wistinetzki (Frankfurt, 1924), secs. 1592–93; *Sefer Rabiah*, sec. 1032, ed. D. Deblitzky (Bnei Brak, 2005), 3:444–45; Israel Ta-Shma, *Kneset Meḥqarim*, vol. 1 (Jerusalem, 2004), 250–53; S. Emanuel, *Shivrei Luḥot*, 224; and my "R. Judah *he-Ḥasid* and the Rabbinic Scholars of Regensburg: Interactions, Influences and Implications," *Jewish Quarterly Review* 96 (2006): 17–37. On the presence of Barukh b. Isaac, author of *Sefer ha-Terumah*, only in northern France, see Emanuel, "Ve-Ish 'al Meqomo Mevo'ar Shemo: Le-Toledotav shel R. Barukh b. Yiẓḥaq," *Tarbiz* 69 (2000): 423–40.

15 See ms. Parma (de Rossi) 929 (Ashkenaz, 1391), fol. 91r: אין אומרים והשיאנו בראש השנה וביום הכיפורים. והא שנחשבים כיום טוב היינו שאין בהם אבילות. וכן כתב מורי הר"ר אברהם ב"ר משה דאין נ"ל לו' והשיאנו לא בראש השנה ולא ביום הכיפורים דאינן רגלים. בתפילות שלנו אין כתו' ובראשי חדשיכם וכו' [בר"ה] . . . ורבינו יעקב בן יקר וכל בני דורו לא התפללו אותו . . . ובתפילות של מורי הר"ר אברהם ב"ר משה היה כתוב ומחקו, וכן סובר ספר חפץ שאין לאומרו. On this issue, cf. *Pisqei ha-Rosh* to tractate *Rosh ha-Shanah*, 4:14.

16 See *Sefer Or Zarua'*, *hilkhot qeri'at Shema*, pt. 1, fol. 11c (section 11, ed. Machon Yerushalayim, 1:47). See also pt. 1, fol. 104c (*she'elot u-teshuvot*, sec. 744, ed. Machon Yerushalayim, 1:628) ,כתב מורי אבי העזרי . . . בתשובתו שהשיב לה"ר אלעזר מווירונא זצ"ל ולמורי ה"ר אברהם מריגנשבורק; *hilkhot Shabbat*, pt. 2, fol. 12a–b (sec. 53, ed. Machon Yerushalayim, 2:65); and Uzi Fuchs, "Iyyunim be-Sefer Or Zarua' le-R. Mosheh me-Vienna" (Master's thesis, Hebrew University, 1993), 16, 18–19, 29, 33–39. It is likely that Isaac b. Moses had left the study hall of Abraham of Regensburg well before R. Abraham expressed his view concerning the issue of *ḥaliẓah* by an apostate,

Moreover, Simḥah of Speyer addresses several halakhic queries to Abraham of Regensburg for his opinion and guidance. Similarly, R. Abraham, along with his colleague Barukh of Mainz (whose view regarding an apostate's *ḥaliẓah* will be discussed shortly), was asked by the Italian Tosafist Eleazar b. Samuel of Verona (a student of Ri of Dampierre) to ratify a particularly challenging and suggestive ruling of his which allowed an *'agunah* to marry another man under difficult circumstances.[17]

Abraham of Regensburg is also mentioned in another passage that has direct bearing on this discussion of the status of an apostate with regard to *ḥaliẓah*. Samuel b. Abraham *ha-Levi* of Worms (known as R. Bonfant), a close student of Simḥah of Speyer (as noted earlier, in chapter 2), cites his teacher regarding whether an apostate is able to divorce his Jewish wife. R. Simḥah adduces a passage from the Jerusalem Talmud (*Qiddushin* 1:1, end, *ḥosheshin le-qiddushav ule-gerushav*), and a geonic ruling in the name of Rav *Kohen Ẓedeq* (*meshummad megaresh et 'ishto mishum de-maqshinan havayah la-yeẓi'ah, mah havayah 'i meqaddesh qiddushin tofsin, 'af [ba-] yeẓi'ah megaresh 'ishto*), according to which an apostate's *qiddushin* and *gerushin* are considered to be effective. R. Simḥah's view in this matter is ultimately a more nuanced one, and will be discussed and further analyzed toward the end of this chapter.

R. Bonfant presents the view of Abraham of Regensburg, about which R. Simḥah raised some questions. The Talmud rules (*Ketubot* 11a) that a minor who had been converted to Judaism (*ger qatan*) by a *beit din* acting on his

---

since *Sefer Or Zarua'* (see this chapter, nn. 42–43) makes no mention of R. Abraham's (similar) position.

17 See Urbach, *Ba'alei ha-Tosafot*, 1:434–35, 437–38; *Sefer Rabiah*, sec. 901, ed. Deblitzky, 3:38–42; *Millei de-Bei Hillula 'al 'Inyanei Erusin ve-Nissu'in*, ed. Y. Hershkowitz (New York, 1998), 25–26 (on the nature of *birkat 'erusin*, and the marriage of converts); *Shibbolei ha-Leqet—ha-ḥeleq ha-sheni*, ed. S. Hasida (Jerusalem, 1988), 222–23 (sec. 48: תשובת ר׳ אברהם מרייג[נ]שבורק ישמחו השמים ותגל הארץ לך מורי הרב ר׳ שמחה נר מערבי, מפני שאתה מצוה עלי לדון לפניך על נדר על דעת רבים הנני דן לפניך לפי עניותי נראה וכו׳); and *Derashah le-Pesaḥ le-R. Eleazar mi-Vermaiza*, ed. S. Emanuel (Jerusalem, 2006), editor's introduction, 28 (n. 102). Cf. *Teshuvot u-Pesaqim*, ed. E. Kupfer (Jerusalem, 1973), 255.

behalf can later renounce his conversion if he was not informed about it prior to his attaining the age of maturity (*bar miẓvah*). R. Abraham understands this talmudic passage to mean that if, however, the renunciation of Judaism by one who had converted to Judaism occurs when he was already of *bar miẓvah* age or beyond (*ger she-ḥazar le-suro*), the renunciation has no impact whatsoever on his Jewish status. Moreover, the same is true for a Jew who sought to renounce Judaism through apostasy. Therefore, if an apostate marries a woman and she accepts his *qiddushin*, we recognize those *qiddushin*, and when the apostate gives his wife a *get* (even if he had married her before he became an apostate), the bill of divorce is likewise completely effective (*'ela vadai dineihem ke-Yisra'el bein le-qula bein le-ḥumra*).[18]

Thus Abraham of Regensburg holds that the granting of a bill of divorce by an apostate to his wife and an act of *qiddushin* that he initiates are effective, even as he holds that an apostate is never required to perform *ḥaliẓah*. He rules in these seemingly contradictory ways because, while the apostate is the one who initiates the halakhic states of marriage and divorce (even as the woman must accept his *qiddushin* for the marriage to be valid), this is not the case with respect to *ḥaliẓah*. Rather, the need for *ḥaliẓah* is initiated or caused by his brother's marriage, which the apostate does not control in any way. Even though a *yavam* can typically determine how he wishes to proceed (whether to perform *yibbum* or *ḥaliẓah*), he is not the one who creates the *ziqah* with his brother's widow. According to Abraham of Regensburg, the apostate cannot live with this woman (who is an uncorrupted Jewess), nor can this be tolerated from the standpoint of the larger communal and halakhic ethos as reflected by the notion of *qanna'im pog'in bah*. In addition, it is immaterial for R. Abraham whether the apostate had already apostatized at the time his brother married or only at some later point. The apostate is not the one who initiates the *ziqah*, and an apostate is thus excluded in all cases from performing *ḥaliẓah*, a position that stands completely opposed to the view of Rashi.

---

18 See *Teshuvot u-Pesaqim*, ed. Kupfer, 295–96 (sec. 176); and this chapter, n. 51. Cf. U. Simonsohn, "The Legal Bonds and Social Ties of Jewish Apostates and Their Spouses According to Gaonic Responsa," 424–34.

Another German Tosafist of this period, Barukh b. Samuel of Mainz (d. 1221), also suggests that an apostate does not perform *ḥaliẓah* under any condition. R. Barukh, who served as a leading member of the rabbinic court in Mainz,[19] was the author of a voluminous halakhic work, *Sefer ha-Ḥokhmah*, which is no longer extant. Fragments and remnants of this work indicate that it contained a wealth of responsa, as well as records (or summaries) of the proceedings of the Mainz rabbinical court, in addition to at least partial commentaries on a number of talmudic tractates.[20] In addition R. Barukh composed *Tosafot*, some of which are also included in *Sefer ha-Ḥokhmah*.[21] As noted earlier, R. Barukh and Abraham of Regensburg interacted at least once, at the request of Eleazar of Verona. In a passage where R. Abraham refers to R. Barukh using various honorific terms, there is perhaps an indication that R. Abraham was a student of R. Barukh (who does not appear otherwise to have had any students, even as his son, Samuel Bamberg, was a rabbinic decisor of note). It appears, however, that R. Abraham was actually a bit older than R. Barukh. R. Abraham's laudatory references to R. Barukh as his teacher simply reflect the writing style employed by many Tosafists in referring to their knowledgeable questioners (including younger scholars) as their teachers, as a sign of the esteem in which these scholars were held even by their more senior colleagues.[22]

R. Barukh's position that an apostate does not perform *ḥaliẓah* is found within a lengthy passage in the *Haggahot Mordekhai* to tractate *Yevamot*, which can be further clarified on the basis of other texts, including a responsum by Judah Mintz of Padua (d. 1508).[23] From these sources it emerges that R. Barukh

19 See Urbach, *Ba'alei ha-Tosafot*, 1:425–27; and my "Religious Leadership during the Tosafist Period," 267–69, 274, 287, 300.

20 See S. Emanuel, *Shivrei Luḥot*, 104–53; and cf. my "The Development and Diffusion of Unanimous Agreement in Medieval Ashkenaz," in *Studies in Medieval Jewish Literature*, vol. 3, ed. I. Twersky and J. Harris (Cambridge, MA, 2000), 26–28, 40 (nn. 35–36).

21 See Emanuel, *Shivrei Luḥot*, 120–23; idem, *Me-Ginzei Eiropah*, vol. 1 (Jerusalem, 2015), 327–66; and cf. Urbach, *Ba'alei ha-Tosafot*, 1:428.

22 See Urbach, *Ba'alei ha-Tosafot*, 1:435 (n. 48); *Sefer Rabiah* and *Shibbolei ha-Leqet*, this chapter, n. 16; and Emanuel, *Shivrei Luḥot*, 109 (n. 31).

23 See *Haggahot Mordekhai 'al Massekhet Yevamot*, sec. 107; *She'elot u-Teshuvot*

was familiar with several geonic texts that relate to this matter. According to these geonic passages (as well as the geonic material with which Rashi was familiar), only when the brother had become an apostate prior to the marriage of his brother was there no requirement for him to perform *ḥaliẓah*. Unlike the Geonim, however, R. Barukh maintains that the possible *ziqah* between the brother(s) of a married sibling and his wife is established not at the time of the wedding (*ʾein nissuʾin mappilim*; marriage does not cause the potential *yavam* to be designated) but only at the point where the married brother dies (*ʾela mitah mappelet*). Thus the question whether the potential *yavam* was already an apostate at the time of his brother's marriage is immaterial. By the

---

Mahar"Y (R. Yuda) Minz, ed. A. Siev (New York, 1995), #12 (fols. 46a, 47b = *Mayyim ʿAmuqim* [Berlin, 1778], fols. 21a, 22a; *Mayyim ʿAmuqim* is the second volume of the responsa of Eliyyahu Mizraḥi, who corresponded with Judah Mintz); and *Sheʾelot u-Teshuvot R. Eliyyahu Mizraḥi* (Constantinople, 1560; repr. Jerusalem, 1938), #68 (fols. 231a, 232a). I thank my friend and colleague Prof. Simcha Emanuel for this last reference. See now his *Me-Ginzei Eiropah*, vol. 2 (Jerusalem, 2019), 310–19. To this point, manuscript research within texts of *Sefer Mordekhai* and *Haggahot Mordekhai* has not yielded the precise source of the published *Haggahot Mordekhai* passage. R. Barukh is referred to in this passage only by his initials, ר״ב (which is perhaps what caused modern scholarship to entirely overlook his view): ור״ב הביא ראיה דקיי״ל כר״ח מדתנן פרק בית שמאי וכו׳ . . . והקשה ר״ב מאי שנא ממזר יבם וכו׳. This convention is fairly common, however, throughout *Sefer Mordekhai* and *Haggahot Mordekhai* texts (which are among the most important resources for reconstructing R. Barukh's *Sefer ha-Ḥokhmah*). See, e.g., *Sefer ha-Mordekhai le-Massekhet Qiddushin*, ed. J. Roth (Jerusalem, 1990), 161 (line 20); 224 (lines 204–5); 245 (2); 265 (93); 293 (219); 302 (275), and cf. 300 (line 25); *Sefer ha-Mordekhai le-Massekhet Gittin*, ed. M. Rabinowitz (Jerusalem, 1990), 331 (line 21); 535 (line 373, שאל ר״ב את רא״ם); 684 (line 282), and cf. 541 (line 40); *Sefer Mordekhai ha-Shalem ʿal Massekhet Pesaḥim*, ed. Y. Horowitz (Jerusalem, 2008), 169 (line 2); S. Emanuel, *Shivrei Luḥot*, 105 (n. 8), 110 (nn. 36, 41), 128, 138 (n. 157); and this chapter, n. 35. It should be noted that Barukh b. Isaac, the French Tosafist student of Ri of Dampierre, does not discuss the question of *ḥaliẓah* for an apostate in his *Sefer ha-Terumah*, although he does cite Rabbenu Tam's allowance for an apostate to write a *get* (and even to force the apostate to give his wife a *get*; see *Sefer ha-Terumah* [Jerusalem, 1959], 79, secs. 127–28), which suggests that he agrees with Rashi's approach that the *qiddushin*, *gittin*, and *ḥaliẓah* of an apostate are essentially valid. Thus, he cannot be the R. Barukh to whom the passage under discussion here refers.

time his brother dies, he is surely an apostate, and therefore no *ziqah* with the deceased brother's wife is ever created.

The question of *mitah mappelet* or *nissu'in mappilim* is discussed twice within tractate *Yevamot* (at 13a and at 30b, in a somewhat more muted context). In the medieval period, two early, important Sefardic rabbinic authorities, Rabbenu Ḥanan'el b. Ḥushi'el of Kairwan (d. 1056) and Isaac b. Jacob Alfasi (Rif, d. 1103 in Lucena) ruled in favor of *mitah mappelet* (following the view of the Amoraim, Rava and Rav Ashi), although this remained a decidedly minority view among subsequent *rishonim*.[24]

As far as I can tell, however, no Ashkenazic rabbinic figures until Barukh of Mainz supported this view. Indeed, R. Barukh presents additional support for Rabbenu Ḥanan'el's approach, adducing another proof from a talmudic *sugya* that Rabbenu Ḥanan'el does not mention. This *sugya* (*Yevamot* 108b–109a) deals with a man who had divorced his wife and subsequently remarried her, without the wife's having married another person in between (*maḥzir gerushato*). The question raised by the Talmud is whether this woman would be permitted in such an instance to live with her husband's brother (through *yibbum*) in the event the husband died (and she was childless), considering that she and her husband are presently together as the result of a remarriage. This matter is linked by the *sugya* to the question raised earlier: Is the *ziqah* created when the husband and wife are first married (in which case there may not be a *ziqah* from the remarriage of both partners), or is the *ziqah* created only when the husband dies (in which case the fact that there is a remarriage is not relevant)? The Talmud rules here that *yibbum* is possible (as codified also by Alfasi), which

24 See *Oẓar ha-Geonim*, vol. 7 (*Yevamot*), ed. Lewin, 305 (sec. 32), and see also 37 (to *Yevamot* 22a); *Hilkhot ha-Rif* to *Yevamot* 13a (fol. 3a) and 30b (fol. 8b); and cf. *Sefer ha-Miqẓo'ot*, ed. S. Assaf (Jerusalem, 1947), 11, and G. Blidstein, "Who Is Not a Jew?" 380, n. 39. Cf. *Haggahot Mordekhai li-Yevamot*, sec. 97, for the ruling by Rabbenu Ḥanan'el that an apostate's *qiddushin* are to be treated as fully effective (and this chapter, n. 32). For the unsubstantiated Ashkenazic tradition that Rif was a direct student of Rabbenu Ḥanan'el, see *Sefer ha-Yashar le-Rabbenu Tam* (*ḥeleq ha-teshuvot*), ed. S. Rosenthal (Berlin, 1898), 89, and cf. I. Ta-Shma, this chapter, n. 35.

suggests that it has adopted the position of *mitah mappelet*; the *ziqah* is established at the time of the husband's death. Barukh of Mainz thus identifies additional support for the view of Rabbenu Ḥanan'el, which he also accepts. The state of *mitah mappelet* is so for every case of potential *ziqah*, including all situations involving an apostate. Thus an apostate is never required to perform *ḥaliẓah*.[25]

To be sure the *Haggahot Mordekhai* passage also includes a question raised by Barukh of Mainz about this conclusion: How can a *mamzer* be obligated to perform *ḥaliẓah* (which the Talmud explicitly derives in *Yevamot* 22a, *mi she-yesh lo aḥ mi-kol maqom*), while an apostate (according to R. Barukh's analysis) is not? An apostate's *qiddushin* are valid without any qualification (according to most authorities, as we shall see), while the *qiddushin* of a *mamzer* are valid only according to the rabbinic view that *qiddushin* are effective even when offered by someone with whom marital relations would engender the Torah punishment of being cut off (*karet*).

Although *Haggahot Mordekhai* proposes no answer to this question in R. Barukh's name or otherwise, the parallel material found in the responsum of Judah Mintz cites an answer that appears already in geonic responsa, that the apostate is indeed worse than a *mamzer* in this regard (*garua' mi-kulam*), and shows how the derivation in *Yevamot* 22a could easily and productively have been reworded to include the apostate, which the talmudic *sugya* does not do. Moreover, the *Haggahot Mordekhai* passage (as well as its parallels) goes on to criticize Rashi's position about an apostate's obligation to perform *ḥaliẓah*, based on an inference from a passage in Moses of Coucy's *Sefer Miẓvot Gadol*. All this and more is marshaled in support of the explicit approach of Barukh of Mainz—that an apostate, as opposed to a *mamzer*, is excluded from

25 R. Barukh concludes his proof as follows (*Haggahot Mordekhai li-Yevamot*, sec. 107): ובגמ׳ [יבמות דף קט ע״א] מפרש דפליגי בנישואין מפילין והלכה כחכמים [דלית להו ני׳ שואין ראשונים מפילין] וכן פסק רב אלפס. וא״כ, אפילו המיר לאחרי כן [=לאחר מנישואי אחיו], אינה חולצת. The standard *Tosafot* to *Yevamot* (which originated in northern France; see Urbach, *Ba'alei ha-Tosafot*, 2:620–23) consistently assumed, on the other hand, that *nissu'in mappilin*. See *Tosafot Yevamot* 13a, s.v. *nissu'in*; and *Tosafot Yevamot* 30a, s.v. *ve-ne'esrah*; 84b, *ve-khi*.

performing *ḥaliẓah*—while raising the question whether even the *qiddushin* of an apostate are effective, a matter to which we shall return.[26]

In light of the question raised by Barukh of Mainz from the case of a *mamzer* (and despite the suggested answers), perhaps R. Barukh was simply exploring the possibility that a widow could remarry without receiving *ḥaliẓah* from her apostate brother-in-law, since it was unlikely that an apostate would deign to perform *ḥaliẓah* in any case.[27] It appears, however, from an extant passage about money-lending in his *Sefer ha-Ḥokhmah*, that R. Barukh sought to rule in this way because he firmly believed that an apostate should not be treated as a full Jew by the Jewish community, even as he is in fact still a Jew from his own religious perspective. The passage in *Sefer ha-Ḥokhmah* reads:

> I, Barukh heard that in [northern] France [*Ẓarefat*], they permitted apostates to borrow money [from Jews] at interest, and they allowed apostates to lend money at interest [to Jews]. Their proof comes from the second chapter in tractate *'Avodah Zarah* [26a–b, which deals with the status of heretics and informants, who need not be given any economic support]. The only [economic] obligation in effect is

26 See *Teshuvot Maharaḥ Or Zarua'*, #116, ed. M. Abittan (Jerusalem, 2002), 107, who explains (for the geonic position on an apostate and *ḥaliẓah*) that the rabbinic approbation supporting Jewish marriages (*kol ha-meqaddesh ada'atah de-rabbanan meqaddesh*) was not extended to this situation since the rabbis did not want the widow to live with the apostate under any condition; and therefore *ḥaliẓah* was also not required. With regard to the *qiddushin* of an apostate (and a *mamzer*), however, where the woman had to agree (and both parties were inherently aware of the prohibitions and difficulties involved), the rabbis left it up to the woman to refuse, but did not otherwise void these *qiddushin* if they were offered and accepted. See also *Ḥiddushei ha-Ritva 'al Masskhet Yevamot* (22a), ed. A. Jofen, 497–518; *Arba'ah Turim, Even ha-'Ezer* 44:9. For the *Semag* passage and its analysis, see this volume, chapter 4, n. 13.

27 On this kind of consideration in halakhic decision-making, see, e.g., Gerson Cohen's review of Bentzion Netanyahu, *The Marranos of Spain: From the Late XIVth to the Early XVIth Century According to Contemporary Hebrew Sources* (New York, 1966), in *Jewish Social Studies* 29 (1967): 178–81; and David Berger, "Jacob Katz on Jews and Christians in the Middle Ages," in *The Pride of Jacob: Essays on Jacob Katz and His Work*, ed. J. Harris (Cambridge, MA, 2002), 52–55.

that the lost object of an apostate must be returned [since Deut. 22:3 mandates the return of "all of your brother's losses" (*le-khol 'avedat 'aḥikha*), in which the word "brother" is otherwise superfluous and therefore comes to specifically include the losses of an apostate as well]. But for other things, he is not considered to be your brother. My teacher and relative [*mori qerovi*] was wont to say that when a person pushes away permitted Jewish practices and adopts prohibited ones [*hekha de-shaviq heterah ve-'akhil 'issura*], he is a heretic and should be treated accordingly. But I say that it is [nonetheless] prohibited for [an apostate] to borrow from or to lend to a Jew at interest because who has allowed him [*mi hitir lo*, to transgress these commandments]? And since it is prohibited for him to do so, we also may not lend to him or borrow from him [at interest] because of *lifnei 'ivver* [placing a stumbling block in front of a blind person], similar to the prohibition of handing a cup of wine to a *nazir*.[28]

28 See *Sefer ha-Ḥokhmah*, sec. 151, partially reproduced in S. Emanuel, *Shivrei Luḥot*, 108, from (the uncensored version of) *Shitah Mequbbeẓet* to *Bava Meẓi'a* 71b; and see *Shitah Mequbbeẓet* (*Ḥiddushei Bava Meẓi'a*), vol. 2, ed. Oz ve-Hadar (Jerusalem, 1996), fols. 553b–554a. See fol. 551b for an indication of censorship: מספר החכמה להה"ר ברוך סימן קנא. אני ברוך שמעתי שבצרפת מתירין להלוות לישראלים משומדים ברבית וללות מהם. וראייתם וכו'. ומורי קרובי היה אומר היכא דשביק היתירא ואכיל איסורא זהו מין ומורידין אותו וראייה מגיטין פרק השולח ההוא גברא דזבין נפשיה ללודאי וכו' [גיטין דף מו ע"ב-מז ע"א] זהו מין ומורידין אותו [ע"ז דף כו ע"ב]. ואני אומר בע"כ לדידיה אסור ללות ולהלות לישראל ברבית דמי התיר לו. וכיון דלדידיה אסור, גם לנו אסור להלות לו או ללות ממנו משום ולפני עור וגו' ודמי ללא יושיט אדם כוס לנזיר וכו'. On the connotation of the expression *de-mi hittir lo*, cf. D. Berger, in the previous note. Interestingly, the piece that follows in this section of *Shitah Mequbbeẓet* cites the commentary of Rabbenu Ḥanan'el (loc. cit.), in the name of Rav Shalom Gaon Yisra'el, that it is prohibited to lend to or to borrow from an apostate at interest, since his *qiddushin*, *gittin*, and *ḥaliẓah* are considered to be effective (קידושיו קידושין ולא משתריא מיניה אלא בגט ולגבי גט יהיב לאיתתיה ופטר לה ולגבי אחיו שמת חלץ לה.). Rabbenu Ḥanan'el's commentary concludes: והואיל והרי הוא כישראל לגבי קידושין וגט וחליצה דאמר שמא יתחרט ויעשה תשובה לפיכך אסור ורחמנא אמר לא תשיך לאחיך הילכך אסור. As such, R. Barukh of Mainz's use of Rabbenu Ḥanan'el's ruling on *mitah mappelet* (to exclude the apostate from being a *yavam*) led him to a different explanation and conclusion from those of Rabbenu Ḥanan'el with regard to *ḥaliẓah* by an apostate—a result that is not uncommon, however, within the realm of medieval talmudic and halakhic interpretation.

The teacher and relative to whom R. Barukh refers in this passage is Eli'ezer b. Samuel of Metz (d. 1198), a student of Rabbenu Tam in northern France.[29]

The precept of *ḥaliẓah*—coupled with the issue of money-lending at interest, as raised in this passage—provided R. Barukh with the opportunity to distinguish between the status of the apostate from the perspective of the members of the Jewish community (where he disagrees with the position associated with Rashi) and the apostate's own religious status, for which the notion of *'af 'al pi she-ḥata Yisra'el hu* remains operative. An apostate is not eligible to perform *ḥaliẓah* because he is to be treated as a non-Jew in this regard by the members of the community; his own personal Jewish status is not relevant in this situation. Barukh of Mainz also accepts what his teacher taught—that the apostate's mindset, which led him to partake of prohibited foods and the like at every opportunity (as per *Gittin* 47a), gives him the status of a quasi-heretic who is not to be sustained by the Jewish community (according to *'Avodah Zarah* 26b) as long as he remains religiously outside of it. At the same time, however, R. Barukh held that members of the community cannot act on this determination in order to lend money to him (or borrow from him) at interest because of his ongoing personal status as a Jew who is forbidden to borrow or lend money at interest.

Had R. Barukh allowed money-lending at interest—and the allowance by his teacher, Eli'ezer of Metz, was right in front of him—we might have assumed that he was simply trying to help the larger Jewish community with respect to obstacles generated by the presence of apostates. They do not need to perform *ḥaliẓah* (which significantly eases the plight of the widow), and yet they can be charged interest, which generates additional income for the members of the Jewish community. However, from R. Barukh's stringency with respect to taking interest, and from his dispassionate analysis of why an apostate should not participate in *ḥaliẓah*—along with the question he raised regarding a

29 See Eli'ezer of Metz, *Sefer Yere'im ha-Shalem*, ed. A. A. Schiff (Vilna, 1892–1902), fols. 73b–74a (sec. 156); and Emanuel, *Shivrei Luḥot*, 108 (n. 26). On Eli'ezer of Metz's presence in Germany as well, see this volume, chapter 4, n.11.

mamzer—it appears that R. Barukh's approach to apostasy was more broadly conceptual and ideological.

R. Barukh's views on money-lending involving an apostate, along with a comparison to the position of Eli'ezer of Metz and his teacher Rabbenu Tam (and other northern French Tosafists), will be discussed more fully in the next chapter. However, as a brief point of comparison, Rabiah of Cologne, who also was a student of Eli'ezer of Metz, held that interest can be taken from an apostate even though his *qiddushin* and *get* are effective (and he is required to do *ḥaliẓah* as well). Rabiah explains simply that, although the apostate is to be treated generally as a Jew (*'af 'al pi she-ḥata Yisra'el hu*), "it is appropriate to fine him in monetary matters [which enables interest to be taken from him, *debe-mamona ra'ui le-qonso*]."[30]

The position put forward by Barukh of Mainz concerning an apostate and *ḥaliẓah* is essentially the same as that of Abraham of Regensburg. As we have seen, R. Abraham distinguishes between the *get* and *qiddushin* of an apostate—both of which remain in effect—versus the apostate's inability to perform *ḥaliẓah*. We are now prepared to discuss in more precise detail the lengthy passage in Isaac b. Moses of Vienna's *Sefer Or Zarua'*, which deals with the issue of an apostate and *ḥaliẓah*. As noted earlier, the passage begins with extensive citations from several geonic texts, including a passage from *Sefer Basar 'al Gabbei Geḥalim*, a work that contains material from the geonic period that is cited only by subsequent Ashkenazic authorities, along with a smattering of Ashkenazic material from the eleventh century.[31] The conclusion of

30 See *Sefer Rabiah*, vol. 1, ed. A. Aptowitzer (Jerusalem, 1983), 158–59 (sec. 151) [= ed. Deblitzky, 1:120]; and *Sefer Mordekhai 'al Massekhet 'Avodah Zarah* (sec. 814), although Rabiah does note that there are those who held that the *get* of an apostate is not effective; see this chapter, n. 53. As recorded in *Sefer Mordekhai 'al Massekhet Yevamot*, sec. 39 (end), Rabiah rules (in his *Sefer Avi'asaf*) that the child of a female apostate (and a gentile) is to be treated as a full Jew, with respect to both the effectiveness of his *qiddushin* and the prohibition disallowing a Jew to lend him money at interest. On this passage, see also Joel Sirkes, *Bayit Ḥadash* to *Arba'ah Turim, Yoreh De'ah*, sec. 159, s.v. *meshummad she-kafar* (end). As described earlier, in chapter 2 (n. 35), Rabiah supported a strict series of procedures for a reverting apostate both to verify his sincerity and to effect expiation.

31 See Y. N. Epstein, *Meḥqarim be-Sifrut ha-Talmud ubi-Leshonot Shemiyyot*, vol. 1

this portion of Isaac b. Moses's presentation is that, in a situation where a Jew became an apostate prior to the marriage of his brother, no *ḥaliẓah* is required. R. Isaac asserts that even though the various geonic texts do not adduce explicit proofs from Talmudic *sugyot* to support their position, he is prepared to accept it, and he suggests a rabbinic proof of his own for this approach.[32]

Based on the geonic material cited, Isaac of Vienna then proceeds to add that, if the person in question had been an apostate at the time of his brother's wedding but subsequently repented and remained in that state until the brother died, a *ziqah* between the widow and the now-penitent former

---

(Jerusalem, 1984), 274–77; I. Ta-Shma, *Kneset Meḥqarim*, vol. 4 (Jerusalem, 2010), 213 (n. 3); and cf. A. Grossman, *Ḥakhmei Ashkenaz ha-Rishonim*, 254–57. On this work and its Ashkenazic context, see S. Emanuel, "Sefer Basar 'al Gabbei Geḥalim u-Terumato le-Ḥeqer 'Olamam shel Ḥakhmei Ashkenaz ha-Rishonim," in *Berakhot le-Avraham: Yom 'Iyyun likhvod Avraham Grossman*, ed. Y. Kaplan (Jerusalem, 2018), 23–42; and idem, *Me-Ginzei Eiropah*, vol. 2 (Jerusalem, 2019), 62–69. *She'elot u-Teshuvot R. Eliyyahu Mizraḥi* (this chapter, n. 23) links R. Barukh of Mainz to the passage from *Basar 'al Gabbei Geḥalim*, but this appears in fact to be a conflation of the material found in *Sefer Or Zarua'*.

32 *Sefer Or Zarua'*, *hilkhot yibbum ve-qiddushin*, sec. 605 (this chapter, n. 7), ed. Machon Yerushalayim, 1:494b–496a: כתוב בתשובות הגאונים, שומרת יבם שנפלה לפני משומד לא משתריא לעלמא עד דחליץ לה . . . והכי אמר רב נחשון גאון בר ישראל דקדיש אשה והוה ליה אח משומד בשעת קידושין ומת ההוא בר ישראל בלא בנים, אשתו פטורה מן החליצה ומן היבום כיון דקדים שמדותיה דאח לקידושין . . . משום דנישואין הראשונים מפילים את האשה לפני יבם . . . וכן מצאתי בספר בשר על גבי גחלים . . . ולא משתריא [האשה] לעלמא עד שחלצה מן ההוא יבם משומד . . . אבל [אם] כד נסבה בעל ההוא יבם היה משומד קודם לכן לא צריכה חליצה מיניה, עכ"ל. עוד מצאתי תשובת רבותינו . . . יבמה שנפלה לפני יבם משומד זקוקה ליבם . . . דאמרינן נישואים הראשונים מפילים. אבל ודאי כי נסבה בעל, ההוא יבם משומד הוה קודם לכן, לא צריכה חליצה. זו היא התשובה שמצאנו בה מן הגאונים אע"ג שלא הרבו בראיות, ידענו שתשובתם נכונה והגונה וכדי הם לסמוך עליהם . . . וכן אם מקדש בן ישראל אשה ויש לו אח ישראל ונשתמד, כיון דבשעת קידושין הוה ליה ישראל, אמרינן דזקוקה ליה דכל המקדש אדעתא דהכי מקדש . . . ולהכי אמר נישואים הראושנים מפילים. אבל אם בשעת קידושין אותו יבם משומד היה, מי איכא למימר אדעתא דרבנן מקדש וקיימי רבנן ומתקני מילתא דאית בה לידי תקלה. ותורה שכתבה כי ישבו אחים יחדיו ומת אחד מהם וגו' יבמה יבא עליה, מי קאמ' אפי הוא משומד יבא אליה והא כתיב דרכיה דרכי נועם. אלא מקיש ישיבת אחים להדדי, ומה אם מת אחד מהם ביהדות, אף יבמה יבא עליה ביהדות . . . ואם נפש אדם לומר הרי כבר שנינו [יבמות כב ע"א] מי שיש לו אח מכל מקום זוקק את אשת אחיו לכל דבר . . . לא במשומד קמיירי . . . דאיכא אח משומד זוקק אשת אחיו ליבום, כדמפרשי רבנן דמתיבתא, דקדשה אחיו כשהוא אכתי ישראל . . . ואיכא אח משומד דאינו זוקק אשת אחיו ליבום כי נשתמד מקמי נישואין דאח . . . ולתקנת עגונות חיישינן . . . ואע"פ שלא הוצרכנו לסהודי על תשובת הגאונים שכדאי הוא לסמוך עליהם, כתבנו לידידינו לפי מיעוט דעתנו סמך וראיה.

apostate is created at that time, which can lead in theory to either *ḥaliẓah* or *yibbum*, even though the penitent brother had been an apostate at the time of the marriage itself. R. Isaac supports this added ruling with one of the *sugyot* in *Yevamot* noted earlier (30b), in which Rava and Rav Ashi maintain that the death of the brother is what creates the *ziqah* (*mitah mappelet*) rather than the marriage, noting that Rabbenu Ḥanan'el had decided in favor of this view of Rava and Rav Ashi.[33]

In the final line of this passage, Isaac of Vienna further extends the impact of R. Ḥanan'el's ruling: "For Rabbenu Ḥanan'el, who rules that *mitah mappelet*, if he was an apostate [*mumar*] when his brother dies [even if he had been a (full) Jew at the time of his brother's wedding], he does not perform either *ḥaliẓah* or *yibbum* since [the] death [of his brother] is what creates the *ziqah*, and at the time of [his brother's] death, he was not a Jew [*ubi-she'at mitah lo hayah Yehudi*]."[34] Isaac *Or Zarua'* first employs Rabbenu Ḥanan'el's ruling to address a case wherein the wayward brother repented prior to his brother's death, but he then applies Rabbenu Ḥanan'el's ruling to exclude an apostate (at the time of his brother's death) from performing *ḥaliẓah*, even if the brother had been a proper Jew at the time of the wedding. This application moves beyond the allowance provided by the Geonim, and it is ultimately the same as the position of Barukh b. Mainz. R. Isaac does not explain his reason for adopting the position of Rabbenu Ḥanan'el (as R. Barukh did), although the great esteem in which Rabbenu Ḥanan'el and his interpretations and rulings

33 See ibid., 496a–b: אבל אם היה משומד בשעת נישואי אחיו וחזר בתשובה, ואחר כך מת אחיו והיו שניהם בדת ישראל בשעת מיתה, אז זוקק אשת אחיו לחליצה וליבום אע״פ שהיה משומד בשעת נישואי אחיו . . . וכן נראה בעיני אני המחבר ראובן ושמעון אחים, והמיר ראובן ונשא שמעון אשה בשעת המרה של ראובן, ואחר כך חזר ראובן בתשובה ומת שמעון, הואיל ובשעת מיתת ראובן היה מחזיק שמעון בתשובה, הרי היתה להם ישיבה אחת ביהדות וזוקק אשת שמעון לחליצה שהרי מיתה מפלת. והוה ליה האי ראובן שחזר בתשובה כאלו נולד לאחר נישואי שמעון דאמרי׳ פ׳ ארבעה אחיו [יבמות ל ע״ב] ולרבא הניחא אי סבר לה כרב אשי וכו׳ . . . ומסקנא על כרחו כרב אשי סבירא ליה, ופי׳ ר״ח והלכתא כרב וכרב אשי. וכיון דהלכתא דמיתה מפלת, מעתה אפילו היה משומד בשעת נישואין אחיו, הואיל והיה יהודי בעל תשובה בשעת מיתת אחיו, הרי מיתה מפלת וחולץ או מיבם. ואפשר שגם רב נחשון גאון וספר בשר ע״ג גחלים סוברין כן, שהרי לא ראינו מפורש בדבריהם שאע״פ שחזר בתשובה קודם מיתת אחיו שאעפ״כ יבמתו יוצאה בלא חליצה, אלא שכתבו שהנישואין הראשונים מפילין.

34 See ibid., 496b: ולפר״ח דפסק מיתה מפלת, אפי׳ היה יהודי בשעת נישואי אחיו, אם היה משומד בשעת מיתת אחיו, לא חולץ ולא מייבם שהרי מיתה מפלת ובשעת מיתה לא היה יהודי.

were held in medieval Ashkenaz renders such an explanation largely unnecessary.[35] Indeed, R. Isaac also cites and applies Rabbenu Ḥanan'el's ruling of *mitah mappelet* to a subsequent passage within the same halakhic subject area of *Sefer Or Zarua'* (the laws of *yibbum* and *qiddushin*), in a situation unrelated to apostasy.[36]

Isaac b. Moses does not mention the similar view held by his older contemporary, Barukh of Mainz. This omission is not surprising, however, given that R. Isaac otherwise cites R. Barukh on only a handful of occasions, apparently because he did not study directly with R. Barukh.[37] Nonetheless, the approach taken by Barukh of Mainz and Isaac *Or Zarua'* constitutes a seemingly purposeful trend in German halakhic literature to rule in accordance with Rabbenu Ḥanan'el (and the position of Rava and Rav Ashi) regarding the point at which a *ziqah* is established, and thus to completely remove an apostate from the performance of *ḥaliẓah*. The broader implications of this ruling are also detected in the particular phrasing employed by the author of *Sefer Or Zarua'*, especially when he declares at the very end of the passage that the apostate was "not a Jew" at the time of his brother's death. Isaac *Or Zarua'* does not mean to say that an apostate is literally considered to be a non-Jew in terms of his own religious status; rather his rhetoric indicates that the apostate is completely excluded from performing *ḥaliẓah* as if he were a non-Jew (and his brother's widow is permitted to marry another person), since the widow cannot live with him under any condition.[38]

In two places Isaac *Or Zarua'*'s son, Ḥayyim Eli'ezer, relates to his father's discussion of whether *ḥaliẓah* must be performed by an apostate. In his abridgment of *Sefer Or Zarua'* (known as *Simmanei Or Zarua' or Or Zarua'*

35 On the esteem with which Rabbenu Ḥanan'el's commentaries were held throughout the literature of the *Tosafot*, see I. Ta-Shma, *Kneset Meḥqarim*, 1: 43–61.

36 See *Sefer Or Zarua', hilkhot yibbum ve-qiddushin*, sec. 644, ed. Machon Yerushalayim, 1:534–35: אבל אם מתה גרושתו ואח"כ מת אחיו, גרושתו שריא וחולצת או מתיבמת ואע"ג דבשעת נישואי אחיו לא חזיא ליה . . . וכן מסתבר דהא קיי"ל כרבא פ"ק [דף יג ע"א] . . . דקסבר מיתה מפלת. ובפ' ד' אחין [דף ל ע"ב] כתב בפר"ח דקיי"ל כרבא ורב אשי. הלכך הואיל וקיי"ל מיתה מפלת אע"ג דלא איחזיא ליה בשעת נישואין הואיל ואיחזיא ליה בשעת מיתת אחיו או חולצת או מתיבמת.

37 See S. Emanuel, *Shivrei Luḥot*, 141.

38 Cf. Jacob Katz, *Halakhah ve-Qabbalah*, 266.

Qaẓar),[39] R. Ḥayyim, as was his wont, reduces the lengthy passage described earlier to a few lines:

> R. Naḥshon Gaon, *Sefer Basar 'al Gabbei Geḥalim* and the responsa of our rabbis [*teshuvot rabbotenu*] rule that a [potential] *yavam* who is an apostate at the time of his brother's marriage [and is still in this state when his brother dies] does not form a *ziqah* with his brother's wife, and she is allowed to marry anyone else [*muteret la-shuq*] without *ḥaliẓah*. And even if he repents after his brother dies, we do not pay attention to this. According to the commentary of Rabbenu Ḥanan'el, however, even if [the apostate] had been an upstanding Jew [*yehudi kasher*] at the time of his brother's wedding, if he was an apostate when his brother died, he does not perform either *ḥaliẓah* or *yibbum*.[40]

R. Ḥayyim understood from his father's presentation that the ruling of Rabbenu Ḥanan'el was highly significant and useful, even as R. Isaac expended a great deal of effort (and space) in first presenting and discussing the geonic view. Thus in R. Ḥayyim's abridgment of *Sefer Or Zarua'*, the position of Rabbenu Ḥanan'el is treated as equal (in terms of the space devoted to it and its significance) to the ruling of the Geonim, which excludes the apostate from *ḥaliẓah* only in a more limited way. Indeed, in at least one version of his *Or Zarua' Qaẓar*, R. Ḥayyim, when presenting his father's approach, rules explicitly in accordance with Rabbenu Ḥanan'el.[41]

---

39 See this chapter, n. 6.

40 See *Sefer Or Zarua'*, ed. Machon Yerushalayim, 1:494b, in the margin [= *Pisqei Or Zarua' le-Rabbenu Ḥayyim b. Yiẓḥaq me-Vienna*, ed. M. J. Blau, 1:117, sec. 18]: רב נחשון גאון וספר בשר על גבי גחלים ותשובות רבותינו פוסקי׳ דיבם שהיה משומד בשעת קידושי אחיו ועדיין כשמת אחיו הוא עומד בשמדותו, אינו זוקק את אשת אחיו ליבום ופטורה לשוק בלא חליצה, ואפי׳ חזר לאחר מיתת אחיו לא אשגחינן ביה. ולפר״ח, אפי׳ היה יהודי בשעת נישואי אחיו, אם היה משומד בשעת אחיו אינו לא חולץ ולא מייבם. See also ms. Vatican 148, fol. 138v; ms. British Museum 532, fols. 114r–v; and ms. Bodl. 881, fol. 153c.

41 See *Haggahot Mordekhai 'al Massekhet Yevamot*, sec. 107 (where R. Ḥayyim's work is referred to as *Or Zarua' Qaẓar*: כתב אז״ק וזה לשונו . . . וקיי״ל כרבינו חננאל עכ״ל

As recorded in one of his responsa, R. Ḥayyim was asked to clarify his father's stance in this matter. Did Isaac *Or Zarua*ʿ rule in this matter like "the view of our northern French teachers" who, following the approach of Rashi, required the apostate to perform *ḥaliẓah* in all situations, or did R. Isaac agree with those who were "lenient, *ke-divrei ha-matirim*," that the apostate does not have to do *ḥaliẓah* at all?[42] R. Ḥayyim's rabbinic questioner confesses that he finds the lenient possibility difficult to understand. The precise identity of these "lenient ones" is not divulged in R. Ḥayyim's response, although this term perhaps refers to those who supported the geonic position. Based on what we have just seen, however, it is also possible that this term refers to those rabbinic scholars in Germany (such as Abraham of Regensburg and Barukh of Mainz) who excluded an apostate from performing *ḥaliẓah* in all instances, in full opposition to the approach taken in northern France.

In the discussion of his father's position, R. Ḥayyim mentions the ruling found in *Sefer Miẓvot Gadol* in the name of Eliʿezer of Metz (whose view was noted earlier), that it is permitted to lend money to an apostate as long as he has not recanted, since he is not "your brother." R. Ḥayyim continues by noting that "as such, with regard to *yibbum* as well, an apostate is not to be involved because there, too, the Torah refers to brothers [in Deut. 25:5, 'When brothers dwell together and one of them dies and she has no child . . . her *yavam* shall perform levirate marriage']." Although R. Ḥayyim goes on to point out that the connotation of the word "brother[s]" is not precisely the same in both these contexts within the Torah—in one instance it connotes a biological sibling,

אר"ז); ms. Bodl. 650, fol. 253r; and *Teshuvot Mahari Minẓ*, #12 (this chapter, n. 23). Judah Mintz concludes that Isaac *Or Zarua*ʿ fully supports the position of Rabbenu Ḥanan'el over the geonic view, because he refers to it already in his discussion of the case of an apostate who repented before his brother died.

42 See *Teshuvot Maharaḥ Or Zarua*ʿ, #114, ed. Abittan, 105a: על דבר הזקוקה למשומד שנש־
תמד בשעה שנתקדשה כדברי רבותינו הצרפתים . . . אם הכריע מורינו רבינו אביך בספרו כדברי המתירים
אם לא כי טעמם לא היבנו. וטעם האוסרים מבורר דמשומד ישראל מקרי כמו שכתב רש"י בתשובה.
R. Ḥayyim lived in various locales in Germany and Austria (and points east), including Wiener Neustadt, Prague, Regensburg, Mainz, and perhaps Cologne. However, the suggestion that he resided for a time in France cannot be substantiated. See N. Goldstein, "R. Ḥayyim Eliʿezer b. Isaac *Or Zarua*ʿ—His Life and Work," 23–26.

while in the other it refers to a fellow Jew who is required to observe the same set of *miẓvot*—R. Ḥayyim nonetheless links them to explain his father's position as part of a unified, larger approach.[43]

Reference to the cohort of German rabbinic decisors concerning an apostate and *ḥaliẓah* (of which Isaac *Or Zarua*ʻ was a part) can be detected in a responsum sent by Isaiah b. Mali di Trani (RID, d. c. 1240) to Isaac *Or Zarua*ʻ. In this responsum RID implores R. Isaac (*ḥalilah ḥalilah lekha ve-ḥullin hu lekha me-ʻasot ka-davar ha-zeh*), on the basis of a number of halakhic sources, not to side with those who ruled that a *yevamah* who had fallen before an apostate does not require *ḥaliẓah*:

> For an apostate [*meshummad*] is akin to a full Jew [*ke-Yisraʼel gamur hu*], whether to marry or to divorce, whether to be excluded from *yibbum* or whether to require it. It is not reasonable to revoke his holiness [as a Jew] from him so that he becomes like a complete non-Jew. Rather, he is to be called a wicked Jew, whose marriage is binding and whose bills of divorce and *ḥaliẓah* are considered effective as they are for all Jews, and he creates a *ziqah* with the *yevamah* and must discharge it.

RID also chides Isaac of Vienna for being swayed by the geonic view, which appears to be against talmudic law. Indeed, RID concludes his plea: "Do not become one of the lenient [*min ha-meqilim*], who permits a Torah prohibition

43 See *Teshuvot Maharaḥ Or Zarua*ʻ, #116, ed. Abittan, 106–107b: ועל דבר הזקוקה למשומד כתב רבינו אבא מארי בשם הגאונים דכל היכא דנשתמד קודם נישואי אחיו המת שאינה זקוקה לו ולא בעיא חליצה מיניה, דנישואין הראשונים מפילים וההיא שעתא לאו אחיו הוא. ואתה כתבת כי טעם האוסרים מבורר דמשומד ישראל מקרי ולא היא, שכך כתב בספר המצות [סמ״ג] אומר רבינו אליעזר ממיץ . . . משומד להכעיס מותר להלוותו ברבית שהרי גם ברבית כתיב כי ימוך אחיך וגומ׳ אל תקח מאתו נשך ותרבית. והא דאמר בסנהדרין חטא ישראל, אף על פי שחטא ישראל הוא, דוקא לענין דברים דלא כתיב בהו אחוה כגון לענין קידושין וגיטין . . . עכ״ל. ומעתה, גם לענין ייבום לא תיזקק למשומד דאחים כתיבי והא לאו אחיו הוא. ואעפ״י שאין כל כך ראיה מכאן, כי דוקא בשאין הפסוק מדבר באחוה ממש אלא שקורהו אחיו מחמת שאחיו הוא במצות שייך לומר כן, אבל כשמדבר באחוה ממש כמו גבי ייבום, אין למעט משומד מטעם דלאו אחיו מקרי וכתיב הלא אח עשו ליעקב. Cf. Israel Isserlein, *Terumat ha-Deshen* (*Teshuvot*), secs. 219, 223; and G. Blidstein, "Who Is Not a Jew?" 380–81 (n. 42).

with impunity [*be-yad ramah*] without any proof from the Talmud."[44] RID penned an additional responsum in this matter (in defense of some of his earlier remarks), in which he asserts axiomatically that "even though an apostate has done evil and has blasphemed and given himself to idolatry, he cannot be stripped of his *qedushat Yisra'el*."[45]

RID was broadly aware of Tosafist materials from both northern France and Germany. He studied in Speyer at the turn of the twelfth century with Isaac *Or Zarua*''s teacher, Simḥah b. Samuel, where he was also exposed to the teachings of a number of German rabbinic figures who had studied with Rabbenu Tam. Moreover, even after he returned to Italy, RID remained in written contact with both R. Simḥah and Isaac *Or Zarua*',[46] although this particular exchange between R. Isaiah and R. Isaac cannot be dated with any precision. Nonetheless, Isaiah di Trani's heartfelt request to R. Isaac that he not place himself among the lenient ones in this matter suggests that there was in fact a group of contemporary rabbinic authorities who had adopted a markedly

---

44 See *Teshuvot ha-RID le-Rabbenu Yeshayah di Trani ha-Zaqen*, ed. A. Y. Wertheimer (Jerusalem, 1975), 326 (#64): חלילה חלילה לך וחולין הוא לך מעשות כדבר הזה . . . ולא תהיה משכלה הזאת תחת ידך, כי המשומד כישראל גמור הוא חשוב לכל דבר איסור בין לקדש בין לגרש בין לפטור מן הייבום בין לזקוק לייבום, דלא כל הימנו להפקיע עצמו מן הקדושה ולהיות כגוי גמור אלא ישראל רשע מקרי וקידושיו קידושין וגיטו גט וחליצתו חליצה ככל בר ישראל וזוקק ופוטר . . . והיאך נניח דברי התלמוד ונתפוש דברי הגאונים . . . ואני ראיתי בדבריך שגם כבודך מגמגם על דבריהם ממאי דאמרי׳ בפרק שני דיבמות [דף כב ע״א] דכל הפוטר זוקק והמשומד פוטר דישראל רשע הוא וקידושיו קידושין . . . אלא ודאי הדברים מחוורים כשמלה שבין זה ובין זה זוקק, שכיון שאם קידש קידושיו קידושין, הרי הוא כבר ישראל גמור לכל דבריו ופוטר מן היבום וזוקק לייבום . . . בבקשה ממך אל תהיה מן המקילין ומתירין איסור תורה ביד רמה בלי שום ראייה מן התלמוד. . . . Although RID may have been referring specifically to the geonic presentation itself (which was indeed somewhat short on talmudic prooftexts; see this chapter, n. 42), RID generally seeks to decide all matters of Jewish law based on the strength of the available talmudic prooftexts. See my "Progress and Tradition in Medieval Ashkenaz," *Jewish History* 14 (2001): 287–91, 303–5.

45 See *Teshuvot ha-RID le-Rabbenu Yeshayah di Trani ha-Zaqen*, ed. A. Y. Wertheimer, 486 (#99): יפה למדנו מכל זה השיטה שישראל משומד אע״פ שהרשיע וכפר והפקיר עצמו לע״ז, לא כל הימנו להפקיע קדושת ישראל מעליו.

46 See Ta-Shma, *Kneset Meḥqarim*, vol. 3 (Jerusalem, 2005), 20–25, 40–43; S. Emanuel, *Shivrei Luḥot*, 154–55, 164–65; and *Perushei Nevi'im u-Ketuvim le-Rabbenu Yeshayah ha-Rishon mi-Trani*, ed. A. Y. Wertheimer, vol. 1 (Jerusalem, 1959), editor's introduction, 54–55.

more lenient approach to apostasy and the need for *ḥaliẓah* than that of Rashi and his successors in northern France.[47]

Although there were a number of leading German rabbinic figures who continued to follow Rashi's approach regarding *ḥaliẓah* (including R. Meir of Rothenburg, who spent much of his student years in northern France studying with the Tosafist teachers Ezra of Moncontour, Samuel of Falaise, Yeḥi'el of Paris, and Samuel of Evreux),[48] the three German Tosafists from the late twelfth and early thirteenth centuries who have been identified with the position that an apostate does not perform *ḥaliẓah*—Abraham of Regensburg, Barukh of Mainz, and Isaac *Or Zarua'*—considered the notion of *'af 'al pi she-ḥata Yisra'el hu* to be effective only to a limited extent. The apostate is still considered to be a Jew for himself and his own religious identity, but his status as a Jew vis-à-vis others (and the larger Jewish community) has been significantly weakened and compromised.[49]

---

47 At one point RID writes that it was Rabbenu Tam (rather than Rashi) who prohibited money-lending to an apostate at interest (*Teshuvot ha-RID*, ed. Wertheimer, 330; although see ibid., n. 32, for the editor's suggestion that the text of the responsum should be emended here from Rabbenu Tam to Rabbenu Shelomoh). RID cites the position that a returning apostate does not require ritual immersion in the name of unspecified Geonim (ibid., 329) rather than from any Ashkenazic sources. Indeed, RID does not mention the names of any other German Tosafists in his presentation to Isaac of Vienna. He does take brief notice of the view of Rava (against the conclusion of R. Naḥshon Gaon) that *mitah mappelet* (ibid., 331), although he mentions this only to highlight the inconsistency within the geonic view, as Rashi had done. On RID's fealty to Rashi's larger position with regard to apostates, see this chapter, n. 62.

48 See Urbach, *Ba'alei ha-Tosafot*, 2:527–28.

49 See also Rabiah's formulation in *Sefer Or Zarua'*, *pisqei Bava Batra* sec. 103, ed. Machon Yerushalayim, vol. 3, fol. 437b (and this volume, chapter 4, n. 28), concerning the inability (in practice) of an apostate to inherit: וכן כתב מורי ר׳ אליעזר בן יואל הלוי שכמו שהוא מוריש לבניו, כך יורש את אביו, דאף על פי שחטא ישראל הוא. אך יש כח ביד חכמים להפקיר ממונו, דהפקר בית דין הפקר כדאמרי׳ . . . יהבינן לה קנס . . . אף על פי שיש לחלק בין קנס לירושה מיהו בכל ענין ראוי לקונסו דהבא על הכותית קנסוהו כדאיתא פרק שור שנגח ובירושלמי פ״ב דע״ז גרסינן להלין כותאי דקסרי, מותר להלוותן ברבית מפני שקלקלו מעשיהם. Cf. *Sefer Or Zarua'*, secs. 102, 104–5; *Teshuvot R. Natrona'i ben Hilla'i Gaon*, ed. Brody, 2:544–47; G. Blidstein, "Who Is Not a Jew?" 382–84; S. Goldin, *Ha-Yiḥud veha-Yaḥad*, 93; and Edward Fram, "Perception and Reception of Repentant Apostates in Medieval Ashkenaz

Indeed, another leading German Tosafist during this same period, Simḥah of Speyer, even considered taking a further step. As briefly noted earlier, R. Bonfant (Samuel *ha-Levi* of Worms) comments that his teacher Simḥah of Speyer did not agree with the view of Abraham of Regensburg (that an apostate cannot renounce his halakhic status as a Jew moving forward) and its underlying talmudic basis. The Talmud rules (*Ketubot* 11a) that a *ger qatan*, a minor who was converted by a rabbinic court but never told of his conversion prior to his *bar miẓvah*, can subsequently reject everything he did as a Jew at any time after his conversion as a minor. Abraham of Regensburg reasoned by inference that an older convert to Judaism—that is, one who converted after the age of majority and who now wishes to renounce his conversion—as well as a Jewish apostate cannot reject what they had done in the past as Jews nor what they might do in the future.

Simḥah of Speyer, however, suggests that perhaps these individuals could indeed reject whatever Jewish observances and rituals they might perform moving forward, after they had readopted their prior religion or become apostates from Judaism. Thus if an apostate now writes and gives his wife (whom he had married prior to his becoming an apostate) a bill of divorce, that *get* may not be valid. Indeed, if the apostate offers a woman *qiddushin*, that *qiddushin* is valid only *le-ḥumra*, as a stringency, because of the doubts raised (*de-'i qaddish, qiddushav qiddushin ve-zehu le-ḥumra . . . ve-davka le-ḥumra ne'emar de-ḥosheshin le-qiddushav*), according to R. Simḥah's understanding of a *sugya* in the first part of tractate *Yevamot* (16b).[50] A *get* is nonetheless required, but

---

and Premodern Poland," *AJS Review* 21 (1996): 300 (n. 5).

50 This understanding (and position) is fairly uncommon in this period. See Isaac b. Abba Mari of Marseilles, *Sefer ha-'Ittur* (*'ot quf, qiddushin, ha-ḥeleq ha-sheni*, fol. 78a); *Arba'ah Turim, Even ha-'Ezer*, 44:9 (and *Beit Yosef* ad loc.); *Semaq mi-Ẓurikh*, ed. Har-Shoshanim, 2:87 (sec. 179); and see also ibid., 2:157–58 (sec. 182, end), for the similar view of an otherwise unidentified *'ish levi mi-Narbonne* (referred to also by *Teshuvot Mahariq*, #175; and in *Teshuvot u-Pisqei Mahariq ha-Ḥadashim*, ed. E. D. Pines [Jerusalem, 1970], 90). Cf. *Sefer Or Zarua'*, pt. 1, sec. 604, ed. Machon Yerushalayim, 494; *Haggahot Mordekhai 'al Massekhet Yevamot*, secs. 97, 107; *She'elot u-Teshuvot Maharashdam* (Jerusalem, 2007), *Even ha-'Ezer*, sec. 10; and in this volume, chapter 4, n. 13.

the apostate may not be capable of writing and giving that *get* because his status as a Jew has been severely diminished. R. Simḥah adds that, because the apostate is still to be treated as a Jew, albeit only as a matter of stringency, he also cannot be charged interest on a loan.

R. Bonfant notes that Simḥah of Speyer found a responsum by Rav *Kohen Ẓedeq* Gaon in which he rules that an apostate may effectively give his wife a *get*, since marriage and divorce are linked inextricably by the Torah in halakhic terms (*maqshinan havayah li-yeẓi'ah*). Additionally, R. Simḥah notes that the only diminution regarding the status of an apostate indicated by a Torah verse (and its rabbinic exegesis) is found regarding the status of a *kohen* who had apostatized and remains in that state. Nonetheless, R. Simḥah remained uncomfortable with the position espoused by Abraham of Regensburg, and his final word on the subject is that an apostate has the status of a Jew only *le-ḥumra* (*she-'ein lo din ke-Yisra'el le-gamrei 'ela le-ḥumra*).[51] Significantly, Eli'ezer of Metz, the teacher of Simḥah of Speyer, also defines the status of the *qiddushin* of an apostate based on the *sugya* in *Yevamot* 16b, which suggests that an apostate's betrothal is not fully effective and is recognized only *le-ḥumra*. Again, however, a *get* is required to dissolve such a betrothal or marriage.[52]

R. Simḥah's contemporary in the Rhineland (and a fellow student of Eli'ezer of Metz), Rabiah of Cologne, was also aware of a contemporary rabbinic view

---

51 See *Teshuvot u-Pesaqim*, ed. Kupfer, 295–96 (sec. 176), and cf. G. Blidstein, "Who Is Not a Jew?" 369, 372 (n. 12), 377 (n. 24). R. Simḥah's formulation concludes: אבל שאר ישראל שנשתמד או גר שחזר לסורו יכול למחות מאותה שעה שנשתמד שאין לו דין ישראל לגמרי אלא לחומרא. Cf. Menaḥem ha-Meiri, *Beit ha-Beḥirah 'al Massekhet Yevamot* (16b), ed. S. Dickman (Jerusalem, 1992), 69. In the course of his remarks, R. Simḥah employs both the phrase חוששין לקידושיו (based on a passage in the Talmud Yerushalmi) and the phrase found in *Yevamot* 16b, גוי שקידש בזמן הזה חוששין לקידושיו שמא מעשרת השבטים הוא. Cf. *Haggahot Mordekhai li-Yevamot*, sec. 107, which considers the *qiddushin* of an apostate to be effective as per *Qiddushin* 49a, *harei 'at mequdeshet li 'al menat she-'ani ẓaddiq, 'afilu rasha gamur mequdeshet shema hirher teshuvah be-da'ato*. Similarly, Abraham of Regensburg presumes that both the *qiddushin* and *gittin* of an apostate (and an adult convert who had renounced Judaism) are effective because his (technical) status as a Jew has not been diminished (ודאי דיניהם כישראל בין לקולא בין לחומרא).

52 See *Sefer Yere'im ha-Shalem*, sec. 156 (this chapter, n. 29). See also ms. Bodl. 678, fols. 114d–115a, cited in Emanuel, "Teshuvot ha-Ge'onim ha-Qeẓarot," 448, n. 43.

that held that the *get* of an apostate is not effective. Rabiah does not endorse this position, noting that Rabbenu Tam reports in a responsum the he had executed (*'asah*) *gittin* for more than twenty apostates in northern France.[53]

---

53 See *Sefer Rabiah*, 1, sec. 151 (this chapter, n. 27): ויש שמחמירין בגט ואומרים כי קידושי תורה שקידש בעודו ישראל אין יכול להפקיע משמדותו מידי דהוי אשפוי ונשתטה . . . ואין הנידון דומה לראיה זו, ed. Deblitzky, 1:120. See also *Teshuvot Maimuniyyot le-hilkhot 'ishut*, #12 (= ms. Moscow 155 [#6835], fol. 40v, with variations: ואני ראיתי מעשה שמשומד נתן גט לאשתו שקידשה כשהיה ישראל גמור ולא ראיתי שום מרבותי שהיו מספקין בדבר. וגם בתשובת ר"ת [ספר הישר, סי' כה, מהדורת רוזנטל, עמ' 42–45] כתב שמשומד נותן גט ולא חילק בדבר); and *Sefer Mordekhai 'al Massekhet Yevamot*, sec. 38 (= ms. Vercelli C1, fol. 291d, ונ"ל דאפילו קידש בעודו ישראל ושוב בהמרתו יהב גט, הוי גט. ויש מרב[ו]תא שנסתפקו בגט שניתן בהמרתו), which cite Rabiah's lost halakhic work, *Sefer Avi'asaf*. In the *Teshuvot Maimuniyyot* passage, Rabiah identifies Nathan b. Yeḥi'el of Rome (author of *Sefer ha-'Arukh*), along with his brother Abraham, as questioning the efficacy of a *get* given by an apostate if he had married his wife prior to his apostasy. Cf. S. Goldin, *Ha-Yiḥud veha-Yaḥad*, 87, 99 (who describes the situation in northern France as well, where the *gittin* of apostates were considered fully effective); and Urbach, *Ba'alei ha-Tosafot*, 81–82. At the same time, however, Rabiah also cites the ruling of Rav *Kohen Ẓedeq* (noted also by Simḥah of Speyer, this chapter, at n. 51) and R. Amram Gaon that not only is the *get* of an apostate valid, but an apostate can also serve as a witness for a *get* if an observant Jew is not available. However, the leniency about an apostate serving as a witness is rejected strongly by Rabiah; and cf. this chapter, n. 51 (end). (In ms. Bodl. 678, fols. 195r–v = ms. JTS Rab. 673 [#41418], fols. 194r–v, this passage is assigned to ראי"ה = R. Eli'ezer [b. Joel] *ha-Levi*.) Both R. Simḥah and Rabiah required a returning apostate to undergo immersion, and Rabiah was especially demanding in this matter. See *Teshuvot u-Pesaqim*, ed. Kupfer, 290–91, sec. 71; my "Returning to the Jewish Community in Medieval Ashkenaz: History and Halakhah," in *Turim*, ed. M. A. Shmidman (New York, 2007), 81–87; and this chapter, n. 27. On the seemingly large concentration of apostates in northern Europe during the twelfth century reflected in Rabbenu Tam's report, see A. Grossman, *Ḥasidot u-Mordot*, 363, 431–32, who notes that Rabbenu Tam's responsum indicates that bills of divorce on behalf of apostate husbands were also authorized by German rabbinic authorities during the eleventh century. See also *Teshuvot u-Pesaqim*, ed. Kupfer, 296, n. 16*; *Maḥzor Vitry*, ed. S. Hurwitz, 779–80, sec. 134 (from *Sefer Terumah*, this chapter, n. 23); Urbach, *Ba'alei ha-Tosafot*, 82; and David Malkiel, "Jews and Apostates in Medieval Europe—Boundaries Real and Imagined," *Past and Present* 194 (2007): 7–9. In the late thirteenth century, however, Yedidyah b. Israel of Nuremberg, a younger colleague of Meir of Rothenburg who also studied in northern France, reports that apostasy occurred infrequently (*va-'afilu 'aḥat minei 'elef 'ein kofer*), although this phrase is perhaps an exaggeration. See I. A. Agus, *Teshuvot Ba'alei ha-Tosafot*, 238 (secs. 128); but cf. *Teshuvot ha-Rosh*, 32:8; and Agus, ibid.,

Yet such a view nonetheless moves beyond assigning a decidedly lower Jewish status to an apostate only with respect to a levirate marriage, as R. Abraham, R. Barukh of Mainz, and R. Isaac *Or Zarua*ʿ had advocated. The diminution in status according to this kind of approach extends to even more basic issues, such as the effectiveness of an apostate's initiation of marriage and divorce, as Simḥah of Speyer's discussion indicates. However, it is suggestive that no northern French Tosafists raised any of these more limiting possibilities concerning the Jewish status of an apostate with regard to bills of divorce (*gittin*) or even with respect to *ḥaliẓah*.[54]

Indeed, a striking example of the extent to which northern French rabbinic figures maintained that the notion of *ʾaf ʿal pi she-ḥata Yisraʾel hu* remains central in determining all aspects of an apostate's status as a Jew can be seen in the following ruling (*pesaq*) of the late-thirteenth-century Tosafist and halakhist Isaac b. Joseph of Corbeil (d. 1280). Isaac of Corbeil asserts that when the food of an apostate from Judaism is cooked by a non-Jew, the food cannot be consumed by a Jew. At the same time, however, he rules that if an apostate lights a fire that is then used by a non-Jew to cook or bake, the food is not considered to be *pat* (or *tavshil*) *ʿakkum* (as would also be the case if a practicing Jew lit the flame) due to the principle of *ʾaf ʿal pi she-ḥata Yisraʾel hu le-ḥumra* (from the strict perspective), which also accounts for why an apostate cannot lend money at interest to a Jew.

R. Isaac's use of the term *le-ḥumra* in this passage appears to be almost the opposite of its use by Simḥah of Speyer (and other German Tosafists) cited earlier. His ruling, that it is prohibited for the apostate to lend money at interest because of the principle of *ʾaf ʿal pi she-ḥata Yisraʾel hu*, comports with the view of several other northern French Tosafists, as we shall see in the next chapter.[55] However, R. Isaac concludes his ruling by noting that the family members of this apostate should not shield or otherwise think well of the apostate, since

235 (sec. 127), for a case described by a contemporary of Yedidyah of Nuremberg, Asher b. Yeḥiʾel (Rosh), in which a group of women apostatized due to their fear of death but subsequently reverted.

54 Cf. G. Blidstein, "Who Is Not a Jew?" 374–82.

55 See this volume, chapter 4, nn. 9, 15; and cf. this chapter, at n. 29.

the Torah indicates (Lev. 20:5) that the Almighty looks most unfavorably at both the heinous sinner and his family, which Isaac of Corbeil understands to refer to a family that protects or otherwise covers for a sinner in their midst or derives benefit from him.[56]

Another aspect of the laws of *yibbum* and *ḥaliẓah* provided Ashkenazic rabbinic authorities with an additional opportunity to consider the status of an apostate. The Talmud debates (*Yevamot* 3a–b) whether a wife who has been designated as potentially unfaithful to her husband (a *safeq sotah*) must nonetheless be formally released through *ḥaliẓah* by her husband's brother if the husband subsequently passes away. The Amora Rav holds that a *sotah* is not included in the *ḥaliẓah* requirement, nor was this requirement in place if any one of the deceased brother's other wives was a *sotah* (referred to by the Talmud as a *ẓarat sotah*). The Talmudic *sugya* asserts that, according to the Mishnah, the presence of such a woman does not affect these requirements, and *ḥaliẓah* must take place.

A passage in the late-thirteenth-century *Sefer Mordekhai* applies this analysis (and debate) to the case of a female apostate, positing that in effect she has the status of a *sotah*, since she has completely abandoned her observance of Judaism. Thus she does not require *ḥaliẓah* according to Rav's view that a *sotah* is exempt. According to the other view in that *sugya*, however, *ḥaliẓah*

56 The passage is recorded in ms. Paris BN 407 (#27901), fol. 237a, in a collection of *pesaqim* from both Pereẓ b. Elijah of Corbeil and Isaac of Corbeil, but it is explicitly attributed to Isaac of Corbeil in *Semaq mi-Ẓurikh*, ed. Y. Har-Shoshanim (Jerusalem, 1979), *miẓvah*, 219 [2], 2:345, sec. 231: בשם ר״י מקורביל שאסור לאכול מפת או מתבשיל של משומד אם בשלוהו גוים כמו מפת ישראל אם לא הכשירו ישראל או המשומד כי אף על פי שחטא הוא ישראל הוא לחומרא. וכן אסור לתת לו רבית. והמחפה עליו (שבועות דף לט ע״ב) והמפאר עליו מפני שהוא קרובו והניאותים ממנו, עליהם נאמר (ויקרא כ:ה) ושמתי אני את פני באיש ההוא ובמשפחתו. נראה לי פירוש אותו שהוא ממשפחתו ומחפה עליו. See also S. Emanuel, *Shivrei Luḥot*, 203–4; and cf. *Pitḥei Teshuvah* to *Yoreh De'ah*, 12:1. Although several manuscript variants of *Semaq mi-Ẓurikh* omit the phrase about money-lending (#4367, ms. Paris 388, fol. 99b [*miẓvah* 220]; #4360, ms. Paris 381, fol. 89a [*miẓvah* 213]; #21838, Bodl. 879, fol. 174b; #5655 ms. British Museum 515, fols. 139b–140a [*miẓvah* 219]; #13898, ms. Parma de Rossi 172, fol. 137a [*miẓvah* 219]), a similar number of manuscripts include it (#21839, ms. Bodl. 880, fol. 238r [*miẓvah* 224]; #13900, ms. Parma de Rossi 583, fol. 37 [*miẓvah* 221]; #1731, ms. Berlin [Steinchneider] 37 [*miẓvah* 213], fols. 146r–b; and #10150, Vienna [National Library] 20, fol 268d).

is required. Placement of a female apostate in the category of a *sotah* is surely suggestive in and of itself, even as the passage proceeds to note that the halakhic ramifications of this discussion are quite significant (*ve-hora'ah gedolah teluyah ba-davar*) and provides a detailed example. If the husband of a wife who had apostatized marries another woman and then dies without having had any children, the second wife is considered a *ẓarat sotah* (based on the apostasy of the first wife). Thus, according to Rav, she can marry another man without *ḥaliẓah*. According to the approach of the Mishnah, however, either *yibbum* or *ḥaliẓah* is necessary, although the latter is recommended in this instance (*ve-tov ha-davar she-taḥloẓ ve-lo tityabbem*).[57]

An actual case in a similar vein, ostensibly from northern France during the twelfth century, is recorded in manuscript. The husband of a woman who had apostatized died, and the woman subsequently reverted (*ḥazrah*). R. Jacob rules that she does not require *ḥaliẓah* from her deceased husband's brother, since she is definitely considered to be a *sotah* (*sotah vadda'it*), in accordance with the position of Rav, which was the way that Rivan (רבינו יב"ן, Rashi's son-in-law Judah b. Nathan) had ruled. However, R. Eli'ezer holds that the *halakhah* in this matter is not in accordance with Rav but rather with the approach of the Mishnah. Thus, just as this woman would have been required to receive a *get* to marry another man, so too does she require *ḥaliẓah* in this instance, even if she was considered a *sotah* during the period of her apostasy.[58]

57 See *Sefer Mordekhai 'al Massekhet Yevamot*, sec. 1 (end, to *Yevamot* 3a); ms. Vercelli C1 (#30923), fol. 285c; ms. Cambridge Add. 490 (#1684), fol. 69v; ms. Parma de Rossi 929 (#13795), fol. 230a; ms. Vienna 73 (#1470), fol. 271a; ms. Toronto FR 5-011 (#9934, formerly London Sassoon 534), fol. 129d; and cf. *Terumat ha-Deshen*, #219.

58 See ms. Bodl. 844 [#21605], fol. 75a, published in *Teshuvot Maharam mi-Rothenburg va-Ḥaverav*, ed. S. Emanuel, 448 (sec. 151). Regarding the period this passage reflects (and the identity of the rabbinic scholars involved), another passage found in ms. Bodl. 844 (fols. 70d–71a; see *Teshuvot Maharam*, ed. Emanuel, 411–12) juxtaposes halakhic rulings by Eli'ezer b. Nathan of Mainz (Raban) and Rivan. (Rivan's commentary to *Bava Meẓi'a* is referenced on fol. 27 of this manuscript; see *Teshuvot Maharam*, ed. Emanuel, 293.) See also Urbach, *Ba'alei ha-Tosafot*, 120, who presents a passage in *Teshuvot Ḥakhmei Ẓarefat ve-Lothaire* (sec. 1) in which R. Yom Tov, a son of Rashi's son-in-law Judah b. Nathan (Rivan), asks his brother R. Eli'ezer

The association of female apostasy with promiscuity, even when the conversion of a particular woman to Christianity (and her baptism) was forced, is at the center of a question that emerged in connection with the persecutions that occurred in Frankfurt in 1241. A betrothed woman, an *'arusah*—who is bound to her groom and cannot live with anyone else even as she is not yet permitted to live with her husband—was among a group of Jewish women who were taken captive and held by Christians for a period of time. Several rabbinic authorities expressed their opinions about whether this woman could be returned to her status as an *'arusah* (with whom the final act of marriage, *nissu'in*, could now be completed by her groom) following her ransom or release, or whether she was prohibited to him because of what had transpired. Complicating this particular case was the fact that the groom had already proceeded to marry another woman.[59]

Isaac b. Moses *Or Zarua'* of Vienna ruled that, even if the woman had been captured and taken by the Christians against her will—and even if, in addition, there was no firm evidence that she had relations with Christians—she was to be viewed as having defiled her *'erusin* vow and could not remain with her

---

to solicit a halakhic ruling from their distinguished relative, Rabbenu Tam. This family group would account for all the names in the passage being discussed. In addition, Rabbenu Tam refers in his *Sefer ha-Yashar* to a talmudic comment by Rivan (*ḥeleq ha-ḥiddushim*, ed. S. Schleschinger [Jerusalem, 1974], sec. 327); and to R. Eli'ezer (sec. 390; and see also sec. 655). In sec. 766, Rabbenu Tam argues against Yom Tov b. Judah in the case of a bill of divorce issued by an apostate. See also *Sefer ha-Yashar* (*ḥeleq ha-Teshuvot*), ed. Rosenthal, 42–47 (secs. 25–26); Urbach, *Ba'alei ha-Tosafot*, 121–22; and A. Reiner, "Rabbenu Tam u-Bnei Doro: Qesharim, Hashpa'ot ve-Darkhei Limmudo ba-Talmud" (PhD diss., Hebrew University, 2002), 183–87. As such, it is likely that we are dealing here with a twelfth-century incident that occurred in northern France.

59 For a thorough review of the various rabbinic positions taken, see Rachel Furst, "Captivity, Conversion, and Communal Identity: Sexual Angst and Religious Crisis in Frankfurt, 1242," *Jewish History* 22 (2008): 179–221. See also G. Blidstein, "Ma'amadan ha-Ishi shel Nashim Shevuyot u-Meshummadot," *Shenaton ha-Mishpat ha-'Ivri* 3–4 (1976–77): 86–100; and my "Meshummadot Nesu'ot she-Ḥazru: Heteran li-Bnei Zugan ha-Yehudi ve-Nokhri lefi Meqorot Ẓefon Ẓarefat ve-Ashkenaz Bimei ha-Benayim," in *Halakhah u-Mishpat: Sefer ha-Zikkaron li-Menaḥem Elon* (Jerusalem, 2018), 604–5.

'arus. Although R. Isaac makes fleeting reference to the parameters of a *sotah* in his response, the crux of his argument in this instance rests on the status of a female who has been captured by non-Jews, and it accords with talmudic law in situations where there is little hope that she can survive her imprisonment and be saved (*Ketubot* 26a–b). For R. Isaac, once this woman was baptized (*mishe-qiblah mayim teme'im*), it must be assumed that the Christians had their way with her and defiled her, since she was too fearful and concerned about her own physical security to resist their advances.[60]

Four other lesser-known rabbinic authorities, including Samuel b. Abraham *ha-Levi* of Worms, R. Bonfant (who, like Isaac *Or Zarua'*, was a student of Simḥah of Speyer, as noted earlier), maintain that the betrothed woman's forced baptism and period of captivity do not render her forbidden to her groom. Indeed, once she had been baptized, her chastity is actually protected by her Christian captors so that she can be eligible for a proper Christian marriage. Moreover, for R. Bonfant, the overriding presumption was that Jewish women who were forcibly converted and violated against their will remained absolutely loyal to their husbands, irrespective of any defilement the baptism may have caused.

It is interesting that Isaac *Or Zarua'* was among those German Tosafists who excluded male apostates from performing *ḥaliẓah* under any condition (since they are not considered full Jews in this matter),[61] while R. Bonfant

60 See *Sefer Or Zarua'*, pt. 1, sec. 747, ed. Machon Yerushalayim, 643–46: דהא סתם גוים וגויות מפקירות ואינם בושים ואדרבה משקיבלה מים טמאים היו גסים בה והיא כל שעה יריאה למרוד בהם ומטנפים בה. Cf. the responsum of R. Hai in *Teshuvot Ge'onei Mizraḥ u-Ma'arav*, ed. J. Mueller (New York, 1959), sec. 87 [= *Oẓar ha-Geonim*, ed. B. M. Lewin, vol. 8 (*Ketubbot*) (Jerusalem, 1939), 356 (sec. 789)]: a female apostate does not inherit from her husband's assets "because she is akin to a *zonah* [*she-otah meshummedet hi ke-zonah*]."

61 See this chapter, nn. 32–34. *Sefer Or Zarua'* (pt. 2, sec. 97, ed. Machon Yerushalayim, fol. 143) raises the question of whether an apostate can serve as a *mohel*. Isaac *Or Zarua'* expresses uncertainty in this regard (*lo yadana mai edon beh*), but he suggests that, at least in theory, he can serve in this capacity according to both the view that anyone who is included in the commandment to be circumcised may serve as a *mohel* and the view that any Jew who was circumcised may serve as a *mohel*. R. Isaac suggests that such an allowance is indicated because when

apparently did not agree with this exclusion.[62] As this chapter has shown, the tendency to limit the Jewish status of an apostate in significant ways, at least with respect to the members of the Jewish community as represented by the issue of *ḥaliẓah*, was supported by a complement of noteworthy Ashkenazic talmudists.

---

the Talmud (*'Avodah Zarah* 27a) discusses these views and the differences among them, it could have easily raised the question of an apostate serving as a *mohel* and yet it does not. As Moses Isserles reads R. Isaac's uncertainty (see *Darkhei Mosheh* to Y. D. 264:2), "*Sefer Or Zarua'* is unsure as to whether a circumcision performed by an apostate is valid, or whether he is considered to be like a non-Jew in this regard."

62 See this chapter, nn. 18, 51. In contrast to a local rabbinic authority, another student of Simḥah of Speyer, Isaiah di Trani (RID), *Teshuvot ha-RID*, ed. Wertheimer, 285–88 (sec. 58), strenuously opposed permitting "a woman who had apostatized and remained among the non-Jews for a lengthy period of time" to live with her Jewish husband once again after her return, although in this instance the woman had apostatized voluntarily. In RID's view, "She thereby defiled herself and is prohibited to her husband forever." At the same time, however, as noted in this chapter (n. 44), RID required an apostate to perform *ḥaliẓah* in all instances.

4

ECONOMIC ISSUES AND THE IMPLICATIONS FOR OTHER AREAS OF JEWISH LAW

Money-Lending at Interest

As discussed in the previous chapter, the German Tosafist Barukh b. Samuel of Mainz ruled that an apostate does not perform *ḥaliẓah* under any condition, since he is not recognized as one who is able to fulfill this precept. While the apostate's personal status as a Jew is guided and determined by the principle of *'af 'al pi she-ḥata Yisra'el hu*, which remains operative, the Jewish community at the same time is to view him as akin to a non-Jew with respect to *ḥaliẓah*.[1]

R. Barukh's assessment of the status of an apostate in the context of *ḥaliẓah* dovetails with the position he took in his *Sefer ha-Ḥokhmah* about why an apostate cannot lend money to Jews (or borrow from them) at interest. Although from their perspective the members of the Jewish community are not required to sustain an apostate (and thus in theory can lend money to him at interest without violating any prohibition), because the apostate from his own religious perspective is still considered to be a Jew (since *'af 'al pi she-ḥata Yisra'el hu*), other Jews may not lend to him at interest (or borrow money from him at interest) due to the prohibition of *lifnei 'ivver lo titein mikhshol* (lit., do not place a stumbling block before the blind). They would thereby be directly

1 See this volume, chapter 3, n. 23.

facilitating his performance of a prohibited act, for which the apostate from Judaism nonetheless remains liable and culpable.[2]

Barukh of Mainz's formulation of the prohibition against taking interest from an apostate (or paying him interest) is decidedly more elaborate than that of his twelfth-century German Tosafist predecessor, Eli'ezer b. Nathan of Mainz (Raban, d. c. 1170).[3] Like Rashi, Raban prohibits the taking of interest from an apostate because of a broad application of the principle of *'af 'al pi she-ḥata Yisra'el hu*—whatever his religious shortcomings, the apostate is still a part of the Jewish people. In this same passage, Raban also prohibits a Jew from selling improperly slaughtered animals (or animals otherwise rendered non-kosher because of internal organ damage, *terefot*) to an apostate because of *lifnei 'ivver*, lest the apostate eat from the meat of these animals. However, Raban, in contrast to Barukh of Mainz, expresses no concern for the violation of *lifnei 'ivver* with regard to lending money to an apostate at interest, as R. Barukh did. For Raban, an apostate may not participate in any kind of usurious transaction simply because of his ongoing standing as a member of the Jewish people.[4]

---

2 See *Sefer ha-Ḥokhmah*, sec. 151; Simcha Emanuel, *Shivrei Luḥot* (Jerusalem, 2006), 108; *Shitah Mequbbeẓet 'al Massekhet Bava Meẓi'a* (71b), ed. Oz ve-Hadar, vol. 2 (Jerusalem, 1996), fols. 553b–554a; and this volume, chapter 3, n. 28. There is a passage in which R. Barukh (ר"ב) is cited as allowing interest to be taken from apostates in practice, but a different Hebrew initial (ר"צ) appears in older and ostensibly more reliable textual witnesses, and may well refer to Isaac [יצחק] of Dampierre; see S. Emanuel, *Shivrei Luḥot*, 108, n. 25. See ibid., 109, for the nuanced approach taken by R. Barukh's teacher, Moses *ha-Kohen* of Mainz, with regard to whether a Jew who does not observe the commandments may be taken advantage of (*'ona'ah*), in either economic or personal contexts.

3 See *Sefer Raban*, ed. Ehrenreich, *Bava Meẓi'a* (71a), fol. 204a (= ed. D. Debitzky [Bnei Brak, 2012], vol. 3, 159, sec. 457): *'aval ger ẓedeq lo de-hu Yisra'el gamur ve-khen me-Yisra'el meshummad 'asur dikhtiv* [Joshua 7:11; and see also *Sanhedrin* 49a], *ḥata Yisra'el 'af 'al pi she-ḥata Yisra'el hu ve-khen 'asur limkor lo [la-meshummad] terefah mishum lifnei 'ivver lo titein mikhshol*. See also ms. Bodl. 566 (#19437), fols. 59v–60r (cited in this volume, chapter 1, n. 18).

4 Although Raban's grandson, Rabiah, allows interest to be taken from an apostate, he notes his grandfather's opposing view and suggests that it can perhaps be supported from *'Avodah Zarah* 26b, where the Talmud's scriptural exegesis requires

The "teacher and relative" referred to by R. Barukh in his formulation, who allowed lending money to an apostate at interest, is Eli'ezer b. Samuel of Metz (d. 1198), a Tosafist student of Rabbenu Tam and author of *Sefer Yere'im*.[5] Jacob Katz maintains that Eli'ezer of Metz (as well as his teacher Rabbenu Tam) permitted the lending of money to apostates at interest (and ostensibly the possibility to borrow from them at interest as well) on the basis of a limited exclusion, rather than on a systemic diminution of the status of an apostate, since both Leviticus 25:36 and Deuteronomy 23:20–21 specify that interest may not be taken or received only from one who is "your brother [*'aḥikha*]." For Katz, this allowance by Rabbenu Tam and Eli'ezer of Metz was mainly a practical one, to allow Jewish money-lenders in northern France to profit from apostates as well.[6]

However, as noted at the end of the previous chapter, Eli'ezer of Metz asserts that the *qiddushin* made by an apostate are considered effective, albeit not in a full or complete way (based on *Yevamot* 16), even as a *get* was nonetheless required to dissolve them. Moreover, in allowing interest to be taken from an apostate, Eli'ezer of Metz maintains that his wanton violation of Jewish law

the lost object of an apostate to be returned to him. Rabiah redirects this proof to support his own position (that the return of a lost object can be done only for a *meshummad* or *mumar le-te'avon* and not for a *mumar* or *meshummad le-hakh'is*); see also *Sefer Or Zarua', pisqei Bava Meẓi'a*, sec. 99, ed. Machon Yerushalayim, fols. 219–20. However, Rabiah suggests that his grandfather's ruling about not selling slaughtered animals that were sickly (*trefot*) to an apostate may well be correct. See *Teshuvot Maimuniyyot le-Sefer Mishpatim*, sec. 36.

5 See Emanuel, *Shivrei Luḥot*, 107–8; and Urbach, *Ba'alei ha-Tosafot*, 1:154–64.

6 See Katz, *Halakhah ve-Qabbalah*, 262, 266; idem, *Exclusiveness and Tolerance*, 71–72 [= *Bein Yehudim le-Goyim*, 79]. Katz asserts that the position of Rabbenu Tam and his students represents a return to a geonic position (allowing the taking of interest) that had been rejected by Rashi. However, as Simcha Emanuel has shown based on a series of textual clarifications, the Geonim across the board—and followed by Rashi—prohibited lending to an apostate at interest. Thus, Rabbenu Tam and Eli'ezer of Metz were the first halakhic authorities to allow this practice. See Emanuel, "Teshuvot ha-Ge'onim ha-Qeẓarot," in *'Atarah le-Ḥayyim: Studies in Talmudic and Rabbinic Literature in Honor of Prof. H. Z. Dimitrovsky*, ed. D. Boyarin et al. (Jerusalem, 2000), 447–49; and cf. G. Blidstein, "Who Is Not a Jew?—The Medieval Discussion," *Israel Law Review* 11 (1976): 385–87.

renders him like a *min* (heretic, or a *mumar le-hakh'is*). In Leviticus 25:35, the Torah instructs a Jew to support and strengthen his fellow Jew (lit., his brother) when he becomes needy (*ki yamukh 'aḥikha*; and see also Deut. 15:7). As the Torah continues (Lev. 25:36), money lent to him for this purpose cannot be returned at interest because he is a brother who needs to be sustained (*'al tiqqaḥ me-'itto neshekh ve-tarbit . . . ve-ḥei 'aḥikha 'immakh*). Since an apostate is not considered to be the brother of other Jews (in terms of the requirement to sustain him) because of his sinfulness (according to the *sugya* in *'Avodah Zarah* 26a–26b), charging him interest is permitted.[7]

Regardless whether the economic factor was as critical in the Rhineland as in northern France,[8] Barukh of Mainz does not endorse the view of Eli'ezer of Metz, which permits lending at interest to an apostate. At the same time, however, R. Barukh also does not agree with the view of Rashi and Raban, which did not countenance lending at interest to (or from) an apostate in any way because the dictum *'af 'al pi she-ḥata Yisra'el hu* requires that the apostate be treated fundamentally like any other Jew with regard to this (and all other) prohibitions.

Moses b. Jacob of Coucy (d. c. 1255), the author of *Sefer Miẓvot Gadol*, who flourished in northern France a generation after Barukh of Mainz, presents the same distinction (and practical conclusion) on lending at interest to an apostate, in the name of his northern French Tosafist colleague and contemporary Samuel b. Solomon of Falaise (d. c. 1245). According to Samuel of Falaise as well, it is prohibited to lend money at interest to an apostate because of the prohibition of *lifnei 'ivver*. At the same time, however, Moses of Coucy, citing the ruling (and the derivations) of Eli'ezer of Metz in his *Sefer Yere'im*,

7 See *Sefer Yere'im ha-Shalem*, ed. A. A. Schiff (Vilna, 1892–1902), fols. 73a–74a (sec. 156, end); ms. Bodl. 678, fols. 114r–115; and Emanuel, "Teshuvot ha-Ge'onim ha-Qeẓarot," 448, n. 43. See also A. M. Gray, "R. Eliezer of Metz's Twelfth-Century Exclusion from Charity of the Jewish *Avaryan be-Mezid* ('Deliberate Transgressor')," in *Approaches to Poverty in Medieval Europe*, ed. S. Farmer (Turnhout, 2016), 67–89.

8 See, e.g., Haym Soloveitchik, *Halakhah, Kalkalah, ve-Dimmu Aẓmi* (Jerusalem, 1985), 59–65; 97–101; S. Emanuel, *Shivrei Luḥot*, 129, 148–49, 262; *Teshuvot u-Pesaqim*, ed. E. Kupfer (Jerusalem, 1973), 171–72 (sec. 108).

maintains that it is permitted to lend to an apostate at interest. R. Moses also adduces a passage in the Talmud Yerushalmi (*'Avodah Zarah* 5:4, first noted by Ri *ha-Zaqen* of Dampierre, as will be seen in a moment) to further support this allowance, noting that when the Cutheans subverted their religious actions (and lost their status as true converts, *gerei 'emet*, based on their revealed idolatrous practices), it became permitted to lend to them at interest.[9]

To be sure, Moses of Coucy (still citing Eli'ezer of Metz) notes that the policy of treating an apostate as a non-Jew is limited only to the issue of lending money at interest (and perhaps returning a lost object to him as well), where the Torah specifically associates this precept and its prohibitions with brotherhood (*she-harei le-gabbei ribbit 'aḥvah ketiv beh*). When it comes to initiating marriage and divorce, however (where the Torah does not specifically mention the characteristic of brotherhood), Moses of Coucy asserts that the apostate's actions are considered fully effective, a ruling that is also found elsewhere in *Sefer Miẓvot Gadol*.[10]

Indeed, with the possible exception of Eli'ezer of Metz (who studied with Rabbenu Tam but also had strong affinities with rabbinic scholars and

9 See *Sefer Miẓvot Gadol* (Venice, 1547), fol. 207b, *'aseh* 162 (the precept of giving charity); ms. Parma (de Rossi) 93, fols. 227d–e; ms. Paris BN Heb. 370, fols. 405d–406a; ms. British Museum 506, fols. 188b–c; ms. Paris BN Heb. 374, fols. 283a–b; ms. Paris Mazarine 4472, fols. 201b–c; Bodl. 864, fols. 160c–d; ms. Vatican 144, fol. 89e; and *Teshuvot Maimuniyyot le-Sefer Mishpatim*, #36 (end). Samuel b. Solomon of Falaise's position is also recorded in his name in the summary of the *Semag* passage contained in *Qiẓẓur Sefer Miẓvot Gadol le-R. Avraham b. Ephraim*, ed. Y. Horowitz (Jerusalem, 2005), 131; and in a number of manuscripts of *Sefer Mordekhai* to tractate *'Avodah Zarah* (e.g., ms. Budapest 2°1, fol. 229a; ms. Parma 929, fol. 216v; ms. Vienna 72, fol. 181c; ms. Vatican 141, fol. 125f; and ms. Vercelli C1, fol. 112a). However, in the standard *Sefer Mordekhai 'al Massekhet 'Avodah Zarah* (sec. 814), this position appears in the name of Eli'ezer b. Solomon. Eli'ezer b. Solomon posed a question to Rabbenu Tam that is recorded in *Sefer ha-Yashar* (see Urbach, *Ba'alei ha-Tosafot*, 1:61–62), and he authored two *seliḥot* for Rosh Hashanah and the ten days of penitence (see *Maḥzor Vitry*, ed. S. Hurwitz [Jerusalem, 1938], 566; Leopold Zunz, *Literaturgeschichte der synagogalen poesie* [Berlin, 1865], 293–94; and *Seder ha-Seliḥot* [*Minhag Lita*], ed. D. Goldschmidt, 226–28 [Jerusalem, 1965], sec. 84).

10 See *Semag*, *'aseh* 48, fol. 125c: ישראל משומד שקידש, אף על פי שעבד עבודה זרה מרצונו, הרי אלו קידושין גמורין וצריכה ממנו גט כדאיתא בפרק החולץ.

scholarship in the Rhineland),[11] there does not seem to have been a single northern French Tosafist who was prepared to consider the apostate as a non-Jew (or as less than a full Jew) with regard to marriage and divorce, or in situations that involved *ḥaliẓah*.[12] A passage in *Haggahot Mordekhai* to tractate *Yevamot* cites the German Tosafists Barukh of Mainz and Isaac *Or Zarua'* as holding that an apostate is not meant to do *ḥaliẓah* (in accordance with Rabbenu Ḥanan'el view that *mitah mappelet). Haggahot Mordekhai* further suggests that Moses of Coucy would also agree with this ruling, based on the notion that *ḥaliẓah*, like money-lending, is specifically linked by the Torah to brotherhood (*'aḥvah*). In addition, an unidentified R. Samson is said to have held this position for a similar reason, since the only way that lending money to an apostate at interest can be prohibited is through the principle of *lifnei 'ivver*, which suggests that an apostate is not a brother and therefore cannot perform *ḥaliẓah* either. However, the compiler of the *Haggahot Mordekhai* gloss then retracts the claim about Moses of Coucy, based on an explicit passage in *Sefer Miẓvot Gadol* that deals with the effectiveness of the *get* of an apostate.[13]

---

11 See my "From Germany to Northern France and Back Again: A Tale of Two Tosafist Centers," in *Regional Identities and Cultures of Medieval Jews*, ed. J. Castaño et al. (London, 2018), 154–56, 160 (n. 42).

12 In his *Sefer Mordekhai Qatan*, R. Samuel Schlettstadt notes that Moses of Coucy, along with Meir of Rothenburg and Rashi, required an apostate to perform *ḥaliẓah*. See, e.g., ms. Vatican 324 (#8635), fols. 229a–b; ms. Hamburg 194/Heb. 247 (#1051), fols. 96r–v; ms. Toronto Friedberg 3–004 (#70562), fol. 97v; and ms. Paris BN 408 (#30735), fol. 46r. *Semag* is also included in this group of authorities by *Semaq mi-Ẓurikh*, ed. Har-Shoshanim, 2:157, sec. 182 (end), n. 221; and see the statement by R. Samuel in the next note (דסמ"ג ס"ל דמומר זוקק).

13 See *Haggahot Mordekhai* to *Yevamot*, sec. 107 (and this volume, chapter 3, nn. 23, 50). Rabbenu Samson in this passage might connote Samson b. Joseph of Falaise, Rabbenu Tam's brother-in-law (see Urbach, *Ba'alei ha-Tosafot*, 1:61, 118), or even Samson of Sens, although there is no other evidence associating either of these two early French Tosafists with this view on *lifnei 'ivver* and the apostate. Indeed, although it is possible that this view, which is attributed by *Sefer Miẓvot Gadol* to Samuel b. Solomon of Falaise (with whom Moses of Coucy was in direct contact; see Urbach, *Ba'alei ha-Tosafot* 1:461, 465), was expressed in northern France already in a prior generation, the more likely possibility is that Samuel of Falaise's name somehow became transposed or otherwise garbled and emerged as R. Samson. Cf. *Tosafot ha-Shalem*, ed. J. Gellis, vol. 2 (Jerusalem, 1985), 192 (secs. 8–9);

A responsum by Ri of Dampierre, cited in his name in several texts and reflected in a number of others, permits a Jew to lend money to an apostate with interest (echoing Rabbenu Tam and Eli'ezer of Metz),[14] since there is no

---

and this chapter, n. 9. The one who seeks to advance this new understanding of Moses of Coucy's view, referred to only as ר״ם, then concludes: מכל אלה היה נראה להתיר יבמה שנפלה לפני מומר בלא חליצה. As indicated, however, the overall compiler, perhaps R. Samuel Schlettstadt himself (see S. Emanuel, *Shivrei Luḥot*, 318), asserts that Moses of Coucy in fact requires an apostate to perform *ḥaliẓah*, since there is a *ziqah*: ולי ההדיוט הכותב נ״ל דסמ״ג ס״ל דמומר זוקק שהרי במצות לגרש כתב וז״ל מי שיש לו אח מ״מ אפילו ממזר ואפילו עובד עבודה זרה עכ״ל. The passage to which the compiler refers is found in *Semag*, *'aseh* 51, fol. 135d (and cf. *Yevamot* 22a, in the Mishnah), and the compiler also refers the reader to his commentary at the end of *Bava Qamma*. Cf. ms. Halle (University Library) Yb Fol. 7 (#14637), fols. 162b–c (ומעשה כזה אירע ולא רצו רבותינו לתמוך להסכים עם מורי הר״ר מרדכי לפוטרה [בלא כלום] כי אמרו אין לעשות כנגד רש״י . . . מתוך זה הבלבול נתגלגלה היבמה והלכה לדראון והמשומד לא רצה לחלוץ); and see also the preceding note. The parallel passage in *Teshuvot Mahar"Y [R. Yuda] Minẓ*, ed. A. Siev (New York, 1995), 47–48 (sec. 12) cites Rabbenu Tuvyah as the one who suggests that Moses of Coucy does not require an apostate to do *ḥaliẓah*. Although this perhaps refers to Moses of Coucy's Tosafist colleague Tuvyah b. Elijah of Vienne (whose initials are ר״ט, which may well be the more accurate acronym than ר״ם), I have been unable to this point to locate this assessment of *Semag* in any other source. Cf. Shmuel Kahn, "R. Mordekhai b. Hillel ha-Ashkenazi," *Sinai* 15 (1945): 69. R. Tuvyah was the teacher of Abraham b. Ephraim, author of *Qiẓẓur Semag*, which includes a number of R. Tuvyah's rulings, several of which may be relevant to this discussion. See *Qiẓẓur Semag*, ed. Y. Horowitz (Jerusalem, 2005), 79–80, 85, 87, 89, 131; and cf. Urbach, *Ba'alei ha-Tosafot* 1: 487 (n. 35), 488–91.

14 Rabbenu Tam's ruling that allowed money-lending to an apostate at interest is cited by Ri in his responsum on this matter; at one point Ri notes that he received this ruling in Rabbenu Tam's name from his father, R. Samuel. In addition to the notion that an apostate should not be sustained according to *'Avodah Zarah* 26b, the Talmud there also excludes the full-fledged apostate from having his lost objects returned as a brotherly provision (as per Deut. 22:1–3). This clearly allows for an apostate to be charged interest by Jews as well. Ri also notes that Rashi's position against taking interest from apostates is found in "collections [*quntresim*] of Rashi's responsa," and in the "writings of R. Shemayah in the name of Rashi, where the student [R. Shemayah] ruled in accordance with Rashi [based on the principle *of 'af 'al pi she-ḥata Yisra'el hu*]." See the next note, and see also *Sefer ha-Yashar le-Rabbenu Tam* (*ḥeleq ha-ḥiddushim*), ed. S. Schlesinger (Jerusalem, 1959), 434, sec. 743; *Shibbolei ha-Leqet—ha-ḥeleq ha-sheni*, ed. S. Ḥasida (Jerusalem, 1988), 185–86 (sec. 46); and this chapter, n. 16. *Shibbolei ha-Leqet* notes that Isaiah di Trani prohibited the taking of interest from apostates (in accordance with Rashi's approach).

requirement for a Jew to support or sustain an apostate. Leviticus 25:36, which prohibits lending at interest to a Jew, concludes with the phrase, "And your brother shall [thereby] be able to live with [and to be sustained by] you [*ve-ḥei 'aḥikha 'immakh*]." The Talmud (*Bava Meẓi'a* 62a) derives from this phrase that interest should always be returned to (and never be taken from) a brother, "so that he will be able to live [comfortably] with you." According to the Torah, this courtesy, however, need not be extended to an apostate, and certainly not to "the apostates of today [*ha-meshummadim shel 'akhshav*], who are submerged among the gentiles [*she-metuma'in* (with an *'ayin*) *bein ha-goyim*]. . . . They cleave to the ways of the nations and are submerged among them, practicing idolatry and forsaking the Torah completely, which renders them completely like a gentile [*ke-goy gamur*], even with respect to not having to sustain them." And so, Ri rules, interest can be taken from them.

Ri further indicates that the scriptural and talmudic derivations he has marshaled lead to this conclusion "even if [the apostate] is not submerged among the gentiles [*'afilu lo hayah metuma bein ha-goyim*]." Additional support for charging interest to an apostate is presented by Ri from the Talmud Yerushalmi passage (*'Avodah Zarah* 5:4 concerning the Cutheans, which *Sefer Miẓvot Gadol* later cites as well). Ri adds, however, that the precept of *lifnei 'ivver* prohibits a Jew from borrowing from an apostate at interest, since the Jewish borrower in that situation is leading the apostate into the prohibition of the usurious transaction. In this respect Ri is undercutting part of the leniency first proposed in northern France by his uncle and mentor, Rabbenu Tam.[15]

See this volume, chapter 3, n. 62.

15 Ri's responsum, which deals with the apostate son of a Jewess who had apostatized, is (partially) reproduced (based on ms. Berlin [Staatsbibliothek, Or. Phillip] 1392, fols. 189r–190r) in Urbach, *Ba'alei ha-Tosafot*, 1:242–44; and see also ms. Parma De Rossi 929, fol. 144r. The fullest version of Ri's responsum is found in *Shibbolei ha-Leqet—ha-ḥeleq ha-sheni*, ed. S. Ḥasida, 186–90 (sec. 46); and see also *Teshuvot R. Yiẓḥaq ben Shmu'el mi-Dampierre*, ed. P. Roth and A. R. Reiner (Jerusalem, 2020), 94–98 (sec. 61). Additional texts that cite this responsum in the name of Ri (or his position anonymously, including *Tosafot 'Avodah Zarah* 26b, s.v. *va-'ani*) are listed by Urbach, ibid, n. 56*. To this list should be added ms. Hamburg 45 (#1041), fol. 151 (1) r, sec. 6, although in this instance Ri's view is expressed simply as a ratification of the position taken by Rabbenu Tam: ופסק ר"ת

Although this last part of Ri's approach is consonant with this aspect of Barukh of Mainz's ruling (and Ri was the first among those Tosafists to acknowledge that a returning apostate should undergo immersion, as noted in chapter 2),[16] Ri is not departing from the essential French Tosafist position that permits a Jew to lend money to an apostate (which R. Barukh rejects in practice), while at the same time treating the apostate like any other Jew with respect to all marital matters, including *ḥaliẓah*. Indeed, even Samuel of Falaise, who appears to have agreed with the restrictive position of Barukh of Mainz regarding lending to an apostate at interest (and the impact of *lifnei*

דמותר ליקח ריבית מן המשומדי׳ דכדאי׳ בע״ז המינים והמוסרים מורידין ולא מעלין וכו׳ . . . מותר לעכב ביה ולא קרינא ביה לאחיך ואתה מותר . . . הוא הדין נמי מותר ליקח ממנו ריבית. וכן פסק רבינו יצחק. See also *Tosafot ha-Rosh le-'Avodah Zarah*, loc. cit., s.v. *le-khol*; *Ḥiddushei Talmidei Rabbenu Yonah 'al Massekhet 'Avodah Zarah*, ed. H. Zarkowski (Brooklyn, NY, 1955), 36–37 (which attributes the Yerushalmi passage to Elḥanan ben ha-Ri); *Ḥiddushei ha-Ramban 'al Massekhet Bava Meẓi'a* (71b), ed. M. Hershler et al. (Jerusalem, 2002), 401–4; *Pisqei ha-Rosh, Bava Meẓi'a*, 5:55; *Sefer Mordekhai 'al Massseket Bava Meẓi'a*, sec. 335 (= ms. Vercelli C1, fols. 46a–b); *Ḥiddushei ha-Ritva 'al Massekhet Bava Meẓi'a* (71b), ed. S. Raphael (Jerusalem, 1992), 590–91; *Ḥiddushei ha-Ritva 'al Massekhet 'Avodah Zarah* (26b), ed. M. Goldstein (Jerusalem, 1982), 106–7; and cf. Simcha Goldin, *Ha-Yiḥud veha-Yaḥad*, 91–92. Several of these texts suggest that Ri's position is based on a talmudic construction (related to the assets of minors, which may be lent to other Jews at interest [*Bava Meẓi'a* 70a]) that a Jew cannot borrow at interest from another Jew only when the lender is prohibited from extending the loan to him at interest. Since members of the Jewish community are permitted to lend to an apostate at interest, he is permitted to pay that interest to them without violation. However, the apostate, from his perspective, is not permitted to lend at interest to other Jews, and so they cannot accept a loan from him at interest because of the prohibition of *lifnei 'ivver*. (The phrase *le-'inyan she-lo le-haḥayot* as used by Ri in this responsum refers to the fact that an apostate need not be supported or sustained, not that proper atonement for apostasy can be achieved only through death, as suggested by Micha Perry, *Massoret ve-Shinnui* [Bnei Brak, 2011], 189.)

16 See ms. Vercelli C1, fol. 291v: אבל האי משומד יודע הו[א] שכל זמן שאי[נו] טובל ומקבל עליו דברי חכמים הוא מוחזק כגוי [ואוסר יין במגעו]. לכך לא צריך ג׳ לקבל לפניהם דבקל יש לנו לדעת ששב אל בוראו כיון שנוהג עצמו כדת יהודי[ת]. See also *Tosafot Bekhorot* 31a, s.v. *ve-kulan she-ḥazru; Tosafot Shanẓ 'al Massekhet Bekhorot*, ed. Y. D. Ilan (Bnei Brak, 1997), 61–62; *Shitat ha-Qadmonim 'al Massekhet 'Avodah Zarah*, ed. M. J. Blau (New York, 1969), 45 (*A. Z.* 7a); and cf. *Tosafot 'Avodah Zarah* 64b, s.v. *'ein*; and this volume, chapter 2, nn. 5, 9.

'ivver on this restriction), does not extend or link this issue to other areas of Jewish law.[17]

Among the German Tosafists, Rabiah of Cologne's position would seem to be the closest to the French approach. To be sure, he required quite a bit from reverting apostates (in terms of both purification and verification), describing the apostate as "like a convert,"[18] and he also categorizes apostates as similar to non-Jews with respect to land acquisition and ownership.[19] Rabiah allows

---

17 Samuel of Falaise is cited in *Semag* only with respect to lending money at interest to an apostate, since that was the specific matter under discussion. However, if lending to an apostate at interest is prohibited because of *lifnei 'ivver*, borrowing from him at interest may also be prohibited for this reason (even as the role of the Jewish borrower is more passive). The Tosafist teachers of Samuel of Falaise (Judah Sirleon, Solomon of Dreux, and Barukh b. Isaac, the author of *Sefer ha-Terumah*) were all students of Ri, and it is possible that Samuel of Falaise simply intended to extend Ri's view along similar lines. In any case it is unlikely that Samuel of Falaise derived his view from Barukh of Mainz, since the period between approximately 1175 and 1215 (corresponding roughly to the later days of Ri and his students) has recently been shown to be one when the major Tosafist centers in Germany and northern France were largely cut off from one another; see my "From Germany to Northern France and Back Again: A Tale of Two Tosafist Centers," 149–71. Thus Barukh of Mainz was aware of the view of his teacher, Eli'ezer of Metz, which followed that of Rabbenu Tam and reflected a prevalent practice in northern France allowing money-lending (or borrowing) at interest with an apostate. (And he could also have been aware of Rabbenu Tam's view through Rabbenu Tam's student, Moses *ha-Kohen* of Mainz; see S. Emanuel, *Shivrei Luḥot*, 108.) But Barukh of Mainz seems to have been unaware of the more limiting view held by Ri (and his use of *lifnei 'ivver*) precisely because of the general absence of contact between northern France and Germany just described; see my "From Germany to Northern France and Back Again," 152–53 (n. 16).

18 See this volume, chapter 2, nn. 34–35.

19 In his *pesaqim* to tractate *Bava Qamma* (*Sefer Or Zarua'*, pt. 3, sec. 272, ed. Machon Yerushalayim, 86; and see also *Sefer Rabiah*, ed. D. Deblitzky [Bnei Brak, 2005], vol. 3, 377–79, sec. 1007), Isaac of Vienna presents the case of a Jew who bought land from an apostate which he then kept under his control for three years, ostensibly establishing a *ḥazaqah* that supports his acquisition. However, another Jew came forward to claim that this *ḥazaqah* was not effective because the apostate had forcibly extracted this parcel of land from him (*'anas mimenu ha-qarqa*), and he had raised an objection in this regard during the three-year period as well. The case was brought before R. Isaac's teacher, Rabiah, who ruled that the *ḥazaqah* in this case was effective, even though the Talmud in tractate *Bava Batra* (35b) rules that

loans to be made to apostates at interest, as Rabbenu Tam (and his students) did, and yet he (like the French Tosafists) also held that the *qiddushin* and *get* of an apostate are effective. Indeed, Rabiah specifically rejects the view that the *get* given by an apostate might not be valid since it is akin to a *get* given by a husband who was originally sound but is now unbalanced (*'ashfuye ve-nishtateh*).[20] Rabiah separates these different areas of precepts (as the French Tosafists did, albeit for a different reason) by noting that, with regard to an apostate's money, it is appropriate to fine the apostate (*ra'ui le-qonso*) by allowing Jews to charge him interest (which now belongs to the lender through the agency of *hefqer beit din hefqer*). In support of this Rabiah cites the Yerushalmi passage in tractate *'Avodah Zarah* that Ri had adduced, and he notes other talmudic examples where this kind of monetary loss was imposed on other religious deviants. However, no such mechanism (or halakhic reasoning) exists through which to undermine the effectiveness of an apostate's *get*, nor is such action warranted.[21]

---

a Jew who tries to establish a *ḥazaqah* involving the actions of a non-Jew will not be successful since (as Rashbam explains in his commentary there) a non-Jew will often seize property by force, and a Jew is typically afraid to protest. In this case, however, the Jewish buyer may keep the field because the original Jewish owner showed that he was not afraid to object to the actions of the apostate in taking his field. However, he did not follow up and raise this same objection at the required intervals according to the halakhic procedures for establishing land ownership. Although in this case the field was lost by the original Jewish owner for technical halakhic reasons, it is clear that Rabiah relates to and treats the apostate in the same way he would a non-Jew in this type of situation.

20 See *Teshuvot Maimuniyyot le-Seder Nashim*, #12; and *Sefer Mordekhai 'al Massekhet Yevamot*, sec. 38 (= ms. Vercelli C1, fol. 291d, citing Rabiah's *Sefer Avi'asaf*); and this volume, chapter 3, n. 30.

21 See *Sefer Rabiah*, ed. Deblitzky, 1:120 (at the end of sec. 151 [corrected by ms. London Beit ha-Din u-Beit ha-Midrash 11, #4682]): ירושלמי פ"ה דע"ז הלין כותאי דקיסרי מותר להלוותם בריבית מפני שקילקלו מעשיהם. וראיתי בתשובת רבינו נתן בעל הערוך ואחיו ר' אברהם הא דאמרי' בישראל משומד אע"פ שחטא ישראל הוא לענין גט וחליצה. ויש שמחמירים בגט ואומרים שקידושי תורה שקידש בעודו ישראל אינו יכול להפקיע משמדותו וכו'. ואין הנדון דומה לראיה זו דבממונא ראוי לנו לקונסו. ודמי להא דאמרי' בפרק שור שנגח שור של ישראל שנגח שור של כותי פטור דקניס ר' מאיר דאע"ג דלדידיה גירי אמת הם כדי שלא יטמעו בהן וכו'. והא דאמרי' במס' ע"ז (דף כו ע"ב) אני שונה לכל אבידת אחיך לרבות את המשומד מיירי במשומד אוכל נבילות לתיאבון ולא להכעיס שאדוק בע"ז. This passage should be supplemented by a related formulation attributed to Rabiah

As has been demonstrated in the previous chapter, for Barukh of Mainz, Abraham of Regensburg, and Isaac *Or Zarua*ʿ of Vienna, the diminished religious status of an apostate extends with regard to *ḥaliẓah* (and other matters as well) beyond the economic realm, which remained the limit for the Tosafists of northern France. Moreover, the distinguished German Tosafist Simḥah of Speyer goes so far as to assert that the Jewish status of the apostate is such that his *qiddushin* are valid only because of stringency (*le-ḥumra*), and for this same reason, a Jew may not take interest on a loan made to an apostate.[22]

Northern French Tosafists such as Moses of Coucy, who permitted interest to be taken from an apostate, nonetheless distinguish between this allowance and the *qiddushin* of an apostate, which were completely valid. Indeed, even Eliʿezer of Metz, who is not as certain about the ability of an apostate to offer fully valid *qiddushin*, and at the same time permits interest to be taken from an apostate because he is a *mumar le-hakhʿis* and akin to a *min*, treats these issues as fundamentally separate components. Simḥah of Speyer, however, perhaps even more than Barukh of Mainz (who focused especially on *ḥaliẓah*), sought to align these various aspects to the greatest extent possible, in order to characterize the apostate as a unified (if complex) figure of religious deviance[23] whose return to the Jewish community required immersion as a significant act of repentance.[24] However, it should be stressed again that those French Tosafist formulations that cite the *sugya* in tractate *ʿAvodah Zarah* 26b (and

in *Teshuvot Maimuniyyot le-Sefer Mishpatim*, #36. Rabiah begins by noting the position of his grandfather Raban (this chapter, n. 4), who prohibited lending to an apostate at interest. In support of his opposing view, Rabiah cites the Yerushalmi passage that Ri had adduced, which allows interest to be charged to an apostate. He concludes that "it is appropriate to fine the apostate [by extracting] his money through *hefqer beit din hefqer*. In doing so, the rabbis turn this money into a gift [a *mattanah*, for the Jewish lender], and it is not considered interest [*ribbit*]." Interestingly, it appears that Rabiah is the only Tosafist to explicitly mention the mechanism of *hefqer beit din hefqer* with regard to lending to an apostate at interest. See also this chapter, n. 28, regarding inheritance.

22 See this volume, chapter 3, n. 50.

23 See *Teshuvot u-Pesaqim*, ed. E. Kupfer, 295 (וה"נ ישראל שנשתמד . . . ודוקא לחומרא נאמ' דחוששין לקידושיו וגם שלא ליטול ממנו ריבית).

24 See this volume, chapter 2, n. 22.

related talmudic texts) to link the apostate categorically to a heretic (*min*) or to a *mumar le-hakh'is* who is not to be sustained or supported (which goes beyond saying that the apostate is not a "brother" solely in the context of the Torah's prohibition against the taking of usury) are still going far beyond anything Rashi and his supporters said (or more precisely, did not say) about the changed religious status of an apostate.[25]

The northern French Tosafist Yeḥi'el b. Joseph of Paris (d. c. 1260), a contemporary of Samuel of Falaise and Moses of Coucy, responded to a question about whether money could be lent to apostates at interest. R. Yeḥi'el cites the ruling of Rabbenu Tam that this is permitted, although many of the texts

---

25 Rashi was aware, of course, of the (uncontested) *sugya* in *'Avodah Zarah* 26b which equates a *meshummad le-'avodah zarah* with a *min*, and maintains that such a person need not be sustained or supported. However, unlike those northern French Tosafists (and others) who applied this *sugya* to allow interest to be taken from an apostate, Rashi, as far as I can tell, employs this talmudic passage only in this one limited context. See *Teshuvot Rashi*, ed. Elfenbein 195–96 (sec. 174), for a question that came before Rashi concerning an apostate's item that had been watched by his Jewish relative. When the apostate asked for his property back, the relative watching the object did not want to return it, and in the interim the apostate died. The (Jewish) relatives who were (legitimately) meant to inherit the apostate's possessions claimed that this object rightfully belonged to them. Although Rashi supports the fact that the relatives who are in a position to inherit from an apostate can do so according to Jewish law (see this chapter, n. 28), he rules that the Jewish court in this case cannot take the object away from the the relative watching the object (and award it to the inheritors), since the apostate is akin to a *min* (*meshummad la-'avodah zarah min hu*) whose assets are considered to be *hefqer*, as per *'Avodah Zarah* 26b. There are differing views within talmudic law as to whether a *min*'s assets may be taken preemptively from him and destroyed, but in this instance the one who was watching the object is considered to have acquired it from the state of non-ownership (*hefqer*). For Rashi an apostate is comparable to a *min* only with respect to his assets, in a case (such as this) where other Jews may be entitled to them. Cf. *Teshuvot Maharam va-Ḥaverav*, ed. S. Emanuel, 745 (sec. 379); *Tosafot Gittin* 34a, s.v. *beit din* (citing Ri); Rashba, *Bava Batra* 106b, s.v. *qanui*; *Beit Yosef* to *Ḥoshen Mishpat*, sec. 283, s.v. *ve-katav 'od*; Marc Saperstein, *Decoding the Rabbis* (Cambridge, MA, 1980), 187–88; and this volume, chapter 1, n. 41. See also ms. Bodl. 566 (#19437), fol. 60b (found within a section that reflects the period and values of Rashi; see this volume, chapter 1, n. 18): אסור לישראל להיות אפטרופא של משומד להוציא ממון מיד חבירו. ואין לבוא על המשומד בעקיפין מפני חילול השם שהגוים לא מעליו ולא מורידין. And cf. ms. Bodl. 678, fol. 195r.

and nuances he includes are similar to those presented by Ri of Dampierre in his responsum. The verse Leviticus 25:36 (which concludes, *ve-ḥei ʾaḥikha ʿimmakh*) links the prohibition of lending at interest to a fellow Jew with the requirement of helping him to live (as explicated in *Bava Meẓiʿa* 62a), but an apostate need not be sustained (*ʾein miẓvah le-haḥayoto u-mamono muttar*, based on *ʿAvodah Zarah* 26b). Moreover, although the Talmud (*Bava Qamma* 119a) prohibits confiscating the money of an informant since he is still within the Jewish community and perhaps will have worthy descendants, the assets of an apostate, who lives among the Christians and is "submerged" (*nishqa*) among them, can be confiscated even by theft, and certainly through the taking of interest. However, R. Yeḥiʾel (again, like Ri) concludes that a Jew cannot borrow at interest from an apostate, since this would contribute to the apostate's benefit (*she-mashbiḥo*).

The student who had asked this question of Yeḥiʾel of Paris suggests that perhaps borrowing from the apostate at interest should be permitted, since the Talmud at the end of this same chapter in tractate *Bava Meẓiʿa* (73b) allows for taking advantage of someone who is behaving improperly in terms of Jewish observance (*she-ʾeino noheg ke-shurah*). Since the apostate is not your brother in this regard, borrowing from him at interest should thus be permitted if it helps the Jewish borrower. Whether or not R. Yeḥiʾel revised his ruling based on this suggestion is unclear, but this passage demonstrates the continuation of the halakhic policies concerning money-lending and apostates along similar interpretational and conceptual lines as those of his Tosafist predecessors and colleagues in northern France. It is worth noting, however, that although R. Yeḥiʾel, like Ri, prohibits the borrowing of money at interest from an apostate, he supplies a different reason for this prohibition. His concern is not that the apostate will be aided directly by the borrower to sin, in violation of the prohibition of *lifnei ʿivver*. Rather, a Jewish borrower should not be providing any kind of profit to an apostate, which reflects a harsher view of the apostate in real terms.[26]

---

26 See *Teshuvot Maharam mi-Rothenburg va-Ḥaverav*, ed. S. Emanuel, 706 (sec. 413), based on ms. Hamburg 45, fol. 184r (sec. 220); and cf. this volume, chapter 3, n. 56.

Apostates and Inheritance

With regard to an apostate's ability to inherit from his Jewish relatives, Jacob Katz notes that "there was unanimous agreement concerning the right of the Jewish community to deny the apostate the inheritance of his Jewish relatives' estate." This meant that a medieval Jewish legal authority could indicate a strong measure of disapproval for apostasy without getting caught up in other halakhic (or economic) considerations, especially since inheritance is purely a matter of disposition of property in the realm of civil law. Inheritance can be guided by judicial principles such as *hefqer beit din hefqer*, as opposed, for example, to usury, which also includes a sensitive Torah prohibition at its core. Indeed, monetary prescriptions such as those that underlie inheritance can easily be set aside by agreed-upon conditions, in accordance with the principle that *matneh ʿal mah she-katuv ba-Torah be-dinei mamonot tenaʾo kayyam* (*Bava Meẓiʿa* 94a).

Nonetheless, Katz maintains that the different justifications put forward by subsequent authorities concerning inheritance can be used to trace the influence of Rashi's position that apostates should not be unduly disadvantaged even with regard to interest and other monetary matters in accordance with the rule of *ʾaf ʿal pi she-ḥata Yisraʾel hu*. Katz's essential argument is that, unlike the Geonim and early Ashkenazic authorities (including Rabbenu Gershom, Meshullam b. Qalonymus, and R. Judah *ha-Kohen* in his *Sefer ha-Dinim*) who held that apostates were prohibited from inheriting according to biblical law (which disinherited Ishmael and Esau in favor of Isaac and Jacob),[27] Rashi held

Within the writings of the Tosafists of northern France, R. Yeḥiʾel's phrasing and prooftexts are closer to those of Ri, while Moses of Coucy follows the formulations of Eliʿezer of Metz, as has been noted (even as Eliʿezer of Metz and Ri were both students of Rabbenu Tam, who had initiated this discussion).

27 See *Oẓar ha-Geonim*, vol. 9 (*Qiddushin*), ed. B. M. Levin (Jerusalem, 1940), 30–35 (secs. 78–88). See also G. Blidstein, "Who Is Not a Jew?" 382–84; Oded Irshai, "Mumar ke-Yoresh bi-Teshuvot ha-Geonim u-Maqbilot ba-Mishpat ha-Nokhri," *Shenaton ha-Mishpat ha-Ivri* 11–12 (1984–86): 435–61; Uriel Simonsohn, "The Legal and Social Bonds of Jewish Apostates and Their Spouses According to Geonic Responsa," *Jewish Quarterly Review* 105 (2015): 422–25, 436–38; *Teshuvot R. Natronai b. Hillaʾi Gaon*, ed. Y. Brody (Jerusalem, 1994), 544–47 (sec. 369);

that this limitation was enacted only on the basis of a talmudic mechanism that operates, in effect, contrary to biblical law. For Rashi the status of a Jew is not significantly changed when he becomes an apostate, and it was only this rabbinic enactment that caused a relatively limited change to occur regarding inheritance. Katz adds that successive and noteworthy Tosafists (as recorded in *Sefer Or Zarua'*), including Isaac b. Asher (Riba) *ha-Levi* of Speyer and Rabiah, agreed with Rashi that an apostate can in fact inherit according to Torah law. They too held that it was only a rabbinic enactment that curtailed an apostate's ability to inherit (with the larger implication that an apostate's status as Jew remains intact according to Torah law), as Rashi had suggested, all of which demonstrates the scope of his continued influence.[28]

However, Riba *ha-Levi* and Rabiah (as noted in chapter 2) were on opposite sides of the larger question as to whether a reverting apostate was required to immerse. Riba held that the apostate is to be treated like all other Jews in this regard. It is therefore not possible for him to undergo immersion upon his return, since Jews from birth never undergo immersion to establish or even reconfirm their status as Jews. Such a rite is prescribed only for converts to Judaism. Rabiah, on the other hand, maintains that a returning apostate is close to being considered and treated as a convert. Thus a reverting apostate must also make a formal acceptance of Jewish observance (*qabbalah*) before a judicial tribunal, in addition to his immersion. The only easement Rabiah provides is that this immersion can take place at night, since the reverting

M. Perry, *Massoret ve-Shinnui*, 158–65; and see also *Teshuvot ha-Rashba*, 7:292; *Arba'ah Turim, Ḥoshen Mishpat*, sec. 283; ms. Vercelli C1, fols. 326d–327b; ms. Bodl. 678, fol. 194c–d [= ms. JTS 673 (#41418), fols. 193c–195a]; Avraham Grossman, *Ḥakhmei Ashkenaz ha-Rishonim* (Jerusalem, 1981), 74. See also ms. Bodl. 566 (this chapter, n. 25): ירושת משומד. המלוה את חבירו ונשתמד [זה שלוה], ומת אביו של משומד, אינו נפרע [המלוה] מנכסי אבי המשומד שאין המשומד יורש את אביו . . . אשת איש שנשתמדה לא ירית לה בעל דכיון דשויא נפשה שלה חתיכה דאיסור׳, נפקא ליה ביה משאר ולא קרינן ביה וירש אותה. והיא אין לה עליו כתובה כלום. This last ruling indicates that, although the husband and his wife who had apostatized were still married according to Jewish law, the economic aspects of the marriage were effectively terminated.

28 See J. Katz, *Exclusiveness and Tolerance*, 72–73 [= *Bein Yehudim le-Goyim*, 79–80]; and this volume, chapter 3, n. 49. See also *Teshuvot Maharaḥ Or Zarua'*, ed. Abittan, sec. 140; and *Semaq mi-Ẓurikh*, ed. Har-Shoshanim, 3:127.

apostate is not absolutely the same as a convert (*ka-ger*, but not actually a *ger*). And yet with respect to inheritance, both Riba and Rabiah ruled, in accordance with Rashi's view and against the position of a number of Geonim and early Ashkenazic predecessors, that the apostate could inherit from his family (just as they could inherit from him) according to Torah law. It was only a rabbinic prohibition, put forward against the apostate as a penalty, which rendered him unable to inherit.

It is reasonable to suggest that in this instance of economic assignment and interaction involving inheritance—as was the case for some Tosafists, including Rabiah, regarding money-lending as well—the thrust of Rabiah's position is to enable practicing, observant Jews to be as financially comfortable as possible. Because Rashi wanted to protect the Jewish status of the apostate at nearly all costs, he was prepared to allow the apostate to inherit on the level of Torah law (if not for the rabbinic injunction), even though this could well mean that other, more distant, family members thereby lost out (in the same way Rashi's position made things harder on the woman who required *ḥaliẓah* from the apostate). Rashi's approach likely held true here for Riba *ha-Levi* of Speyer as well. As cited in *Sefer Or Zarua'*, Isaac b. Asher *ha-Levi* refutes and redefines the earlier position that maintained Esau did not inherit from Isaac in any way.

However, Isaac *Or Zarua'* records that his teacher Rabiah first asserts that an apostate can inherit according to Torah law in accordance with the principle of *'af 'al pi she-ḥata Yisra'el hu*. This posture presumes, without question, the ability of an apostate's Jewish family to inherit from him as well. Rabiah then moves, however, to deny the right of an apostate to inherit in practice, due to the rabbinic application of *hefqer beit din hefqer*, which puts only the apostate at a disadvantage. Indeed, Isaac *Or Zarua'* formulates Rabiah's position by noting that it is worthwhile to withhold inheritance from an apostate as a fine (*bekhol 'inyan ra'ui le-qonso*). *Sefer Or Zarua'* does not mention that Rabiah also allowed money-lending to an apostate at interest (against the position taken by Rashi) as a fine (*qenas*), which was also imposed via the mechanism of *hefqer beit din hefqer*.[29] But the section about inheritance in *Sefer Or Zarua'*

---

29 See this chapter, n. 21.

does cite the passage from the Talmud Yerushalmi (concerning the Cutheans) that Rabiah had noted when allowing a Jew to charge interest to an apostate, in support of the rabbinic elimination of an apostate's right to inherit.

Sefer Or Zarua' continues by noting that, according to Rabiah, even for the geonic position (that an apostate cannot inherit from his family members according to Torah law), a father should be able to inherit from a son who had become an apostate, because there is no reason to fine the father in such an instance (*lamah yiqnesu et ha-'av*). Indeed, even before this part of the presentation in *Sefer Or Zarua'*, Rabiah is cited there as ruling on the question of whether a husband can inherit from his wife who had apostatized and then died—is he still considered her spouse (*she'er*) who inherits from his wife, given that she had lived with a non-Jew during her apostasy and had become forbidden to her husband? Rabiah's response is that the husband does inherit, because "why should we penalize [or fine] the husband [*veha-ba'al lamah neqansin hu*]?" Just as a father inherits the estate of his son who apostatized, so too a husband inherits from his wife, even if they could not have continued to live together. As Isaac *Or Zarua'* subsequently repeats, "Why should the husband lose his ability to inherit?"[30] The thrust of Rabiah's view on inheritance and apostasy is that, while the apostate loses in these various situations, his (or her) family and other Jews who are involved are entitled to benefit as appropriate.

Following his presentation of Rabiah's view on why an apostate cannot inherit, Isaac *Or Zarua'* cites the view of another of his German teachers, Simḥah of Speyer, that even according to the stringent geonic view, a Jewish grandson whose father is an apostate can inherit from his grandfather; the apostate's presence "in the middle" does not affect the grandson even according to Torah law. As *Sefer Or Zarua'* further notes, this allowance was not addressed by Rashi in his responsum dealing with an apostate and inheritance. Both Rabiah and Simḥah of Speyer sought to allow the family to benefit to the greatest extent possible, even though Simḥah of Speyer was also decidedly stringent

30 See *Sefer Or Zarua'*, pt. 3, *pisqei Bava Batra*, sec. 102, ed. Machon Yerushalayim, 436.

with regard to immersion for a returning apostate and the Jewish status of an apostate. This was not, however, Rashi's position at all.[31]

A formulation regarding the apostate and his inheritance by Moses b. Jacob of Coucy in his *Sefer Miẓvot Gadol* is also best understood in the divergent way that has been described. R. Moses's position on inheritance and the apostate is similar to that of Rabiah, even as two additional clarifying phrases are found in his formulation (which owes quite a bit to Maimonides' *Mishneh Torah, hilkhot naḥalot*, 6:12):

> An apostate can inherit from his [fully] Jewish relatives [*qerovav ha-Yisre'elim*]. However, if the rabbinic court wishes to cause this money to be lost to him and to fine him such that he cannot inherit them, so as not to strengthen the hand of evildoers, they have the authority to do so [*ve-'im ra'u beit din le-'abbed mimenu (mamono) u-le-qonso she-lo yirash kedei she-lo le-ḥazzeq yedei resha'im ha-reshut be-yadam*].[32]

In this instance, unlike in the case of lending money at interest to an apostate, *Sefer Miẓvot Gadol* does not need to deal with the issue of whether an apostate is entitled to support (especially since his heirs are not necessarily affected by this issue in any case), nor is there any particular role for *'aḥvah* (brotherhood), as there is with respect to money-lending.[33]

What emerges from this discussion is that, since inheritance is purely a monetary issue, some rabbinic authorities went outside their typical

31 See *Sefer Or Zarua'*, ibid., secs. 437–38 (secs. 103–5); *Sefer Mordekhai 'al Massekhet Qiddushin*, sec. 492, ed. Y. Roth (Jerusalem, 1990), 128–36; *Piseqi ha-Rosh 'al Massekhet Qiddushin*, 1:22–23; *Teshuvot ha-Rosh*, 17:10; *Arba'ah Turim, Ḥoshen Mishpat*, sec. 283. For Simḥah of Speyer's stringencies, see this volume, chapters 2 (n. 22) and 3 (n. 50).

32 See *Sefer Miẓvot Gadol* (Venice 1547), fol. 185c (*'aseh* 96). See also ms. Paris 370 (#20421), fols. 398b–c; ms. Paris Mazarine 4472 (#4411), fol. 163c; ms. Parma de Rossi 93 (#12322), fol. 180d; and cf. *Teshuvot Maharam va-Ḥaverav*, ed. S. Emanuel, 745 (sec. 379).

33 See this chapter, n. 9.

theoretical halakhic definitions concerning the Jewish status of an apostate, to take into account the possible benefits or losses of other family members. Thus it becomes difficult to prove Rashi's potential influence on any of these rabbinic figures based on a survey of their views regarding an apostate and inheritance, as Jacob Katz sought to do. Indeed, it is equally difficult to prove much of anything from this area of Jewish law alone (where all agree that an apostate should not inherit in practice) about what a particular medieval rabbinic figure held more broadly concerning the Jewish status of an apostate (or of a reverting apostate).

Regarding the apostate and money-lending—or the apostate's Jewish status in terms of marriage and divorce, or *ḥaliẓah*—the nexus between the area of Jewish law under consideration and the involvement of an apostate in various other areas (or in terms of the requirements for reversion) was often taken into account, and in a number of cases, these connections generated nuanced explanations. Moreover, even with regard to the discrete question of charging an apostate interest, medieval rabbinic authorities had to decide whether this was permitted or whether it remained prohibited. Once that decision had been made, the only remaining halakhic variable (for those who took the view that it was permitted) was to determine whether the principle of *lifnei 'ivver* was also operant, and to what extent. The results of these decisions usually provide the observer with a fairly clear idea of where that authority stands on the question of the Jewish status of an apostate, precisely because there were few if any other options that could have been selected.

However, when one considers the apostate and inheritance—for which two equally valid and effective rabbinic explanations existed as to why the apostate should not be able to inherit (and no one actually permitted an apostate to inherit)—it is difficult to correlate the particular explanation that an authority chose with his larger view of the halakhic nature of apostasy, except perhaps in the case of Rashi himself. How a particular medieval rabbinic authority denies an apostate's right to inherit does not necessarily reveal his larger view about the halakhic status of an apostate. As we shall now see, this holds true for other areas related to apostates as well, such as the permissibility of a returning apostate to pronounce the priestly blessing, or the ability of an apostate to serve as a witness, among others.

Pronouncing the Priestly Blessing

Rashi (like Rabbenu Gershom of Mainz) was understandably adamant that, in light of the principle of *'af 'al pi she-ḥata Yisra'el hu*, a returning apostate who is a *kohen* could resume pronouncing the priestly benediction (*birkat kohanim*) as soon as he rejoined the Jewish community in observance. Rabbenu Gershom bases his allowance primarily on the need to recognize the efficacy and potency of repentance and to support genuine penitents, which allows the *kohen* to receive the first *'aliyyah* to the Torah once again as well. But Rashi provides support for his position on the basis of talmudic formulations which rule that only visible physical blemishes render a *kohen* unfit to pronounce the priestly blessing (*Megillah* 24b and *Ta'anit* 27a). A significant religious deviation which the *kohen* subsequently renounces can disqualify him only from serving within the *Beit ha-Miqdash* itself.[34]

Although many Tosafists and other subsequent Ashkenazic authorities agreed with this ruling, some did not. However, it cannot be automatically assumed that a rabbinic authority who disagrees holds that a reverting apostate is unable return to where he had been as a Jew, or that he requires additional actions to reacquire his status as a full member of the Jewish community. A *kohen* is born into the *kehunah* and its privileges and perquisites, but he can lose these as the result of violations. In this respect the Jewish priesthood is not precisely the same as an individual's basic status as a Jew, which cannot be lost even temporarily once one has been born a Jew.

As R. Natronai Gaon puts it (according to one version of his responsum),

> If the apostate has repented, it is sufficient for him to be [once again] the same as other ordinary Jews [*dayyo lihyot ki-she'ar Yisra'el*]. But

34 See J. Katz, *Exclusiveness and Tolerance*, 69–70 (and the sources cited) [= *Bein Yehudim le-Goyim*, 77].

> to ascend to the priestly blessing [where the *kohen* recites that he has been sanctified with the holiness of Aaron] and to read first from the Torah . . . this *kohen* has [with his apostasy] already profaned the holiness of Aaron. And if he reads first from the Torah, the Torah is thereby profaned because the other Jews present will say, we have retained our status as observant Jews [*ba'alei mizvot*] while this one has separated himself and removed himself from the community. Now that he has come back, is it not sufficient that he be the same as us?[35]

Moreover, there are several different services or rituals in which a *kohen* played a special role, even after the destruction of the Temple. It should not be assumed, for example, that just as the returning apostate is permitted to offer the priestly blessing (based on an analysis of talmudic *sugyot*), he is also necessarily permitted once again to receive the first *'aliyyah* to the Torah. The latter rite is arguably one that places the *kohen* in a more visible and important public position (*serarah*), which perhaps should not be restored to a Jew who had apostatized.[36] Finally, there are those who maintain, based on a different understanding of the underlying talmudic texts, that it is not so simple to distinguish between a *kohen* serving in the Temple and one who pronounces the priestly blessing in the synagogue. A serious religious breach such as apostasy, which brings a person into contact with a form of idolatry, cannot be overlooked in either context, even if the *kohen* in question has repented.[37] In sum, the special characteristics of the priestly benediction may not be a

---

35 See *Teshuvot R. Natronai*, ed. Brody, 140–42 (sec. 35). In the other version of this responsum, R. Natronai does allow the repentant apostate who is a *kohen* to eat *ḥalah* gifts because, even though a *kohen* may be blemished in a way that prohibits him from performing the priestly duties and services, he is still entitled to partake in the priestly gifts. Cf. this volume, chapter 1, n. 5. R. Natronai may have been the source for Yosef b. Samuel Tov Elem's stringent view as well. See A. Grossman, *Ḥakhmei Ashkenaz ha-Rishonim*, 225 (n. 70); and cf. M. Perry, *Massoret ve-Shinnui*, 186.

36 This is the view of Solomon b. Abraham of Montpellier, in a responsum written to Naḥmanides. See this volume, chapter 6, n. 14.

37 This appears to be the view of Maimonides in *Mishneh Torah, hilkhot tefillah u-nesi'at kappaim*, 15:3.

reliable indicator of how Jewish an apostate is (or was) in broader halakhic terms and contexts, and we may find seeming inconsistencies in the ways different rabbinic authorities deal with this issue within their own thinking.

Thus, for example, Rabiah, who was quite strict with returning apostates—even as he held that marriage and divorce undertaken between a Jewish apostate to Christianity and a Jewess was valid—is one of those Tosafists who rules that a returning apostate cannot resume pronouncing the priestly blessing. Rabiah points to a geonic ruling, perhaps that of R. Natronai, as his source. At the same time, however, Rabiah rules that only a known and habitual murderer (*bi-mefursam u-mu'ad le-kakh tadir*) who is a *kohen* may not pronounce the priestly blessing. If, however, a *kohen* commits a murder (or an act of adultery) in a chance encounter (*she-ba be-miqreh le-yado*), he is permitted to pronounce the priestly blessing. Rabiah acknowledges the disparity in these situations, remarking that there is indeed a greater degree of strictness in the case of an apostate: "Repentance is sufficient, except in the case of an apostate."[38] Indeed, it would seem that even one encounter with apostasy is one too many.

Rabiah's student Isaac *Or Zarua'* who, as noted earlier, records a number of Rabiah's ruling about apostates, cites Rabbenu Gershom's lenient approach regarding an apostate who is a *kohen* rather than the strict view of Rabiah. At the end of this passage, Isaac *Or Zarua'* raises the possibility that a *kohen* who practiced idolatry cannot return to the priestly service (which is Rabiah's view), concluding nonetheless, in accordance with the view of Rabbenu Gershom, that such a *kohen* can return to pronounce the priestly blessing and to receive the first *'aliyyah* to the Torah, even if he cannot return to the Temple service itself.[39]

However, in a lengthy responsum that Isaac of Vienna composed about whether a murderer who repented can serve again as a prayer leader (*sheliaḥ ẓibbur*), R. Isaac relates to Rabiah's view somewhat differently and adds some important additional information. On the basic question that was asked,

38 See *Sefer Rabiah*, ed. Deblitzky, 4:267 (sec. 1155). See also *Haggahot Maimuniyyot* to *Mishneh Torah, hilkhot tefillah*, 15:3 (in the previous note); and Isaac *Or Zarua*'s report of Rabiah's view (in the following note) concerning the kind of murderer or adulterer who can return to pronounce the priestly blessing.

39 See *Sefer Or Zarua'*, pt. 2, sec. 412, ed. Machon Yerushalayim, 470–71.

R. Isaac rules, in accordance with his teacher Simḥah of Speyer, that once the sinner has repented and immersed himself (which constitutes an act of atonement and affliction for his past prohibited actions), he is ready to resume his position as a prayer leader as before. Indeed, once he has had thoughts of repentance and admitted his sin, the Almighty immediately forgives him. The procedure of immersion is necessary only to nullify any negative consequences for the penitent that his sinful act might have set in motion.

Isaac *Or Zarua*ʿ concludes that even a willful murderer can once again serve in this capacity if he has properly repented, and he is not comparable to someone who has worshiped idolatry, which renders a *kohen* a *baʿal mum* (a blemished *kohen*, as per the scriptural derivation recorded in *Menaḥot* 109a). It is unclear at this point in the passage whether R. Isaac means that the *kohen* who has served idolatry becomes a *baʿal mum* only in terms of his serving in the Temple or whether this means he cannot pronounce the priestly blessing in other locales as well. But Isaac *Or Zarua*ʿ continues by reporting what he learned from his teacher Rabiah (*kibbalti mi-mori Rabbenu Avi ha-ʿEzri*): When the Talmud (*Berakhot* 32b) states that a murderer cannot pronounce the priestly blessing, this is only the case if he has not repented. If, however, he has repented for his crime, he may bless the Jewish people with the priestly blessing, as per the passage in the Talmud Yerushalmi (*Gittin* 5:9), which asserts that if members of the congregation are concerned that a *kohen* is an adulterer or a murderer (and is thus not worthy of giving the priestly blessing), the Almighty assures them that He is the one who provides the blessing (Nu. 6:27). Apparently still citing his teacher Rabiah, Isaac *Or Zarua*ʿ posits "that wherever we can rectify a [teaching in the] Yerushalmi with our Talmud [Bavli], we do so in order not to have to maintain that they are at odds with each other."

This Yerushalmi passage, which Rabiah himself had also cited, easily accounts for his comment that it is necessary to be stricter with apostates than with other grave sinners. If the members of the congregation accuse *kohanim* of two cardinal sins, murder and adultery, the Almighty intervenes, since it is He who actually provides the blessing and not the *kohanim*.

However, this passage does not include the scenario in which the *kohen* is suspected by the congregation to be worshipping idolatry, nor does it indicate that he too can return to give the priestly blessing under the aegis of the Almighty.

Rabiah's caveat—that only if the untoward act (of murder) takes place once ("by chance") can such a *kohen* resume giving the blessing but not if the *kohen* was a serial violator, since the Almighty's support would be unimaginable in such a situation—is also completely understood in light of the Yerushalmi passage. Because the priestly blessing is integrally linked to the congregation and is not simply a matter of the *kohen*'s own ritual performance, an apostate may be at a distinct disadvantage in this situation, even if he has reverted and repented, while an erstwhile *sheliaḥ ẓibbur* who had once killed someone unintentionally and without malice can resume his role. Both Rabiah and his student Isaac *Or Zarua*ʿ acknowledge with respect to resuming the priestly blessing that there is a difference between the cardinal sins of murder and adultery on the one hand and serving idolatry or apostasy on the other.[40]

Whether Isaac *Or Zarua*ʿ fully agrees with his teacher's view, it is tempting to suggest that Rabiah's stringent handling of an apostate who was a *kohen* is largely a reflection of his suspicion of returning apostates and his uncertainty about their standing more generally. However, there are some additional textual considerations in this matter that have not been fully explored. *Tosafot* to tractate *Sotah*, which were compiled in Germany during the period of Rabiah,[41] cites the view of the *She'iltot* (in *parashat Koraḥ*) that "a *kohen* who worshipped idolatry should not pronounce the priestly blessing. He is worse than a murderer whom the Talmud instructs (*Berakhot* 32a) not to pronounce

40 See *Sefer Or Zarua*ʿ, pt. 1, sec. 112, ed. Machon Yerushalayim, 105–7. Note that *Arba'ah Turim*, *Oraḥ Ḥayyim*, sec. 128, cites this Yerushalmi passage in connection with Rabbenu Gershom's responsum. Cf. Simcha Assaf, "Qoveẓ shel Igrot R. Shmu'el ben Eli u-Bnei Doro," *Tarbiz* 1:2 (1930): 48–49, for a geonic ruling that allowed someone who had committed a heinous sin and repented to serve as a prayer leader.

41 See *Tosafot Sotah* 39a, s.v. *ve-khi*; and see also E. E. Urbach, *Ba'alei ha-Tosafot*, 637–39. As Urbach notes, Y. N. Epstein held that the compiler of these *Tosafot* was none other than Barukh b. Samuel of Mainz.

this blessing." This is the position of Rabiah, and it may well be the geonic source for his ruling to which he had alluded.[42]

Simḥah of Speyer adduces a proof from the *Sifra* to *parashat Emor* (at the end of *parshata* 1) that a *kohen* who has strayed from the ways of the Jewish community (*peresh mi-darkhei ha-ẓibbur*) is no longer thought of as a *kohen* (*lo neḥshav ke-kohen*) but is still considered a Jew.[43] Similarly, R. Simḥah, who is even more negative than his contemporary Tosafist colleague Rabiah about the Jewish status of an apostate,[44] stresses that a *kohen* who is a murderer cannot pronounce the priestly blessing, but only if he persists in performing this heinous crime (*'omed be-mirdo*, or perhaps if he does not repent). If, however, he committed only a one-time, unintentional murder, he may continue to pronounce the priestly blessing. R. Simḥah also cites the Yerushalmi passage just discussed as proof for his position in this matter, since only a rebellious sinner is to be excluded from pronouncing the blessing according to this passage. Unlike Rabiah, however, Simḥah of Speyer also allows a reverting *kohen* to resume pronouncing the priestly blessing even though here too he is almost as demanding as Rabiah with regard to immersion for a reverting apostate.[45] Indeed, Samson of Sens, who like Rabiah sought to actually verify the sincerity of a returning apostate's intentions,[46] also allows a reverting apostate to pronounce the priestly blessing, as does Moses of Coucy,[47] whose views

42 This passage is not found in extant versions of *She'iltot*, but (German) Tosafists were surely familiar with this work. See Urbach, *Ba'alei ha-Tosafot*, 395, 551; S. Emanuel, *Shivrei Luḥot*, 66, 77–78 (n. 123); and *Tosafot Ketubot* 4b, s.v. *pashit*. *Tosafot Menḥot* 109a, s.v. *lo*, cites this same view (*hemir dato lo yisa 'et kappav ve-lo yiqra rishon . . . de-ha 'aḥleh li-qedushateh*) in the name of *Sefer Ve-Hizhir*, just prior to citing Rashi's view that a reverting *kohen* can resume this benediction. See also *Ḥiddushim 'al ha-Torah le-Rabbenu Tam u-Beit Midrasho*, ed. A. Shoshana (Jerusalem, 2017), 236–37; Urbach, *Ba'alei ha-Tosafot*, 713; Israel Ta-Shma, *Kneset Meḥqarim*, vol. 1 (Jerusalem, 2004), 34–35, 78; *Tosafot Shabbat* 135b, s.v. *kegon she-laqaḥ*; *Temurah* 12b, s.v. *she-'ein*; and *Tosafot ha-Rosh* to *Ḥullin* 106b, s.v. *'amar Rav*.

43 See *Teshuvot u-Pesaqim*, ed. E. Kupfer, 296 (sec. 176).

44 See this volume, chapter 3, n. 50.

45 See this volume, chapter 2, n. 22.

46 See ibid., n. 20.

47 The views of Simḥah of Speyer, Samson of Sens, and Moses of Coucy are all

on the Jewish status of apostates have been shown to be generally compatible with those of Rabiah.[48] The range of different options (and texts) that relate to the reverting apostate and the priestly blessing—and the involvement of the congregation in that blessing—allows for an array of positions that are not necessarily so well integrated or aligned with the larger question of an apostate's status as a Jew.[49]

Apostates as Witnesses

The Talmud establishes in tractate *Sanhedrin* (25b) that sinners who are liable for lashes and other severe punishments for their misdeeds cannot serve as witnesses until they have properly repented. Moreover, in instances where they stole or subverted funds, it is necessary for them to restore their ill-gotten gains, and to demonstrably refrain from pursuing these inappropriate activities any further. We had occasion in the second chapter to note the opinion of Riẓba of Dampierre that, in the case of an apostate, although it is certainly best for him to try to restore any ill-gotten gains that had come his way while he was living as a Christian, his sincere repentance is effective even if he is not able to accomplish these monetary restitutions.[50] Rashi rules in a

recorded in the *Haggahot Maimuniyyot* passage, this chapter, n. 38. See also *Sefer Miẓvot Gadol*, *'aseh* 20.

48 See this chapter, nn. 20–21.

49 Cf. M. Perry, *Massoret ve-Shinnui*, 189–91. The position of Meir of Rothenburg (see Meir b. Barukh of Rothenburg, *Teshuvot, Pesaqim u-Minhagim*, ed. I. Z. Kahana, vol. 1 [Jerusalem, 1957], 157 [sec. 92])—that a returning apostate should not be told to ascend to pronounce the priestly blessing, but that if he does go up on his own he should not be removed or stopped—is another of the many "compromise" halakhic positions that Maharam took (across different areas of Jewish law) so that he did not have to rule against his leading predecessors but rather could take their differing views into account (*la-ẓet yedei kol ha-shitot*). See my "Compromise and Inclusivity in Establishing *Minhag* and *Halakhah*: Contextualizing the Approach of R. Meir of Rothenburg," in *Minhagim: Custom and Practice in Jewish Life*, ed. S. Goldin et al. (Berlin, 2019), 53–71.

50 See this volume, chapter 2. n. 18. Cf. this volume, chapter 6, n. 11, for the view of Solomon b. Abraham of Montpellier. Repentance is a critical first step toward reinstatement, but additional afflictions and remorse are necessary for the returning

responsum on whether former converts who had become Christian under duress and then returned to the Jewish community could testify about something that occurred while they were still in the state of forced apostasy. This is another of the very few instances where Rashi distinguishes in halakhic matters between forced and voluntary apostates.[51]

Rashi's position is that it depends on how the court that is presently hearing and collecting evidence evaluates the status of these apostates under duress. If the court determines that they continued to observe Jewish law and practices (*dat Mosheh*) in private or when they were alone, and are not suspected of transgressing sins willfully but only under pressure from the Christians, their testimony can be accepted. However, if it is determined that they sinned wantonly (*mufqarim ba-ʿaverot*) during their apostasy, in situations where they were not being compelled to do these sinful acts by non-Jews (*she-lo ʾanasum goyim ʿaleihem*), they are not now able to testify about what occurred at that time, even though they have by now regretted what they did and repented appropriately (*she-ḥazru bahen ʾaḥar zeman teshuvah hogenet*). Rashi bases his ruling on a *Baraita* (*ʿArakhin* 17b [end], and *B. B.* 128a) specifying that only when witnesses are acceptable from the time the incident occurred until now is their testimony accepted. However, in cases where a witness was "kosher" at the beginning (when the incident occurred) but not at the end (when their testimony is given to a rabbinic court) or vice versa, that testimony is unacceptable. Thus in cases where the forced apostates behaved wantonly at the time the incident occurred, their testimony is unacceptable now, even though they have since returned to the Jewish community and repented.[52]

---

apostate to be once again considered fully trustworthy in both civil and religious matters, including his ability to serve as a witness.

51 See this volume, chapter 1, n. 33.

52 See *Teshuvot Baʿalei ha-Tosafot*, ed. I. A. Agus, 51–52 (sec. 9). It is not included by Israel Elfenbein in his collection of Rashi's responsa. Jacob Katz cites this responsum in his *Halakhah ve-Qabbalah*, 269–60 (n. 28). He maintains that Rashi's approval of a marriage between two forced converts (*ʾanusim*) that was witnessed by two *ʾanusim* (*Teshuvot Rashi*, ed. Elfenbein, 192–93, #171[= *Teshuvot Maharaḥ Or Zaruaʿ* #45]; and see also *Teshuvot Mahariq*, #85) is not, as some have suggested, because Rashi holds that all Jews can automatically serve as kosher witnesses by definition

The late-thirteenth-century Tosafist Yedidyah b. Israel of Nuremberg is the first to cite this responsum in Rashi's name, and he further discusses the level of verification (*ḥazaqah*) that is needed, according to Rashi, to make these determinations.[53]

---

because of the principle of *'af 'al pi she-ḥata Yisra'el hu*. Rather, in that instance, the *qiddushin* has to be respected if it was witnessed by two *'anusim*: i.e., those who returned fully at the first moment they were able do so safely, which is then also a case of *mokhiaḥ sofan 'al teḥillatan*. This rationale is slightly different from what Rashi expresses regarding whether reverted *'anusim* may be reliable witnesses for events they observed while still apostates. But that is likely because the *qiddushin* between the *'anusim* is itself fundamentally valid for Rashi. As such, the witnesses are providing only verification rather than their own testimony. Indeed, in the marriage case Rashi also maintains that, even if the witnesses were apostates who behaved wantonly with Christian women, this did not disqualify their testimony in this matter (after they have returned) because of the talmudic principle *he-ḥashud 'al ha-'arayot kasher le-'edut 'ishah* (*Sanhedrin* 26b); i.e., verifying *qiddushin* does not require such high-level testimony. As Rashi further notes, witnesses to matters of divorce are held to a higher standard than those who witness the marriage (ה"מ לאפוקה אבל לעיולה מהימני). Nonetheless, Rashi is equally clear in his other responsum concerning broader *'edut* privileges for a returning apostate. Wanton behavior on the part of the apostates (if it was not coerced by Christians) at the time the event in question was witnessed *does* disqualify the apostates from giving testimony, even if they later return fully. See also *Teshvot Rashi*, ed. Elfenbein, 194 (#173), which states that an apostate is not reliable concerning prohibitions (*'eino ne'eman be-'issurim*) because he is suspect (*ḥashud*) in their regard (as is his wine). See also Rami Reiner, "Mumar Okhel Nevelah le-Te'avon Pasul: Mashehu 'al Nosaḥ u-Perush Bidei Rashi," in *Lo Yasur Shevet mi-Yehudah: Studies Presented to Professor Simon Schwarzfuchs*, ed. J. Hacker and Y. Harel (Jerusalem, 2011), 327.

53 See Avigdor Haneman, "Hilkhot 'Agunot: Halakhah be-Hishtanutah—Mishpat, Parshanut, Historiyyah ve-Ḥevrah" (PhD diss., Ben-Gurion University of the Negev, 2018), 62–63; Agus, *Teshuvot Ba'alei ha-Tosafot*, 242, 245; Judah b. Asher, *Teshuvot Zikhron Yehudah*, #92, ed. A. M. Havazelet (Shaalvim, 2005), 112–27; and *Semaq mi-Ẓurikh*, ed. Har-Shoshanim, 2:157 (*miẓvah* 182, end). Like Haneman, Rachel Furst has recently closely examined a group of rabbinic views on the validity of testimony provided by apostates in the case of a husband who had been killed during a persecution in Wurzburg in 1298. If accepted, this testimony would allow the wife to remarry. The rabbinic views offered include those of Yedidyah of Nuremberg and Ḥayyim *Or Zarua'* (to be discussed shortly). See Furst, "A Return to Credibility? The Rehabilitation of Repentant Apostates in Medieval Ashkenaz," in *On the Word of a Jew*, ed. N. Caputo and M. Hart (Bloomington, IN, 2019), 201–21.

In a lengthy responsum, Isaiah di Trani (RID, a student of Simḥah of Speyer), argues that a current apostate (*mumar*) cannot be relied on if he testifies that a woman's husband had died, and she is therefore now free to marry any other Jewish man. This is so even if the apostate is considered to be *mesiaḥ lefi tumo* (lit., speaking innocently and without guile), and is offering testimony where he has no interest or stake, a situation in which even a non-Jew is typically believed if he offers such testimony in the case of a potential *'agunah*. At the end of his responsum, RID notes that, in the particular case that had come before him, there was indeed a monetary incentive for the apostate to testify in this way (which RID does not fully describe). However, RID's position is that even if the apostate had no incentive to lie, he is disqualified (*pasul*) from serving as a witness as a matter of Jewish evidentiary law, and under any condition.

While other (unnamed) rabbinic figures involved in this case were prepared to allow the testimony of a witness who was otherwise disqualified even according to Torah law, if that testimony was judged to be *mesiaḥ lefi tumo*, RID maintains that such a lenient stance may be possible if the potential witness regularly transgresses only one area or type of sin (*rasha le-davar eḥad*). However, the testimony of an apostate who has denied the Creator in a wanton way (*she-kafar be-Borei 'Olam le-hakh'is*), and is "completely filled with abomination and stain as he transgresses the entire Torah [*ve-hu male kol 'avel ve-shimẓah ve-'over 'al kol divrei Torah*]," cannot be believed under any condition. RID further assumes that the apostate has an ulterior motive in this instance, and his testimony is thus not considered to be without guile (*lefi tumo*) in any case. The apostate seeks to allow the wife to "go free" and to be unfettered in her ability to marry someone else. A non-Jew who does not know or understand Jewish law can be considered *lefi tumo* in such a situation, but an apostate cannot.[54]

54 See *Teshuvot ha-RID*, ed. A. Y. Wertheimer (Jerusalem, 1975), 273–84 (sec. 57). RID derives support from a comment by Rabbenu Ḥanan'el (*Yevamot* 114b) stating that an apostate, like a thief, is disqualified from testifying in such matters of marriage under any condition. Eli'ezer b. Nathan of Mainz (d. c. 1170), *Sefer Raban*, ed. D. Deblitzky (Bnei Brak, 2012), 3:481 (sec. 519, end), rules that a minor who

RID appears to have a rather low opinion of *meshummadim* as potential witnesses, although to be sure the apostate in this case is a "wanton apostate" and not someone who is secretly or privately practicing Judaism. Rashi would likely agree that the testimony of such an apostate who shows no sign of remorse is unacceptable.[55] Indeed, the views of Rashi and RID regarding apostates are similar across a series of issues: *Qiddushin* offered by apostates are valid, they must do *ḥaliẓah*, they may not be charged interest, and reverting apostates do not require immersion.[56]

Ḥayyim b. Isaac *Or Zarua'*, on the other hand, was ostensibly more accepting than Rashi in a situation involving former apostates who had converted under duress and were now testifying about the death of a husband so that his wife could remarry.[57] In R. Ḥayyim's view, as long as these *'anusim* have fully returned and can assert now that they are testifying truthfully about what occurred then, they are believed, even if they were eating non-kosher food (*nevelot u-terefot*) at the time they witnessed the event. To permit an *'agunah* to remarry, it is not necessary (as in most other cases) for the witnesses to have been upstanding Jews at the time they witnessed the event. What is required is that we can know that the truth is in accordance with what the witnesses are saying now (*lo be-'inan 'edut raq she-neda sheha-kol hu 'emet kemo she-hu 'omer 'attah*). To be sure, as Ḥayyim *Or Zarua'* notes, Rabiah would not agree

---

is *mesiaḥ lefi tumo* can be relied upon in such matters; Isaac Alfasi (Rif, d. 1103, to *Yevamot* 122a [folio 46b in the standard pagination]) holds that the testimony of a thief (a *rasha*) who is *mesiaḥ lefi tumo* is accepted (against the view of Rabbenu Ḥanan'el), since he is no worse than a non-Jew. Rabiah, however, was hesitant to rule this way (in his *Sefer Avi'asaf*). A Jewish *rasha* (as opposed to a non-Jew) nonetheless knows the nature of Jewish law and life (*yodea' be-tiv Yisra'el*), and he is therefore perhaps conniving or directing his testimony rather than being *mesiaḥ lefi tumo* as it appears. This approach is similar to Isaiah di Trani's regarding the testimony of an apostate. See *Sefer Or Zarua'*, pt. 1, sec. 697, ed. Machon Yerushalayim, 589, where the views of Rabiah and Raban are juxtaposed.

55 See A. Haneman, "Hilkhot 'Agunot," 45–52.

56 See *Teshuvot ha-RID*, 323–32 (sec. 64); and see also 285–88 (sec. 58). Cf. my *The Intellectual History and Rabbinic Culture of Medieval Ashkenaz* (Detroit, MI, 2013), 243.

57 See *Teshuvot Maharḥ Or Zarua'*, ed. Abittan, 82–84 (sec. 91).

that a current apostate (including one who was forcibly converted, an *ʾanus*) is considered to be a *mesiaḥ lefi tumo*, because his testimony is perhaps being shaped by his own interests.[58] However, in the case before R. Ḥayyim, the witness asserts that he is now testifying truthfully and is otherwise upstanding.

The acceptability of an apostate's testimony is guided by a variety of halakhic qualifications and standards that are first and foremost connected to evidentiary rules and tolerances: for example, whether an apostate's testimony is truly considered to be *mesiaḥ lefi tumo* and whether testimony offered for an event that occurred during apostasy can be accepted to allow a potential *ʿagunah* to remarry. Thus the status of an apostate's testimony depends on factors that are different from (and in some ways beyond) a fundamental assessment or gauge of the religious and communal standing of an apostate or the nature of apostasy. As with inheritance and the priestly blessing, when an apostate's status significantly impacts the fate or fortunes of others, a different and often greater level of verification or achievement may be required than in situations where apostates are being evaluated only in terms of their own immediate religious status and how they relate to or interact with other Jews in more discrete ways.[59] These same kinds of considerations underlie the ruling by Joseph of

58 See this chapter, n. 54, for Rabiah's position. Regarding a question that arrived from Ashkenaz (and presents the lenient view of Alfasi against the stricter view of Rabiah's *Sefer Aviʾasaf*), Rashba (*Sheʾelot u-Teshuvot*, 2:32) rules that a forced apostate's testimony is acceptable if he is *mesiaḥ lefi tumo*, but only if he was never observed eating non-kosher food voluntarily (not under duress), and only if he begins to offer his testimony on his own. If, however, he comes to court to offer it, or if he offers it initially in response to a question, he is not considered *mesiaḥ lefi tumo* but rather is considered to be framing his testimony. Cf. *Teshuvot u-Pesaqim*, ed. Kupfer 286 (and n. 39, on a responsum by R. Paltoi Gaon concerning testimony about captured Jewish women who were not forced to engage in sexual relations, and its acceptance within Ashkenazic sources); *Shaʿarei Teshuvot Maharam b. Barukh*, ed. M. A. Bloch (Berlin, 1891), 187–88 (sec. 80); and this volume, chapter 3, n. 53.

59 Note the position of Rashi concerning an apostate's property in the hands of other Jews, cited in this chapter, n. 25; and Ri's assertion (this volume, chapter 2, n. 5) that allowing a returning apostate to perform *sheḥitah* (or other kinds of ritual acts) on behalf of others requires additional verification, beyond what is needed for him to be able to return to the community. The French Tosafist Samson of Sens (this volume, chapter 2, n. 20) is one of the few medieval rabbinic authorities

Lincoln, a contemporary of Yeḥi'el of Paris, that an apostate, as well as a Jew who is suspected without doubt of having committed adultery, is disqualified from being appointed as an agent to receive (and transfer) a bill of divorce from a husband to his wife.[60]

---

who wished to elevate the levels of verification and performance necessary for the return of an individual apostate, although Rabiah (this volume, chapter 2, n. 35) was also supportive of this effort. Cf. *Haggahot Maimuniyyot, hilkhot 'issurei bi'ah*, 18:2 [1], for the case of a *kohen* and his wife who had apostatized willingly and later reverted. Although it would seem that, in her state of apostasy, the woman becomes irrevocably prohibited to her *kohen* husband (as a *zonah*), just as a married woman who apostatizes willingly cannot return to her Jewish husband (even if he is not a *kohen*), R. Samson rules in a responsum that in this instance the man and woman may continue to live together as a married couple once they have returned to the Jewish community. The essence of his reasoning is that in this situation the modesty and values of loyalty that characterized their marriage previously remain in place even during their period of apostasy, as is the case for married couples who are Christian. See G. Blidstein, "Ma'madan ha-Ishi shel Nashim Shevuyot u-Meshummadot," *Shenaton ha-Mishpat ha-'Ivri* 3–4 (1976–77): 61–66; and my "Meshummadot Nesu'ot she-Ḥazru: Heteran li-Bnei Zugan ha-Yehudi veha-Nokhri lefi Meqorot Ẓefon Ẓarefat ve-Ashkenaz Bimei ha-Benayim," in *Halakhah u-Mishpat: Sefer ha-Zikkaron li-Menaḥem Elon*, ed. A. Edrei et al. (Jerusalem, 2018), 599–60. Cf. *Teshuvot ha-Rosh*, 32:8.

60 See *Semaq mi-Ẓurikh*, ed. Y. Har Shoshanim, 2:127 (sec. 225, end): משומד פסול להביא הגט וישראל החשוד בודאי על העריות ואינו משומד לעבודה זרה פסול להביא הגט ולומר בפני נכתב ובפני נחתם עכ״ל תרומה חדשה; and cf. this volume, chapter 6, n. 35. Adducing a different passage in *Semaq mi-Ẓurikh* (3:277, sec. 97) that cites *Terumah Ḥadashah* (in a procedural matter about the salting of meat), Urbach, *Ba'alei ha-Tosafot*, 511, suggests that this may well be the name of the collection of halakhic rulings produced by Joseph of Lincoln during the mid-thirteenth century. See also ms. JTS Rab. 645 (#39324), fols. 29r–b; ms. Bodl. 781 (#20138), fols. 68r–v, and 72r. This work contains other rulings and cases concerning both the giving of *gittin* and the procedures for ritual slaughter (Urbach, *Ba'alei ha-Tosafot*, 509–10, n. 86; 511, n. 92). Indeed, *Semaq mi-Ẓurikh*, 2:130 (sec. 233) records a case that came before Joseph (Ri) of Lincoln about a woman who willfully committed adultery with a Christian and apostatized but subsequently reverted and left for a faraway place (*ve-ḥazrah bah ve-halkhah li-medinat ha-yam*). The woman's mother complained to Joseph of Lincoln that her (former) son-in-law had married another woman but did not wish to divorce her repentant daughter (which would prevent her from now marrying another Jew). R. Joseph prevailed upon the son-in-law to willfully divorce his first wife, and he designated himself as an agent to accept the *get* on her behalf. R. Joseph instructed the husband to appoint him to this role (which would immediately permit the woman to remarry),

and to then immediately appoint another agent to bring the *get* to his first wife in her faraway locale. All this would transpire without the first wife's prior knowledge. Although the Tosafist R. Judah of Meaux (or perhaps Metz) held that such a divorce (of which the woman being divorced was initially unaware) cannot be finalized until the woman actually receives the *get*, "many *gedolei Ẓarefat* acknowledged (and agreed to) the ruling by R. Joseph of Lincoln." See Urbach, *Ba'alei ha-Tosafot*, 510; my "Meshummadot Nesu'ot she-Ḥazru," 600, n. 24; ms. Parma de Rossi 172 (#13898), fol. 90r; ms. Paris BN 381 (#4360), fol. 58v; ms. Berlin 37 (#1731), fol. 91v; ms. Bodl. 880 (#21839), fol. 122r; and cf. ms. Vercelli C1, fol. 354v; *Minḥat Yehudah*, ed. H. Touitou (Jerusalem, 2012), editor's introduction, 75; and I. Levi, "Un reuceil de consultations de rabbins," *Revue des etudes juives* 44 (1902): 82, sec. 22. I hope to return to the rulings of Joseph of Lincoln in a separate study.

5

BETWEEN JEWS AND CHRISTIANS

Doctrinal and Societal Changes

We have just seen that not every area of medieval Ashkenazic *halakhah* referring to apostates and apostasy necessarily yields a consistent evaluation by the rabbinic authors on the essential religious nature of these phenomena. Nonetheless, the preceding chapters have traced a series of significant changes and movement in the views of the Tosafists and other Ashkenazic rabbinic authorities about the status of apostates and the prohibition on money-lending, the performance of *ḥaliẓah*, and the requirements and rites that should accompany reversion, including immersion and the extent to which objective verification is necessary. Although there are distinctions within the changes themselves, along with a number of nuanced differences between northern France and Germany, these various reevaluations all adhere to an identifiable timeline. New interpretative initiatives and rulings on the part of Tosafists, which added requirements for a returning apostate and considered the ongoing apostate to be more removed from the Jewish community than before, begin to appear in the late twelfth and early thirteenth centuries, and they take firmer shape as the thirteenth century progresses.

Although these discussions are firmly grounded in the vast expanse of talmudic and rabbinic literature, as were all Tosafist endeavors within the realm of Jewish legal interpretation, the following question should be raised in light of these noticeable results and their fairly uniform chronology: Were these changes solely the result of talmudic and other exegetical and interpretative considerations, or were there also temporal factors that contributed to these newer rabbinic views and adjustments?

Before we formulate an answer to this question on the basis of noticeable shifts in the relationship between Jews and Christians in medieval Europe during this period, and in the new ways that Judaism and Christianity had begun to perceive the other, it is helpful to note a similar chronological curve in two related matters: the limiting of Rabbenu Tam's lenient approach regarding the halakhic consequences of sexual relations that transpired between a (now-reverting) female apostate and a non-Jew; and evolving rabbinic attitudes regarding the acceptance of converts to Judaism in northern Europe.

In describing how the leading northern French Tosafist Jacob b. Meir Tam (1100–1171) dealt with the challenging halakhic situations posed by the ongoing presence of apostates from Judaism, Ephraim Urbach writes that "Rabbenu Tam attempted to ease the return of apostates to the Jewish fold. Thus, it is reported that he permitted a Jewess, who had apostatized and engaged in sexual relations with a Christian prior to her reversion, and whose Jewish husband had divorced her, to be married to her former Christian partner who himself had converted to Judaism."[1]

The *Tosafot* passages that record the position taken by Rabbenu Tam also note the strong objections to his ruling that were put forward by one of his senior students, Isaac b. Mordekhai (Ribam) of Bohemia. In Ribam's view, the relations the Jewess had with her lover while he was a Christian disqualify her from returning not only to her Jewish husband but also to her former lover who converted to Judaism, in accordance with the talmudic principle (*Sotah* 27b) that a married woman who commits adultery becomes prohibited both

1 See E. E. Urbach, *Ba'alei ha-Tosafot* (Jerusalem, 1980), 1:82. Even Rashi was not prepared to go this far in easing the return of the female apostate under such circumstances; see this chapter, n. 11. On romantic entanglements between Jews and Christians, see the literature cited in Paola Tartakoff, "Testing Boundaries: Jewish Conversion and Cultural Fluidity in Medieval Europe, c. 1200–1391," *Speculum* 90 (2015): 732 (n. 13); and see also J. R. Miller, "Sexual Relationships between Christians and Jews in Medieval Germany According to Christian Sources," *Iggud: Selected Essays in Jewish Studies* 2 (2005): 19*–32*.

to her husband and to the one with whom she had illicit sexual relations (*ke-shem she-ʾasurah la-baʿal kakh ʾasurah la-boʿel*).[2]

Passages in *Sefer Miẓvot Gadol* by Moses of Coucy (d. c. 1255) and in the late-thirteenth-century *Sefer Mordekhai* (and in the glosses to this work known as *Haggahot Mordekhai*) intimate that Rabbenu Tam's nephew and influential successor, Isaac b. Samuel (Ri) of Dampierre agreed with the stringent view of Ribam, although Ri's position cannot be confirmed on the basis of direct statements made by him.[3] At the same time, however, several

---

2 See *Tosafot Ketubot* 3b, s.v. *ve-lidrosh*; *Tosafot ha-Rash mi-Shanẓ ʿal Massekhet Ketubot*, ed. A. Liss (Jerusalem, 1973), 6; *Tosafot ha-Rosh ʿal Massekhet Ketubot*, ed. A. Lichtenstein (Jerusalem, 1999), 17–19; *Tosafot Sanhedrin* 74b, s.v. *ve-ha*; *Tosafot ha-Rosh ʿal Massekhet Sanhedrin* (74b) in *Sanhedrei Gedolah* (vol. 3), ed. B. Lipkin (Jerusalem, 1970), 204–5; and *Tosafot Yeshanim Yoma* 82a, s.v. *huz*, ed. A. Arieli (Jerusalem, 1993), 179–80. This last passage attributes the stringent position to Isaac b. Meir (Rabbenu Tam's brother), due perhaps to a different (but imprecise) reading of the acronym Ribam. See Urbach, *Baʿalei ha-Tosafot*, 1:199; *Sefer Mordekhai ha-Shalem ʿal Massekhet Sanhedrin*, ed. Y. Horowitz (Jerusalem, 2009), 142, n. 9 (*ve-Ribam ʾaḥiv*); and the citation from *Sefer Miẓvot Gadol* discussed in the next note. See also Simcha Goldin, *Apostasy and Jewish Identity in High Middle Ages Northern Europe* (Manchester, 2014), 53–54, 87–88, where Ribam is misidentified as R. Yaakov b. Mordechai. The so-called *Tosafot Shanẓ* on the printed page of the Talmud to *Sotah* 26b [= *Tosafot Evreux ʿal Massekhet Sotah*, ed. Y. Lifshitz (Jerusalem, 1969), 70] associates Rabbenu Tam with the stringent position, and does not attribute the more lenient view to anyone; cf. *Tosafot ha-Rosh ʿal Massekhet Sotah*, ed. Lifshitz, 50–52. On Ribam as a senior student of Rabbenu Tam who studied first with Isaac b. Asher (Riba) *ha-Levi* of Speyer (d. 1133), see Urbach, ibid., 1:196–98.

3 See Moses of Coucy, *Sefer Miẓvot Gadol* (*Semag*), *lo taʿaseh* 121 (Venice, 1547), fol. 42a (= *Sefer Miẓvot Gadol ha-Shalem*, ed. Machon Yerushalayim, vol. 2 [Jerusalem, 2003], 224–25, and see esp. at n. 36). Just prior to this possible reference to Ri, *Semag* (and see esp. ms. Vatican 144, fol. 63c) records the views of Rabbenu Tam, Ribam, and Ri on a related matter: the status of a woman who had been captured by gentiles (based on *Ketubot* 26b; cf. this chapter, at nn. 11–12). See also *Sefer Mordekhai ha-Shalem ʿal Massekhet Sanhedrin*, sec. 720, ed. Horowitz, 139; Chaim Dickman, "Sefer Mordekhai ha-Shalem," in *Sefer Zikkaron ha-Ẓvi veha-Ẓedeq* (Beʾer Sheva, 2000), 38 (based on ms. Vienna 72); ms. Bodl. 778, fols. 244a–b; ms. Bodl. 667, fols. 12b–13a; ms. Vatican 141, fols. 144b–d; *Haggahot Maimuniyyot, hilkhot ʾissurei biʾah*, 18:2 [1] (*ve-ʾein nirʾeh le-Ri ve-[gam] le-Ribam*). Cf. *Tosafot Bava Batra*, s.v. *ʾispelida*; and *Sefer Or Zaruaʿ*, pt. 3, *pisqei Bava Batra*, sec. 11, ed. Machon Yerushalayim, 372.

northern French Tosafist formulations point to an additional—and even more striking—leniency offered by Rabbenu Tam in this context. If the reverting female apostate wished to return instead to her husband (rather than to resume living with her former paramour), she can do so, assuming that the husband did not wish to divorce her (and that he was not a *kohen*, since the wife of a *kohen* cannot remain with her husband if she had been tainted in any way by sexual relations outside the marriage, including those with a non-Jew).[4]

Thus, for example, the *Tosafot Yeshanim* to tractate *Yoma* compiled by Moses of Coucy (on the basis of the *Tosafot* of his teacher Judah Sirleon [d. 1224], a student and successor of Ri) records that, in addition to allowing the returning female apostate to marry her former non-Jewish paramour who had converted to Judaism, Rabbenu Tam also ruled that "the Torah nullified [*afqereh*] the seed of an idolater so that his relations do not prohibit a woman from returning to her husband." Indeed, neither part of the principle "just as she is prohibited to her husband, she is also prohibited to the adulterer" is applicable.[5] Using similar terms, a composition known as *Tosafot she-'al ha-Alfas* asserts at the beginning of tractate *Ketubot* that, according to Rabbenu Tam, sexual relations with a gentile do not have the legal standing to render a woman forbidden to her husband. Thus she also cannot become forbidden to her paramour if he has undergone conversion, even as it is obvious that only one of these relationships can be allowed to continue.[6]

4 The Provençal talmudic commentator Menaḥem b. Solomon *ha-Meiri* (d. 1316), in his *Beit ha-Beḥirah 'al Massekhet Ketubot* (3b), ed. A. Sofer (Tel Aviv, 1968), 18, and in *Beit ha-Beḥirah 'al Massekhet Sanhedrin*, ed. A. Sofer (Jerusalem, 1971), 279, cites the view of "a few of the northern French rabbis" (= Rabbenu Tam) that "the relations of a non-Jew are not considered relations that prohibit the woman to her husband, and they therefore do not prohibit her to her paramour."

5 See *Tosafot Yeshanim*, this chapter, n. 2; on the dating and provenance of these *Tosafot*, see Urbach, *Ba'alei ha-Tosafot*, 1:477–78.

6 See *Tosafot she'al ha-Alfas le-Rabbenu Mosheh b. Yom Tov mi-Londres, Massekhet Ketubot*, in *Shitat ha-Qadmonim 'al Massekhet Qiddushin*, ed. M. Blau (New York, 1970), 326 (from ms. Paris BN 314): *lo mitsera be-bi'at goy, de-bi'ato 'einah bi'ah*. Although Urbach, *Ba'alei ha-Tosafot*, 1:495–97, discounts Blau's assessment that Moses b. Yom Tov of London is the author or compiler of this composition, he

As a point of comparison, Rabiah's father, Joel b. Isaac *ha-Levi* of Bonn (d. c. 1200), ruled leniently in the case of a Jewess who had freely gone off with Christians and remained in their home for three days, until she was extricated through the payment of a bribe. R. Joel *ha-Levi* held that she was permitted in this instance to return to her husband; the relatively short duration of her stay and the fact that no conversionary activity is even intimated undoubtedly figured prominently in his ruling.[7] There is no doubt that Rabbenu Tam's rulings in these matters were the most far-reaching among rabbinic authorities in both northern France and Germany, through the twelfth century and beyond.

However, later thirteenth-century texts did not understand Rabbenu Tam's position in this way, a development that is likely the result of a limiting approach that developed over time.[8] According to these later sources, Rabbenu Tam maintains that if a woman voluntarily had sexual relations with a non-Jew while married to a Jew, her husband was required to divorce her, and she could not return to him. At the same time Rabbenu Tam held that relations with a non-Jew are not considered in halakhic terms to be the same as relations with a Jewish adulterer, to whom she would remain prohibited even after her

---

agrees that this commentary contains material from a series of northern French (and English) Tosafists.

7 See *Sefer Rabiah*, ed. D. Deblitzky (Bnei Brak, 2005), 3:107 (sec. 928); *Sefer Or Zarua'*, pt. 1, *hilkhot yibbum ve-qiddushin*, sec. 615 (Zhitomir, 1862), fol. 84a [= ed. Machon Yerushalayim (Jerusalem, 2010), fol. 506b]; and cf. Blidstein, "The Personal Status of Apostate and Ransomed Women in Medieval Jewish Law" [Hebrew], *Shenaton ha-Mishpat ha-'Ivri* 3–4 (1976–77): 61. Indeed, the brief duration and absence of evidence for promiscuity (or apostasy) in this situation suggest to Ḥayyim b. Isaac *Or Zarua'* that R. Joel was prepared to allow the wife to return to her husband in this instance even if he was a *kohen*. See *Teshuvot Maharaḥ Or Zarua'*, ed. M. Abittan (Jerusalem, 2002), 93–94 (sec. 103).

8 See the *Mordekhai* passage and its variants listed in this chapter, n. 3 (*mi-tokh kakh pasaq Rabbenu Tam de-'eshet 'ish she-hemirah datah ve-nis'et la-nokhri ve-ḥazrah ve-nigreshah min ha-Yisra'el ve-shuv nitgayyer ba'alah ha-nokhri, ve-hittir Rabbenu Tam laqaḥat 'otah le-'ishah*). See also *Encyclopedia Talmudit*, 5:298–299; and Gerald Blidstein, "The Personal Status of Apostate and Ransomed Women in Medieval Jewish Law," 52 (n. 51); R. Israel Isserlein, *Terumat ha-Deshen*, pt. 1, sec. 219, ed. S. Abittan (Jerusalem, 1991), 162; and Ḥayyim Yosef David Azulai (*Ḥida*, d. 1806), *Teshuvot Ḥayyim Sha'al*, #49.

husband had divorced her. Thus a female apostate who had returned to the Jewish community and was divorced by her husband can continue to live with her former non-Jewish paramour if he had converted.

Even this degree of leniency, however, is striking, and surely reflects Rabbenu Tam's desire to ease the path of an apostate's return to Judaism, as Urbach had noted. Given the sensitive nature of this enterprise, Yeḥi'el b. Joseph of Paris (d. c. 1260) and Asher b. Yeḥi'el (Rosh, a student of Meir of Rothenburg who fled to Spain from Germany in the early years of the fourteenth century) ratified Rabbenu Tam's allowance for the repentant woman to remain with her former paramour who had converted, while noting that their permissive rulings flowed from different lines of halakhic reasoning than those of Rabbenu Tam. R. Yeḥi'el maintained that the Christian paramour who had now converted to Judaism may remain with the woman who had reverted because, as a convert, "he is akin to a newborn" (*Yevamot* 97b) and is therefore not culpable according to Jewish law for his relationship with this woman when she was still married to her first husband.[9] Rosh also stresses that Rabbenu Tam's ruling cannot be employed to allow the woman to return to her husband. His modification of Rabbenu Tam's approach is recorded in both their names in the *Arba'ah Turim* of Rosh's son, Jacob b. Asher.[10]

---

9 See *Sefer Mordekhai 'al Massekhet Sanhedrin*, sec. 720 (end), ed. Y. Horowitz (Jerusalem, 2009), 142; and *Sefer Semaq mi-Ẓurikh*, ed. Y. Har-Shoshanim (Jerusalem, 1973), 2:50 (sec. 93). Isaac of Corbeil (d. 1280) went so far as to suggest that the approach of his father-in-law, Yeḥi'el of Paris, is ultimately insufficient to permit the woman to remain with her former paramour: "For even if the former non-Jew who converted is permitted to remain with this woman because he is 'akin to a newborn child' [due to his conversion], how are we able to now permit the woman to have relations with the convert [since she had prohibited relations with him as an adult Jewess]?" See ms. Cambridge Add. 3127 (#17556), fol. 167v (in the upper margin); and S. Emanuel, *Shivrei Luḥot*, 206–7.

10 See *Pisqei ha-Rosh* to *Ketubot*, 1:4 (end: *ve-nir'ah li le-qayyem pesaq Rabbenu Tam ve-lo mi-ta'ameh*); Jacob b. Asher, *Arba'ah Turim, Even ha-'Ezer*, sec. 178 (*hilkhot sotah*), end. Although parallel passages in *Pisqei ha-Rosh* and (the *Tosafot Shanẓ*-based) *Tosafot ha-Rosh* occasionally diverge (owing to the different origins and purposes of these works; see, e.g., Judah Galinsky, "Ha-Rosh ha-Ashkenazi bi-Sefarad: Tosafot ha-Rosh, Pisqei ha-Rosh, Yeshivat ha-Rosh," *Tarbiz* 74 [2005]: 389–421), Rosh adds this same support for Rabbenu Tam's view in *Tosafot ha-Rosh* to *Ketubot*

However, no other rabbinic authorities in thirteenth-century Germany employed—or even referred to—Rabbenu Tam's ruling that allowed a willful apostate to return and marry her former lover if he converted. It seems that on the whole German rabbinic authorities at this time were more comfortable with the approach associated with Rashi, that willful apostasy automatically prohibits a woman to her Jewish husband even if she had repented fully and returned, and with the view of Ribam, that sexual relations with a non-Jew outside an existing Jewish marriage were considered adulterous.[11]

Thus Isaiah b. Mali di Trani (RID), who studied with Simḥah b. Samuel of Speyer and was also familiar with a number of Rabbenu Tam's teachings as presented by his German students, chides a local rabbinic figure to be stringent in a case where a woman had apostatized and remained among Christians for a lengthy period of time (*nishtamdah ve-ʿamdah bein ha-goyim yamim rabbim*). After she returned to the Jewish community, the woman lived with her husband as before (*ve-hi ʿomedet taḥat baʿalah u-meshamashto ke-vatḥilah*). Since she had apostatized willingly and was therefore forbidden to her husband forever, R. Isaiah deems this result completely unacceptable, referring to it as "an evil sickness that has occurred in your community [*raʿah ḥolah shamati she-naʿasah bi-qehalkha . . . ki kevan she-merẓonah halkhah ve-ʿamdah ʿim ha-goyim ki hifqirah ʿaẓmah ve-neʾesrah (le-baʿalah) ʿolamit*]." R. Isaiah asserts that if the woman had willingly apostatized, it is also assumed that she willingly had relations with gentiles, regardless of whether there were witnesses to that effect.[12]

(3b) and *Sotah* (26b); cf. this chapter, n. 2. Cf. *Teshuvot ha-Rosh*, 32:8; and G. Blidstein, "The Personal Status of Apostate and Ransomed Women," 100–102.

11 See this chapter, n. 2, and this volume, chapter 1, n. 35; and cf. S. Goldin, *Apostasy and Jewish Identity*, 87. Rabbenu Tam's older German contemporary, Eliʿezer b. Nathan (Raban), goes so far as to suggest that a child born from relations between a married Jewish woman and a non-Jew, where the Jewess had been a willing participant (*be-raẓon*), may not be fully Jewish. See *Sefer Raban* to *Yevamot* 45b, ed. D. Deblitzky (Jerusalem, 2008), 3:434 (sec. 509).

12 See *Teshuvot ha-RID*, ed. A. Y. Wertheimer (Jerusalem, 1967), 285–88 (responsum 58); and see also G. Blidstein, "The Personal Status of Apostate and Ransomed Women," 53–54 (n. 59), and 59–60. On RID's career and presence in Ashkenaz, see Israel Ta-Shma, *Kneset Meḥqarim*, vol. 3 (Jerusalem, 2005), 9–43.

By the mid-thirteenth century in northern Europe, the possibility that a reverting female apostate could be permitted to return to her Jewish husband if her apostasy had been willful no longer existed, although some northern French Tosafists were still prepared to permit her to marry her former lover if he had converted. If a woman had apostatized under duress (without her husband), and lived in close quarters with Christians for a lengthy period of time, any halakhic strategy employed to allow her to return to her husband was predicated on a determination that she had not had sexual relations rather than on Rabbenu Tam's approach that such relations were not to be considered to be halakhically adulterous. In short, Rabbenu Tam's leniencies in these matters, which greatly discounted the halakhic impact of sexual encounters with Christians under these various circumstances, were by now almost nowhere to be found.[13] The chronological pattern of these developments dovetails with the various changes in the attitudes of rabbinic figures toward apostates that we have noted to this point, and German Tosafists on the whole seem to have been stricter than their northern French counterparts as well.[14]

Another relevant area of change in Ashkenazic rabbinic thinking has to do with the acceptance of converts to Judaism. Evidence for successful conversion to Judaism in northern France and Germany during the high Middle Ages can be found within the rabbinic literature of this period, a welcome development given the virtual absence of archival material that might shed light on this phenomenon.[15] I have argued, however, that this literature suggests

13 For further discussion of these leniencies and others found within Tosafist literature, see my "Nesu'ot Meshummadot she-Ḥazru: Heteran li-Bnei Zugan ha-Yehudi veha-Nokhri lefi Meqorot Ẓefon Ẓarefat ve-Ashkenaz Bimei ha-Benayim," in *Halakhah u-Mishpat: Sefer ha-Zikkaron li-Menaḥem Elon*, ed. A. Edrei et al. (Jerusalem, 2018), 593–606. Cf. Shalem Yahalom, "Mehemnut Historit be-Sifrut ha-Tosafot," *Madda'ei ha-Yahadut* 54 (2019), 205–08.

14 Cf. my *The Intellectual History and Rabbinic Culture of Medieval Ashkenaz* (Detroit, MI, 2013), 38–84.

15 See Jacob Katz, *Bein Yehudim le-Goyim* (Jerusalem, 1960), 84–88 [= *Exclusiveness and Tolerance* (Oxford, 1961), 77–82]; Ben Zion Wacholder, "Cases of Proselytizing in the Tosafist Responsa," *Jewish Quarterly Review* 51 (1961): 288–315;

that the Tosafists in northern France, beginning with Ri of Dampierre, were more welcoming and tolerant of prospective converts over time. This can be seen not only with regard to the interpretation of narrative talmudic passages but also in the ways they framed and discussed the halakhic requirements for conversion.[16]

Dedicated converts to Judaism tended to reach out to, or be brought to the attention of, leading Tosafists in both northern France and Germany. In turn these rabbinic figures, who were often impressed with the achievements and devotion of the converts, welcomed them into their own homes and offered guidance. However, from the days of Ri and beyond, northern French Tosafists dealt in detail with the procedural questions of how a particular conversion should be performed and with actual problems and issues that arose during the conversion process. They did not simply put forward talmudic interpretations or larger, theoretical halakhic prescriptions in these matters.

German Tosafists, on the other hand, mainly commented on the relevant Talmudic *sugyot* and issued halakhic rulings based on those *sugyot*, but their efforts tended to be demonstrably less innovative or reflective than those of their northern French counterparts. The German rabbis often presented or summarized the talmudic material with little or no comment, and did not make efforts to correlate (or to qualify) the talmudic requirements in ways the northern French authorities did. Moreover, there does not appear to have been a single instance in which a German Tosafist discusses or puts forward the case

---

Kenneth Auman, "Conversion from Christianity to Judaism in the Middle Ages" (Master's thesis, Yeshiva University, 1977); and Avraham (Rami) Reiner, "Ha-Ger: Ha-Omnam Aḥikha Hu? Li-She'elat Ma'amad ha-Gerim bi-Qehillot Ashkenaz ve-Ẓarefat ba-Me'ot ha-Yod Alef—ha-Yod Gimmel," in *Ta-Shma—Meḥqarim le-Zikhro shel Yisra'el M. Ta-Shma*, ed. M. Idel et al. (Alon Shvut, 2011), 747–69 [= idem, "L'attitude envers les proselytes en Allemagne et en France du XIe au XIIIe siècle," *Revue des Etudes Juives* 167 (2008): 99–119]. Auman's study traces developments in southern Europe as well, and also cites evidence from Christian sources throughout Europe, noting, however, that these sources sometimes appear to contain exaggerations or even fabrications.

16 See my "Approaches to Conversion in Medieval European Rabbinic Literature: From Ashkenaz to Sefarad," in *Conversion, Intermarriage, and Jewish Identity*, ed. A. Mintz and M. Stern (New York, 2015), 217–57.

of a potential convert (i.e., prior to his or her conversion) whose process of conversion generated a specific halakhic problem or query.

There are two additional considerations that may help to explain these differences between the writings of the rabbis of northern France and of Germany during the twelfth and thirteenth centuries on both the theoretical and practical levels—differences that are supported by the smaller number of converts to Judaism overall who appear to have been accepted by the Jewish communities in Germany as compared to those in northern France.[17] The first is the value or consideration of lineage, *yiḥus*, and its role in the development and ongoing existence of the Jewish communities in northern France and Germany. As Avraham Grossman has demonstrated in several studies, this concept or value was an exceptionally powerful one in Ashkenaz from the eleventh century onward. Although the rabbinic circles of northern France also placed significant value on this consideration, the rabbinic families of Germany were even more committed to it.[18]

Ri of Dampierre was aware, on the basis of a talmudic formulation, of the differences between *gerim* and those born as Jews in terms of the possibility of

17 Among the learned converts who surfaced in northern France during this period, mention should be made of R. Yehosefyah *ha-Ger*, who composed a number of *piyyutim*, and R. Avraham (b. Avraham) *ha-Ger*, whose well-known opinion on the usefulness of *gerim* in urging other Jews to fufill the commandments is cited in *Tosafot Qiddushin* 71a, s.v. *qashim*; see also E. E. Urbach, *Ba'alei ha-Tosafot*, 1:226. Interestingly, Avigdor Katz of Vienna, who studied in Germany but hailed originally from northern France, cites the approach of Avraham b. Avraham in the name of his own learned French ancestor, Menaḥem b. Pereẓ of Joigny, a Tosafist student of Rabbenu Tam. See *Perushim u-Pesaqim le-R. Avigdor*, 361: ופי׳ רבינו זקיני מיונ״י קשים הם לישראל כספחת לפי שהם מחייבים לישראל שהרי הגר שבא מטיפה פסולה הוא ירא ה׳ ומערה נפשו למצות קונו ק״ו לישראל שהיה להם לעשות כמה וכמה רצון אביהם שבשמים; cf. *Perushim u-Pesaqim*, 75, 94–97; and Israel Ta-Shma, *Minhag Ashkenaz ha-Qadmon* (Jerusalem, 1992), 204.

18 See A. Grossman, *Ḥakhmei Ashkenaz ha-Rishonim* (Jerusalem, 1981), 400–415; idem, "Yiḥus Mishpaḥah u-Meqomo ba-Ḥevrah ha-Ashkenazit be-Ashkenaz ha-Qedumah," in *Peraqim be-Toledot ha-Ḥevrah ha-Yehudit Bimei ha-Benayimu ba-'Et ha-Ḥadashah*, ed. I. Etkes et al. (Jerusalem, 1980), 9–23; idem, "Yerushat Avot ba-Hanhagah ha-Ruḥanit shel Qehillot Yisra'el Bimei ha-Benayim ha-Muqdamim," *Zion* 50 (1985): 207–20; idem, *Ḥakhmei Ẓarefat ha-Rishonim* (Jerusalem, 1995), 281.

their receiving the presence of the *Shekhinah*. Nonetheless, there was little if any discussion within northern France about the practical application of this kind of larger spiritual principle, and there is no indication that marrying converts who had been accepted into Judaism and who had expended full effort and intent during their conversion (in Ri's words, *mit'amẓin le-hitgayyer*, based on Ruth 1:18) constituted a diminution in any way in the status of the Jew who married them. Thus northern French rabbinic authorities did not hesitate to rule leniently on behalf of potential converts, and to deal with them benevolently even before they had completed the conversion process. Although no German halakhist would necessarily disagree once the conversion process had been completed, it was left to Ri of Dampierre to exclaim (in a halakhic context) that *gerim* are considered full members of the Jewish people with regard to all precepts.[19]

On the other hand, *Sefer Ḥasidim* and the contemporary German Tosafist Rabiah (responding to his father, R. Joel *ha-Levi*) enunciated an identifiable hierarchy in this regard. Rabiah utilizes the term *muvḥar shebe-'aḥikha* (the chosen ones among your brothers) in identifying the members of the larger Jewish community who must be especially careful in terms of marriage partners and thus may not marry a *giyyoret* (a female convert) or a *shifḥah kena'anit* (a female maidservant).[20] The *ḥakham* in *Sefer Ḥasidim* counsels individuals about instances when it is appropriate to marry women with "defective" or lesser *yiḥus* (lineage). In one such instance *Sefer Ḥasidim* actively follows the Mishnaic and talmudic prescription (in tractate *Yevamot*) that an impotent man should marry a *giyyoret*.[21] Given the extra measure of sensitivity to these

19 See *Tosafot Yevamot* 109b, s.v. *ra'ah 'aḥar ra'ah; Haggahot Mordekhai 'al Massekhet Yevamot*, sec. 110 (end); ms. Vercelli C1 (#30923), fol. 291d; ms. JTS Rab. 526 (#39216), fol. 190v; ms. Moscow Guenzberg 1329 (#47575), fol. 148v; *Tosafot Bava Meẓi'a* 111b, s.v. *mi-gerkha* ("*ve-khi be-khol ha-miẓvot 'ein ger ẓedeq bikhlal Yisra'el?*"); and Urbach, *Ba'alei ha-Tosafot*, 237 (n. 41).

20 See *Sefer Rabiah*, ed. D. Deblitzky (Jerusalem, 2005), 3:421, 423–34.

21 See Ephraim Shoham-Steiner, *Ḥarigim Be'al Korḥam* (Jerusalem, 2008), 230–34; *Sefer Ḥasidim (Parma)*, sec. 1911–1912; Semag, *lo ta'aseh* 118; *Pisqei ha-Rosh li-Yevamot* 8:1–3; and *Arba'ah Turim, Even ha-'Ezer*, sec. 5:1. All report the talmudic (and Mishnaic) rulings (*Yevamot* 75b–76b) that an impotent Jew may marry

considerations of *yiḥus* found among the Jewish communities in Germany, it is possible to understand the relative stringency or inflexibility that German Tosafists and other rabbinic decisors displayed with regard to the talmudic regulations governing conversion (and their relative silence on actual cases or issues of potential converts), even as they fully welcomed those who were able to make it through this arduous process.

There is also an apparent difference in the ways the Jewish communities in Germany and northern France interacted with Christian society regarding conversion. Conversion to Judaism was a grave offense throughout Latin Christendom during the medieval period, and there are a host of doctrinal and other texts that speak strongly against it.[22] However, during the late twelfth century, when efforts to prevent conversion to Judaism were largely in the hands of local bishops, and during the first half of the thirteenth century,

---

a *giyyoret*. The discussion in these sources revolves around whether the impotence was genetic or if it was caused by injury or medical procedure, and there is no indication (except in *Sefer Ḥasidim*) that this ruling was being followed in practice. Talmudic exegesis regarding the question of whether קהל גרים איקרו/לא איקרו קהל (see, e.g., *Qiddushin* 73a and *Yevamot* 77b, and see also *Tosefta Qiddushin* 5:1) does not appear to have directly impacted these discussions.

22 See, e.g., Solomon Grayzel, *The Church and the Jews in the XIIIth Century* (New York, 1966), 22–26, 59–60, 199–200; idem, *The Church and the Jews in the XIIIth Century*, vol. 2, ed. K. Stow (New York, 1989), 13–17, 102–3, 122–23; Robert Chazan, *Church, State, and Jew in the Middle Ages* (West Orange, NJ, 1980), 191–94; J. M. Ziolkowski, "Put in No-Man's Land: Guibert of Nogent's Accusations against a Judaizing and Jew-Supporting Christian," in *Jews and Christians in Twelfth-Century Europe*, ed. M. A. Signer and J. Van Engen (Notre Dame, IN, 2001), 110–22; J. R. Rosenbloom, *Conversion to Judaism: From the Biblical Period to the Present* (Cincinnati, OH, 1978), 71–83; and the varied examples collected in K. Auman, "Conversion from Christianity to Judaism," 20–43. The monk Rigord of St. Denis, in accounting for Philip Augustus's expulsion of the Jews from the royal realm in 1182, included the following claim: "When they made a long sojourn there, they grew so rich that they claimed as their own almost half of the whole city, and they had Christians in their homes as menservants and maidservants, who were open backsliders from the faith of Jesus and judaized with the Jews." See R. Chazan, *Medieval Jewry in Northern France* (Baltimore, MD, 1973), 43–45 (and this chapter, n. 40); and cf. W. C. Jordan, *The French Monarchy and the Jews* (Philadelphia, 1989), 9–10, 33–37.

when responsibility for enforcement of this restriction shifted to the mendicant orders, there is evidence suggesting that both the local bishops and the mendicant friars were generally in closer proximity to the Jewish communities in Germany (and were thus able to have a greater impact there) than they were to the Jewish communities of northern France.[23]

Indeed, while there is little mention in Jewish sources about Christian pressure against conversion to Judaism in northern France, there are several explicit and strongly worded reflections of this concern in Germany. A mid-thirteenth-century halakhic compendium, *Sefer Asufot* (whose anonymous author is linked to both Rabiah and Eleazar of Worms), writes that at present it is a dangerous, life-threatening act (*sakkanat nefashot*) to convert

---

23 On the bishops who monitored conversions, see, e.g., Alfred Haverkamp, "Baptised Jews in German Lands during the Twelfth Century," in *Jews and Christians in Twelfth-Century Europe*, ed. Signer and Van Engen, 255–310. On the monasteries and the Jews of Germany, see, e.g., J. D. Young, "Neighbors, Partners, Enemies: Jews and the Monasteries in Germany in the High Middle Ages" (PhD diss., University of Notre Dame, 2011), esp. 183–92, which documents the "neighborly relations" (and close proximities) between Jews in Germany and various monks and friars during the early thirteenth century, which also meant that anti-Christian behavior could be monitored more closely. See also Jeremy Cohen, *The Friars and the Jews* (Ithaca, NY, 1982), 229–34. In his German vernacular sermons, the Franciscan friar Berthold Von Regensburg (who was active c. 1240–1270) railed against the Jews who collaborated to lead the faithful astray, in very specific and intimate terms: "A Jew wants to make conversation with you, so that you might therefore become weaker and weaker in your belief. . . . He has thought out for a long time how he will converse with you, in order that you might thereby become even weaker in your faith. For the same reasons, it is declared by scripture and the papacy that no unlearned man should speak with a Jew." In 1233 Pope Gregory IX admonished the German clergy regarding Christians who "of their own free will adopt their [the Jews'] faith, following their rites and permit themselves to be circumcised, publicly professing themselves Jews." See S. Grayzel, *The Church and the Jews in the XIIIth Century*, 199. In the same year, the Church Council in Mainz "excommunicated such Christians as choose to live in Jewish homes in order to act as their servants," and ordered their colleagues to do so as well, "to make this decision thoroughly observed by their subjects." See Grayzel, ibid., 325; and cf. P. Tartakoff, "Testing Boundaries: Jewish Conversion and Cultural Fluidity in Medieval Europe," 740; idem, *Conversion, Circumcision, and Ritual Murder* (Philadelphia, 2020), 24–27.

anyone to Judaism, while a passage in the slightly earlier *Sefer Ḥasidim* indicates that the circumcision of a potential convert could not be performed because the Jews of his town feared doing so, lest the Christians become aware of it.[24] Meir of Rothenburg (d. 1293) describes in a responsum the case of four Jews who were ordered by the ruling authorities to testify under oath about the identity of a fifth Jew who was a *ger*; they faced confiscation of their property if they did not tell the truth. Although they would have been permitted to swear falsely (to the effect that the fifth Jew was not a convert) or to otherwise prevaricate in their responses since this situation posed a real danger to life (*sakkanat nefashot*), they testified truthfully that he was indeed a convert.

Maharam notes that, most fortuitously, this *ger* was not burned at the stake, adding that the heavens had great mercy on him, since R. Meir would have believed that "not one in a thousand is saved [from this fate], since when apostates [from Judaism to Christianity] testify against a convert [to Judaism] he is burned, how much more so when Jews testify against him." Instead the *ger* in this instance was assigned a very stiff monetary penalty, for which the other Jews involved were required to repay him, according to R. Meir. However, it was R. Meir's great astonishment that the *ger* escaped the fate of being burned

24 See *Sefer Asufot*, ms. Montefiore 134, fol. 85r [= *Zikhron Berit la-Rishonim*, ed. J. Glassberg (Berlin, 1892), 132: כ״ש בזמן הזה שהיא סכנת נפשות שאין מגיירין]; and *Sefer Ḥasidim* (*Parma*; *SḤP*), ed. J. Wistinetzki (Frankfurt, 1924), sec. 214: גר שבא להתגייר וכבר קיבל עליו כל המצות, מצות עשה לעשות ומצות לא תעשה שלא לעשות, ומבקש שימולו אותו. ובני העיר יראים למולו ויהיה בבית יהודי דר עד שימולו אותו והיה מאכילו נבילות וטריפות כי אמר כל זמן שלא מל ולא טבל הרי הוא כנכרי וכו׳. In the parallel passage in *Sefer Ḥasidim* (*Bologna*), ed. R. Margoliot (Jerusalem, 1957), sec. 690, the reason the circumcision was delayed (because of fear on part of the community) is not found, perhaps reflecting a level of censorship. An even stronger expression of this fear is found in the fifteenth-century *Sefer Maharil: Minhagim shel Rabbenu Ya'aqov Moelin* (d. 1427), ed. S. Spitzer (Jerusalem, 1989), 627 (*liqqutim*), sec. 61: אמה. הבא להתגייר עכשיו בינינו בין האומות והישראל מתיירא שיפרסם ויבוא לידי סכנה, מותר לדחותו. ואם מחזיק בו מלהניחו עד שיגיירנו מותר לגלות למושל למען הציל עצמם וכל ישראל מן הסכנה; and cf. this volume, chapter 1, n. 27. For passages in *Sefer Ḥasidim* that express the concern of the Jewish communities about Christian authorities who might try to thwart the reversion of an apostate (or otherwise mete out punishments), see this volume, chapter 1, n. 21.

at the stake in this instance (a punishment that was apparently otherwise enforced), which is the most striking aspect of his responsum.[25]

A responsum by Ḥayyim Eli'ezer, son of Isaac *Or Zarua'* and a student of Meir of Rothenburg, mentions the case of a certain Rabbi Isaac who circumcised converts to Judaism; as a result, his community incurred a very serious charge (an *'alilah*, which included the threat of physical persecution) by the Christian authorities.[26] Taken together these various rabbinic sources suggest that the pressure brought to bear by Christians in Germany when their co-religionists sought to convert to Judaism often involved much more than sharp rhetoric.[27]

Although manuscripts of *siddurim* and *maḥzorim* from northern France as well as western and eastern German rites from the thirteenth and fourteenth

---

25 See *Teshuvot Maharam b. Barukh defus Prague*, #103; and see also I. A. Agus, *R. Meir of Rothenburg* (New York, 1947), 2:666–67 (#772); and K. Auman, "Conversion from Christianity to Judaism," 24–25, 33–34.

26 See *Teshuvot Maharaḥ Or Zarua'*, #142 (end), ed. M. Abittan (Jerusalem, 2002), 133: אכן אם הקהל באו מחמת כן לעלילה ואפילו יחיד שבא מחמת כן לעלילה שסבורין הגויים שהוא עשה זה המעשה וידוע להם בוודאי שיהודי אחד עשה כן אכן אינם יודעים מי עשהו ובאים להעליל על זה אתה עשית, מותר לו לומר לגוים פלוני עשה ולא אני. ואפילו אם העושה לא נתכוין לרעה אלא לדבר מצוה, כעובדא דרבינו יצחק שמל גרים ומתוך כך באו הקהל לידי עלילה. Ṛ. Hayyim concludes by indicating that this episode was (also) recorded in his father's *Sefer Or Zarua'* (to which he composed an abridgment). Although this material has not been located within any extant versions of *Sefer Or Zarua'*, perhaps due to censorship (cf. J. Katz, *Bein Yehudim le-Goyim*, 84, n. 53), a brief reference to this situation is found in *Pesaqim le- Rabbenu Ḥayyim b. Yiẓḥaq Or Zarua'*, ed. M. Blau (New York, 1997), vol. 2, 377 (sec. 33): ר׳ יצחק מל גרים ומתוך כך באו הקהל לידי עלילה. ומר מאיר אמר לשר דיבור המביא את ר׳ יצחק לידי הפסד, מר מאיר פטור. ואפילו אם מסר את ר׳ יצחק להדיא על דבר זה. This passage was inserted between the end of *hilkhot ẓedaqah* and the beginning of *hilkhot ḥalah*. See also *Teshuvot Maharaḥ*, ed. Abittan, 275 (*teshuvot ḥadashot mi-ktav yad*), #14: וכן דן אבא מארי בר׳ יצחק שמל גרים אפי׳ מזכירו בפירוש כדי להציל עצמו, וראייה משבע בן בכרי וכן הסכימו כל הגדולים.

27 Isaac *Or Zarua'* spent part of his student days in northern France (see Urbach, *Ba'alei ha-Tosafot*, 1:436–39; and Uzi Fuchs, "Iyyunim be-Sefer Or Zarua' le-R. Yiẓḥaq b. Mosheh of me-Vienna" [Master's thesis, Hebrew University, 1993], 12–40), but he lived for the most part, and certainly during his mature years, as a leading rabbinic authority in Germany and Austria. His son, R. Ḥayyim, lived in a variety of locales in Germany and Austria; but there is no evidence that he was ever in northern France. See Noah Goldstein, "R. Ḥayyim Eli'ezer ben Isaac Or Zarua'—His Life and Work" (DHL diss., Yeshiva University, 1959), 23–26.

centuries retain the blessings to be recited at the circumcision of a *ger*, their presence in these liturgies may be akin to what is found in *Sefer Asufot*. The laws and procedures for conversion must be "kept on the books" as a bona fide part of the halakhic and ritual process. Nonetheless, the extent to which these blessings had occasion to be recited in medieval Germany remains unclear, even as their recitation in northern France during this period appears to have been more common.[28]

In any case, the positive attitude toward accepting dedicated converts, and the efforts to make their transition easier from both the halakhic and communal perspectives—which appear to have become fully developed in northern France—began during the period of Ri of Dampierre and then ran through the thirteenth century. This is precisely when the more demanding and restrictive measures for apostates who sought to revert were developed, accompanied also by the downgrading of the status of those who became and remained apostates from Judaism. Given the ever-widening gap between Judaism and Christianity at this time, rabbinic authorities at least in northern France sought to ease the way for dedicated converts from Christianity—who had demonstrated their deep commitment to Judaism—to be embraced by the Jewish community. At the same time those apostates who sought to revert to Judaism were now challenged to renounce their dalliance with Christianity in a more pronounced way, and even to openly state and demonstrate their religious recommitment. Concomitantly, those apostates who chose to remain attached to the Christian community and did not demonstrate any interest in reversion were considered

28 See, e.g., ms. Parma (de Rossi) 605 (#13061; a *maḥzor* of the western Ashkenazic rite), fol. 143r; ms. Cluny Museum 12290 (#14772; a Worms *siddur*), fols. 68v–69r; ms. Jerusalem NLI 4°682 (B398; an eastern Ashkenazic rite), fol. 41r; ms. Parma 3518 (#14025; a northern French *maḥzor*), fol. 15r; ms. Parma (de Rossi) 854 (#13017; an Italian rite), fol. 154v; and ms. Moscow-Guenzberg 1230 (#48939; a Spanish/Aragonese *mahzor*), fol. 169r. On the incidence and significance of interpretational, methodological, and halakhic differences between the Tosafists in northern France and Germany, see this chapter, n. 14, and see also my "From Germany to Northern France and Back Again: A Tale of Two Tosafist Centers," in *Regional Identities and Cultures of Medieval Jews*, ed. J. Castaño et al. (London, 2018), 149–52.

by these same rabbinic authorities as having gone over to the "other side" in a profound and even visceral way.

There are several significant and fairly widespread temporal factors and changes in Christian views and doctrines that arose during this period which might well have impacted rabbinic thinking about apostates from Judaism (and about conversion to Judaism). Robert Chazan has drawn attention to the list presented by the rabbinic author and chronicler Ephraim b. Jacob of Bonn (d. 1197) in his *Sefer Zekhirah*. This work documents eleven small-scale but nonetheless intense persecutions that took place in northern Europe between 1171 and 1196, in which Jews were killed in a particularly harsh or cruel manner, and Jewish property and assets were taken and destroyed in unprecedented ways. Half of these incidents took place in the Rhineland or elsewhere in Germany: Cologne in 1171, Boppard (1180), Neuss (1186), Speyer (1196), and again in Boppard and in Austria (also in 1196). Two incidents occurred in northern France, beginning with the ritual murder charge in Blois in 1171, and two occurred in England. Ramifications from the Third Crusade were also felt in Germany around 1190. And already in 1147 in Wurzburg, Jews were accused by Christians of an act of ritual murder just a few years after the first medieval European ritual murder charge had been leveled in Norwich, England (in 1144). The larger collection of incidents, which occurred nearly a hundred years after the First Crusade, was precipitated, according to Chazan, by the deepening Christian perception of the Jews as enemies.[29]

It stands to reason that an apostate who joined the Christian community in the late twelfth century or early thirteenth century would be seen by rabbinic authorities, as well as by the Jewish community at large, in an increasingly unfavorable light. The growing rabbinic demand for a demonstrative act of contrition for a reverting apostate—which would show in a more graphic way that a significant line had been crossed, whether the apostasy had been

29 R. Chazan, *Medieval Stereotypes and Modern Antisemitism* (Berkeley, CA, 1997), 53–78; idem, *Fashioning Jewish Identity in Medieval Western Christendom* (Cambridge, 2004), 356–58. On the ritual murder charge in Wurzburg, see *Sefer Zekhirah: Seliḥot ve-Qinot le-R. Ephraim b. Ya'aqov*, ed. A. M. Habermann (Jerusalem, 1970), 22–23.

motivated by venal or more ideological considerations—is well understood in light of this series of events and others, and the worsening perceptions that accompanied them.

Even more significant is the formulation of Pope Innocent III in 1201, in his letter to the Archbishop of Arles, which effectively expands the meaning of voluntary conversion to Christianity to include even those who were baptized only as a last-ditch means of avoiding death.[30] Innocent's new interpretation, which addressed a problem that had been raised at several points during the twelfth century,[31] meant that virtually every Jewish apostate to Christianity

30 See Solomon Grayzel, *The Church and the Jews in the XIIIth Century*, vol. 1 (New York, 1966), 101–3; and cf. ibid., 92–93. In 1199, Innocent III instructed a bishop to make sure that a convert from Judaism and his daughter had sufficient food and clothing. He writes to others in this regard at the same time (and again in 1201, 1206, and 1213) to ensure that former Jews who converted to Christianity had what they needed (and sometimes more), and that they were able to marry into the Christian community. See also Shlomo Simonsohn, *The Apostolic See and the Jews: History* (Toronto, 1991), 52–57, 79, 98–99, 154–56. Innocent's active approach was continued by Honorius III, Gregory IX, and Innocent IV (see Grayzel, ibid., 136–39, 164–67, 212–13, 220–21, 222–25, 248–49, 255–57, 284–85). Gregory IX in particular attempted to make sure that no Jew regretted his decision to convert (by providing support, granting benefices and prebends, and ensuring that a convert to Christianity suffered no loss of any property they had acquired as Jews); and these practices continued into the 1240s and beyond. See Rebecca Rist, *Popes and Jews, 1095–1291* (Oxford, 2016), 208–12; and see also Chaviva Levin, "Jewish Conversion to Christianity in Medieval Northern Europe: Encountered and Imagined, 1100–1300" (PhD diss., New York University, 2006), 89–91, 241–57.

31 As a result of the First Crusade, the forced baptism of Jews (including children) became an important issue for theologians and canon lawyers. See Kenneth Stow, "Conversion, Apostasy and Apprehensiveness: Emicho of Flonheim and Fear of the Jews in the Twelfth Century," *Speculum* 76 (2001): 911–33; S. Grayzel, *The Church and the Jews in the XIIIth Century*, vol. 2 (Detroit, MI, 1989), 4–7; Kenneth Pennington, "Gratian and the Jews," *Bulletin of Medieval Canon Law* 31 (2014): 111–24; and cf. Deena Klepper, "Pastoral Literature in Local Context: Albert of Diessen's *Mirror of Priests* on Christian-Jewish Coexistence," *Speculum* 92 (2017): 701–8. Popes in both the twelfth and thirteenth centuries issued letters to individuals in response to questions about protecting Jews from forced conversion. For additional Church discussions during the twelfth and thirteenth centuries, see Simonsohn, *The Apostolic See and the Jews*, 42, 253–57, 349–50. Against Thomas Aquinas, who held that children could not be baptized against their parents' will,

was considered according to Christian dogma to be a willing Christian. Constitution 70 of the Fourth Lateran Council in 1215 required that a convert to Christianity give up the Jewish rite completely. Indeed, in light of this rule, and with the support of several European monarchs, friars began to set up "Houses of Converts," where converts from Judaism could be instructed in Christianity and be shielded from attempts by other Jews to bring them back to Judaism.[32]

Moreover, a bull promulgated by Pope Clement IV in 1267 states that a convert to Christianity who reverts to Judaism—even if he had been baptized against his will—is to be treated as a heretic, and a passage in the *Schwabenspiegel* dictates that a baptized Jew who denies the Christian faith and continues to practice Judaism is to be burned as a heretic.[33] As we have seen, thirteenth-century Ashkenazic rabbinic formulations refer to ritual immersion as a means of removing the impurity of Christianity (*zuhama*), or as a demonstrative sign of change in status (*la'asot hekkera*), which might well mean that this requirement was seen on some level, even by the rabbinic leadership, as a necessary form of un-baptism.[34]

John Duns Scotus (c. 1266–1308) held that children could be taken from their parents and baptized.

32 See S. Simonsohn, *The Apostolic See and the Jews*, 267, 275; R. Rist (this chapter, n. 30); and *The Church in the Medieval Town*, ed. T. R. Slater and G. Rosser (London, 1998), 50–51; Lauren Fogle, *The King's Converts* (Lanham, MD, 2019), 21–28, 77–82, 130–39.

33 See S. Grayzel, *The Church and the Jews in the XIIIth Century*, 2:14–15, 102–4, 122; S. Simonsohn, *The Apostolic See and the Jews*, 345–48; Edward Fram, "Perception and Reception of Repentant Apostates in Medieval Ashkenaz and Premodern Poland," *AJS Review* 21 (1996): 304–5; Jeremy Cohen, *The Friars and the Jews*, 48–49; Bernard Rosenzweig, "Apostasy in the Late Middle Ages in Ashkenazic Jewry," *Dine Israel* 10–11 (1981–83): 70–71. However, papal policy in this matter was not monolithic. Cf. J. M. Elukin, "The Discovery of Self: Jews and Conversion in the Twelfth Century," in *Jews and Christians in Twelfth-Century Europe*, ed. Signer and Van Engen, 63–76; and Haverkamp, "Baptised Jews in German Lands During the Twelfth Century," 260–67, 291–98.

34 For references in Jewish polemical literature, chronicles, and *piyyut* during this period to the baptism as pollution (*tinnuf*) or defilement (*shemez̧*), whose waters are characterized as putrid or having stench, see, e.g., S. L. Einbinder, *Beautiful Death* (Princeton, NJ, 2002), 34–35; David Berger, *The Jewish-Christian Debate in the High Middle Ages* (Philadelphia, 1979), 94, sec. 78; and Elisheva Carlebach, *Divided Souls* (New Haven, CT, 2001), 18. Cf. this volume, chapter 6, nn. 1–2.

We should also bear in mind that, unlike the more demanding physical forms of *tiqqunei teshuvah*, which were often accompanied by some type of public humiliation, ritual immersion would not have been seen as an especially arduous rite of reentry into the Jewish community, especially if it could be undertaken privately by the penitent. Nonetheless, at least some of the Tosafists and Ashkenazic rabbinic authorities who supported the need for ritual immersion were positing the existence of a gap between the apostate and the Jewish community that Rashi and other rabbinic figures did not recognize.

As the texts presented in chapter 2 have shown, the practice of ritual immersion for a returning apostate in northern France and Germany during the twelfth and thirteenth centuries enjoyed a good deal of rabbinic approbation and even encouragement. The identification of the Jews as a central and unique enemy of Christendom—and that apostates from Judaism to Christianity were now considered by the Church, or by the papacy at least, to be irrefutably Christian—seems to have created a significant moment in the history of *halakhah* with regard to the status of apostates in Ashkenazic society. Included among the German Tosafists and halakhists in the first third of the thirteenth century who required or supported immersion for a reverting apostate are Rabiah, Simḥah of Speyer, and Eleazar of Worms, all of whom were teachers of Isaac *Or Zarua'* of Vienna, and contemporaries of Abraham of Regensburg and Barukh of Mainz. R. Abraham, R. Barukh, and R. Isaac *Or Zarua'*, who maintained that an apostate was not required to perform *ḥaliẓah* at all (and was incapable of doing so from the halakhic perspective), may also have arrived at their (new) policy on the basis of larger halakhic and social considerations that were tied to a reassessment of the nature of apostasy. Just as Rashi's initial use of and support for the principle of *'af 'al pi she-ḥata Yisra'el hu* (and its application to individual Jews) were likely undertaken, at least in part, as a response to the increased number of conversions among Jews in the Rhineland and elsewhere owing to the First Crusade, these German Tosafists may have adjusted their halakhic positions in light of contemporary events as well, as a means of strengthening their communities and protecting them from further spiritual if not physical damage at the hands of the Christian majority and its authorities.

The sequence of persecutions highlighted in *Sefer Zekhirah* did not occur in a vacuum. Recent studies have drawn attention to the newly articulated and pernicious accusations that churchmen leveled against Jews in this period and in the decades before. Already in the first quarter of the twelfth century, Rupert, abbot of Deutz (Cologne, d. 1129), harshly characterizes the Jews as a highly jealous and particularistic people, marked by greed and irrationality. Rupert reiterates again and again that Jewish hands are covered in the blood of Jesus, and that they begrudged Christians the salvation that Jesus had brought them. Moreover, Jews show only contempt for all other peoples as well; they are truly and irrevocably at odds with Christendom.[35]

In even sharper and more vituperative tones, Peter the Venerable (Petrus Venerablis), abbot of Cluny (d. 1156), contends that the Jews had become the archenemies of Christianity, and the gap that existed between the two religions was widened and sharpened as a result. Writing to the early Capetian ruler Louis VII (who himself sought to severely punish apostates from Christianity who sought to revert to their original religion) in support of the Second Crusade, Peter attacks the Jews as "vile blasphemers and far worse than the Saracens, not far away from us but right in our midst," who blaspheme, abuse, and trample on Jesus and the sacraments "so freely and insolently and with impunity." He continues, "How can zeal for God nourish God's children if the Jews, enemies of Jesus and of the Christians remain totally unpunished?" Peter concludes with a paraphrase of the verse in Psalms 139:21, "O Lord shall I not hate those who hate you and be consumed with enmity for your enemies?" In light of his shrill charges, Peter goes on to say that he did not wish for

35 See David Timmer, "Biblical Exegesis and the Jewish-Christian Controversy in the Early Twelfth Century," *Church History* 58 (1989): 309–21; Anna Sapir Abulafia, "The Ideology of Reform and Changing Ideas Concerning Jews in the Works of Rupert of Deutz and Hermannus Quondam Iudeus," *Jewish History* 7 (1993): 44–57; idem, *Christians and Jews in the Twelfth-Century Renaissance* (London, 1995), 123–40; and J. C. Schmitt, *The Conversion of Herman the Jew* (Philadelphia, 2003), 130–40.

Christians to physically attack the Jews, but he calls for depriving the Jews of much of their assets: "Let their lives be spared but their money taken away." In short, Peter sought to punish the Jews for the crucifixion through severe financial impositions.

In his treatise *Against the Inveterate Obduracy of the Jews*, in which Peter also cites and attacks the Talmud, he characterizes the Jew as a wretched enemy of God, a reprehensible blasphemer, and an agent of the devil. Indeed, the lies and deceits of the Jews have surpassed even those of Satan, the father of lies. Judaism itself is described as perfidy, perversity, wickedness, and deception. Moreover, perhaps expanding on a claim made by Odo, abbot in Tournai and later Bishop of Cambrai (d. 1113), some thirty years before,[36] Peter, citing Psalms 49 and Isaiah 6 in support of his claim, argues that a Jew is not human but instead animal-like: "Indeed, I dare not designate you a man, lest I lie. For I see that in you is extinguished, indeed buried, that which separates animals and beasts and raises man above them—reason." In Peter's view the "Jewish beast" is guided by the "reprehensible" Talmud, which causes the rejection of the teachings of the prophets.[37] Although the approaches of Rupert and Peter

---

36 See Anna Sapir Abulafia, "Twelfth-Century Christian Expectations of Jewish Conversion: A Case Study of Peter of Blois," *Aschkenas* 8 (1998): 50; and see also ibid., 45–46, 69–70. Cf. I. M. Resnick, *Marks of Distinction* (Washington, DC, 2002), 40–41. For a similar degree of rancor in the writings of Guibert of Nogent, see Gilbert Dahan, "Saint Anselme, les juifs, le Judaisme," in *Les Mutations socioculturelles au tournant XIe-XIIe siècles* (Spicilegium BeccenseII), ed. R. Foreville (Paris, 1984), 521–34; *A Monk's Confession: The Memoirs of Guibert of Nogent*, trans. P. J. Archambaut (University Park, PA, 1996), 82 (n. 133); and Jay Rubinstein, *Guibert of Nogent: Portrait of a Medieval Mind* (New York, 2002), 115, 120.

37 See Peter the Venerable, *Epistolae* 130, in *Letters*, ed. G. Constable (Cambridge, MA, 1967), 1:327–30; idem, *Adversus Iudeorum inveteram duritiem*, ed. Y. Friedman (Turnhout, 1985), 125–26; and idem, *Against the Inveterate Obdurancy of the Jews*, trans. I. M. Resnick (Washington, DC, 2013), 211. See also Amos Funkenstein, "Changes in the Patterns of Christian Anti-Jewish Polemic" [Hebrew], *Zion* 33 (1968): 137–43; Gavin Langmuir, *Toward a Definition of Antisemitism* (Berkeley, CA, 1990), 197–208; Anna Sapir Abulafia, *Christians and Jews in the Twelfth-Century Renaissance*, chapter 6; Jeremy Cohen, *Living Letters of the Law: Ideas of the Jew in Medieval Christianity* (Berkeley, CA, 1999), 245–70; Ryan Szpiech, *Conversion and Narrative* (Philadelphia, 2013), 70–73, 82–86; Giacomo Todeschini, "The Origin of a Medieval Anti-Stereotype: The Jews as Receivers of Stolen Goods," in

were not adopted uncritically by subsequent Christian thinkers in their theological writings, there is no doubt that these Church figures introduced a new element of blatant animus into the medieval Christian attack on the Jews and Judaism. It is difficult to imagine that the Jews in northern France remained unaware of Peter's words and sentiments (or of other Christians for whom they resonated), given Cluny's central place in the expansive network of Benedictine monasteries on the one hand, and the frequent social and economic (if not polemical) interactions between Christians and Jews on the other. The same holds true for the teachings of Rupert as well.[38]

Indeed, Haym Soloveitchik, citing earlier studies by Gavin Langmuir, maintains that the hatred of Christians for Jews moved between the First and Second Crusades from a "rational" form of anti-Judaism to a visceral hatred. The ritual murder charges that became almost commonplace during the second half of the twelfth century reflect these developments, as do the increasing references in popular literature to the Jews as grotesque and satanic figures. In Soloveitchik's view, as a result of these developments, leading French Tosafists, including Rabbenu Tam and Ri, rejected available leniencies with regard to the handling of Christian wine, which also would have eased economic dealings involving this wine.[39] Again, is it likely that the range of increasingly

---

The Jewish-Christian Encounter in Medieval Preaching, ed. J. Adams and J. Hanska (New York, 2015), 240–47; R. Chazan, *From Anti-Judaism to Anti-Semitism* (Cambridge, 2016), 119–34; I. M. Resnick, Preface to *Jews in Medieval England*, ed. M. A. Krummel and T. Pugh (Palgrave, 2017).

38 See Resnick, *Marks of Distinction*, 39–40. His conclusion is that "Peter's attack on the rationality of the Jews . . . likely influenced a much larger circle." On the exchange of ideas between Jews and Christians in northern Europe at this time, see my *The Intellectual History and Rabbinic Culture of Medieval Ashkenaz*, 84–110; and cf. Isaac Gottlieb, "Rupert and Rashi," *Journal of the Ancient Near Eastern Society* 33(2018): 23–59. Jeremy Cohen, *The Friars and the Jews*, 43, writes that "the most predominant attitude of the friars [whose work began in earnest during the first half of the thirteenth century] toward the Jews was marked by an aggressive missionary spirit and often violent animosity."

39 See Haym Soloveitchik, *Yeinam* (New York, 2016), 109–21. See also Alyssa Gray, "R. Eliezer of Metz's Twelfth-Century Exclusion from Charity of the Jewish *Avaryan be-Mezid* ('Deliberate Transgressor')," in *Approaches to Poverty in Medieval Europe*, ed. S. A. Farmer (Turnhout, 2016), 85; P. Tartakoff, "Testing Boundaries:

negative attitudes toward apostates that has been documented with regard to *ḥaliẓah* (and other halakhic issues) in Germany, and the increased religious requirements placed on a returning apostate in both Germany and northern France, also reflect (or respond to) these changes in Christian attitudes and rhetoric concerning the Jews. Throughout much of his reign, Louis VII granted promises to the Jews for their physical safety and assorted economic and communal privileges, yet he decreed in 1144 that converts to Christianity were forbidden to revert to their prior religion under penalty of exile or even death, although there is no evidence that this decree was subsequently applied with any consistency.[40]

Within Ashkenazic society the apostate was becoming something of a spiritual enemy as well. The apostate at the very least was seen as an ally of the increasingly hostile enemy of the Jews that Christianity had become.[41] German

---

Jewish Conversion and Cultural Fluidity in Medieval Europe," 736–37; and cf. A. Grossman, "Bein 1012 le-1096: Ha-Reqa ha-Tarbuti veha-Ḥevrati le-Qiddush ha-Shem be-TaTN"U," in *Yehudim mul ha-Ẓelav*, ed. Y. T. Assis et al. (Jerusalem, 2000), 61–65. For a rather remarkable passage associated with Ri which has gone virtually unremarked in modern scholarship, see *Tosafot 'Avodah Zarah* 26a, s.v. *'avodat kokhavim*. In discussing the conditions under which Jews may enter the homes of gentiles to be healed (*le-rappotam*, which he was prepared to allow; cf. *Haggahot Maimuniyyot, hilkhot ma'akhalot 'asurot* 14:2), Ri nonetheless prohibits leaving young children alone in these homes for two reasons: the fear that they will be physically harmed (*shefikhut damim*); and, if the children are somewhat older, that they may be drawn into heresy (*yamshikhum le-minut*). The second reason is not mentioned by the Talmud and does not appear in the *Tosafot* variants. Cf. Moses of Coucy, *Sefer Miẓvot Gadol, lo ta'aseh* 45 (Venice, 1547), fol. 10c; and *Teshuvot R. Yiẓḥaq ben Shmu'el mi-Dampierre*, ed. Roth and Reiner, 93–94 (sec. 60).

40 See Kenneth Stow, *Jewish Dogs: An Image and Its Interpreters* (Stanford, CA, 2006), 90–91, 112–13; R. Chazan, *Medieval Jewry in Northern France*, 32–33, 37–38, 40–41, 44–45; and cf. D. Berger, "Jacob Katz on Jews and Christians in the Middle Ages," in *The Pride of Jacob: Essays on Jacob Katz and His Work*, ed. J. Harris (Cambridge, MA, 2002), 54–55.

41 Cf. E. Fram, "Perception and Reception of Repentant Apostates," 307–9; and R. Reiner, "Ha-Ger: Ha-Omnam Aḥikha Hu," this chapter, n. 15. See also S. Einbinder, *Beautiful Death*; and D. Berger, *The Jewish-Christian Debate in the High Middle Ages*, this chapter, n. 34.

Tosafists took the lead in incorporating these views, thereby limiting the doctrine of *'af 'al pi she-ḥata Yisra'el hu* in several ways. French Tosafists and rabbinic figures adjusted their position vis-à-vis the apostate to a lesser extent, perhaps because they remained more loyal, at least to a degree, to the earlier view developed by Rashi.[42] Only with regard to money-lending at interest did several northern French Tosafists in the second half of the twelfth century suggest a significant deviation from Rashi's approach, in both theory and practice. By the middle of the thirteenth century, however, there is mounting evidence in northern France as well for the rising tensions in rabbinic circles concerning the status of an apostate. This emerges from the Tosafist academy at Evreux, which mandated the immersion of a reverting apostate as a thinly disguised reversal of his baptism, comparing the immersion of a reverting apostate in halakhic terms directly to the requirement for immersing a Canaanite slave at the point of his release, when he becomes a fully obligated member of the Jewish religious community.

To be sure, certain rabbinic determinations about the halakhic status of an apostate were made without necessarily taking the larger changes in the relationship between Judaism and Christianity (and Jews and Christians) into account. Rabbinic decision-making must proceed first and foremost along established halakhic lines. As we have seen especially at the end of the last chapter, there are points of interaction among apostates, former apostates, and other Jews where the halakhic decision was made not so much according to the status of an apostate as a Jew in the larger sense, but rather in light of the halakhic procedures and rabbinic prerogatives that were involved. This was the case for distributing inheritance and accepting testimony, and in situations where the returning apostate may not be entitled to return to all of his earlier

42 Although he will disagree with Rashi at times, Isaiah di Trani was generally quite devoted to Rashi's comments and views, frequently referring to Rashi as the *moreh* in both his talmudic and biblical commentaries and writings. RID's loyalty is clearly manifest with respect to the status of an apostate. Like Rashi, RID held that it was fundamentally prohibited to lend to an apostate at interest, that an apostate must perfom *ḥaliẓah*, and that a returning apostate need not immerse himself in a ritual bath. See *Pisqei ha-RID le-Masskhet 'Avodah Zarah* (Jerusalem, 2006), 40–41 (and see also *Tosafot ha-RID* to *'Avodah Zarah* 26b), and this volume, chapter 4, n. 56.

roles (such as pronouncing the priestly blessing), even as he can be readmitted to the Jewish community as a member in good standing. Nonetheless, the changing societal and religious factors that affected halakhic considerations of apostasy which have been outlined in this chapter can also account for the pronounced tendency during the thirteenth century to limit Rabbenu Tam's allowances concerning a female apostate who had relations with a non-Jew but now sought to return, and for the increased support for converts from Christianity to Judaism during this same period.

The approaches toward apostates maintained by Rashi and his Tosafist critics in both Germany and northern France were debated anew from the fourteenth century onward.[43] Indeed, the present study demonstrates that the sharp distinction made by Jacob Katz between the Middle Ages and the early modern period regarding the image and perception of the apostate—that an apostate was considered to be less Jewish by both halakhic authorities and Ashkenazic society as a whole only in the latter period, as the societal gap between Judaism and Christianity changed with the onset of modernity—must be reconsidered.[44]

To this point we have encountered quite a few examples and situations already during the medieval period where Tosafists treated active apostates and those who sought to revert in a more exclusionary and demanding way

---

43 See B. Rosensweig, "Apostasy in the Late Middle Ages in Ashkenazic Jewry," 55–79; Emese Kozma, "Seder Teshuvah li-Meshumadim she-Ḥozrim la-Yahadut be-Austriah ba-Me'ah ha-Ḥamesh 'Esreh," *'Alei Sefer* 24–25 (2015): 189–95; and E. Fram, "Perception and Reception of Repentant Apostates," 316–21. See also Shlomo Spitzer, "Pisqei Rabbotenu shebe-Ashkenaz be-Dor ha-Samukh li-Gezerat Quf Tet," *Moriah* 8:2–3 (1978): 6 [sec. 18]; *Teshuvot Maharil he-Ḥadashot*, ed. Y. Satz (Jerusalem, 1977), 347–48 (sec. 207); *She'elot u-Teshuvot Mahariq*, #85; and *Teshuvot u-Pisqei Mahariq he-Ḥadashim*, ed. E. Pines (Jerusalem, 1970), 90–91.

44 See J. Katz, *Exclusiveness and Tolerance*, 48–51 [= *Bein Yehudim le-Goyim*, 50–52], and idem, *Halakhah ve-Qabbalah*, 267–69. Cf. Elisheva Carlebach, *Divided Souls*, 28–29; idem, "Early Modern Ashkenaz in the Writings of Jacob Katz," in *The Pride of Jacob*, ed. J. Harris, 77; and idem, "'Ich will dich nach Holland schicken': Amsterdam and the Reversion to Judaism of German-Jewish Converts," in *Secret Conversions to Judaism in Early Modern Europe*, ed. M. Muslow and R. H. Popkin (Leiden, 2004), 51–59.

than their Ashkenazic predecessors had. Indeed, recognition that this range of views existed already during the thirteenth century goes a long way toward explaining some seemingly anomalous responses of certain rabbinic figures and Church authorities alike.

In the two final chapters, which extend into the late medieval and early modern periods, the impact of the talmudic and halakhic formulations by the Tosafists will be assessed. As we have seen, in the aftermath of the First Crusade and the subsequent anti-Jewish violence and Church pressures that dotted the twelfth and thirteenth centuries, the Tosafists developed, adjusted, and expanded the teachings of Rashi and others on the nature of apostasy and the halakhic status of apostates in some rather suggestive ways. Well before the riots of 1391, episodes of both forced and voluntary conversion began to increase in Spain as well. Leading Spanish rabbinic authorities who received quite a bit of Ashkenazic talmudic and related rabbinic writings over the course of the thirteenth century mobilized this newer and more focused material to provide support and guidance for their own policies concerning apostates. Interestingly, as the modern period begins, the Spanish halakhic material about apostates, which was derived in large measure from Ashkenazic approaches and sources, makes its way to Eastern Europe. This material sets the tone there for rabbinic policy concerning apostates, on occasion to an even greater extent than the original Ashkenazic formulations themselves.

Leading rabbinic decisors in Germany and Austria during the fifteenth century also encountered a fair amount of apostasy, along with continuing Christian pressure on those Jews who had apostatized to guard against their return to Judaism. As we shall see, R. Israel Isserlein and his close colleagues also made significant use of the earlier Tosafist materials to address these situations. However, as devoted Ashkenazic Jews who sought to associate themselves with the teachings and practices of Ashkenaz in its heyday,[45] these rabbinic authorities were a bit more concerned with explaining why they rejected the approach of Rashi, which occurred in more than a few instances.

---

45 See Yedidya Dinari, *Ḥakhmei Ashkenaz be-Shilhei Yemei ha-Benayim* (Jerusalem, 1984), 9–21.

6

REVERTING APOSTATES IN CHRISTIAN SPAIN

Sources and Strategies

An Ashkenazic rationale for the immersion of a reverting apostate appears in the rabbinic literature of Spain around 1300, although it has gone largely unnoticed. In an article published four decades ago, Joseph Shatzmiller discussed a ceremony or rite that Yosef Hayyim Yerushalmi had highlighted a decade earlier, which was found in the confessor's manual of the inquisitor Bernard Gui (dating from the early 1320s in southern France). According to the information Bernard received and gathered from lapsed Christians, a Jew who converted to Christianity but subsequently decided to return to Judaism was required to undergo a ritual immersion (*tevilah*) with rather extensive and even harsh preparations, accompanied by a renunciation of the Christian religion and a declaration of faith to the dictates of the Torah.[1]

Shatzmiller, following Yerushalmi, suggests that this ceremony might best be thought of as a kind of "counter-baptism" or "de-Christianization" rite, especially given that, prior to the immersion of the one who wished to return, "Jews would rub sand over his entire body, but especially on his forehead, chest and arms, that is, on the places which during baptism received the holy

1 See Y. H. Yerushalmi, "The Inquisition and the Jews of France in the Time of Bernard Gui," *Harvard Theological Review* 63 (1970): 363–67; J. Shatzmiller, "Converts and Judaizers in the Early Fourteenth Century," *Harvard Theological Review* 74 (1981): 63–77.

chrism." However, Shatzmiller then presents texts from two leading Spanish rabbinic authorities on this issue. Two similar responsa are found in the large collection of *Teshuvot ha-Rashba* (Solomon b. Abraham ibn Adret of Barcelona, d. c. 1310), both of which appear to rely heavily on geonic statements; indeed, the second of these texts begins with the phrase "*nish'al ha-gaon*" (the gaon was asked). In response to the question of whether a reverting apostate (*meshummad she-ḥazar bo, mi she-nistammed ve-roẓeh laḥzor*) requires immersion (*tevilah*) or *malqot* (the administering of lashes), these texts maintain that, because any number of grave sins may have been transgressed by the apostate, the giving of lashes is advised, but immersion is not required since this person had been born a Jew (*nolad bi-qedushah*). The second texts adds that the reverting apostate must also publicly accept membership in the Jewish community and recommit to Jewish observances (*'akh ẓarikh she-yeqabbel 'alav divrei ḥaverut be-farhesya*); he should express regret for what he has done (*ve-yitḥaret mi-mah she-'asah*). From that point on there is no reason to suspect any duplicity in this matter on the part of the returnee (*u-mikan va-'elakh 'ein ḥosheshin le-ha'aramah be-'inyan zeh*).[2] Recognizing that southern France and northern Spain shared many cultural affinities and connections within both the Jewish and Christian communities,[3] Shatzmiller nonetheless concludes that for Rashba, while a public act of rejoining the Jewish community and its observances is required (aspects of which include flagellation, confession, and sincere repentance), immersion is considered superfluous.[4]

Shatzmiller compares Rashba's position to that of his student, Yom Tov b. Abraham Ishvilli (Ritva, d. c. 1325), who disagrees. As has been noted, Ritva (in his Talmudic *ḥiddushim* to tractate *Yevamot*, 47b) asserts that, although immersion is not required according to the letter of the law (*shurat ha-din*),

---

2 See *She'elot u-Teshuvot ha-Rashba*, 5:66, 7:411.

3 See also Pinchas Roth, "Regional Boundaries and Medieval Halakhah: Rabbinic Responsa from Catalonia to Southern France in the Thirteenth and Fourteenth Centuries," *Jewish Quarterly Review* 105 (2015): 72–98.

4 Cf. *Teshuvot ha-Rashba ha-Meyuḥasot la-Ramban*, #180, and *Shibbolei ha-Leqet le-R. Ẓidqiyyah b. Avraham ha-Rofeh mi-Romi*, part 2, ed. S. Ḥasida (Jerusalem, 1988), 198 (sec. 147).

a rabbinic requirement or enactment mandates that the reverting Jew must immerse himself, *mishum ma'alah*, which Shatzmiller renders as "for the sake of perfection." Moreover, in a prior passage in his *ḥiddushim* to tractate *Yevamot* (not cited by Shatzmiller), Ritva indicates that, although apostates who seek to return to their previous, proper Jewish status (*meshummad[im] u-ba'u laḥzor le-kashrutan*) do not require immersion at all (*ve-'einam ẓerikhim tevilah kelal*), the prevailing custom is nonetheless to immerse them (*'aval nahagu le-hatbilam*). Ritva's formulations comport with the material found in Bernard Gui's inquisitorial record. In addition to the two additional personal depositions that Yerushalmi located—confirming the basic thrust of Bernard's words concerning the need for immersion—Shatzmiller adduces another document from the Provençal inquisition during this period in Marseilles, and it also describes a required immersion as part of the re-judaization process.[5]

In light of these diverse sources suggesting that immersion for returning apostates had become the rule in southern France and northern Spain by the early fourteenth century, Shatzmiller concludes that Rashba was not necessarily describing the actual practice of his day when he writes that lashes were to be administered but that immersion was not required. Rather, Rashba is

5 See Shatzmiller, "Converts and Judaizers in the Early Fourteenth Century." See also Ram Ben-Shalom, *Yehudei Provence: Rennaisance be-Ẓel ha-Knesiyyah* (Raanana, 2017), 254–56; and *Ḥiddushei ha-Ritva 'al Massekhet Yevamot* [47b], ed. R. A. Jofen (Jerusalem, 1988), 330–32: *ve-Yisra'el she-ḥata ve-ḥazar bi-teshuvah, de-kulei 'alma shurat ha-din 'eino ẓarikh tevilah 'ela qabbalat [ḥaverut] bifnei beit din le-khatḥila, ve-'af 'al pi khen hu tovel mi-derabban mishum ma'alah dumya de-tevilat 'eved me-shuḥrar she-'ein tevilato 'ela mi-derabbanan, ve-khen katuv be-Tosafot ha-'aḥaranot.* This passage is reproduced by Yosef Ḥaviva in his *Nimmuqei Yosef* to *Yevamot* 47b (fol. 16b in the pagination of the Rif), s.v. *ve-katav ha-Ritva*. Ritva maintains that acceptance (*qabbalah*) before a rabbinic tribunal is advisable *a priori*, but the absence of such an acceptance does not undermine the process. See this volume, chapter 2, n. 54. Similarly, in another formulation about immersion, found in his *ḥiddushim* to *Yevamot* [16b] (ed. Jofen, 358), Ritva notes that it is ostensibly sufficient for reverting apostates to accept Jewish practices (once again) before a *beit din* (*mistabra be-qabbalat ḥaverut lifnei beit din sagi le-hu*), before concluding that the common practice is to immerse them; Shatzmiller appears to have been unaware of this additional formulation by Ritva.

offering a legal opinion or instruction (based primarily on geonic materials) that there is actually no need for immersion at all. Rashba's view is that even if an immersion is undertaken simply for the sake of completion or "perfection," such an immersion would imply a degree of recognition of the Christian sacrament of baptism. This practice was perceived by Rashba to be significantly flawed, and he therefore sought to eliminate it.

There is also, however, an important dimension in the transmission of rabbinic literature that is reflected in the differing views of Rashba and Ritva. Shatzmiller notes that one of Rashba's responsa "might represent some editorial effort on the part of Solomon ibn Adreth," and the other appears to be an almost verbatim quotation of the earlier geonic responsum. In fact, given the heavy editing of many sections of Rashba's published responsa, it is most likely that these are versions of geonic responsa that found their way into Rashba's responsa corpus (as did other geonic responsa).[6]

Although such an editorial history would render Shatzmiller's assessment of Rashba's view a bit imprecise, the more crucial point is that, until the comments of Ritva in his *ḥiddushim* to tractate *Yevamot*, it is difficult to point to a single rabbinic formulation that was composed in Christian Spain on the question of what was required of returning apostates. What can be found within the larger Islamic or Sefardic milieu are several geonic responsa (which may well refer to apostates who practiced Islam rather than Christianity),[7] some

---

6 See Simcha Emanuel, "Teshuvot ha-Geonim ha-Qeẓarot," in *'Atarah le-Ḥayyim: Meḥqarim be-Sifrut ha-Talmudit veha-Rabbanit Likhvod Professor Ḥaim Zalman Dimitrovsky*, ed. D. Boyarin et al. (Jerusalem, 2000), 447–49; and idem, "Kitvei Yad shel Teshuvot ha-Rashba she-Bidei Ḥakhmei ha-Me'ot ha-Ḥamesh 'Esreh–ha-Tesha 'Esreh," *Jewish Studies Internet Journal* 13 (2015): 1–46.

7 See *Oẓar ha-Geonim*, vol. 7 (*Massekhet Yevamot*), 111–12 (secs. 258–60); Uriel Simonsohn, "Are Gaonic Responsa a Reliable Source for the Study of Jewish Conversion to Islam? A Comparative Analysis of Legal Sources," in *Jews, Christians, and Muslims in Medieval and Early Modern Times*, ed. A. E. Franklin et al.(Leiden, 2014), 121–38; idem, "The Legal and Social Bonds of Jewish Apostates and Their Spouses According to Gaonic Responsa," *Jewish Quarterly Review* 105 (2015): 417–39; and Moshe Yagur, "Zehut Datit u-Gevulot Qehillatiyyim be-Ḥevrat ha-Genizah (Me'ot ha-10–13): Gerim, 'Avadim, Mumarim" (PhD diss., Hebrew University, 2017), 137–38.

of which ultimately entered rabbinic collections in Christian Spain perhaps as a reflection of the geonic-Andalusian nexus that was evident within Spain through the twelfth century and beyond.[8] At the same time, however, Rashba did compose several responsa dealing with how an apostate is to be viewed and treated while still in a state of apostasy (in which he invokes the principle of *'af 'al pi she-ḥata Yisra'el hu*),[9] including a suggestive ruling that permits the ritual slaughter performed by a Jew who had apostatized under the fear of death (*me-yir'ah . . . mi-paḥad she-yaharguhu*).[10]

---

8 See Bernard Septimus, *Hispano-Jewish Culture in Transition* (Cambridge, MA, 1982), 80, 85–92, 95–101, 106–9.

9 See *She'elot u-Teshuvot ha-Rashba*, 1:194 (money may be lent to an apostate at interest, citing the supporting view of R. Abraham [b. David of Posquieres]); see *Teshuvot u-Pesaqim le-Rabad*, ed. Y. Kafih (Jerusalem, 1964), 173, sec. 126 (even as the *qiddushin* and *get* of an apostate are effective). See also *Teshuvot ha-Rashba*, 1:242, 1:1162; *Teshuvot ha-Rashba ha-Meyuḥasot la-Ramban*, #142; and *She'elot u-Teshuvot ha-Rashba he-Ḥadashot mi-Ketav Yad* (ed. Machon Yerushalayim, 2005), 148, sec. 212 (citing the responsum of Rabbenu Tam [*Sefer ha-Yashar*, sec. 25] on how he arranged for apostates to give *gittin*); and 154, sec. 222 (an apostate must perform *ḥaliẓah* irrespective of whether he apostatized before or after his brother's marriage [which is the view of Rashi]; this act is effective just as an apostate's *get* is effective); 1:661 (an apostate is considered to be like a non-Jew regarding his presence within an *'eruv*); 7:292 (an apostate does not inherit, citing R. Hai and other Geonim). See also 7:179 (this volume, chapter 2, n. 64, citing his teacher Rabbenu Yonah b. Abraham); ms. Bodl. 820, fols. 22v–25v; and cf. Yiẓḥak Brand, *Mihu Ḥiloni? Qeri'ot Hilkhatiyyot* (Jerusalem, 2012), 62–63; and J. Katz, *Halakhah ve-Qabbalah* (Jerusalem, 1986), 267.

10 See *Teshuvot ha-Rashba*, 7:41 (= ms. Bodl. 820, fol. 22v), based on *Gittin* 45b. Rashba similarly permits ritual slaughter performed by a convert to Judaism who had returned to his prior observances (*ger she-ḥazar le-suro*) under the same pressures; any Jewish wine these individuals touched is permitted, although Rashba asserts that they should have given their lives rather than accept an idolatrous religion even under duress. Cf. *She'elot u-Teshuvot ha-Rivash* (d. 1408, Barcelona, Saragossa, Valencia, Algiers), ed. D. Metzger (Jerusalem, 1993), 5–8 (secs. 4, 6; but cf. sec. 11); and B. Netanyahu, *The Marranos of Spain* (Ithaca, NY, 1999), 22–32. The essence of Rashba's leniency, albeit only with respect to a *ger she-ḥazar le-suro*, is recorded in ms. Bodl. 844, fol. 82c, published in *Teshuvot Maharam mi-Rothenburg va-Ḥaverav*, ed. Emanuel, 484 (sec. 184; and see the parallels in *Sefer Orḥot Ḥayyim*, noted by Emanuel). This manuscript was copied in Ashkenaz in 1375 and contains a good deal of Ashkenazic material from the thirteenth century

One noteworthy formulation about the process for a returning apostate which originated outside of Spain involved Rashba's predecessor and teacher, Naḥmanides (Ramban, d. 1270). It is preserved in two parallel manuscripts and has been published no fewer than three times during the past century.[11] In this instance Ramban asks the question of Solomon b. Abraham of Montpellier (*min ha-Har*, d. c. 1240), who is perhaps best known for his heavy involvement in the Maimonidean controversy of the 1230s.[12] R. Solomon was a major teacher of Ramban's cousin, Rabbenu Yonah b. Abraham of Gerona (d. 1263), and Ramban refers to R. Solomon as "my colleague [*ḥaveri*], *ha-Rav he-Ḥasid* R. Solomon of Barcelona," indicating that R. Solomon spent some time in Barcelona as well.[13]

(see Emanuel's introduction, 77–88), including tens of sections from Isaac b. Moses of Vienna's *Sefer Or Zarua'*. *Sefer Or Zarua'*, pt. 1, sec. 555 (ed. Machon Yerushalayim), fol. 462, rules that a Torah scroll written by a *ger she-ḥazar le-suro maḥmat yir'ah* is permitted for use, assuming that in fact "his heart is still pointed toward heaven, *libbo la-shamayim*." This ruling is also recorded by Ḥayyim *Or Zarua'* in his *Simmanei Sefer Or Zarua'*, ibid. (and in *Sefer Mordekhai*, at the end of *halakhot qetanot le-massekhet Menaḥot*, fol. 13c in the standard pagination), although there is also no mention in these passages of an apostate who was coerced. This is also the case for *Tosafot ha-Rosh 'al Massekhet Gittin* (45b), s.v. *she-ḥazar le-suro*, ed. H. B. Rabin (Jerusalem, 1974), 167. However, in his *Yam Shel Shelomoh* to tractate *Ḥullin*, 1:7, Solomon Luria (Maharshal) cites the allowance of the ritual slaughter done by a Jew who apostatized under duress, as found in Rashba's responsum. See also Moses Isserles, *Darkhei Mosheh* to *Yoreh De'ah* 124:3; and *Beit Yosef* to *Yoreh De'ah*, sec. 119, s.v. *katav ha-Rashba*.

11 See ms. Bodl. 2343 (#21407, fourteenth-century Provence), fols. 50r–51r [= ms. Parma de Rossi 166 (#13913), fols. 35v–36v]; Adolf Neubauer, *Israelietische Letterbode* 3 (1878): 1–3; Menashe Grossberg, *Gevul Menashe* (Frankfurt, 1899), 5–9; and H. S. Sha'anan, *Moriah* 9, 11–12 (1980): 3–4. (The Parma manuscript provides several corrections for Sha'anan's transcription of the Bodleian manuscript.)

12 Cf. P. Roth, "Halakhah u-Biqqoret bi-Derom Ẓarefat: R. David b. Sha'ul 'al Hilkhot Yayn Nesekh," *Tarbiz* 83 (2015): 439–63. On Solomon of Montpellier's activities as a decisor of Jewish law, see ibid., 440–41; and ms. Moscow RSL 525 (#47856), fols. 261b–262b (in a case of *terefot*), published in *Sefer ha-Me'orot le-R. Meir ha-Me'ili mi-Narbonne 'al Massekhet Ḥullin*, ed. M. Y. Blau (New York, 1964), 237–41; and ms. Bodl. 781 (#20318), fols. 93v–95r, 100v–101r.

13 See I. Ta-Shma, *Kneset Meḥqarim*, vol. 2 (Jerusalem, 2004), 86 (n. 53), 111 (n. 5); and B. Septimus, *Hispano-Jewish Culture in Transition*, 28, 63–64, 99–100.

The wording of Naḥmanides' question is no longer extant, but R. Solomon's response exists in full. He notes that it is not always possible to ascertain the sincerity of a returning apostate, especially when the individual in question confesses (*mitvaddeh*) and seeks forgiveness when he is among Jews and partakes of their food while still spending time among Christians and eating with them as well.[14] R. Solomon's guidelines are that a returning apostate must "publicly repent without any coercion [*ẓarikh she-yashuv be-farhesya me-ʾelav be-lo shum ʾones*], and must remain among us and perform the *miẓvot* as he once did."

According to Solomon of Montpellier, these commitments entitle the returning apostate to be considered a *baʿal teshuvah*, without need for immersion or any physical affliction (*be-lo tevilah u-belo shum yissur*). However, for such a person to be considered completely trustworthy and reliable (*kasher le-gamrei*), to be believed as a witness and to be trusted in all matters of *ʾissur ve-heter*, the repentant apostate must undergo a prescribed regimen of afflictions and display remorse "in accordance with what is prescribed by the *beit din* in his city. Once he has accepted those afflictions and has regretted his sin, he is considered to be fully reliable in all matters." However, at no point in this process is immersion mandated by R. Solomon.

At the end of his response to Naḥmanides, R. Solomon notes (and questions) the ruling of R. Natronai Gaon according to which a *kohen* who apostatized but subsequently returned to Jewish practice may not offer the priestly blessing. R. Solomon agrees with the suggestion (apparently made by Ramban in his question) that moving forward this *kohen* should not be able to receive the first *ʿaliyyah* to the Torah, since this contains an element of dominion (*serarah*). However, his ability to offer the priestly blessing together with his fellow *kohanim*, as even those who are physically blemished (*baʿalei mumin*) are permitted, should be restored.[15]

R. Solomon's overall view with respect to the returning apostate is fully consonant with that of the Geonim as found in the responsa collection of

---

14 Cf. this volume, chapter 2, n. 64.

15 Cf. this volume, chapter 4, nn. 35–36.

Rashba. Immersion is not required, but public reacceptance of the *mizvot* (through both word and deed) is. In addition, the returning apostate must undergo forms of physical affliction or *malkot* to achieve the full measure of trustworthiness, credibility, and expiation. R. Solomon's citation of the geonic material at the end of his responsum further suggests that he is working within a geonic framework. He cites no other post-talmudic authorities with regard to returning apostates, although Maimonides is cited, *inter alia*, with respect to the treatment of full-fledged apostates and heretics (*minim*).

It is instructive to compare R. Solomon's approach in this matter with those of the northern French Tosafist Isaac b. Samuel (Ri) of Dampierre and his students, as discussed earlier, in chapter 2. In one version of his responsum, Ri recounts the case of a Jew from Troyes who had returned to Judaism. Two Jews apparently queried him quite rigorously about the sincerity of his repentance, and he withdrew from them in fear. Subsequently, he became a servant (*shamash*), which brought him into contact with Jewish wine, and Ri was asked about the halakhic status of these wines, since the touch of an apostate typically renders them unfit for Jewish use. Ri responds that the wines are kosher, because the former apostate knows that "as long as he has not immersed himself and accepted upon himself the dicta of the rabbinic authorities, his status is considered as that of a non-Jew. As such, it is not necessary to convene a tribunal of three before whom he must accept Judaism once again, since it is easy for us to verify that he has returned to his Creator, for he now conducts himself in accordance with the Jewish religion."

For Ri, at least in this version of his response, the act of ritual immersion by a returning apostate not only serves as a means of expiation but also confirms that he is no longer regarded by the Jewish community as having a status akin to that of a non-Jew. This immersion does not have to be undertaken in the presence of a rabbinic body or tribunal, but it does serve to alert and bind the former apostate to his renewed status and responsibilities. In Ri's formulation, ritual immersion is seen as a means of indicating and ensuring the returning apostate's compliance with the requirements of Judaism (in addition to the acceptance of the words and dictates of the rabbis and living once again as a practicing Jew), if not as a means of "undoing" his baptism.

However, Ri's student Isaac b. Abraham of Dampierre (Riẓba) did not recognize at all the need for a former apostate to immerse so that the wine he touched could be permitted, especially since the apostate in question had been seen observing the Sabbath again, at least publicly. Moreover, Riẓba's brother, Samson b. Abraham (Rash) of Sens, thought that additional verification of the reverting apostate's sincerity was needed in such a case, which an immersion was surely not able to provide.[16]

For Solomon of Montpellier as well, immersion was not the way to achieve sufficient verification in the eyes of others, nor was it even a part of the expiation process. Public repentance and living within the community were meant to provide a level of confidence concerning the sincerity of the former apostate's return. For the Geonim lashes (*malqot*) were also a necessary consideration, ostensibly as a means of both expiation and deterrence. Solomon of Montpellier also mandated physical afflictions, but only for the returning apostate to achieve a higher degree of credibility in other religious matters.

However, for whatever reason, R. Solomon's responsum to Naḥmanides is not cited by any subsequent Spanish rabbinic authorities. Moreover, although a number of Provençal rabbinic figures already in the late twelfth century (most notably Asher of Lunel) were aware of rulings issued by Isaac of Dampierre[17]—as were other Spanish and Provençal authorities by the early years of the thirteenth century, including several who had actually traveled north to study in Ri's *beit midrash*[18]—Ri's ruling about the appropriateness of a penitent

16 See this volume, chapter 2, nn. 18–20.

17 R. Asher in fact corresponded with Ri. See Urbach, *Ba'alei ha-Tosafot* (Jerusalem, 1984), 236–27; Israel Ta-Shma, *Ha-Sifrut ha-Parshanit la-Talmud*, vol. 2 (Jerusalem, 2000), 147–50; and my "Talmudic Studies," in *The Cambridge History of Judaism*, vol. 6 (The Middle Ages: The Christian World), ed. R. Chazan (Cambridge, 2018), 602.

18 Bernard Septimus, *Hispano-Jewish Culture in Transition*, 32–35; I. Ta-Shma, *Kneset Meḥqarim*, 2:119–20; Shalem Yahalom, *Bein Geronah le-Narbonah* (Jerusalem, 2013), 192–94, 243–47, 256–58; and my "Talmudic Studies," 602–4.

apostate undergoing immersion also seems to have remained unknown in these areas. Indeed, even at the end of the thirteenth century, all that appears to have been available to Spanish authorities such as Rashba are texts and views of the Geonim.

In a responsum about the Jewish status of an apostate with respect to his liability for illicit sexual relations, Naḥmanides discusses the ability of an apostate to effect *qiddushin* (and *gittin*) and to perform *ḥaliẓah*, along with his ability to receive inheritance, maintaining that in all such matters where Torah laws and prohibitions are involved, the apostate is to be viewed as a Jew. With regard to economic issues, however, Ramban notes that an apostate's lost objects need not be returned to him, nor must a Jew pay him damages according to the requirements of Jewish law. In addition, it is permitted to lend money at interest to an apostate, against the view of Rashi (which is noted), although Ramban does not cite any authorities by name for these allowances.[19]

However, in his Talmudic *ḥiddushim*, in which he often cites teachings and interpretations of the Tosafists, Ramban refers to the fact that the permission to charge interest to an apostate was issued by Rabbenu Tam, and he cites the Yerushalmi passage that had first been noted by Ri of Dampierre (who is not named) to support this approach. Indeed, Ramban also adopts Ri's position (again, without citing him by name) that one should nonetheless not borrow money from an apostate at interest because this causes the apostate to transgress, and the Jewish borrower thereby violates the prohibition of *lifnei ʿivver*.[20] Nonetheless, Ramban concludes the responsum with the following request: "This is my view in this matter, although nothing from the words of the earlier authorities has reached me [*ve-lo higgiʿani me-divrei ha-rishonim*]. You should search in the responsa of the Geonim and in the works of R. Judah [of Barcelona], and let me know if even a kernel of material is to be found there."

19 See Simcha Assaf, *Teshuvot ha-Ramban*, in *Sifran shel Rishonim* (Jerusalem, 1935), 56–58 (sec. 2).

20 See *Ḥiddushei ha-Ramban ʿal Massekhet Bava Meẓiʿa* (71b), ed. A. R. Hishrik et al. (Jerusalem, 2012), 461–64. See also *Teshuvot ha-Ramban ha-Meyuḥasot la-Rashba*, #142; *Teshuvot ha-Meyuḥasot*, #224; *Teshuvot ha-Rashba*, 1:194; and Shalom Albeck, "Yaḥaso shel Rabbenu Tam li-Beʿayot Zemanno," *Zion* 19 (1954): 139–40 (n. 67).

Ramban openly admits that he has little earlier rabbinic data on these issues from within the geonic or Sefardic rabbinic worlds, and he asks the questioner to let him know if there is any relevant material to be found in works from these authorities and areas.[21]

Solomon of Montpellier similarly was unaware of earlier sources in these matters. Only what was found in geonic works was known to him, and even that repository of knowledge was somewhat spotty. Perhaps R. Solomon was aware of (and agreed with) the view of the early German Tosafist Isaac b. Asher *ha-Levi* (Riba, d. 1133), as cited in *Tosafot Pesaḥim* and elsewhere, that one who was born a Jew cannot undergo immersion at any time as a means of confirming his Jewishness. The Geonim, however, developed their similar view prior to (and independent of) Riba. Although none of these authorities refers to the principle of *'af 'al pi she-ḥata Yisra'el hu* in denying the need for immersion, this rationale appears within geonic writings even before the significant attention given to it by Rashi, and it is possible that this principle played a role in the development of the nonimmersion position, as Shatzmiller has suggested.[22]

As has been demonstrated in the second chapter of this study, Ri's espousal of the need for immersion by a returning apostate was the precursor to a series of Tosafist formulations (found mainly in manuscript) in both Germany and northern France from the early thirteenth century onward which ratifies this need and expands on it. Although some of these formulations (such as that of Simḥah of Speyer and his student Samuel of Worms, known also as R. Bonfant) and at least one version of Ri's own formulation focused on the immersion as a means of expiation and perhaps an un-baptism as well, others concentrated on identifying the immersion mainly as a deterrent. However, at this time the

21 See Assaf, *Teshuvot ha-Ramban* (op. cit., n. 19): זהו דעתי בענין זה ולא הגיעני מדברי הראשונים כלום. ואתה חפש בתשובות הגאונים ובספרי ה"ר יהודה [מברצלונה] ואם שורש דבר נמצא בם הודיעני. Cf. I. Ta-Shma, *Ha-Sifrut ha-Parshanit la-Talmud*, 2:49; and my "Talmudic Studies," 594–95.

22 For Riba's view, see this volume, chapter 1, n. 19. For the geonic espousal of *'af 'al pi she-ḥata Yisra'el hu*, see *Teshuvot u-Pesaqim*, ed. E. Kupfer (Jerusalem, 1973), 290; *Oẓar ha-Geonim*, vol. 7 (*Yevamot*), 35 (responsa, sec. 80).

only Ashkenazic formulation that requires the reacceptance of *mizvot* before a rabbinic tribunal, in addition to the immersion (which could take place at night), is attributed to the German Tosafist Rabiah. Unlike Ri and R. Simḥah and other Tosafists, Rabiah apparently wished to formalize the return of the apostate in a more public way, unusual in Ashkenaz (except perhaps for Samson of Sens's suggested approach) but reminiscent in this respect of the geonic position, as well as that of Solomon of Montpellier.[23]

With this background, we are now prepared to look more carefully at the formulation of Ritva in his *ḥiddushim* to *Yevamot* 47b (reproduced earlier in this chapter in n. 5). In his opening comments Ritva takes note of the basic geonic position. No immersion for the returning apostate is necessary, but it is best, at least *a priori* (*le-khatḥilah*), to have a public reacceptance of his membership in the Jewish community, specifically in the presence of a rabbinic court (*beit din*). As noted in our discussion of the Ashkenazic materials in chapter 2, *ḥaverut* is an allusion to the talmudic requirement that when an *'am ha-'arez* with respect to ritual purity is elevated to the status of a *ḥaver* who can now handle ritually pure foods without any difficulty, this change in status is made in the presence of a rabbinic court.[24]

In the second part of Ritva's formulation, however, ritual immersion, which was apparently being done, is deemed to be a rabbinic requirement, *mishum ma'alah*. This is compared by *Tosafot 'aḥaronot*, some type of later *Tosafot*, to the talmudic requirement (in *Yevamot* 47b) that an *'eved kena'ani* must undergo immersion when he goes free. A search of the standard *Tosafot* to *Yevamot*, along with the rich variant *Tosafot* texts that have been published in recent years,[25] yields no such requirement or formulation. The talmudic

23 See this volume, chapter 2, nn. 20, 27, 34–35; and cf. chapter 3, n. 50.

24 The third manuscript version of Ri's responsum (ms. Leipzig 1119), written in a fifteenth- or sixteenth-century Spanish hand (see this volume, chapter 2, nn. 16–17), maintains the need for a *qabbalah* on the part of the reverting apostate, at least in front of individuals, rather than the need for immersion, which was an integral part of Ri's initial formulation. Perhaps the Spanish origins of this manuscript contributed to the shifting of these requirements.

25 See *Tosafot Maharam ve-Rabbenu Perez*, ed. H. Porush (Jerusalem, 1991); *Tosafot Yeshanim ha-Shalem*, ed. A. Shoshana (Jerusalem, 1994); and see also *Tosafot*

discussion, which is remarked on by some of these *Tosafot* texts, deals with the need for an *'eved kena'ani*—who is immersed and circumcised when he enters into this state of servitude, causing him also to become obligated in *miẓvot* to an extent (*meḥuyyav be-miẓvot ke-'ishah*)—to undergo an additional immersion when he is freed. He then becomes obligated in all *miẓvot*, like all other Jewish males. These *Tosafot* texts posit that this second immersion is rabbinic in nature,[26] but there is no discussion about a returning apostate in this context.

However, a *Sefer Mordekhai* manuscript (cited in chapter 2, in connection with the responsum of Ri) contains another gloss that reports the view of *Tosafot Shitah*, an appellation most often associated with interpretations that emanated from the Tosafist study hall at Evreux (c. 1250) or with the *Tosafot* produced in the *beit midrash* of their student Pereẓ b. Elijah of Corbeil (d. 1297).[27] The *Tosafot Shitah* passage specifically extends the requirement of immersion for the released *'eved kena'ani* to a reverting apostate who had repented. This passage invokes the principle of *'af 'al pi she-ḥata Yisra'el hu* at the outset, and then asserts that the returning apostate must nonetheless undergo an immersion *la'asot hekkera*, to make a distinction or demarcation.[28] This is precisely the rabbinic requirement (and the *Tosafot* source) for immersion to which Ritva refers, and which he characterizes as *mishum ma'alah*. The returning apostate is not going from a state of slavery to one of freedom, but he is

---

ha-Rosh, ed. Y. D. Bar-Ilan (Jerusalem, 2016).

26 For the position that this immersion is required according to Torah law, see *Ḥiddushei ha-Ramban*, ad loc., which views this immersion as a requirement from the Torah that is akin to the immersion of a convert to Judaism; and see this volume, chapter 2, n. 51.

27 See my "Rabbinic Conceptions of Marriage and Matchmaking in Christian Europe," in *Entangled Histories: Knowledge, Authority, and Jewish Culture in the Thirteenth Century*, ed. E. Baumgarten et al. (Philadelphia, 2017), 28 (n. 28); and this volume, chapter 2, n. 55.

28 See ms. Vercelli C1, fol. 291v (in the left-side margin): ואחד עבד המשוחרר צריך טבילה. תי' אמאי זקוק טבילה שניה כשמשחררי' אותו. והלא אי' טעון לחזור ולהסיף ממנו דם ברית. וי"ל דההיא מדרבנן כדי לעשו' הכיר' בין עבוד' לחירות דה"נ ישראל משומד אע"פ שחטא ישראל הוא ואפ"ה כששב צריך טבילה. וכן משמ' פ' השולח שלא בעי טבילה אלא מדרבנן דקאמ' הכותב שטר אירוסי' לשפחתו וא וצאי בו והתקדשי בו יש בלשון הזה ל' שחרור והוי מקודש' אע"ג שלא טבלה. תוס' שיטה.

similarly transitioning (and now returning) to a different and higher status, as a fully recognized and religiously obligated member of the Jewish community. *Mishum ma'alah* does not mean "for the sake of perfection" but is rather a reflection of the reverting apostate's newly elevated status.

As I have demonstrated elsewhere, Ritva had access to Tosafist material that was not available to Ramban, or even to Ritva's teacher and senior colleague Rashba. The main source for Ritva's awareness of these additional Tosafist materials is the *Tosafot Rabbenu Pereẓ*. However, Rabbenu Pereẓ and his closest colleagues—Meir of Rothenburg, Yeḥi'el of Paris, and Isaac of Corbeil—all studied in the Tosafist academy at Evreux; and material from Evreux is prominently featured elsewhere in Ritva's *ḥiddushim* as well. Although it is not possible to consistently identify the term *Tosafot 'aḥaronot* in *Ḥiddushei ha-Ritva* with materials that came from this study hall, there can be no doubt that the *Tosafot Shitah* passage from Evreux, or perhaps from the *Tosafot* of Rabbenu Pereẓ, is Ritva's source in this instance.[29]

The attractiveness of this Tosafist position for Ritva is fairly obvious. In the near-total absence of earlier European sources concerning the reversion process for an apostate—and in contradistinction to the geonic responsa (as well as the ruling by Solomon of Montpellier) that present requirements for a returning apostate but do not offer any firm talmudic prooftexts or anchors for these practices—*Tosafot Shitah* identifies an overarching rabbinic requirement that neatly and convincingly mandates immersion for the returning apostate as well, which was by now the practice in Spain in any case.

29 See my "Between Ashkenaz and Sefarad: Tosafist Teachings in the Talmudic Commentaries of Ritva," in *Between Rashi and Maimonides*, ed. E. Kanarfogel and M. Sokolow (New York, 2010), 249–73. Note Rashba's responsum (7:179), which cites Rabbenu Yonah in the name of *Ḥakhmei Ẓarefat* with regard to the status of an apostate who flitted between the Jewish and Christian communities (*mi-pi Rabbenu Yonah she-shama lifsoq le-ḥakhmei Ẓarefat ki meshummad la-'avodah zarah ha-holekh mi-maqom le-maqom ve-'ein 'anu yod'im 'im yehudi hu 'im lav)*; and see this volume, chapter 2, nn. 64–65. Rabbenu Yonah studied with the Tosafist brothers of Evreux; see Urbach, *Ba'alei ha-Tosafot*, 479; my *"Peering through the Lattices": Mystical, Magical, and Pietistic Dimensions in the Tosafist Period* (Detroit, MI, 2000), 62–67; and I. Ta-Shma, *Kneset Meḥqarim*, 2:109–17.

Ritva is the first Sefardic talmudist and rabbinic authority to embrace a distinctly Ashkenazic derivation regarding immersion for a returning apostate. If Rashba was indeed expressing his own view (and not simply parroting the Geonim), the difference between these views does not revolve around the issue of how Jewish the apostate was per se, since the *Tosafot Shitah* passage cited by Ritva enunciates and espouses the principle of *'af 'al pi she-ḥata Yisra'el hu* as well. Nor is this discussion necessarily about the efficacy of baptism, since the geonic view that immersion is not required applies equally to those who had apostatized to Islam prior to their return. Rather, it is about the development of a Spanish rabbinic position that does not simply rely on earlier sensibilities or popular practice but is based instead on a clear and identifiable talmudic locus.[30]

As a result of the societal pressures, heightened rhetoric, and sharpened Christian ideology concerning the Jews that developed in the aftermath of the First Crusade and became more virulent during the twelfth century (as described in the previous chapter), Ashkenazic authorities—taking their cue from Rashi but not necessarily adopting his specific positions—sought to develop halakhic policies to deal with the return of forced and willful apostates, as well as the status of apostates who remained connected to Christianity. Until the mid-thirteenth century, the Ashkenazic rationales for immersion were based for the most part on considerations such as repentance and deterrence, and perhaps the reversal of baptism. As we have seen, beyond the northern French Tosafists who argued for the permissibility of taking interest from apostates, several German Tosafists began to offer broader halakhic rationales to nullify the apostates' status as Jews with respect to a number of other precepts and issues. At the same time, however, Ri's student Isaac b. Abraham of Dampierre (Riẓba, d. 1209) and other Ashkenazic authorities continued to maintain the more welcoming position put forward by Rashi in these matters. Yet much of the Ashkenazic material

30 Cf. *Ḥiddushei ha-Ritva 'al Massekhet Yevamot* 22a, ed. Jofen, 499–518, where Ritva rules against the geonic position that an apostate need not perform *ḥaliẓah* if he had already apostatized at the time of his brother's marriage. Cf. *Ḥiddushei ha-Rashba*, ad loc.

that developed after Rashi appears to have remained relatively unknown in Spain (and even in southern France) until the late thirteenth century and beyond.[31]

Rabbenu Tam and his students' allowance that it was permitted to lend money to an apostate at interest (and the restriction that some French Tosafists imposed on borrowing money from an apostate) is one of the few explicit rulings concerning apostates to emerge from northern Europe and make its way to Spain already in the days of Ramban.[32] Ritva's derivation and justification of immersion for a reverting apostate are other significant examples of this movement of rabbinic interpretations and rulings.

---

31 See this chapter, nn. 9–10. See also *Teshuvot ha-Rashba ha-Meyuḥasot la-Ramban*, #180, which cites the moderate view of Riẓba of Dampierre concerning reverting apostates (see this volume, chapter 2, n. 18), along with the somewhat less moderate view of Eleazar of Worms (this volume, chapter 2, n. 39).

32 See this chapter, n. 20; and this volume, chapter 4, n. 15. Ritva cites the same Tosafist names and conclusions (and Ramban as well); see *Ḥiddushei ha-Ritva ʿal Massekhet Bava Meẓiʿa* [71b], ed. S. Rephael (Jerusalem, 1997), 590–91; and *Ḥiddushei ha-Ritva ʿal Massekhet ʿAvodah Zarah* [26b], ed. M. Goldstein (Jerusalem, 1982), 106–7; and see also this volume, chapter 2, n. 51. In his *ḥiddushim* to *Yevamot* 22a–b, ed. Jofen, 499–518, Ritva ratifies the *qiddushin*, *get*, and *ḥaliẓah* of an apostate. In this instance he cites the geonic view that *ḥaliẓah* is not required if the brother had apostatized prior to his brother's wedding. His conclusion is that it is best to require *ḥaliẓah* in all cases, but he mentions neither Rashi nor Maharam of Rothenburg in this connection. See also *Ḥiddushei ha-Rashba ʿal Massekhet Yevamot* (ad loc.), ed. S. Dickman (Jerusalem, 1989), 128–29. Similarly, when Ritva discusses the issue of why an apostate does not inherit, he cites only the Geonim and Maimonides. See *Ḥiddushei ha-Ritva ʿal Massekhet Yevamot* [62a], ed. Jofen, 578–79. Note that, just prior to his comment to *Yevamot* 47b about (*qabbalah* and) immersion for a reverting apostate (with the latter requirement based on *Tosafot ʾaḥaronot*; see this chapter, n. 5), Ritva (ed. Jofen, 428–29) writes that an apostate's *qiddushin* and *get* are effective, as they are for any Jew (and even to end a marriage to a Jewish woman that he initiated while an apostate). In addition, "It is reasonable to think [*mistabra*] that he is considered to be like a Jew in terms of the modes and rules of acquisition and obligation that are effective for him [*be-haqnaʾotav ve-ḥiyyuvav kulam ke-Yisraʾel hu nidon*]. However, if the law of the kingdom [*din ha-malkhut*] is that [an apostate from Judaism to Christianity] buys and sells as a non-Jew does [*she-hu qoneh u-maqneh ke-goy*], [this is so] because of [the principle of] *dina de-malkhuta dina*."

At no point during the twelfth and thirteenth centuries does there seem to have been an absence of apostates in northern Spain (Catalonia and Aragon) or Languedoc. Solomon of Montpellier and Naḥmanides, corresponding during the first half of the thirteenth century about immersion and other questions concerning the status of apostates, were clearly reacting to facts on the ground. And the presence of apostates in these areas certainly increases in the late thirteenth century and early fourteenth century, as Jews are expelled from various lands and locales in northern Europe and severely persecuted in others.[33]

And yet at the end of his commentary to *Pereq ha-Mevi* in tractate *Gittin*, Abraham b. Isaac of Montpellier (who exchanged halakhic letters with R. Menaḥem b. Solomon *ha-Meiri* of Perpignan in 1314 and was a contemporary of Ritva) assesses the status of an apostate in certain halakhic contexts without mentioning any other medieval authorities. An apostate is disqualified from delivering a *get* because he is like a gentile (*harei hu ke-goy*). Similarly, R. Abraham writes that an apostate's status in terms of participating in an *'eruv* is equivalent to that of a gentile. Even though the principle of *'af 'al pi she-ḥata Yisra'el hu* is applicable in a few matters (*bi-qeẓat milei*), these are in situations from which other Jews should not otherwise benefit. For example, with regard to *qiddushin*, a Jewish woman married to an apostate would be prohibited to all others if the groom had not apostatized. Therefore, she is

33 See Paola Tartakoff, *Between Christian and Jew: Conversion and Inquisition in the Crown of Aragon, 1250–1391* (Philadelphia, 2012), 24–31, 63–75, 117–31; Ram Ben-Shalom, *Mul Tarbut Noẓrit: Toda'ah Historit ve-Dimmui 'Avar be-Qerev Yehudei Sefarad u-Provence Bimei ha-Benayim* (Jerusalem, 2007), 208–13; and Pinchas Roth, "Later Provençal Sages—Jewish Law and Rabbis in Southern France, 1215–1348" [Hebrew] (PhD diss., Hebrew University, 2012), 258–61. Roth presents a multifaceted case (found in ms. Paris BN 1391 [#34252], fols. 87v–88r) about a husband who had apostatized in northern France and then went to live in the home of another (male) apostate, where he subsequently died. His wife had made her way to southern France, where she called upon the homeowner (who had subsequently reverted to Judaism) to testify as to the death of her husband so that she would be free to marry again. Issues of *mesiaḥ lefi tumo* with respect to the former apostate are raised as well. On the acceptability of these types of testimony involving a former apostate, cf. this volume, chapter 4, nn. 53–54.

still considered to be prohibited based on the *qiddushin* offered by the apostate because other Jews cannot benefit as a result of his apostasy. Similarly, interest cannot be taken from an apostate because, had the apostate not sinned, charging him interest would be prohibited. However, where other Jews do not benefit from the sin of apostasy, the apostate is like a complete gentile (*havei goy gamur le-khol devarav*). R. Abraham points to a prooftext from tractate *Sanhedrin* (60a). At the same time, however, the mother of an apostate need not undergo *yibbum* or *ḥaliẓah* (if his father died), because although the apostate is a *rasha* and an idolater, he is his father's progeny and inherits according to Torah law.[34]

In light of these gaps in halakhic precedent regarding apostates and apostasy, Ritva understandably took full advantage of a Tosafist text, the *Tosafot Shitah* passage, to account for the practice of immersing an apostate who sought to revert, which was different from what geonic authorities had recommended.[35] Ritva's formulation about immersion for a reverting apostate, including its Tosafist roots, and his *a priori* recommendation (*le-khatḥilah*) for the former apostate to formally reaccept observance of the precepts before a rabbinic court (*qabbalat divrei ḥaverut bifnei beit din*) as well, are then cited verbatim by the commentary to Alfasi's *Halakhot* known as *Nimmuqei Yosef*. The author of this commentary, Yosef Ḥaviva of Barcelona, was active during

34 See *Perush R. Avraham min ha-Har 'al Massekhtot Nedarim ve-Nazir*, ed. M. Y. Blau (New York, 1962), 245: ולענין ישראל משומד מסתברא דהוי פסול לשליחות הגט משום דמשומד הרי הוא כגוי . . . ואינו מבטל רשותו בשבת אלא צריך לשכור הימני כמו ששוכרין מגוי. וכל שכן לשאר מילי, הילכך פסול לשליחות. ואע״ג דאמרינן בקצת מילי אעפ״י שחטא ישראל הוא, הני מילי במילתא דלא הוי הנאה לישראל כגון הא דקידושין שאם לא חטא היא אסורה לכל העולם, השתא נמי דחטא אוסרה. ולא יהנה ישראל על שעבר זה הרשע עבירה שיועילו לו מעשיו לכל העולם עכשיו כמו שהיא אסורה אילו לא חטא. וכן אסור נמי ליקח מזה ריבית מזה הטעם, שהרי קודם שחטא היה אסור ליקח הימנו ריבית וכן אסור לתת לו רבית. אבל היכא דלא שייך הנאה לישראל מחמת מה שחטא, הוי כגוי גמור לכל דבריו. ובפרק ארבע מיתות [דף ס ע״ב] גבי רבשקה אמרינן שמפני שישראל משומד היה, קרעו כשבירך את השם ואם היה גוי היו פטורין מלקרוע. וזה ראוי כדכתבינן. וודאי ישראל משומד פוטר את אמו מן החליצה ומן היבום שאעפ״י שחטא ישראל הוא וזרע אין לה אמר רחמנא והרי יש לה. ואע״פ שהוא רשע ועובד ע״ז, זרעו הוא ויורש את אביו דבר תורה. Cf. Ram Ben-Shalom, *Yehudei Provence: Renaissance be-Ẓel ha-Kenesiyyah* (Raanana, 2017), 304–5; and this volume, chapter 4, n. 60.

35 Ritva also refers to apostates and their status in his responsa. See *She'elot ha-Ritva*, ed. Y. Kafih (Jerusalem, 1959), especially #159.

the late fourteenth and early fifteenth centuries, and he cites *Ḥiddushei ha-Ritva* with noticeable frequency. As Paola Tartakoff has shown, on the basis of extensive archival research in documents from the Crown of Aragon, both apostasy and repeated attempts to return to Judaism were in evidence there by 1340, well before the extensive persecutions of 1391.[36]

In sum, the comparison of Rashba's responsa to the commentary of Ritva undertaken by Shatzmiller is important not only because of what it may tell us about the internal Spanish rabbinic debate concerning returning apostates but also because it highlights the impact Ashkenazic talmudic scholarship had on the communities of northern Spain in this matter. Indeed, Jacob b. Asher of Toledo (d. 1349), who does not cite from the *ḥiddushim* of his Spanish contemporary Ritva in his *Arba'ah Turim*,[37] states simply (and without attribution) in *Yoreh De'ah* (sec. 267, in complete accordance with the geonic view) that a repentant apostate does not require immersion but does require lashes (*ke-Yisra'el mumar she-'ein ẓarikh tevillah 'ela malqot*); yet Yosef Karo (d. 1575) in his *Beit Yosef* (at the end of the next section, *Yoreh De'ah*, 268) cites the full *Nimmuqei Yosef* passage (including the names of Ritva and *Tosafot*), concluding that the returning apostate requires immersion *mi-derabbanan, mishum ma'alah*, just as a freed *'eved kena'ani* does.[38]

Moreover, the *Nimmuqei Yosef* passage is also a favored source for Yosef Karo's Eastern European contemporaries, Moses Isserles in his gloss to *Shulḥan 'Arukh* (*Yoreh De'ah*, 268:2), and Solomon Luria (Maharshal) in his *Yam shel Shelomoh* (*'al Massekhet Yevamot*, 4:52, end, although neither he nor Isserles notes that this approach actually originates in a *Tosafot* text), as it was for other leading rabbinic figures in Eastern Europe during the early

36 See *Nimmuqei Yosef* to *Yevamot* (47b), this chapter, n. 5; and P. Tartakoff, this chapter, n. 33. On *Nimmuqei Yosef*, see I. Ta-Shma, *Ha-Sifrut ha-Parshanit 'al ha-Talmud*, 2:90 (and the literature cited in n. 154).

37 Cf. my "Between Ashkenaz and Sefarad: Tosafist Teachings in the Talmudic Commentaries of Ritva," 249 (n. 36), 266 (n. 87).

38 Cf. *Beit Yosef*, *Yoreh De'ah*, sec. 267, s.v. *teshuvah le-ga'on*, which mentions the geonic view that immersion is not required. Indeed, in *Shulḥan 'Arukh*, 267:8, a *Yisra'el mumar* is characterized as requiring lashes but not immersion.

sixteenth century and beyond.[39] Overall the *Tosafot Shitah* passage formulated at the Tosafist academy at Evreux (or by its students) struck a deep chord. It is ironic that this *Tosafot* passage, as cited by *Nimmuqei Yosef*, was later brought back to the Ashkenazic milieu in the early modern period, where it became a touchstone for rabbinic policy there concerning returning apostates as well, even if not all the rabbinic authorities at that time were aware of its Ashkenazic origins.[40]

Interestingly, a similar pattern of rabbinic transmission and influence can be detected regarding conversion in Christian Spain. On the one hand, Spanish archival evidence (of the kind not found for Ashkenazic lands) suggests that there was a steady trickle of converts that increased throughout the thirteenth century and into the fourteenth century, especially after 1340, but well before the calamitous Christian persecutions and attacks of 1391.[41] On the other

---

39 Isserles writes that the reverting apostate should be immersed, and he should accept the commandments before a rabbinic tribunal of three; in his gloss to *Shulḥan ʿArukh, Yoreh Deʿah*, 267:8, Isserles notes that there are those who require immersion for a returning apostate, לכתחלה ... ולמעלה בעלמא, citing *Nimmuqei Yosef* with no mention of acceptance before a *beit din*. However, Yoel Sirkes (d. 1640), *Baḥ*, *Y. D.* 267, s.v. *teshuvah le-gaon*, following Maharshal, requires immersion (alone), and mentions *Nimmuqei Yosef* as the source (but not *Tosafot*). Sirkes also notes that Maharshal wrote that the common practice is to completely shave off the hair of a returning apostate prior to his immersion. See also Joshua Falk (d. 1614), *Perishah* to *Arbaʿah Turim, Yoreh Deʿah* 267, section 3, who cites *Tosafot*, along with *Nimmuqei Yosef* in the name of Ritva, as requiring immersion. The two leading seventeenth-century Eastern European commentaries to *Shulḥan ʿArukh* also require immersion, although they mention no medieval sources; see *Taz, Y. D.* 267:5 (citing *Derishah* and Maharshal), and *Shakh*, ibid., sec. 15. See also *Magen Avraham, Oraḥ Ḥayyim*, 326:8. On the lesser availability of *Ḥiddushei ha-Ritva* as compared to the *Nimmuqei Yosef* commentary, see I. Ta-Shma, *Ha-Sifrut ha-Parshanit la-Talmud*, 2:69–74, 90–91. See also Ḥayyim Yosef David Azulai (*Ḥida*, d. 1806), *Birkei Yosef* (Vienna, 1859), *Even ha-ʿEzer*, fol. 1b (1:11:4), who cites a passage from Ritva's *ḥiddushim* to tractate *Yevamot* on the basis of a manuscript.

40 Cf. Y. H. Yerushalmi, "The Inquisition and the Jews of France in the Time of Bernard Gui," 371–74; and this volume, chapter 1, at n. 11.

41 See P. Tartakoff, *Between Christian and Jew: Conversion and Inquisition in the Crown of Aragon*, 24–31, 119–28, 135–39. Similarly, K. Auman, "Conversion from Christianity to Judaism in the Middle Ages" (Master's thesis, Yeshiva University,

hand, however, it is difficult to find any sustained nontheoretical discussion of the requirements, rituals, or procedures for prospective *gerim* in the responsa of either of the two leading rabbinic figures at this time.[42] Both Ramban and Rashba comment on the central talmudic *sugyot* in *Yevamot* (45b–47a) in their *ḥiddushim*, but there is no suggestion that any of this analysis was being implemented on a practical level, and no actual cases are mentioned or even indicated.[43]

Although the interpretive Talmudic *ḥiddushim* produced in Spain during the thirteenth century do not typically lend themselves to the inclusion of cases that arose, the presence of converts in Christian Spain, as indicated by the archival literature, coupled with the relative silence of Spanish responsa and commentaries regarding the process of ongoing conversion, suggest that, unlike the situation in northern France, conversions were being carried out in Spain at a more local rabbinic level, with less awareness or input on the part of the leading rabbinic scholars of the day. This possibility is perhaps a reflection of the less insular and more cosmopolitan nature of Hispano-Jewish society, as compared to its Ashkenazic counterpart, and of the existence of a more formal communal rabbinate in Spain already at this time.[44]

1977), 54–57, maintains that Christian Spain was close to northern France in terms of the number and incidence of actual conversions by individuals, even as the Church appears to have been more concerned with thwarting proselytizing in northern France.

42 See, e.g. *Mafteaḥ ha-She'elot veha-Teshuvot shel Ḥakhmei Sefarad u-Ẓefon Afriqah*, ed. M. Elon (*ha-Mafteaḥ ha-Histori*), vol. 1 (Jerusalem, 1981), 111; vol. 2 (Jerusalem, 1987), 22–23. See also Yitzhak Baer, *A History of the Jews in Christian Spain* (Philadelphia, 1978), 1:417 (n. 79, end); and Auman, "Conversion from Christianity to Judaism in the Middle Ages."

43 A predecessor of Ramban in Christian Spain, Meir *ha-Levi* (Ramah) Abulafia of Toledo (c. 1165–1244), is cited by Yeroḥam b. Meshullam (a student of Asher b. Yeḥi'el [Rosh], who also resided in Toledo) as endorsing the approach of the northern French Tosafists with regard to the number of judges who must be present at the various phases of the conversion process and the issue of immersion at night. See Yeroḥam b. Meshullam, *Sefer Toledot Adam ve-Ḥavvah* (Venice, 1553), *netiv sheloshah ve-'esrim, ḥeleq revi'i* (fols. 200a–b).

44 See, e.g., J. Katz, *Halakhah ve-Qabbalah*, 201–12; my "Rabbinic Attitudes toward Nonobservance in the Medieval Period," in *Jewish Tradition and the Nontraditional*

Nonetheless, Ritva's *ḥiddushim* represent once again something of a departure. Ritva was the first talmudist in Christian Spain to justify a significant procedure for monitoring the return of penitent apostates to the Jewish community based on a talmudic construct as formulated in a variant *Tosafot* text of which he was aware. Similarly, with regard to conversion, Ritva brings together a series of unified regulations within his *ḥiddushim* to tractate *Yevamot* that guide and support the efforts of a duly constituted *beit din* to supervise conversions that are shaped by Ashkenazic approaches.[45]

Ritva's halakhic policies concerning conversion to Judaism, like those regarding penitent apostates, were copied (mostly in his name) and preserved in Yosef Ḥaviva's late-fourteenth-century commentary, *Nimmuqei Yosef*.[46] As noted, this commentary survived the ensuing centuries better than the *ḥiddushim* of Ritva did, and *Nimmuqei Yosef* is the conduit through which

---

Jew, ed. J. J. Schacter (Northvale, NJ, 1992), 32–35; my "The Rabbinate in Pre-Modern Judaism," in *Encyclopedia of Religion*, ed. Lindsay Jones (Detroit, MI, 2005), 11:7578–7581; and Y. T. Assis, *The Golden Age of Aragonese Jewry: Community and Society in the Crown of Aragon, 1213–1327* (London, 1997), 101–7, 139–42, 299–307, 311–14.

45 See my "Approaches to Conversion in Medieval European Rabbinic Literature: From Ashkenaz to Sefarad," in *Conversion, Intermarriage, and Jewish Identity*, ed. A. Mintz and M. Stern (New York, 2015), 237–40. To be sure, Ritva does not follow these approaches with complete consistency, just as he does he not adopt many of the rulings found in earlier Sefardic sources in this instance (such as the codes of Rif and Rambam), or even the positions of his more immediate predecessors, Ramban and Rashba.

46 Regarding immersion for a returning apostate, see *Nimmuqei Yosef* to *Yevamot* 47b (fol. 16b in the pagination of the Rif), *ve-katav ha-Ritva* (and this chapter, n. 5). On conversion, see *Nimmuqei Yosef* to *Yevamot* 45b (fol. 15b in the pagination of the Rif), s.v. *mi lo tavil le-qeryo* (that the immersion of a convert must take place before a duly constituted court of three under all conditions); *NY* to *Yevamot* 46b (fol. 16a in the pagination of the Rif), s.v. *'ein matbilin ba-laylah* (that the immersion of a convert may not take place at night); *NY* to *Yevamot* 47a (fol. 16a), s.v. *u-modi'in 'oto* (that if the convert was not informed prior to his conversion about some of the specific *miẓvot* he must observe—but that he had accepted the *miẓvot* generally—the conversion is nonetheless valid); and *NY* to *Yevamot* 24b (fol. 5b in the pagination of the Rif, end; that those who convert with ulterior motives do not invalidate their conversions).

Ritva's approaches became available to subsequent rabbinic decisors.[47] Ultimately, however, the *Shulḥan 'Arukh* mediates in these matters of conversion between the approaches of Maimonides and those of the (northern French) *Tosafot*. The voice of the *rishonim* from northern Spain is barely heard in this matter, as was also the case regarding the requirements for a returning apostate.[48]

Instances of Sefardic reliance on earlier Ashkenazic authorities with respect to apostates and apostasy can also be detected in later periods. Solomon b. Simeon Duran (Rashbash, d. 1467, Algiers) writes in a responsum about what the children of *'anusim* must do when they wish to repent. He begins with a lengthy discussion of the principle *'af 'al pi she-ḥata Yisra'el hu*, including the citation of a passage from the *ḥiddushim* of Rashba to tractate *Yevamot* (22a), which support his firm conclusion that the *qiddushin* of these forced converts are valid. Their children who seek to return are therefore not considered to be in the category of converts to Judaism (*gerim*).[49] Rashbash then cites "students of Rashi" who held that interest cannot be taken from the son of a female apostate. He notes that Rabbenu Tam, who allowed interest to be taken from apostates, did so only because there is no need to support apostates, even though they are still considered to be Jewish brethren, and that is what Naḥmanides concludes (in his *ḥiddushim* to *Bava Meẓi'a* 71b) as well.[50] Rashbash also writes that, since these children of apostates are not converts, they do not require immersion to rejoin the community, even if they had not been circumcised until this point. He cites the writings of "*Rabbanei Ẓarefat*," which, based on the content and style, perhaps refers to the responsum of Isaac b. Abraham (Riẓba) of Dampierre indicating that an apostate does not require either immersion or (re)-acceptance before a judicial tribunal of three

47 See *Beit Yosef* to *Yoreh De'ah*, sec. 268 (end), s.v. *Ba'al Halakhot*; and cf. this chapter, n. 39.

48 See *Shulḥan 'Arukh*, *Yoreh De'ah*, sec. 268. Only the ruling in *Y. D.* 268:4, that the immersion of a convert at night is acceptable after the fact, is (partially) attributed by *Be'er ha-Golah* to *Ḥiddushei ha-Rashba li-Yevamot* (46b).

49 Cf. this chapter, nn. 54 and 64.

50 See this chapter, n. 20.

(as a convert does). He then proceeds to discuss the circumcision that will need to be performed in this case and its blessings.[51]

Similarly, Rashbash asserts that an uncircumcised apostate who repented and was then circumcised is not considered a *ger* but rather a *ba'al teshuvah*, as is a female apostate who reverts.[52] In another responsum Rashbash rules, on the basis of Sefardic sources and rabbinic figures including Rabbenu Ḥanan'el, Maimonides, and Naḥmanides, that apostates who have not returned cannot inherit.[53] Elsewhere, however, he rules in this way by citing the early Ashkenazic rabbinic figures R. Meshullam and R. Judah *ha-Kohen* (in his *Sefer ha-Dinim*), noting that this was also the view of Rambam, Rosh, and Moses of Coucy, in his *Sefer Miẓvot Gadol*.[54]

David ibn Zimra (Radbaz, d. 1573), writing in the late sixteenth century regarding immersion for returning apostates in Egypt (*'anusim*, from Islam),

51 See *She'elot u-Teshuvot ha-Rashbash*, ed. M. Sobel (Jerusalem, 1998), 71–73, #89 [= ms.Bodl. 820, fols. 25b–26b]. Cf. *Pitḥei Teshuvah, Yoreh De'ah* 268, sec. 10. For the responsum of Riẓba of Dampierre, see this volume, chapter 2, n. 18.

52 See *She'elot u-Teshuvot ha-Rashbash*, 160, #223 (end). In another responsum, 324, #393, Rashbash heartily ratifies the effectiveness of the *qiddushin* made by an apostate as a foregone conclusion, without providing much data in support.

53 See *She'elot u-Teshuvot ha-Rashbash*, 264–65, #235.

54 See ibid., 354, #418. Rashbash's father, Simeon b. Ẓemaḥ Duran (d. 1444), also cites a number of Ashkenazic sources in his rulings concerning apostates, albeit to a lesser extent. See, e.g. *She'elot u-Teshuvot Tashbeẓ*, ed. Y. Katan et al. (Jerusalem, 2007), 1:61, regarding the apostate's inability to inherit (citing Geonim and Rambam); 3:40, regarding the effectiveness of a *get* issued by an apostate (citing Rambam and *Arba'ah Turim*); and again in 3:43 (61–62), citing Rabbenu Tam, Ri, and Rambam. In 2:139, mourning the son of an apostate born to a Jewish mother is discussed, but substantive sources are not presented. In 3:47, the *qiddushin* of an apostate are discussed, and the conclusion is that these are effective. Geonic sources, Rashi, and *ḥiddushei ha-Rashba* to *Yevamot* are cited, as is *Arba'ah Turim*. Ramban's allowance to lend to an apostate with interest (as found in his *ḥiddushim* to *Bava Meẓi'a*) is discussed, as is the view of the *Sefer ha-'Ittur* (*ot quf, qiddushin, ha-ḥeleq ha-sheni*, fol. 78a), that an apostate's *qiddushin* are not effective. The *halakhah*, however, follows the *Arba'ah Turim* and the other authorities cited. Cf. B. Netanyahu, *The Marranos of Spain*, 72–75; and Dora Zsom, "Wine Produced and Handled by Converts: The Rulings of the Ribash, the Tashbez, and the Rashbash," in *Studies in Responsa Literature*, ed. V. Bányai and S. RáKomoróczy (Budapest 2011), 47–77.

cites only the views of two German Tosafists, Simḥah of Speyer and Riba of Speyer. Although the immersion is meant to achieve a state of repentance and is thus not absolutely obligatory as a ritual act (*ʾein bo mishum miẓvah ve-ʾeino meʿakkev*)—and, per *Pesaḥim* 92b, no subsequent immersion is ever required for a Jew who underwent circumcision as a Jew—this immersion should nonetheless be done, because these apostates are moving from a state of impurity as practicing non-Jews to a state of purity as observant Jews. At the same time, however, Radbaz recommends that any of the children of the *ʾanusim* who have not been circumcised should also be immersed at the time of their circumcision.[55]

In another responsum Radbaz discusses the status of children of apostates (*bnei mumarim*, referring apparently to *conversos* or New Christians from Spain or Portugal) who had fled to Turkey (*Togarmim*) and then traveled to Alexandria to do business. The question was whether, in the course of business dealings with them, it is permitted to lend them money at interest. In this instance Radbaz begins by citing Rashi's responsum that this is prohibited, since *ʾaf ʿal pi she-ḥata Yisraʾel hu*. Ri (of Dampierre), however, permitted this to be done because they are not considered "your brethren" (*ʾaḥikha*), and Jews are therefore not

55 See *Sheʾelot u-Teshuvot ha-Radvaz*, 3:858 (415), where the answer begins: *Katvu be-shem Rabbenu Simhah z"l de-kol baʿalei teshuvah ẓerikhin tevilah*. R. Simḥah's ruling is also cited (and applied) in a responsum that briefly discusses *conversos* (*le-mi she-nitmeʿu ʾavotav dorot ve-dorei dorot ve-hineh shav el ha-Shem she-yitbol*), which was added to *Teshuvot Zikhron Yehudah le-R. Yehudah b. ha-Rosh*, ed. A. Y. Havazelet (Jerusalem, 2005), 159 (sec. 16), and was likely composed by a late-fifteenth-century Spanish authority (see ibid., 153, and the editor's introduction, 44). In this instance R. Simḥah's position is cited from *Shibbolei ha-Leqet* (*hilkhot rosh ha-shanah*, sec. 283; ed. S. Buber [Vilna, 1887], fol. 133b), that one who immerses himself prior to Rosh Hashanah and Yom Kippur for expiation should pronounce a blessing on this immersion, since all pentitents require immersion. The later Spanish passage notes that there was resistance to this practice as it was applied to returning *conversos*, "because those whose ancestors were submerged [*she-nitmeʿu*] and are now seeking to return will not even want to immerse without a blessing since they say that they are full Jews [*yehudim gemurim*]." The conclusion appears to be that immersion without a blessing is sufficient, and that those who support the extreme leniency being sought by those who are returning (that there is no need to undergo immersion) are in the wrong.

obligated to support them (*le-haḥyoto*). Thus in this regard there is no problem of *lifnei 'ivver lo titein mikhshol*. However, a Jew may not borrow money from them, because that causes the *conversos* to sin for no reason (and there is the problem of *lifnei 'ivver*, as Ri had suggested). Similarly, *Sefer Miẓvot Gadol* (סמ"ג = *Sefer ha-Miẓvot le-R. Mosheh mi-Coucy*) holds that you cannot lend at interest to a *mumar 'okhel nevelot le-te'avon*, but you may to a *mumar le-hakh'is*, because he is not your brother (*'aḥikha*). In all such matters you may treat him as a non-Jew; only in matters such as *gittin ve-qiddushin* (where brotherhood is not specifically mentioned) should he be treated as a Jew. In short, this is a fine summary of the view of *Sefer Miẓvot Gadol*.[56]

Radbaz notes that both Ramban and Rashba (in their Talmudic *ḥiddushim*) held this way as well in matters of lending at interest to and from apostates. Even though the forefathers of these Turkish merchants who travelled to Alexandria were considered *'anusim*, their descendants are now considered to be in the category of *mumar le-hakh'is*, because if they wanted to, they could have returned to the practice of Judaism (*dat Yisra'el*) as others had done, especially given that they were coming from (and returning to) secure lands (*'araẓot betuḥim*), where they were able to do as they chose. According to Ri and *Semag*, these *mumarim* could be treated this way because they had denied the God of Judaism and embraced idolatry. They could be treated as non-Jews with regard to charging interest; their *gittin* and *qiddushin* were considered effective only as a matter of stringency (*le-ḥumra*). With regard to interest, however, rabbinic law permits other Jews to charge them interest as a penalty for what they have done. Indeed, Radbaz even cites the passage in the Talmud Yerushalmi about the Cutheans which Ri had adduced to support his view.[57]

Yom Tov b. Moses Ẓaḥalon (d. c. 1640 in Safed, although his family had Spanish roots) rules that a returning apostate does not require immersion; this is required only of a convert to Judaism. Indeed, he writes that "we have

---

56 See *Teshuovt ha-Radvaz*, 4:1086 (12); and this volume, chapter 4, nn. 9–10, 15.

57 On the relative stringency of Radbaz's position in his day with respect to *conversos*, see B. Netanyahu, *The Marranos of Spain*, 72 (n. 187). Cf. Y. H. Yerushalmi, *From Spanish Court to Italian Ghetto* (New York, 1971), 194.

never heard that a Jewish apostate who repents must immerse himself." He subsequently cites the *Nimmuqei Yosef* passage to tractate *Yevamot* (which cites *ḥiddushei ha-Ritva*), arguing that immersion is a rabbinic requirement, as it was for an *'eved kena'ani* who had been freed. But Ẓaḥalon also cites a geonic ruling (from a later source) that no immersion is required, which is how he concludes.[58] Ẓaḥalon rules in another responsum that an apostate must perform *ḥaliẓah* with the wife of his deceased brother, based on the views of several Geonim as well as that of Isaiah di Trani (RID).[59] He rejects the view of his questioner (citing the approach of Isaac b. Sheshet, Rivash, d. 1408) that, because these *conversos* violate the Sabbath systematically (*meḥalelei Shabbat*), the witnesses for the marriage are also *conversos*, and a priest officiates at every aspect of these weddings, no real *qiddushin* occurs and there is therefore no *ziqah* created which then requires *ḥaliẓah*.[60]

At the same time, however, Ẓaḥalon includes in his responsa collection the views of a number of his contemporary rabbinic colleagues on the same issue. Isaac Gershon served in Venice at the end of the sixteenth and in the early seventeenth century, before returning around 1625 to Safed (where he had been born). His responsum includes a rabbinic discussion involving two brothers who were descended from *'anusim* in Portugal and now living in Greece. A hundred and twenty-five years had passed since the initial *'anusim* in this family had appeared. By now, however, most of the family members have "forgotten the principles of Jewish marriage" (*nishtakaḥ torat qiddushin*), and some are not formally married at all. Moreover, they worship as Christians and publicly violate the Sabbath.

However, one of these two brothers married his wife under a rabbinic aegis, *ke-dat Mosheh ve-Yisra'el*, but he subsequently died childless. His wife sought out her husband's brother, asking him to come to Venice, given that a period of safe travel was in effect (for which all *'anusim* had paid their ruler a

58 See *She'elot u-Teshuvot Maharit Ẓaḥalon he-Ḥadashot* (Jerusalem, 1981), vol. 2, 199–200 (sec. 207).

59 See *She'elot u-Teshuvot Mahariẓ ha-Yeshanot*, #148, ed. Machon Yerushalayim (Jerusalem, 2016), 440–43.

60 See *She'elot u-Teshuvot Rivash*, ed. D. Metzger, 6–8 (#5–6).

large sum to be able to move around freely), but the brother repeatedly refused. These *ʾanusim* now were considered by many authorities to be like gentiles, because they worship Christianity and violate the Sabbath. The brother had been asked to come three times—which he would have been able to do safely—but he refused to do so, claiming that he could not leave his (non-Jewish) wife and family. The question was whether the initial *qedushat Yisraʾel* that existed within this family (and its weddings) more than a century ago was still in effect, and therefore *ḥaliẓah* would be required (since a *ziqah* exists)—they were still brothers, as Jacob and Esau were, even though they conducted themselves like non-Jews—or whether they should be considered as two Arab or Christian brothers.

Isaac Gershon rules in accordance with the latter suggestion (and against the view held by Yom Tov Ẓaḥalon), that there is in fact no *ziqah*. In doing so he refers to a series of late medieval rabbinic authorities, expressing particular angst regarding the view of Joseph ibn Lev (d. c. 1580 in Istanbul), who considered *converso* descendants of this type to be Jews as far as the requirement of *ḥaliẓah* is concerned.[61] In making his case, Isaac Gershon notes the strict position of Isaiah di Trani regarding the need for *ḥaliẓah* where an apostate is involved.[62] But he points to the view of R. Sherira Gaon, which suggests that *ḥaliẓah* is not required if the parents (or other ancestors) of the brothers involved were not married according to Jewish law. He notes that *Sefer ha-ʿIttur*, *Sefer Mordekhai*, and *Sefer Or Zaruaʿ* all endorse this position,[63] as do *Arbaʿah Turim*, Rashba, and the *Maggid Mishneh*.[64]

Moreover, Isaac Gershon asserts that neither Rashi nor Maharam of Rothenburg, who typically required an apostate to perform *ḥaliẓah* with his

61 See *Teshuvot Yosef ibn Lev*, 1:15.

62 See this volume, chapter 3, nn. 44–45.

63 See Isaac b. Abba Mari of Marseilles, *Sefer ha-ʿIttur* (end, *get ḥaliẓah*, fol. 6b); *Sefer Mordekhai ʿal Massekhet Yevamot*, secs. 28–29; *Sefer Or Zaruaʿ* (sec. 605); and this volume, chapter 3, nn. 7, 50. See also Meir Benayahu, "R. Yiẓḥaq Gershon," *Asufot* 13 (2001): 9–25 (esp. 19).

64 See *Arbaʿah Turim, Even ha-ʿEzer*, sec. 157 (and see also *Beit Yosef*, s.v. *karav*); *Ḥiddushei ha-Rashba* to Yevamot 22a, ed. H. Dickman (Jerusalem, 2005), 128–29; and *Maggid Mishneh, hilkhot yibbum*, 1:6.

brother's wife in all cases,[65] would make this demand in such a situation. He adds that, according to Rivash (as noted earlier), these weddings are presided over only by a priest; nothing approaching proper *qiddushin* is offered (*de-'ein netinat davar me-'ish le-'ishah*) but "only words" (*raq devarim be-'alma*). Here too, key resources for this discussion emerge in particular from Ashkenazic sources composed during the twelfth and thirteenth centuries, which played an outsized role in setting many of the halakhic policies for dealing with apostasy, as we have seen.[66]

65 See this volume, chapter 3, n. 11. The similar view in this matter of *Terumat ha-Deshen* (sec. 223) is also cited. See this volume, chapter 7, n. 30.

66 See *She'elot u-Teshuvot Mahariz ha-Yeshanot*, #148, 437–40; and cf. B. Netanyahu, *The Marranos of Spain*, 75, n. 194.

7

THE RESPONSA AND RULINGS OF ISRAEL ISSERLEIN AND HIS CONTEMPORARIES

THE PREVIOUS CHAPTER TRACED the impact of developments in Ashkenazic halakhic policy concerning apostasy and reversion on Spanish (and Sefardic) rabbinic literature, from the late thirteenth century and beyond. In this chapter we will discuss the development of subsequent views within Ashkenaz itself. Israel b. Petaḥyah Isserlein of Austria (1390–1460, known also by the Hebrew acronym מהרא״י) was one of the leading talmudists and halakhists in his day, and among the most outstanding rabbinic legal minds and authors in central Europe in the period after the Black Death. Ashkenazic rabbinic leaders in this period generally considered themselves to be *batra'ei*, later authorities whose major goal was to recover and restore the rulings and traditions of the earlier period. Their leading predecessor in this and other respects was Meir b. Barukh (Maharam) of Rothenburg, whose death in custody in 1293, during a period of severe restrictions and persecution, effectively marked the end of the highly productive Tosafist period that began in the twelfth century.[1]

1 See my "Preservation, Creativity, and Courage: The Life and Works of R. Meir of Rothenburg," *Jewish Book Annual* 50 (1992–93): 249–59; and my "1286: R. Meir b. Barukh (Maharam) of Rothenburg, the leading rabbinic figure of his day, is arrested in Lombardy and delivered to Rudolph of Habsburg," in *Yale Companion to Jewish Writing and Thought in German Culture, 1096–1996*, ed. S. L. Gilman and J. Zipes (New Haven, CT, 1997), 27–34.

The wave of intolerance that swept through a number of German cities during the early fifteenth century also reached the leading Austrian Jewish settlements in Vienna and Wiener Neustadt. Some four hundred Jews were killed in Vienna in 1420–21 during the reign of Albert V. The rest of the community was banished, except for a minority of its members who accepted baptism. This large-scale persecution became known as *Gezerat Vienna*. Although rulers and religious authorities allowed apostates to return to Judaism and reiterated that Christians should not force Jewish children to convert without their parents' consent, the edict of the Jews' expulsion from Vienna and other areas under Albert's dominion was repeated twice during the reign of his son Ladislaus. The expulsion was recanted only when Frederick III became the Holy Roman Emperor in 1458. As points of comparison, the Jews were also expelled from Iglau (Moravia) in 1426, and there was a series of expulsions at this time from Bavaria as well. In 1496 the Jews were banished from Wiener Neustadt, where Isserlein served from just prior to 1450, when he arrived from Marburg. A bull from Pope Paul II in 1469, specifically addressed to the Austrian clergy, called for the just treatment of the Jews.[2]

Nonetheless, despite recurring episodes of persecution, Jewish economic and communal life continued apace in a number of different regions within Austria. The numerous responsa and other legal rulings and writings of Isserlein that have survived cover many topics and themes unrelated to the deterioration of Jewish life. They served as a most significant resource for Moses Isserles and other leading halakhists in Eastern Europe during the sixteenth and seventeenth centuries. In addition to his legal reasoning and conclusions, Isserlein preserved texts and rulings from earlier Ashkenazic works that might

2 See Shlomo Eidelberg, *Jewish Life in Austria in the Fifteenth Century* (Philadelphia, 1962), 18–27; Y. Y. Yuval, *Ḥakhamim be-Doram* (Jerusalem, 1989), 61–62, 68–69; Martha Keil, "What Happened to the 'New Christians'? The 'Viennese Geserah' of 1420–21 and the Forced Baptism of Jews," in *Jews and Christians in Medieval Europe: The Historical Legacy of Bernhard Blumenkrantz*, ed. P. Buc et al. (Brepols, 2016), 97–114; Emese Kozme, "Sidrei Teshuvah li-Meshummad she-Ḥazar le-Yahadut be-Austriyyah ube-Germanyah ba-Me'ah ha-Ḥamesh 'Esreh," *'Alei Sefer* 24–25 (2015): 197–98. Overall, however, papal bulls and policies from the fifteenth century concerning the Jews are somewhat contradictory.

otherwise have been lost, which contributed further to the high esteem in which his legal writings were held.[3]

The title of Isserlein's collection of responsa, *Terumat ha-Deshen*, is itself instructive. The phrase *terumat ha-deshen*, literally the offering of the ashes, connotes in biblical and rabbinic literature the priestly service of cleaning the ashes off the altar in the Temple each morning. This task was considered a necessary and even laudable part of the daily service, despite its seemingly mundane purpose. In the mind of its fifteenth-century author, the title of this work may also have been intended to mean "a contribution from the ash heap," a self-effacing wording that reflects the author's inclination toward pronounced piety and asceticism (as we shall see), as well as the overall tendency of the rabbinic scholars of this period to present themselves as less important than their illustrious predecessors.[4]

Moreover, the numerical value (*gematria*) of the word *deshen* equals 354, which corresponds to the number of days in the lunar year and is precisely the number of responsa Isserlein included in his initial collection. This detail, in addition to other considerations (most names and other identifying features are typically omitted), gave rise to the belief, first enunciated in Eastern Europe in the early seventeenth century, that Isserlein's well-organized responsa were composed artificially and not necessarily in response to actual questions.

It is likely, however, that the questions were essentially the ones Isserlein actually received, which he then reshaped and presented in ways that allowed him to include the clear analyses he wished to record for posterity. More than fifty of the questions and issues in the responsa section also appear in some form within the nearly 270 halakhic rulings (*ketavim u-pesaqim*) that form the second part of Isserlein's collected work, suggesting that there is a strong measure of realia within his responsa as well. Recent studies have renewed the discussion about the proper order of Isserlein's responsa, and the degree to which they were stylized.[5]

---

3 On Isserlein's halakhic writings, see Yedidya Dinari, *Ḥakhmei Ashkenaz be-Shilhei Yemei ha-Benayim* (Jerusalem, 1984), 297–313.

4 See Dinari, ibid., 20–21, 34–40; and see also Yuval, *Ḥakhamim be-Doram*, 408–23.

5 See Edward Fram, "Al Seder ha-Teshuvot ba-Mahadurah ha-Mudpeset shel Sefer Terumat ha-Deshen," *'Alei Sefer* 20 (2009): 81–96; and Pinchas Roth, "Ha-Siman

These bibliographic issues have relevance for the texts in *Terumat ha-Deshen* that deal with apostates. It is clear from Isserlein's responsa and other rulings—including the reportage of his devoted student Joseph b. Moses in his *Leqet Yosher*, as well as the responsa of Isserlein's student and slightly younger colleague, Israel Bruna (d. 1480), among other contemporary rabbinic figures in Germany and Austria—that conversion to Christianity, willfully or under duress, was not an isolated or otherwise uncommon phenomenon at this time. There were cases of problematic bills of divorce given by *meshummadim* and instances of *ḥaliẓah* in which an apostate was involved, along with the presence of converts to Christianity who sought to return to the Jewish community, although the total number of cases in all these areas actually documented within the responsa literature of the period is not especially large.[6]

It is fairly evident that the possibility for Jewish apostates to revert to Judaism, regardless of what had led them to accept Christianity initially, was becoming increasingly difficult. As in earlier periods, the Church—and Christian society more broadly—looked quite unfavorably on *relapsi* (Christian converts who had reverted to Judaism) and took various steps to inhibit this movement. This meant that the Jewish community in turn had to consider whether Jews who sought to revert within a particular area or region might unduly endanger themselves or the communities as a whole. As a bull from the generally tolerant Pope Martin V—who had published a bull in 1422 in the aftermath of *Gezerat Vienna*, ordering that Jews be protected—indicates, the Church hierarchy did not approve of apostates from Christianity acting as Jews or mingling with Jews.[7] At the same time, however, rabbinic authorities during this period were also dealing with questions about whether an

---

he-Ḥaser be-Sefer Terumat ha-Deshen," *'Alei Sefer* 21 (2010): 179–81.

6 See Eidelberg, *Jewish Life in Austria*, 27–31; Bernard Rosensweig, "Apostasy in the Late Middle Ages in Ashkenazic Jewry," *Dine Israel* 10–11 (1981–83): 55–67; Dinari, *Ḥakhmei Ashkenaz be-Shilhei Yemei ha-Benayim*, 113–16; and Yuval, *Ḥakhamim be-Doram*, 37, 43–44, 66–67, 83, 165–66, 185, 193.

7 See E. Fram, "Perception and Reception of Repentant Apostates in Medieval Ashkenaz and Premodern Poland," *AJS Review* 21 (1996): 314, n. 57.

apostate from Judaism could be charged interest, whether he renders Jewish wine forbidden to drink, whether he could serve as a *Shabbes goy*, whether meat that had been rendered non-kosher through a less than effective *sheḥitah* could be sold to him, whether a Jew (or the synagogue) could accept charity from him, and whether a Jew could play (cards, or perhaps gamble, *lisḥoq*) with him.[8]

To complicate matters further, R. Isserlein complains in one of his *pesaqim* about the incidence of *reqim u-poḥazim*, derelicts and scoundrels, who return to Judaism with less than complete contrition and sincerity in order to benefit in some personal way from their reversion.[9] Moreover, while a number of Jews who had been forcibly baptized in Vienna in 1420–21 immediately returned to Judaism with the permission of the Christian authorities, Isserlein describes in detail a case that occurred some time after 1421, in which a group of Jews who were traveling to attend a wedding were captured and tortured through various means. The result of this complicated episode was that some of the men and women apostatized, while another small group was able to escape and remain as Jews. Isserlein was asked about whether the captured women who had apostatized were permitted to remain with their husbands.

Although the majority of those captured were ultimately put to death, those who had been converted to Christianity were eventually allowed to

8 See Elisheva Carlebach, *Divided Souls* (New Haven, CT, 2001), 26; Eric Zimmer, *Harmony and Discord* (New York, 1970), 163, 165–66; and S. Eidelberg, *Jewish Life in Austria*, 27–30.

9 See *Terumat ha-Deshen, Pesaqim*, #221, ed. S. Abittan (Jerusalem, 1991), 2:420; *Pesaqim*, #138, ed. Abittan 2:379–1 (*she-hayah mumar shetei pe'amim ve-lo 'asah teshuvah kelal ke-'otam ha-reqim ha-sovevim she-hemiru u-pe'amim ḥozrim u-maḥaziqim 'aẓmam ki-yehudim u-pe'amim ke-nokhrim lefi tumatam*). In these *pesaqim*, Isserlein cites the ruling by Maharam of Rothenburg (*Teshuvot Maimuniyyot le-Seder Nashim*, sec. 10), in which Maharam dismisses the testimony by this kind of "flip-flopping" apostate in a similar case; see this volume, chapter 2, n. 47. See also *She'elot u-Teshuvot R. Yisra'el Bruna*, ed. M. Hershler (Jerusalem, 1960), 27–29 (sec. 32); and cf. *She'elot u-Teshuvot R. Ya'aqov Weil* (Jerusalem, 1988), 169 (*dinin ve-halakhot*), sec. 57, which forbids accepting an apostate's gift to the synagogue of candles to be lit on Yom Kippur. Cf. *Sefer Ḥasidim*, ed. J. Wistinetzki, secs. 190, 1476.

return to Judaism, including several women who had apostatized on another occasion and had previously returned to Judaism; Isserlein notes that the Christian captors could have charged these women with an additional violation (of relapsing back into Judaism), but they did not, apparently due to a technicality. In addition, the Jews being held captive were never charged with harboring these relapsed Christians in their midst.[10]

In another responsum R. Isserlein begins by noting that in his day converts to Christianity who wished to revert to Judaism were expected to undergo both ritual immersion and a close shaving or cropping of their hair and beards (*giluaḥ*, by others) as a matter of course. This much earlier practice had become the accepted manner by which the Jewish community conducted and oversaw all such conversions.

Nonetheless, R. Isserlein adduces a somewhat unusual rabbinic source to support the practice. The mid-eleventh-century Provençal exegete Moses *ha-Darshan* of Narbonne linked this practice with the Torah's requirement (Nu. 8:6–7) that the Levites shave off all their hair and then immerse themselves when they assumed the role of the firstborn in the service of the *mishkan*, after the firstborns lost their role due to the sin of the golden calf. This sin, which Moses *ha-Darshan* and other medieval exegetes understood to be one of idolatry (whose practitioners were said to offer up dead carcasses, *zivḥei metim*, rather than holy sacrifices, and who were themselves considered to be spiritually dead), meant that when the Levites took up their new task they had to ceremonially remove or displace this spiritual state of death. The procedures of shaving and immersion served this purpose, because this was precisely how a leper, who was also considered to be spiritually dead (*meẓora ḥashuv ke-met*), was able to purify himself and return to the community after the signs of his leprosy had abated.[11]

10 See *Terumat ha-Deshen, Teshuvot*, #241, ed. Abittan, 1:194–97; E. Fram, "Perception and Reception of Repentant Apostates in Medieval Ashkenaz and Premodern Poland," 317–18; and M. Keil (this chapter, n. 2).

11 See Ḥanan'el Mack, *Mi-Sodo shel Mosheh ha-Darshan* (Jerusalem, 2010), 63–64 (n. 21); 196–97; 228–29. Cf. idem, "The Bifurcated Legacy of Rabbi Moses Hadarshan and the Rise of *Peshat* Exegesis in Medieval France," in *Regional Identities and*

Employing this midrashic-halakhic model, Isserlein now turns to the question before him: Can the shaving of the reverting apostate be performed on the intermediate days of a festival? A strict rabbinic decree mandated that one who did not shave his beard or take a haircut in honor of the festival could not do so during these days lest the person neglect to groom himself properly before the festival began or put it off for some other reason, thus entering the festival in an unkempt state. Isserlein cites a Mishnah that permits a leper and others who require a purification period and process that concludes only after the festival has begun to shave themselves on the intermediate days of the festival. This overrides the rabbinic decree against shaving, because they did not have the opportunity to do so prior to the festival, and it is appropriate to allow them to be restored to a state of full purity and to offer the requisite sacrifices without delay. Isserlein reasons that returning apostates, who are penitents, should also be able to have their hair cut and to be shaved as preparation for their immersion during the intermediate days of the festival, since they cannot participate fully in public prayer services until they shave and are immersed (*she-harei 'ein meẓarfin 'oto le-khol davar shebi-qedushah 'ad she-yegaleaḥ ve-yitbol*).

Terumat ha-Deshen was not the earliest Ashkenazic source to compare and support the practice of shaving a returning apostate prior to immersion on the basis of the preparations made by the Levites and the purification process of a returning leper.[12] Yet to my knowledge it is the first Ashkenazic work to outline the level of separation from participation in religious rituals that a returning apostate must observe prior to his immersion. Isserlein also carefully defines the other halakhic boundaries involved. The absence of shaving

---

Cultures of Medieval Jews, ed. J. Castaño et al. (London, 2018), 73–91. Mack shows that, although R. Moses's forte was midrashic interpretation (which reflects his Provençal background), and he impacted Rashi's Torah commentary to Numbers in particular in this regard, he was also a source of *peshat* interpretation for Rashi.

12 This distinction belongs to the northern French Torah commentary *Ḥizzequni* (c. 1275), and the slightly later iterations found in other compilatory Torah commentaries composed in northern France and Germany, c. 1300; see this volume, chapter 2, n. 45. Nonetheless, *Terumat ha-Deshen* remains the first halakhic (rather than exegetical) composition to do so.

and immersion does not hinder the sincerely penitent apostate's return to Judaism in theory. However, the accepted practice of doing so, which Isserlein bases on the sanctification of the Levites, is characterized by him as *minhag 'avotenu Torah hi*. As such, the performance of these rituals is fully necessary to achieve the proper degree of purification; and this requirement has the power to override the rabbinic decree against shaving, as with a leper who is in the midst of his purification process. Isserlein finds further support for his view in a halakhic ruling by Asher b. Yeḥi'el (Rosh) which allows for the removal of unwanted hair from a newborn child during the intermediate days of the festival even if the child was born before the festival began, since a child is exempt from this decree. The returning apostate should be similarly exempted.

In providing this last comparison, Isserlein is perhaps pointing to the talmudic principle (*Yevamot* 97b) that "a convert to Judaism is considered to be like a newborn child," which would mean that Isserlein, in effect, viewed the reverting apostate as akin to a convert.[13] On the other hand, this may simply be Isserlein's way of adducing further evidence for the exemption of certain people—by virtue of the unique (halakhic) categories in which they are found—from the decree against shaving on the intermediate days of the festival. What is clear, however, is that the rite that mandated the shaving of a reverting apostate seems to have become the norm in Isserlein's day. However, there is no reference here to the rubbing of the chrism sites in particular or to any other of the even more aggressive techniques that were used according to the reports received by Bernard Gui, which preceded this episode by at least a century.[14]

As noted in chapter 2, a formulation by the German Tosafist Simḥah of Speyer and his student Samuel *ha-Levi* of Worms (R. Bonfant) explains that the immersion of a returning apostate allows the returnees to purify themselves from the sins of having lived among Christians and partaken of their food and lifestyle (*kedei she-titaher min ha-'averah*), so that they may return to

13 This view appears in thirteenth-century Germany, in a formulation by Rabiah (d. c. 1225); see this volume, chapter 2, n. 34.

14 See *Terumat ha-Deshen, Teshuvot*, #86, ed. Abittan, 1:76–77. For Bernard Gui's reports, see this volume, chapter 1, n. 9.

a state of repentance in purity (*ve-taḥzor bi-teshuvah be-taharah*).[15] Indeed, the notion of requiring purification at the point of an apostate's return is expressed already in a responsum by the late-twelfth-century Tosafist Ri of Dampierre.[16] However, these sources are not cited by Isserlein, nor are other thirteenth-century Tosafist sources that refer specifically to preparing the returning apostate for immersion by shaving his head and paring his nails.[17] The availability of every one of these earlier texts to Isserlein would be difficult to establish, but it is likely that these practices were so well established by Isserlein's day that there was no need to provide support for their every aspect.

However, R. Isserlein does employ another textual strategy that should also be noted. He makes the point that Rashi cites the approach of Moses *ha-Darshan* in his own Torah commentary. This may be Isserlein's way of indicating that, although one might think the entire immersion practice and analysis Isserlein presents seem to fly in the face of Rashi's promotion of the axiom *'af 'al pi she-ḥata Yisra'el hu*, since Rashi himself cites the approach of Moses *ha-Darshan* regarding the purification of the Levites, the transference of these rites to a returning apostate can be understood as a friendly (or at least not unfriendly) amendment to Rashi's larger view. In any case, as the work of Isserlein's rulings and teachings *Leqet Yosher* further indicates, once the immersion has been undertaken, the former apostate can be immediately reinstated as a member of the Jewish community with whom other Jews can interact freely.[18]

As Edward Fram has noted, it is clear from Isserlein's responsum about shaving an apostate during *ḥol ha-mo'ed* that he did not wish to delay or inhibit in any way the purification process and rites for an apostate who wished to return. This suggests that Christian efforts to prevent the relapse of apostates from Judaism were not as severe as they had been in earlier periods,

---

15 See this volume, chapter 2, n. 28.

16 See ibid., n. 5.

17 See ibid., nn. 37, 38, 44.

18 See *Sefer Leqet Yosher*, ed. J. Freimann (Berlin, 1903), *Yoreh De'ah*, 49: *meshummad keshe-taval le-shem teshuvah mutar le'ekhol ve-lishtot/ve-la'asoq 'immo mi-yad.*

although from Isserlein's responsum about the women who had been captured and apostatized (described earlier), it would seem that this pressure nonetheless was still extant. In any case, Isserlein did not consider the posture of the Christian authorities in these matters to constitute an unacceptable risk once an apostate was committed to returning. Thus he recommended that this process could proceed with dispatch, although it is also possible that he is referring to cases where specific determinations had been made that there was in fact little danger.[19]

Isserlein's desire to smooth the return to the Jewish community of an apostate who sought to revert is borne out by another brief responsum in which he is asked about whether the returning apostate must undergo a penitential regimen (including meaningful physical afflictions) prior to his return.[20] Isserlein was generally very inclined toward these kinds of penances and *tiqqunei teshuvah* and other forms of self-abnegation for a variety of sins—practices that were derived directly from the penitential regimens of *Ḥasidei Ashkenaz*. He prescribed them for others, and he followed many such pietistic practices himself.[21]

In this instance, however, R. Isserlein informs his questioner that these regimens should not be applied too extensively for a returning apostate. Leaving the fold puts the sinner at a far greater negative distance from the practice of Judaism than the performance of other sins (*suro ra yoter mi-ba'al she'ar 'averot*), because the apostate "has become accustomed to living among the Gentiles and fulfilling all of his heart's desires [*be-khol sherirut libbo*]." Thus we must be concerned lest he lash out against the repentance process if it is too arduous (*'ikka le-meḥash pen yeva'et bi-teshuvato*). In support of this

19 See Fram, "Perception and Reception of Repentant Apostates in Medieval Ashkenaz and Premodern Poland," 318–19.

20 See *Terumat ha-Deshen, Teshuvot*, #198, ed. Abittan, 1:141. The question reads: *mumar she-yaẓa min ha-klal ve-ḥazar le-dat 'emet, ẓarikh le-hitkapper be-siggufim gedolim kefi mah she-'avar 'al kol miẓvot sheba-Torah 'o lo ẓarikh kulei hai*. See also *Sefer Leqet Yosher, Yoreh De'ah*, 49.

21 See Ya'akov Elbaum, *Teshuvat ha-Lev ve-Qabbalat Yissurim* (Jerusalem, 1993), 26–29, 34–36; and Y. Dinari, *Ḥakhmei Ashkenaz be-Shilhei Yemei ha-Benayim*, 85–93.

approach, Isserlein points to a passage in *Semaq mi-Ẓurikh* (citing Eleazar of Worms, although Eleazar's name is not mentioned here by Isserlein),[22] which advises not to be overly demanding in prescribing acts of self-abnegation for the returning apostate. Isserlein further notes that "there are no greater and harsher afflictions than what is suffered by the returning apostate each day as he is taken away from the many pleasures in which non-Jews are immersed, and in which he was fully immersed up to this point." Moreover, "he is now once again subject to the many fears, troubles, and evil acts which the other nations inflict on the Jewish people." Prior to his return, he did not have to worry about any of this. "It turns out that his reversion has caused him all of this suffering" (*ve-nimẓa teshuvato goremet lo kol [ha-] siggufim halalu*), and that is a sufficient degree of affliction.

To be sure, as was the case regarding prescriptions attributed to Eleazar of Worms himself about the afflictions that should (or should not) be undertaken by a reverting apostate, there is some conflicting evidence associated with Isserlein, especially as recorded in *Leqet Yosher*.[23] As Emese Kozme has documented, several of Isserlein's contemporaries in Germany and Austria proposed rather extensive regimens of penance for returning apostates that were very much in the spirit of the German Pietists, whose penitential teachings and practices were followed quite closely during this period.[24] Nonetheless, another of Isserlein's *pesaqim* yields, in passing, what amounts to something of a compromise approach for him, making reference to "one who [properly] returns to the true faith [*le-dat ha-'emet*] by immersing, fasting and undergoing lashes, and openly denies idolatry [*ve-kofer la-'avodah zarah be-peh male*]."[25]

---

22 For Eleazar of Worms's formulation, see this volume, chapter 2, n. 39.

23 See *Sefer Leqet Yosher*, ed. Freimann, *Yoreh De'ah*, 49. Cf. Y. Dinari, *Ḥakhmei Ashkenaz be-Shilhei Yemei ha-Benayim*, 91 (n. 102); Y. Elbaum, *Teshuvat ha-Lev ve-Qabbalat Yissurim*, 28 (nn. 21–22); and E. Fram, "Perception and Reception of Repentant Apostates in Medieval Ashkenaz and Premodern Poland," 319, n. 22.

24 See E. Kozme, "Sidrei Teshuvah li-Meshummad ha-Ḥozer bi-Teshuvah be-Austriyyah ube-Germanyah ba-Me'ah ha-Ḥamesh 'Esreh," 195–211.

25 See *Terumat ha-Deshen, Pesaqim*, #221, ed. Abittan 2:420.

Isserlein wanted the reverting apostate to make a strong statement of commitment at the point of his return, after which he was to be welcomed by the Jewish community, presuming that his return otherwise appeared to be sincere. Nonetheless, Isserlein does not seem to have sought or cultivated the return of apostates per se, even as he tried to move the reversion process along once an apostate from Judaism seeking to return came forward. However, as we shall see in a moment, Isserlein does adhere to several of Rashi's rulings that were meant to keep an apostate linked to Judaism when he was outside Jewish society and law. Isserlein occupies a sensitive place between the more demanding rites of return that had increasingly appeared in Western Europe during the thirteenth century—along with attempts to diminish the Jewishness of the apostate in certain ways, which Isserlein was aware of and explicitly rejects—and the more skeptical approaches that emerged in the early modern period in Eastern Europe, which were briefly described toward the end of the last chapter.[26] Leading rabbinic figures in Poland, from the sixteenth century onward, were less generous than Isserlein regarding the Jewish status of the apostate, and they did not necessarily follow his approach of hastening the process of return for those interested in reverting.[27]

Isserlein treats an ongoing apostate as a Jew with respect to the matrimonial issues of *gittin* and *ḥaliẓah* in the way Rashi and most Tosafists did. He allowed an apostate to appoint a Jewish agent to bring a *get* to his wife, making sure that the apostate would not be able to cancel this appointment or otherwise attempt to thwart his wife's receiving the *get*.[28] Isserlein notes the challenges to Rashi's view regarding *ḥaliẓah* posed by several German Tosafists (citing both Abraham of Regensburg and Isaac *Or Zarua*ʿ by name),[29] but he

---

26 See this volume, chapter 6, nn. 38–39.

27 See E. Fram, "Perception and Reception of Repentant Apostates in Medieval Ashkenaz and Premodern Poland," 317–39; and cf. B. Rosensweig, "Apostasy in the Late Middle Ages in Ashkenazic Jewry," 77–79.

28 See *Terumat ha-Deshen*, *Pesaqim*, #42–43, ed. Abittan, 2:340–41. Cf. E. Zimmer, *Harmony and Discord*, 165–66; this volume, chapter 4, n. 60; and this chapter, n. 40.

29 See this volume, chapter 3, nn. 12, 32–34, 41.

openly rejects this position,[30] as did his student Israel Bruna, who served in both Bruen and Regensburg, where he was the target of an apostate's pitched allegations to the authorities.[31] Nonetheless, Mahari Bruna elsewhere notes that R. Isserlein permitted a groom whose brother was an apostate to explicitly stipulate at the wedding ceremony that the marriage would be valid only if it did not result in the apostate brother serving as a *levir (yavam)*. If, however, the only available *levir* turns out to be an apostate, the marriage is retroactively annulled (so that the woman in any case would not require *ḥaliẓah* to be married to another Jew).[32]

Others among Isserlein's rabbinic colleagues followed the view of the Geonim (cited by Isaac *Or Zarua'*, against that of Rashi) that an apostate at the time of his brother's marriage does not have to perform *ḥaliẓah*.[33] Thus, in a responsum written to R. Zalman Katz, Aaron Blumlein of Krems (Austria) ruled that, if the brother was an apostate at the time of the marriage, no *ḥaliẓah* is required.[34] There were also cases in which a widow who had been waiting a rather lengthy period of time for *ḥaliẓah* from an apostate brother without receiving it subsequently married another Jew. Prominent rabbinic authorities, including Isserlein's predecessor Jacob Moelin (Maharil, d. 1427), ruled in cases such as this that no *ḥaliẓah* was now necessary "after the fact."[35]

---

30 See *Terumat ha-Deshen, Teshuvot*, #219, ed. Abittan, 1:161–63; and #223, ed. Abittan, 1:168–71; and see B. Rosenzweig, "Apostasy in the Late Middle Ages in Ashkenazic Jewry," 55–57. See also *She'elot u-Teshuvot Maharil ha-Ḥadashot*, ed. Y. Satz (Jerusalem, 1977), 347–48 (#207).

31 See *She'elot u-Teshuvot R. Yisra'el Bruna*, ed. Hershler, 54–58 (secs. 66–68). On Mahari Bruna's service in the rabbinate, his relationship with Isserlein, and the ensuing expulsions of Jews from the locales in which he served, see Abraham Fuchs, "Ha-Ḥomer ha-Histori bi-She'elot u-Teshuvot R. Yisra'el Bruna" (DHL thesis, Yeshiva University, 1974), 58–66, 71–75, 86–90. See also *Germania Judaica*, vol. 3.2, ed. A. Maimon et al. (Tubingen, 2003), 1193–94.

32 See *She'elot u-Teshuvot R. Yisra'el Bruna*, ed. Hershler, 112 (sec. 184). Cf. B. Rosensweig, "Apostasy in the Late Middle Ages in Ashkenazic Jewry," 47–48; and A. Fuchs, "Ha-Ḥomer ha-Histori bi-She'elot u-Teshuvot R. Yisra'el Bruna," 228.

33 See Rosensweig, "Apostasy in the Late Middle Ages in Ashkenazic Jewry," 63–67.

34 See Y. Y. Yuval, *Ḥakhamim be-Doram*, 59–71, and esp. 66 (nn. 58–59).

35 See *Teshuvot Maharil*, #205, ed. Y. Satz (Jerusalem, 1979), 322–23. In this case, the

Once again, however, there are other instances in which Isserlein does not embrace Rashi's approach concerning apostates. Israel Bruna records his teacher's response to a young man from Passau who had taken an oath not to "play" with any Jews (*shelo liṣhoq ʿim shum yehudi*), but then asked Isserlein if he was permitted to play cards or perhaps to gamble with a certain apostate in Neustadt. R. Isserlein responds that, "although he is still a Jew [in terms of his religious identity] despite his sin, he is not referred to as [or called] a Jew and so the oath does not apply [*ʾaf ʿal pi she-ḥata Yisraʾel hu, mi-kol maqom lo ʾiqrei yehudi ve-lo ḥal ʿalav ha-neder*]." Although this response might be considered a narrow one, given that the situation involves an oath where such technicalities are considered especially significant, Israel Bruna immediately provides a broader talmudic proof that an apostate "who denies the Jewish God and accepts idolatry" is not considered to be a Jew.[36]

Indeed, as recorded in *Leqet Yosher*,[37] R. Isserlein rules that it is permitted nowadays to lend money at interest to apostates, since they are so enmeshed in sin that, even in situations where permissible food is available, they eat prohibited foods (*she-shavqu hetera ve-ʾakhil ʾissura*).[38] As far as inheritance is

---

woman herself spent some time living among Christians as well. Prior to that, however, she had made a number of attempts to secure *ḥaliẓah*. Moreover, her apostate brother-in-law stated that he was a devout Christian, and that any involvement in this Jewish religious act would run counter to his beliefs. See also *Teshuvot R. Yaʿaqov Weil*, ed. Y. S. Domb (Jerusalem, 2001), #54.

36 See *Sheʾelot u-Teshuvot R. Yisraʾel Bruna*, ed. Hershler, 93, sec. 135. See also A. Fuchs, "Ha-Ḥomer ha-Histori," 226–29; E. Zimmer, *Harmony and Discord*, 163–64; B. Rosensweig, "Apostasy in the Late Middles Ages in Ashkenazic Jewry," 69.

37 See *Sefer Leqet Yosher*, ed. Freimann, *Yoreh Deʿah*, 15.

38 *Leqet Yosher*, ibid., notes that there are many rabbinic opinions that permit this, and the questioner had already received the interest payments in this instance. Nonetheless, some punctilious individuals follow the view that this is prohibited. Cf. *Terumat ha-Deshen*, ed. Abittan, 465 (*teshuvot ḥadashot*, sec. 38). On the other hand, like Rashi, Jacob Moelin (Maharil) ruled that it is completely prohibited to take interest from an apostate, since he is still considered to be "your [Jewish] brother" (*ʾaḥikha*) with regard to the effectiveness of his *gittin* and *qiddushin*. See *Sefer Maharil*, ed. S. Spitzer (Jerusalem, 1989), 623 (*liqqutim*, sec. 45); and cf. B. Rosensweig, "Apostasy in the Late Middle Ages in Ashkenazic Jewry," 68–69. *Beit Yosef* to *Yoreh Deʿah* 159:2 allowed the taking of interest from an apostate,

concerned, Isserlein is a bit more circumspect. He adopts the position that the Jewish court should take control of this and act according to what will be most compelling if the apostate should return to the Jewish community.[39]

Isserlein and Zalman Katz, who served as the rabbi of Nuremberg for thirty years (between 1413 and his death in 1444), became involved with the case of an apostate who had worked as a scribe when he was part of the Jewish community. The apostate had left his wife without a *get* when he apostatized. By chance, this apostate ran into his brother-in-law in Wiener Neustadt, who pleaded with the apostate to write his wife a *get*. The apostate agreed, on condition that it would be written immediately and without any delay, since he was about to head off to a business transaction in another locale. The brother-in-law was thus appointed a *sheliaḥ le-holakhah*, an agent to transfer the *get* from the apostate to his wife. However, Isserlein was concerned about the ability of an apostate to appoint such an agent at all, given that this apostate in particular had been an expert scribe who was well-versed in the laws and procedures of *gittin*, including the ways a *get* could be subtly disqualified. Isserlein, who was in charge of producing and supervising the giving of the *get*, required the brother-in-law to travel to Nuremberg to secure the approval of Zalman Katz, who was considered an outstanding expert in such matters, that this *get* was valid. Isserlein sent along a detailed letter explaining why he thought it should be.

Zalman Katz was prepared to rely on the *get* that Isserlein had prepared (and on the agency for the *get* that the apostate had transferred to his brother-in-law). He copied three responsa for Isserlein regarding an apostate granting a *get* which he had received from Maharil, Yoḥanan Treves, and Aaron Blumlein.

---

citing French Tosafists such as Rabbenu Tam. And in his *Shulḥan 'Arukh*, *Yoreh De'ah*, 159:2, Yosef Caro adopts Ri's caveat that interest should not be paid, however, to an apostate (this volume, chapter 4, n. 15). Moses Isserles, however, in both *Darkhei Mosheh* and his glosses to *Shulḥan 'Arukh*, ad loc., cites the ruling of Maharil.

39 See *Terumat ha-Deshen*, *Teshvuot*, #349, ed. Abittan, 306–9; B. Rosenzweig, "Apostasy in the Late Middle Ages in Ashkenazic Jewry," 75–76; Y. Y. Yuval, *Ḥakhamim be-Doram*, 193; and see also ibid., 185 (n. 55).

Isserlein, in turn, ratified the *get* based on Zalman Katz's acquiescence, and he recorded this entire incident and discussion in the *Terumat ha-Deshen*.[40]

In contrast, Jacob Weil (d. c. 1455), a student of Maharil and a contemporary of Isserlein, would not allow such an agency to be created, since he considered the apostate to have severed his relationship with the Jewish people to such an extent that the constructs of Jewish law, including agency and its appointment (*sheliḥut*), could no longer be applied to him. During this period some rabbinic authorities suggested that the agent should be empowered on behalf of the wife to receive the *get* using the principle of *zakhin le-'adam she-lo be-fanav* (a person may be the recipient of a beneficial act or award even if he or she is not present). Others added that, since the apostate in effect had the status of a non-Jew, it was surely better for his wife not to remain with him. Maharil distinguished in this regard between a man who was converted forcibly or under duress (and therefore might well repent) and one who converted willingly (for whom the chance of repentance was much more remote).[41]

Isserlein was involved with the question of how a Jewish husband ought to give a *get* to his wife who had apostatized, noting that in the Rhineland it was not required to give a *get* in such a case. His concern was that, since the wife who had apostatized was undoubtedly having illicit relations with Christians, it was better for her from the halakhic perspective to do so as a single (divorced) woman rather than as a married woman. Thus another person could accept the *get* for her, because it is to her benefit (*u-mezakkeh lah get 'al yedei 'aḥer di-zekhut hu lah*). The sensitivity shown here, to try to minimize the full extent of an apostate's sin and punishment, is noteworthy.[42]

40 See *Terumat ha-Deshen, Teshuvot*, #237, ed. Abittan, 1:188–90. A summary was also recorded by one of Isserlein's students. See *Terumat ha-Deshen, Pesaqim*, #42–43, ed. Abittan, 2:340–41. Cf. Y. Y. Yuval, *Ḥakhamim be-Doram*, 21–24, 43–44; and B. Rosenzweig, "Apostasy in the Late Middle Ages in Ashkenazic Jewry," 59–62.

41 See *Teshuvot Mahari Weil*, ed. Domb, 153–54 (#126), and Weil's *dinin ve-halakhot* (this chapter, n. 9), 165 (sec. 17); and *She'elot u-Teshvot Maharil he-Ḥadashot*, ed. Satz, sec. 206.

42 See *Terumat ha-Deshen, Pesaqim*, #256, ed. Abittan, 2:440–41. See also *She'elot u-Teshuvot Maharil*, #100, ed. Satz, 190–94.

In sum R. Israel Isserlein appears for the most part to have followed the views of the Tosafists of northern France, even though he rarely identifies these sources by name. Indeed, despite his extensive library, it remains difficult to know whether he had access to the full range of Tosafist sources, both French and German, that have been presented throughout this study. Nonetheless, Isserlein strongly supports the practice that a returning apostate should be immersed (describing it as *minhag 'avotenu Torah hi*), but he seems to have downplayed the extent to which a demanding regimen of *tiqqunei teshuvah* should also be required. Since the *qiddushin* of an apostate are effective, an apostate's *get* had to be properly executed, and he was required to perform *ḥaliẓah* if no other brother was available. At the same time, interest on a loan could be taken from an apostate, and Isserlein remained concerned with serial apostates who "flip-flopped" between the Jewish and Christian communities. Indeed, since some things never seem to change, a Jew in this period might exclaim out of personal frustration that he would apostatize if his mother-in-law entered his home; and Isserlein had to deal with the halakhic fallout from such a declaration as well.[43]

To be sure, the fifteenth century was not the same as the thirteenth century in terms of the causes and extent of apostasy. Nonetheless, Isserlein was able to maintain a balanced view with an excellent rabbinic pedigree, which allowed him in turn to negotiate the difficult challenges that apostasy and reverting apostates continued to pose to the Jewish community in his day. As we have seen, a number of his learned rabbinic colleagues were involved in these kinds of decisions and activities as well.

---

43 See *Terumat ha-Deshen, Pesaqim*, #192, ed. Abittan, 406. See also *She'elot u-Teshuvot R. Yisra'el Bruna*, ed. Hershler, 21–22 (sec. 24); Yaakov Guggenheim, "Meeting on the Road: Encounters between German Jews and Christians on the Margins of Society," in *In and Out of the Ghetto*, ed. R. Po-Chia Hsia and H. Lehmann (Cambridge, 1995), 125–37; and M. Keil, "Ritual Repentance and Testimonies at Rabbinical Courts in the Fifteenth Century," in *Oral History of the Middle Ages: The Spoken Word in Context*, ed. G. Jaritz and M. Richter (Krems/Budapest, 2001), 175.

CONCLUSION

Rashi (d. 1105), and to a lesser extent his pre-Crusade predecessor, Rabbenu Gershom of Mainz (d. 1028), favored an approach to apostates that sought to smooth their return to the Jewish community, based on an assumption that their halakhic status as Jews was not significantly diminished by their apostasy even if they had apostatized willingly. These earlier Ashkenazic authorities expected reverting apostates to pledge and demonstrate their repentance and renewed commitment to Jewish observance to the Jewish community once again, but no further requirements were imposed. Moreover, Jews were not permitted to lend money at interest to ongoing apostates or to otherwise harm their basic economic well-being. An apostate's *qiddushin* and *gittin* were considered effective, as was the need for him to do *ḥaliẓah* for his brother's childless widow in all cases, against the geonic view that someone who had apostatized prior to his brother's wedding does not perform *ḥaliẓah*.

To be sure, Rashi agrees that an apostate is ultimately not entitled (by rabbinic law) to inherit from his ancestors, with those assets going instead to other family members, and his testimony while in a state of apostasy can be accepted only under limited conditions, and only where the apostasy occurred under duress. For Rabbenu Gershom, a *kohen* who had apostatized willingly could not return to pronounce the priestly blessings, although, as has been suggested, this particular ritual detail does not significantly alter the larger lenient posture that Rashi and Rabbenu Gershom shared.

The approach favored by Rashi and Rabbenu Gershom during the eleventh century was narrowed and changed in several significant ways by the Tosafists, beginning in the mid- to late twelfth century. In northern France, Rabbenu Tam (d. 1171) and his students Isaac (Ri) of Dampierre (d. c. 1190) and Eli'ezer of Metz (d. 1198) allowed interest to be taken from an apostate not simply because he was no longer considered to be a full "brother" (as in the verse *la-nokhri tashikh ule-'aḥikha lo tashikh*, Deut. 23:21), but because the Talmud (*'Avodah Zarah* 26b) clearly indicates that a heretic-like figure who does not observe Jewish law even when he has the opportunity to do so without any difficulty (a *mumar le-hakh'is*) should not be sustained or supported. However, in recognition of the inherent Jewish identity of an apostate, Ri notes that a Jew cannot borrow money at interest from an apostate, since this would be akin to inducing the apostate to perform a sinful act and would thus violate the prohibition of *lifnei 'ivver lo titein mikhshol.*

To ease the way for returning apostates, Rabbenu Tam allowed a reverting female apostate who had sexual relations with a non-Jew during her apostasy to marry her non-Jewish paramour if he subsequently converted to Judaism. Indeed, Rabbenu Tam also permitted this woman, following her reversion, to return instead to her Jewish husband, assuming that he did not wish to divorce her. However, Rabbenu Tam's students, including Ribam of Bohemia and likely Ri as well, did not support these allowances, which Rashi was also not prepared to countenance. At the same time Rabbenu Tam was also instrumental in overseeing the effective execution of *gittin* that had been authorized by apostates.

Ri of Dampierre supported the practice of immersing a returning apostate whether as a penance, as a means of focusing the reverting apostate on his renewed commitment, or as a form of un-baptism. But Ri openly dismisses the need for a more formal reacceptance of Jewish practices or an explicit verification of the apostate's sincerity as was mandated by the Talmud for an *'am ha-'areẓ* who wished to become a *ḥaver* with regard to ritual purity. Two of Ri's students, however, the brothers Isaac and Samson b. Abraham (Riẓba of Dampierre and Rash *mi-Shanẓ*) proposed in different ways the need for some type of verification.

Successors of Ri and his students in the thirteenth century, including Moses of Coucy (d. c. 1255), Yeḥi'el of Paris (d. c. 1260), and Samuel and Moses b. Shne'ur of Evreux (d. c. 1250), accepted and further explained the positions of their northern French predecessors, grounding these requirements in additional talmudic texts and analysis. The brothers of Evreux (or their direct student, Rabbenu Pereẓ of Corbeil, d. 1297) maintained that the immersion required of a reverting apostate is of the same nature and purpose as the immersion that a freed *'eved kena'ani* had to undergo according to talmudic law. Meir of Rothenburg, who had studied with Samuel of Evreux and was a close senior colleague of Rabbenu Pereẓ, also recognized its necessity.

Moses of Coucy correlates the efficacy of an apostate's *qiddushin* and *gittin* with the allowance to lend money to him at interest, as put forward in Rabbenu Tam's circle. R. Moses also notes the difference of opinion about whether a Jew may borrow money at interest from an apostate, attributing support for Ri's view—that this is a violation of *lifnei 'ivver*—to his Tosafist colleague Samuel of Falaise. This issue is further discussed by Yeḥi'el of Paris as well, although he explains the prohibition against borrowing at interest from an apostate as a means for Jews to avoid enhancing his well-being rather than as a function of *lifnei 'ivver* (i.e., that this will engender further sin on the part of the apostate). Yeḥi'el of Paris, among other contemporary Tosafist colleagues, also reduces Rabbenu Tam's allowance for a reverting female apostate. She may marry her former paramour if he converted to Judaism, but she cannot remain with her Jewish husband under any condition. R. Yeḥi'el also presents a different reason from that of Rabbenu Tam for this allowance, and his son-in-law, Isaac b. Joseph of Corbeil (d. 1280), effectively eliminates it altogether.

German Tosafists in the late twelfth and early thirteenth centuries invested the immersion for a returning apostate with even more meaning and consequence than did their northern France counterparts. For Simḥah of Speyer (d. c. 1230), this immersion is an indispensable means of expiation that must always be undertaken. For Eli'ezer b. Joel *ha-Levi* (Rabiah, d. c. 1225), since the returning apostate is akin to a convert to Judaism (*ka-ger*), the immersion and its intensive preparations—including shaving the head and paring the nails closely, which must also be accompanied by a reacceptance of Jewish beliefs and practices in the presence of a rabbinic tribunal of three—are intended to closely correspond to the halakhic regimen of conversion to Judaism.

Indeed, the only leniency proposed by Rabiah in this regard is that the immersion of a reverting apostate can take place at night (which is unacceptable for the immersion requirement for conversion). Several additional German Tosafist texts endorse immersion as Rabiah had advocated. A northern French source, *Qiẓẓur Semag* (by Abraham b. Ephraim [d. c. 1265], a student of the Tosafist Tuvyah of Vienne), cites Rabiah's approach anonymously. The late-thirteenth-century northern French Torah commentary *Ḥizzequni* refers to the ongoing practice of this rite in the case of reverting apostates in its discussion of the purification of the Levites (Nu. 8:7, which involves shaving the head and immersion) as they assumed their role in the *mishkan*.

Moving beyond their northern French counterparts once again, German Tosafists posited a significantly diminished status of apostates as Jews in the area of *yibbum* and marriage issues more broadly. Abraham of Regensburg (c. 1200), Barukh of Mainz (d. 1221), and Isaac of Vienna (d. c. 1255) maintained (against the view of Rashi, and even beyond the geonic view) that an apostate does not perform *ḥaliẓah* in any situation. Their reasoning and derivations differ slightly, but the emergence of this position is unmistakable, and it is discussed further in the writings of Isaac *Or Zarua*ʿs son, Ḥayyim Eliʿezer (c. 1300). Other German Tosafists (and students of Simḥah of Speyer), such as Isaiah di Trani (d. c. 1240), acknowledge this ruling while disagreeing with its premise, but Simḥah of Speyer himself (along with Eliʿezer of Metz, who taught in the Rhineland and had other connections there) strongly considers the possibility that the *qiddushin* of an apostate are valid only *mi-safeq* (*le-ḥumra*, as per *Yevamot* 15b). R. Simḥah was also unsure about whether the *get* of an apostate is valid. Rabiah was aware of others who espoused this view, even as he himself did not embrace it.

The German Tosafists focused their attempts to weaken the full Jewish status of apostates on matrimonial matters; some regarded the issue of money-lending as less crucial. Indeed, even though in his view an apostate's *qiddushin* were deemed valid only *le-ḥumra*, Simḥah of Speyer remarks that the apostate's questionable status as a Jew in this matter is nonetheless sufficient to prohibit lending money to him at interest. Rabiah suggests that money-lending at interest to an apostate is permitted as a *qenas* (a fine or punishment), which operates under the judicial principle of *hefqer beit din hefqer*, that monies can be reassigned under the direction of rabbinic authority.

Barukh of Mainz's rulings, on the other hand, take a more evenly integrated approach. While an apostate can no longer be considered by other Jews to be an eligible candidate for *ḥaliẓah*, because his status as a Jew in this regard is lacking, the apostate nonetheless remains a Jew from his own religious perspective, and he should not be forced to perform additional sins. Hence money-lending for which interest is charged to him, or paid to him, is prohibited. In some ways this is the inverse of the formulation found in Moses of Coucy's *Sefer Miẓvot Gadol*, and it succinctly reflects the more severe view of apostasy embraced by several German Tosafists. However, even the Tosafists of northern France, with few exceptions, moved well past the position that Jacob Katz identifies and associates with Rashi.

This study has presented a series of historical, doctrinal, and societal patterns and events that can explain the Tosafists' various moves toward stringency regarding apostasy and reversion, along with concomitant changes regarding conversion to Judaism where, at least in northern France, converts were more openly welcomed during this period. The Tosafists' analyses were formulated (and proceeded) along textual and juridical lines. But the trends identified here suggest that larger considerations of how to protect the Jewish communities in northern Europe from the inroads of increased anti-Judaism, and the Christians' outright hatred for the Jews as unrivaled enemies of Christianity, played a major role in the Tosafists' more demanding and restrictive rulings concerning apostates (as compared to those of Rashi and his followers). These concerns might even have determined the extent to which these rulings were accepted by the laity (and dovetailed with existing practices).

The sharp dichotomy Jacob Katz posits between the medieval and early modern periods, which assumes the near-complete absence of more restrictive policies toward apostates (and their reversion) until the later period, cannot be sustained on the basis of the evidence presented in this study, even as the early modern period did see the further expansion of some of these restrictions. The evidence from medieval Christian sources about how the Jews dealt with those who sought to return from Christianity to Judaism (*relapsi*) is based not only on popular practices and culture but also reflects concepts and practices that had the approbation of the rabbinic elite in northern Europe.

At the same time this study sounds a cautionary note about how to assess Tosafist literature and analyses concerning apostates. There are specific areas of Jewish law in which the relevant halakhic considerations allowed and at times even required the Tosafists to consider apostates in a somewhat different way than they did otherwise. Generally speaking, if the physical or spiritual well-being or the assets of other Jews with whom the apostate was not so closely connected or directly involved were at stake, Tosafists could rule in different ways and with a different set of considerations than they did in the larger but more intimate areas on which this study has focused, including the requirements for reversion, matrimonial and *yibbum* matters, and money-lending transactions.

The Ashkenazic views that developed during the Tosafist period in these overarching matters of apostasy and reversion had an interesting and sometimes even surprising *nachleben*. As the phenomenon of apostasy increased in Christian Spain during the thirteenth century and beyond (and well before the calamitous events of 1391 and beyond), Spanish talmudists and halakhists sought precedents that could be helpful to them. Geonic material was apparently all they had available—perhaps together with a Provençal source or two that relied mostly on the same geonic teachings—and much of that material (even where it dealt with Christianity rather than Islam) is not so formally documented on the basis of talmudic law. As Spanish talmudists became aware of the expanded Ashkenazic rulings, they began to rely on them as they did in other areas of Jewish law, and to formulate and anchor more effectively the procedures and restrictions they followed.

A late-fourteenth-century Spanish rabbinic source (*Nimmuqei Yosef*) preserves a *Tosafot Shitah* passage that had been noted earlier by Ritva with regard to the immersion of a reverting apostate, and it provides the textual vehicle through which this requirement was transferred to Eastern Europe in the sixteenth century. Indeed, some of the later authorities in Eastern Europe who cited and supported this passage appear to have been unaware of its distinctly Ashkenazic origins. Among Spanish and Sefardic authorities who dealt with the halakhic status of *conversos* during the fifteenth and sixteenth centuries and beyond, Tosafist sources are often the major, and on occasion the only, rabbinic texts they cite in issuing their rulings.

The challenges posed by apostasy in late medieval Ashkenaz following the Black Death shift, in light of changes in both Church and societal responses. Israel Isserlein and his rabbinic colleagues in the fifteenth century had to develop effective halakhic policies—in this area as in many others—that demonstrated an overall fealty to the heyday of medieval Ashkenazic Jewry and its teachers, but which also had the ability to deal with the contemporary facts and realia they faced. Although R. Isserlein was not nearly as encouraging of returning apostates as Rashi had been, he sought to maintain at least some of Rashi's policies that were identifiable as such.

Where Isserlein disagrees with Rashi, he tries to express his disagreement in a way that does not openly conflict with Rashi's view. Indeed, he bases the ubiquitous practice in his day (*minhag 'avotenu Torah hi*) of immersing a returning apostate on a comment by Rashi regarding the verse in Numbers that describes the Levites' preparations to serve in the *mishkan*. Rashi's comment cites an interpretation of Moses *ha-Darshan* of Narbonne about why both shaving and immersing the Levites were required. While taking note of the dissenting German Tosafist view, Isserlein rules that an apostate must perform *ḥaliẓah* as Rashi and others, including Meir of Rothenburg, had concluded. But Israel Bruna describes how Isserlein authorized a condition to be made at the time of a wedding: If the husband dies and his brother is an apostate at that time, the wedding is retroactively annulled, and thus no *ḥaliẓah* is required. Isserlein permits lending money at interest to a committed apostate, even though his devoted student notes that there were some punctilious Jews who did not do this. On balance Isserlein's views in these matters are closest to those of the Tosafists of northern France. Yet it cannot be assumed that Isserlein had at his disposal the full complement of the Tosafist writings presented and discussed in this study.

With the advent of the modern period, additional changes take place with respect to apostasy and reversion (as noted by Jacob Katz and Edward Fram) in Poland, if not in Germany. It would be interesting and perhaps important to see how the medieval Ashkenazic positions are (or are not) utilized and developed with the further passage of time. The historical and societal situations of the Jewish people in the seventeenth and eighteenth centuries (and beyond) are obviously quite different. Nevertheless, it would be worthwhile to study the extent to which the larger positions put forward by the Tosafists, as identified and treated in this study, beyond the view of Rashi, played a role in these centuries as well.[1] Mindful, however, of the rabbinic dictum *lo ʿalekha ha-melakhah ligmor*, I invite those who specialize in these later periods to take up this challenge.

1 See, e.g., Jakob Goldberg, *Ha-Mumarim be-Mamlekhet Polin-Lita* (Jerusalem, 1986); Deborah Hertz, "Women at the Edge of Judaism: Female Converts in Germany, 1600–1750," in *Studies in Jewish Civilization*, vol. 2, ed. M. Mor (Omaha, NE, 1997), 87–109; B. Z. Kedar, "Continuity and Change in Jewish Conversion to Christianity in Eighteenth-Century Germany" [Hebrew], in *Studies in the History of Jewish Society in the Middle Ages and the Modern Period*, ed. E. Etkes and Y. Salmon (Jerusalem, 1980), 154–70; and this volume, chapter 1, n. 48; chapter 7, n. 27.

APPENDIX

Rabbinic Scholars in Europe during the High Middle Ages

Northern France	**Germany and Central Europe**
Rashi (Solomon b. Isaac, d. 1105)	Rabbenu Gershom (b. Judah of Mainz, d. 1028)
Rashbam (Samuel b. Meir, d. c. 1160)	Riba (Isaac b. Asher) *ha-Levi* of Speyer (d. 1133)
Rabbenu Jacob (b. Meir) Tam (d. 1171)	Raban (Eli'ezer b. Nathan) of Mainz (d. c. 1170)
Ri (Isaac b. Samuel) of Dampierre (d. c. 1190)	Ribam (Isaac b. Mordekhai) of Regensburg/ Bohemia
R. Elḥanan ben ha-Ri (d. 1184)	R. Ephraim b. Isaac of Regensburg (d. 1175)
R. Eli'ezer b. Samuel of Metz (d. 1198)	R. Abraham b. Moses of Regensburg
Riẓba (Isaac b. Abraham) of Dampierre (d. 1209)	Rivaq (Judah b. Qalonymus) of Speyer (d. 1199)
R. Barukh b. Isaac (d. 1211, *Sefer ha-Terumah*)	R. Judah b. Samuel *he-Ḥasid* (d. 1217)
R. Samson (Rash) b. Abraham of Sens (d. 1214)	R. Barukh b. Samuel of Mainz (d. 1221)
R. Judah b. Isaac Sirleon of Paris (d. 1224)	Rabiah (Eli'ezer b. Joel *ha-Levi*, d. c. 1225)
R. Samuel b. Solomon of Falaise (d. c. 1245)	R. Eleazar b. Judah of Worms (d. c. 1230)
R. Samuel b. Shne'ur of Evreux (d. c. 1250)	R. Simḥah b. Samuel of Speyer (d. c. 1230)
R. Moses b. Jacob of Coucy (d. c. 1255)	R. Isaac b. Moses *Or Zarua'* of Vienna (d. c. 1255)
R. Yeḥi'el b. Joseph of Paris (d. c. 1260)	R. Avigdor b. Elijah *Kohen Ẓedeq* (Katz) of Vienna
R. Isaac b. Joseph of Corbeil (d. 1280)	R. Samuel b. Abraham *ha-Levi* (R. Bonfant, d. c. 1275)
Rabbenu Pereẓ b. Elijah of Corbeil (d. 1297)	R. Meir b. Barukh (Maharam) of Rothenburg (d. 1293)

Southern France	Spain
R. Isaac b. Abba Mari of Marseilles (d. c. 1193)	Rabbenu Yonah b. Abraham of Gerona (d. 1263)
Rabad (Abraham b. David) of Posquières (d. 1198)	Ramban (Moses b. Naḥman) of Gerona (d. 1270)
R. Solomon b. Abraham of Montpellier (d. c. 1240)	Rashba (Solomon b. Abraham ibn Adret) of Barcelona (d. c. 1310)
R. Abraham b. Isaac of Montpellier (d. c. 1315)	Ritva (Yom Tov b. Abraham Ishvilli, d. c. 1325)
R. Menaḥem b. Solomon *ha-Meiri* (d. 1316)	Rosh (Asher b. Yeḥi'el, d. c. 1325; fled Germany in 1304)

Italy
R. Isaiah b. Mali di Trani (RID, d. c. 1240)
R. Zedekiah b. Abraham *ha-Rofe* (d. c. 1260)

INDEX OF MANUSCRIPT REFERENCES

The number following each entry is the film number in the electronic catalog (Ktiv) of the Institute for Microfilmed Hebrew Manuscripts (IMHM) at the National Library of Israel.

Berlin (State Library) Or. Qu. 3 (Cat. Steinschneider 37) [f 1731] 50, 98, 136
Berlin (State Library) Or. Phillip 1392 (Cat. Steinschneider 194) [f 1757] 110
Budapest (National Library) 2°1 (f 31445) 74, 107

Cambridge University
Add. 490 (f 16784) 70, 74, 99
Add. 559–560 (f 16848) 50
Add. 3127 (f 17556) 142

Halle (University Library of Saxony) Yb Fol. 7 (f 14637) 109
Hamburg (State and University Library)
45 (Heb. 235) [f 1041] 71, 72, 110, 116
194 (Heb. 247) [f 1051] 108

Jerusalem NLI 4°682 (B 398) 152
Jerusalem NLI 4°6695 [Hechal Shelomoh 45ג] 38

Leipzig (University Library) 1119 (f 74146) 39, 176
London Beit Din 11 (f 4682) 113
London British Museum (Margoliouth)
506 (Harley 5718) [f 4855] 107
515 (Add. 26982) [f 5655] 98
532 (Add. 27297) [f 6085] 89
Or. 9931 (f 6987) 57
London Montefiore 134 (f 7304) 50, 150
London Sassoon 534 [Toronto FR 5-011] (f 9334) 70, 99

Moscow RSL (Guenzburg)
- 155 (f 6835) 96
- 187 (f 6866) 50
- 349 (f 47697) 57
- 525 (f 47856) 170
- 1230 (f 8938) 152
- 1329 (f 47575) 147

NY JTS
- Lutzki
  - 791 (f 24021) 57
  - 794 (f 24024) 57
- Rab.
  - 526 (f 39216) 147
  - 645 (f 39324) 135
  - 673 (f 41418) 96, 118
  - 674 (f 41419) 70

Oxford Bodleian (Neubauer)
- 566 (f 19437) 9, 27, 30, 32, 39, 104, 115, 118
- 650 (f 20566) 90
- 667 (f 20583) 74, 139
- 672 (f 20588) 69
- 678 (f 20583) 4, 95, 96, 106, 115, 118
- 682 (f 20597) 55
- 778 (f 20315) 139
- 781 (f 20318) 135, 170
- 784 (f 20321) 45
- 820 (f 20357) 17, 70, 169, 188
- 844 (f 21605) 43, 99, 169
- 879 (f 21838) 33, 50, 98
- 880 (f 21839) 98, 136
- 881 (f 21840) 89
- 1210 (f 16670) 45
- 2343 (f 21407) 170

Paris BN
- Heb. 314 (f 4328) 140
- Heb. 370 (f 20241) 107, 121
- Heb. 374 (f 4353) 107
- Heb. 381 (f 4630) 33, 50, 98, 136
- Heb. 388 (f 4367) 50, 98
- Heb. 407 (f 27901) 98
- Heb. 408 (f 30735) 108

Heb. 1391 (f 34252) 181
Heb. 1408 (f 24886) 45
Paris Cluny Museum 12290 (f 14772) 152
Paris Mazarine 4472 (f 4411) 107, 121
Parma Palatina (de Rossi)
93 (f 12322) 107, 121
166 (f 13913) 170
172 (f 13898) 50, 98, 136
563 (f 13202) 55
583 (f 13900) 98
605 (f 13061) 152
854 (f 13017) 152
929 (f 13795) 75, 99, 107, 110
Cod. Parma 3518 (f 14025) 152

Toronto (Friedberg) 3–004 (f 70562) 108

Vatican
Ebr. 141 (f 11627) 107, 139
Ebr. 144 (f 223) 107, 139
Ebr. 148 (f 227) 89
Ebr. 183 (f 8698) 45, 55
Ebr. 324 (f 8635) 108
Vercelli (Bishop's Seminary) C1 (f 30923) 17, 34, 39, 53, 60, 70, 74, 96, 99, 107, 111, 113, 118, 136, 147, 177
Vienna (National Library)
20 (hebr. 12a) [f 10150] 98
72 (hebr. 2) [f 10157] 74, 107, 139
73 (heb. 208) [f 1470] 99

Zurich Braginsky 115 [London Beit Din 12] (f 4683) 50

INDEX OF SUBJECTS AND NAMES

Authored works are found under the author's name.

Abraham b. David of Posquières (Rabad), 169n9
Abraham b. Ephraim, 50–51n35; *Qizzur Semag*, 67, 216
Abraham b. Isaac of Montpellier, 181–82
Abraham b. Moses of Regensburg, 97, 114, 156; on *ḥalizah*, 16–17, 73–74, 85, 90, 93, 95, 206, 216
Abulafia, Meir *ha-Levi*, of Toledo (Ramah), 185n43
Albert V (duke of Austria), 196
Alfasi, Isaac b. Jacob (Rif), 80, 133n54, 134n58, 182
'am ha-'arez seeking to become *ḥaver* compared to returning apostate, 11–12, 29–31, 34, 35, 39–40, 43
Amora Rav, 98–99
Amram Gaon, 96n53
apostasy. *See* rabbinic approaches to apostasy and reversion
Arba'ah Turim, 192
Asher b. Yeḥi'el (Rosh), 97n53, 142, 185n43, 188, 202
Asher of Lunel, 173
Avot de-R. Natan, 45, 47, 49, 67
Avraham b. Avraham *ha-Ger*, 146n17
Bamberg, Samuel, 78
baptism: effect on Jewish character of, 3–4; ritual immersion as reversal of, 5, 6, 49, 56, 155, 161, 165–66, 175
bar mizvah, 77, 94
Barukh b. Isaac, author of *Sefer ha-Terumah*, 75, 79n23, 112n17
Barukh b. Isaac of Regensburg, 75;
Barukh b. Samuel of Mainz: on *ḥalizah*, 76, 78–85, 87, 88, 90, 93, 103, 108, 114, 216, 217; on money-lending at interest, 82–85, 103–6, 108, 110, 111, 112n17, 114, 217; on ritual immersion, 156; *Sefer ha-Ḥokhmah*, 78, 82, 103; *Tosafot* by, 127n41
batra'ei, 195
beit din. *See* tribunal, appearance before
Bekhor Shor (Yosef b. Isaac of Orleans), 37n12
Benedict XII (pope; as Jacques Fournier), 6n11
Bernard Gui, 5–6, 10n20, 53, 165, 167
Berthold Von Regensberg, 149n23
betrothals. See *qiddushin* of apostates
Blumlein, Aaron, of Krems, 207, 209

Bonfant (Samuel b. Abraham *ha-Levi*) of Worms, 47–49, 76–77, 95, 101–2, 175, 202
borrowing from an apostate at interest, 110, 116
Bruna, Israel, 198, 207, 208, 219

Caro, Joseph. *See* Karo, Yosef
children: born of female apostates, 46–48, 85n30, 143n11, 188n54; converts to Judaism as minors, 77, 94; newborns, removal of unwanted hair from, 202; reverting children of apostates, 187–88, 189; taken from Jewish parents and converted, 154–55n31, 196
Christian authorities: conversion to Judaism and, 148–51; on forced versus willing conversion to Christianity, 154–55, 196, 199–200; Pope Paul II on just treatment of Jews, 196; reverting Jews and, 5–6, 10n20, 11n21, 27, 31, 40, 155, 160, 199–200, 203–4. *See also* Jewish-Christian relations
Christianity, converts to. *See* converts to Christianity; forced versus willing converts; rabbinic approaches to apostasy and reversion
circumcision: of converts to Judaism, 150, 151–52; *mohel*, apostate serving as, 101–2n61; of reverting children of apostates, 187–88, 189; uncircumcised apostate repenting and being circumcised, 188
Clement IV (pope), 155
converts to Christianity: children taken from Jewish parents, 154–55n31, 196; *conversos* in Spain/Sefardic diaspora, 189–92, 219. *See also* forced versus willing converts; rabbinic approaches to apostasy and reversion
converts to Islam, 179, 188–89
converts to Judaism: Christian responses to, 148–51; circumcision of, 150, 151–52; evolution of acceptance of, 138, 144–53; German versus northern French Tosafists on, 145–49, 152, 153; as minors, 77, 94; paramours of female Jewish apostates, 142–44; returning apostates compared to, in ritual immersion discussions, 12, 28–29, 32, 34, 36, 42, 51, 52, 67, 68; *yiḥus* (lineage), consideration of, 146–48
Crusades, 23, 153, 154n31, 156, 159, 163, 179
Cutheans, 107, 110, 120, 190

David b. Qalonymus of Muenzberg, 51n37
David ibn Zimra (Radbaz), 48–49n32, 188–90
dietary laws. *See* food and wine associated with apostate
divorce: agents of *gets*, apostates as, 135; apostate's ability to divorce Jewish wife, 76–77, 79n23, 94–97, 169n9, 214, 216; delivery of *get* to female apostates, 19, 210; Isserlein and contemporaries on, 198, 206, 209–10, 211; money-lending at interest compared, 105, 113; Rashi on, 9n18; of repentant apostate by Jewish husband, 135–36n60; in Spain/Sefardic diaspora, 174, 180n32, 188n54
Duran, Simeon b. Ẓemaḥ, 188n54
Duran, Solomon b. Simeon (Rashbash), 187–88

Eleazar b. Judah of Worms, 13, 49n33, 53–56, 148, 156, 205; *Sefer Roqeaḥ*, 54
Eleazar b. Samuel of Verona, 76, 78
Eleazar of Strasbourg, 71
Elḥanan b. *ha-Ri*, 30n5, 35–36n11, 111n15
Eli'ezer b. Joel *ha-Levi. See* Rabiah of Cologne
Eli'ezer b. Nathan of Mainz (Raban), 99n58, 104, 106, 114n21, 143n11, 147, 149
Eli'ezer b. Samuel of Metz: on *ḥaliẓah*, 84–85, 90, 95, 216; on inheritance by apostates, 117n26; on money-lending at interest, 105–7, 109, 112n17, 114, 214; narrowing of lenient approach to apostasy under, 214; *Sefer Yere'im*, 105, 106; on testimony by apostates, 132–33n43
Elyaqim *ha-Levi* of Speyer, 69n3
England, persecutions of Jews in, 153
Ephraim b. Isaac, 49n33, 74
Ephraim b. Jacob of Bonn, *Sefer Zekhirah*, 153
Esau and Jacob (biblical figures), 117, 192
Esther (biblical figure): return to Jewish husband, 18; ritual immersion of, 48, 49, 67
'eved kena'ani/shifḥah kena'anit (gentile servant/slave), 59–60, 61, 147, 176–77, 183, 191, 215
Evreux, Tosafist academy at, 161, 177, 178, 184
Evreux brothers (Moses, Isaac, and Samuel b. Shne'ur), 13, 60, 62, 64, 93, 178n29, 214–15
expulsions of Jews: Bruna and, 207n31; from France, 148n22; from German lands, 196; numbers of apostates and, 181
Ezra of Moncontour, 93
Falk, Joshua, 184n39
female apostates: children borne by, 46–48, 85n30, 143n11, 188n54; conversion of non-Jewish paramour, 142–44; German versus northern French Tosafists on, 144; *get*, delivery of, 19; *ḥaliẓah* for, 98–101; held captive by Christians, 45, 48n31, 49, 100–101; marriage to non-Jewish paramour, 138–44; promiscuity, association with, 98–100; return to Jewish husband by, 17–21, 48n31, 102n62, 135nn59–60, 138–39, 142, 199–200, 214; separation period before return to Jewish community, 52; sexual relations with non-Jews, consequences of, 138–44
First Crusade, 23, 153, 154n31, 156, 159, 163, 179
"flip-floppers"/suspect returnees, 44, 58, 63–65, 178n29, 199, 211
food and wine associated with apostate: Isaac b. Joseph of Corbeil on, 97; Isserlein and contemporaries on, 199, 208; Rashi on, 2–3, 19n33, 22, 28n3, 38–39; religious status of apostate and, 22; Ri of Dampierre on ritual immersion and, 28–40; Ritva on, 176; Riẓba on, 10, 12, 42; slaughtered meat, 104, 169, 170n10, 199; suspect returnees/religious "flip-floppers," 64–65; widening over time of gulf between apostate and Jewish community, 25–26
forced versus willing converts: children taken from Jewish parents, 154–55n31; Christian rules regarding, 154–55, 196, 199–200

forced versus willing converts (*continued*)
female returning apostates, sexual and marital status of, 17–21, 144; females held captive by Christians, 45, 48n31, 49, 100–101; Innocent III's expansion of what constitutes voluntary conversion, 154–55; Islam, forced converts to, 48–49n32; Isserlein and contemporaries on, 199–200; marriage between and witnessed by forced converts, 130–31n52; Rashi on, 1, 17–21; reasons for conversion to Christianity, 31, 44; ritual slaughter by forced apostate, 169, 170n10; Torah scroll written by apostate, 170n10
Fournier, Jacques (later Pope Benedict XII), 6n11
France: expulsions of Jews from, 148n22; list of rabbinic scholars by geographic region, 221–22; northern French Tosafists (*see specific Tosafists and subject matter*); persecutions of Jews in, 153
Frederick III (Holy Roman Emperor), 196

gamblers: apostates, gambling with, 208; repentance by, 40, 41–42
gender. *See* female apostates
gentile servant/slave of Jewish master, 59–60, 61, 147, 176–77, 183, 191, 215
Geonim: on *ḥaliẓah*, 15, 69–71, 79, 82n26, 86–87, 90, 92n44, 179n30, 180n32, 207; on inheritance by apostates, 117, 119, 120; on lashing of returning apostate, 173; on money-lending at interest to apostates, 105n6; on priestly blessing, 2n2, 123–24, 125, 127n40, 171; on ritual immersion, 4, 29, 179; Spanish rabbinic responsa and, 168–69, 171–75, 179, 191, 218
German lands: expulsions of Jews from, 196; list of rabbinic scholars by geographic region, 221–22; monks and friars, relations between Jewish communities and, 149n23; persecutions of Jews in, 153, 196
German Tosafists. *See specific Tosafists and subject matter*
Gershom b. Judah of Mainz, 2, 7, 9n18, 69n4, 117, 123, 125, 127n40, 213
Gershon, Isaac, 192–93
get/gittin. *See* divorce
Gezerat Vienna, 196, 198
Gregory IX (pope), 149n23, 154n30
Guibert of Nogent, 63n60, 158n36

Haggahot Mordekhai, 78, 81, 108, 139
Ḥakhmei Ẓarefat, 64
halakhah on apostasy and reversion, x–xi; consistency of, 137; Rashi's impact on, 1, 3; ritual immersion required by, in 16th and 17th centuries, 5, 6. *See also specific topics and rabbis*
ḥaliẓah, apostate's duty of, 15–17, 67–103; Abraham of Regensburg on, 16–17, 73–74, 85, 90, 93, 95, 206, 216; Barukh of Mainz on, 76, 78–85, 87, 88, 90, 93, 103, 108, 216, 217; Bonfant on, 76–77, 95, 101–2; changes over time regarding, 25, 216–17, 219; definition of *ḥaliẓah*, 68; divorce of Jewish wife by apostate and, 76–77, 79n23, 94–97; female apostate/

potentially unfaithful wife, *ḥaliẓah* for, 98–101; geonic leniency on, 15, 69–71, 79, 82n26, 86–87, 90, 92n44, 179n30, 180n32, 207; German Tosafists on, 67–97, 216; Ḥanan'el b. Ḥushi'el of Kairwan on, 80–81, 83n28, 87–88, 89; Hayyim Eli'ezer *Or Zarua'* on, 16n31, 69–73, 88–91, 216; Isaac b. Moses *Or Zarua'* on, 16n31, 69–73, 75, 85–92, 93, 97, 101, 108, 114, 156, 192, 206, 216; Isserlein and contemporaries on, 16, 25n47, 74n12, 206–7, 211, 219; Meir of Rothenburg on, 15–16, 72, 93, 108n12, 192–93; money-lending at interest and, 82–85, 90, 97–98, 103, 108, 111, 114; northern French Tosafists on, 68, 85, 90, 97, 179n30; *qiddushin* of apostates and, 9n18, 61n56, 76–77, 79n23, 80n24, 81–82, 83n28, 85, 88, 94–95, 216; Rashba on, 169n9, 192; Rashi on, 2, 9n18, 15–16, 68–71, 77, 90, 93, 108n12, 119, 169n9, 192–93, 206; RID on, 16n31, 91–92, 93n47, 102n62, 191, 216; Ritva on, 180n32; Simḥah of Speyer on, 17n31, 71–72, 216; in Spain/Sefardic diaspora, 174, 191–93; suspect returnees/religious "flip-floppers," 63n62, 68n1, 71; *yibbum* versus, 68n2, 71, 80, 87, 90, 99

Ḥanan'el b. Ḥushi'el of Kairwan, 80–81, 83n28, 87–88, 89, 188

Ḥayyim b. Ḥanan'el *Kohen*, 9n18

Ḥayyim Eli'ezer b. Isaac *Or Zarua'*: on conversion to Judaism, 151–52; on *ḥaliẓah*, 16n31, 69–73, 88–91, 216; on ritual immersion, 46; on sexual relations between female apostate and non-Jew, 141n7; on testimony of apostates, 133–34; on Torah scroll written by apostate, 170n10

ḥazaqah, 112–13n19

Henry IV (Holy Roman Emperor), 23

Hezekiah b. Manoaḥ (*Ḥizzequni* Torah commentary), 56–57, 68, 201n12, 216

ill-gotten gains, requirement to return, 23n42, 41–42, 129

immersion. *See* ritual immersion

impotent Jew allowed to marry *giyyoret*, 147–48n21

inheritance by apostates, 93n49, 117–23, 188n54, 208–9

inheritance from apostates, 115n25, 120

Innocent III (pope), 154–55

Isaac b. Abba Mari of Marseilles, 16–17n31, 94n50

Isaac b. Abraham. *See* Riẓba of Dampierre

Isaac b. Asher *ha-Levi* of Speyer (Riba), 9, 118–19, 175, 189

Isaac b. Jacob of Bohemia (Ri *ha-Lavan*), 75

Isaac b. Joseph of Corbeil, 10n20, 97–98, 142n9, 178, 215

Isaac b. Meir, 139n2

Isaac b. Mordekhai of Bohemia (Ribam), 20, 74, 138–39

Isaac b. Moses *Or Zarua'* of Vienna: on betrothed woman held captive by Christians, 100–101; on female apostate returning to Jewish husband, 19n34; on *ḥaliẓah*, 16n31, 69–73, 75, 85–92, 93, 97, 101, 108, 114, 156, 192, 206, 216; on inheritance by apostates, 118, 119–21; *mohel*, on apostate serving as, 101–2n61

Isaac b. Moses (*continued*)
on money-lending at interest, 112n19, 114; northern French studies of, 151n27; on priestly blessing, 125–27; on ritual immersion, 46, 49n33, 156
Isaac b. Samuel of Dampierre. *See* Ri of Dampierre
Isaac b. Sheshet (Rivash), 191, 193
Isaiah b. Mali di Trani. *See* RID
Ishmael (biblical figure), 117
Islam, apostatization to/reversion from, 179, 188–89
Isserlein, Israel, and his contemporaries, 195–211, 219; apostasy and reversion, incidence of, 197–99; *batra'ei*, self-image as, 195; on divorce, 198, 206, 209–10, 211; earlier Tosafist materials used by, 163, 195, 203, 211, 219; on food and wine associated with apostate, 199, 208; on forced versus willing converts, 199–200; on *ḥaliẓah*, 16, 25n47, 74n12, 206–7, 211, 219; on inheritance by apostates, 208–9; on money-lending at interest, 199, 208, 219; on penitential regimens, 204–6, 211; persecution and anti-semitism experienced by, 195–97; on *qiddushin* of apostates, 211; on religious status of apostates, 206, 208; on ritual immersion, 8, 200–204, 211; on suspect returnees, 199, 211; *Terumat ha-Deshen*, 196–98, 201, 210
Isserles, Moses, 5, 11n21, 25n47, 102n61, 183, 184n39, 196

Jacob and Esau (biblical figures), 117, 192
Jacob b. Asher of Toledo, *Arba'ah Turim*, 183
Jacob b. Meir Tam. *See* Rabbenu Tam
Jewish-Christian relations, 23–24, 137–63, 217; acceptance of converts to Judaism, 138, 144–53; chronological shifts in, 137–38; growth in Christian concern with converts/apostates, 154–55; Jews entering Christian homes, Ri on, 160n39; monks and friars, Jewish relations with, 149n23, 159n38; persecutions and anti-semitism, 153–54, 157–60, 163, 179–80, 195–97; porous nature of boundaries between communities, 30, 63–65; ritual immersion and, 155–57; sexual relations between female apostate and non-Jew, halakhic consequences of, 138–44; in Spain, 163; spiritual enemy, view of apostate as, 160–62
Joel b. Isaac *ha-Levi* of Bonn, 141, 147
John Duns Scotus, 155n31
Joseph b. Moses, *Leqet Yosher*, 198, 203, 205, 208
Joseph ibn Lev, 192
Joseph of Lincoln, 134–35
Judah b. Nathan (Rivan), 99
Judah *ha-Kohen, Sefer ha-Dinim*, 117, 188
Judah *he-Ḥasid*, 45, 55n43, 75
Judah of Meaux/Metz, 136n60
Judaism, converts to. *See* converts to Judaism

Karo, Yosef: *Beit Yosef*, 183; *Shulḥan 'Arukh*, 183, 209n38
Katz, Avigdor, of Vienna, 52, 68, 146n17
Katz, Jacob: on changes over time in rabbinical approaches, 23–26, 162, 217, 220; on *ḥaliẓah*, 15, 16, 25, 69, 74n12; on

inheritance by apostates, 117–18, 122; on Jewish-Christian relations, 23–24; on money-lending at interest, 14, 15, 105, 217; on Rashi versus Tosafist halakhists on ritual immersion, ix, x, 1, 4–5, 14, 17, 62; on testimony by apostates, 130n52; un-baptism, on ritual immersion as form of, 6
Katz, Zalman, of Nuremberg, 207, 209–10
kohen: female apostate returning as wife of, 140, 141n7; as part of married couple apostatizing together, 135n59; as returning apostate (*see* priestly blessing, resumption of pronouncing)
kosher food. *See* food and wine associated with apostate

Ladislaus (duke of Austria), 196
lashes administered to returning apostate, 7, 29n4, 43, 129, 166, 167, 173, 183, 205
lineage *(yiḥus)* and converts to Judaism, 146–48
Louis VII (king of France), 157, 160
Luria, Solomon (Maharshal), 5, 170n10; *Yam shel Shelomeh*, 183

Maggid Mishneh, 192
Maharam. *See* Meir b. Barukh of Rothenburg
Maharil (Jacob Moelin), 207, 208n38, 209, 210
Maharshal. *See* Luria, Solomon
Maḥzor Vitry, 70
Maimonides, 124n37, 172, 180n32, 188
Mainz, Council of (1233), 149n23
marriage questions: economic aspects of marriage, apostasy terminating, 118n27; forced converts, marriage between, witnessed by forced converts, 130–31n52; impotent Jew allowed to marry *giyyoret*, 147–48n21; non-Jewish paramour, female apostate's marriage to, 138–44; return to Jewish husband by female apostate, 17–21, 48n31, 102n62, 135nn59–60, 138–39, 142, 199–200, 214; validity of marriage between apostate and Jewess, 125; *yibbum*, 68n2, 71, 80, 87, 90, 99, 182, 216, 218; *ziqah*, 2, 15, 68, 70, 72, 77, 79–81, 86–89, 91, 109n13, 191, 192. *See also* divorce; *ḥaliẓah*, apostate's duty of; *qiddushin* of apostates
married couples apostatizing together: *kohen* in, 135n59; presumed not to have strayed sexually, 52n38, 135n59; ritual immersion for, 58
Martin V (pope), 198
meat, slaughtered, 104, 169, 170n10, 199
Meir b. Barukh of Rothenburg (Maharam): on converts to Judaism, 150–51; on *ḥaliẓah*, 15–16, 72, 93, 108n12, 192–93; Isserlein and contemporaries, as predecessor of, 195, 219; on priestly blessing, 129n49; Rabbenu Pereẓ and, 178; on ritual immersion, 4, 7, 20, 57n46, 58–62, 215; on suspect returnees/religious "flip-floppers," 63, 199n9
Menaḥem b. Pereẓ of Joigny, 146n17
Menaḥem b. Solomon *ha-Meiri*, 140n4, 181
Menasheh son of Hezekiah (biblical figure), 54
Meshullam b. Qalonymus, 117, 188
meshummad, as term, 3–4n5

Mintz, Judah, of Padua, 78, 79n23, 81
Mizraḥi, Eliyyahu, 79n23
miẓvah, ritual immersion for returning apostates as, 29, 32n7, 33, 34, 44, 172, 177
Moelin, Jacob (Maharil), 207, 208n38, 209, 210
mohel, apostate serving as, 101–2n61
money-lending at interest to apostates, 14–15, 103–16; borrowing from an apostate at interest versus, 110, 116; brotherhood factor in, 22n42, 106, 107, 115, 116, 190; changes over time regarding, 215; geonim on, 105n6; German Tosafists on, 112–14, 216–17; *ḥaliẓah* and, 82–85, 90, 97–98, 103, 108, 111, 114; Isserlein and contemporaries on, 199, 208, 219; Northern French Tosafists on, 103–12, 114–16; Rashi on, 2, 14, 93n47, 104, 105n6, 106, 109n14, 115, 174, 179; in Spain/Sefardic diaspora, 169n9, 174–75, 179–80, 182, 187, 188n54, 189–90
money-lending at interest to other Jews, 41–42
Mordekhai b. Hillel. See *Sefer Mordekhai*
Moses b. Jacob of Coucy: on *ḥaliẓah*, 81; on inheritance by apostates, 117n26, 121; Jewish-Christian relations and, 139, 140; on money-lending at interest, 106–8, 114, 115, 215, 217; on priestly blessing, 128–29; on *qiddushin* and *gittin*, 215; on ritual immersion, 50n35, 214; *Sefer Miẓvot Gadol*, 106, 107, 108, 121, 139, 188, 190, 217; Spanish/Sefardic rabbis and, 188, 190
Moses b. Yom Tov of London, 140–41n6
Moses *ha-Darshan* of Narbonne, 8, 56, 200, 201n11, 203
Moses *ha-Kohen* of Mainz, 112n17
Moses of Zurich, 50–51nn34–35
Moses Zaltman b. Joel, 74
mumar, as term, 3–4n5

Naḥmanides. *See* Ramban
Naḥshon Gaon, 89, 93n47
Nathan b. Yeḥi'el of Rome, 96n53
Natronai Gaon, 2n2, 123–24, 125, 171
northern French Tosafists. *See specific Tosafists and subject matter*

Odo of Tournai/Cambrai, 158

Paltoi Gaon, 134n58
paring nails and shaving prior to ritual immersion, 5, 8, 50, 51, 57, 67–68, 200–204, 215
Paul II (pope), 196
penitential regimens: Eleazar of Worms on, 54–55, 56, 205; Isserlein and contemporaries on, 204–6, 211; Judah *he-Ḥasid* on, 45n21; lashes, 7, 29n4, 43, 129, 166, 167, 173, 183, 205; ritual immersion, as repentance, 28, 32, 34, 35, 37n12, 38, 40–43, 46, 49–50, 54–55, 60–62, 67; *Sefer Ḥasidim* on, 12; Simḥah of Speyer on, 49
Pereẓ b. Elijah of Corbeil, 13, 60, 62, 177–78, 215
Peter the Venerable of Cluny, 157–59; *Against the Inveterate Obduracy of the Jews*, 158
Philip Augustus (king of France), 148n22
pietism and Pietists, 11, 45, 49, 53, 58, 204, 205
priestly blessing, resumption of pronouncing, 123–29; forced versus willing converts, 19;

geonim on, 2n2, 123–24, 125, 127n40, 171; Rashi on, 2, 9n18, 18; in Spain, 171
purification, ritual immersion as, 7, 8, 38, 45, 47–48, 49, 52, 56, 200–203

qiddushin of apostates: female betrothed held captive by Christians, 100–101; *ḥaliẓah* and, 9n18, 61n56, 76–77, 79n23, 80n24, 81–82, 83n28, 85, 88, 94–95, 216; Isserlein and contemporaries on, 211; money-lending at interest and, 105, 113, 114; Rashba on, 169n9; Rashi on, 3, 9n18; ritual immersion and, 61n56; Ritva on, 180n32; in Spain/Sefardic diaspora, 174, 181–82, 187, 188n52, 188n54; testimony of apostates and, 131n53, 133

Rabad (Abraham b. David of Posquières), 169n9
Raban (Eli'ezer b. Nathan of Mainz), 99n58, 104, 106, 114n21, 143n11, 147, 149
Rabbenu Ḥanan'el, 132n54
Rabbenu Tam (Jacob b. Meir Tam): Christian wine, on handling of, 159; on divorce, 79n23, 96n53, 100n58, 169n9, 214; on female apostates, 20–21, 138–44; *ḥaliẓah* and, 74, 75, 84, 85, 169n9; later Tosafists influenced by, 215; on money-lending at interest, 93n47, 105, 109, 110, 112n17, 115, 174, 180, 187, 213–14; narrowing of lenient approach to apostasy under, 213–14; RID and, 92; ritual immersion and, 9n18, 33n8, 36n11, 37n12
rabbinic approaches to apostasy and reversion, ix–xi, 1–26, 213–20; changes over time in, 8–14, 23–26, 213–20; female apostates' return to Jewish husband, 17–21; frequency of apostasy and reversion incidents, 40, 96n53; *ḥaliẓah*, 15–17, 67–103 (see also *ḥaliẓah*, apostate's duty of); inheritance by apostates, 93n49, 117–23, 188n54, 208–9; inheritance from apostates, 115n25, 120; Isserlein and contemporaries, 195–211, 219 (*see also* Isserlein, Israel, and his contemporaries); Jewish-Christian relations affecting, 23–24, 137–63, 217 (*see also* Jewish-Christian relations); list of rabbinic scholars by geographic region, 221–22; money-lending and, 14–15, 103–16 (*see also* money-lending at interest to apostates); priestly blessing and, 123–29 (*see also* priestly blessing, resumption of pronouncing); Rashi's influence on Tosafists regarding, ix–x, 1–4, 21, 161, 163, 179, 213–14; religious status of apostate Jews, 21–22; requirements for return, 7, 22, 23, 42–43; ritual immersion, ix–x, 4–14, 27–65 (*see also* ritual immersion); in Spain/Sefardic diaspora, 165–93, 218–19 (*see also* Spain/Sefardic diaspora); testimony of apostates, 19n33, 58, 129–35; timeline for changes and reevaluations in, 137; widening over time of gulf between apostate and Jewish community, 25–26. *See also specific rabbis*

Rabiah of Cologne (Eli'ezer b. Joel *ha-Levi*): on divorce, 216; on divorce of Jewish wife by apostate, 95–97; on inheritance by apostate, 93n49, 118–20; on inheritance from apostates, 120; on marriage between apostate and Jewess, 125; on money-lending at interest, 85, 104–5n4, 112–13, 216–17; on priestly blessing, 125–29; on ritual immersion, 13, 50–51, 56, 67, 68, 118–19, 215–16; on testimony of apostates, 133–34; on tribunal appearance, 176; on verification and performance requirements for returning apostates, 135n59
Radbaz (David ibn Zimra), 48–49n32, 188–90
Ramah (Meir *ha-Levi* Abulafia of Toledo), 185n43
Rambam. *See* Maimonides
Ramban (Naḥmanides): frequency of conversion in Spain and, 185; on inheritance by apostates, 188; on money-lending at interest, 180, 187, 190; on priestly blessing, 124n36; on requirements for returning apostate, 170–71; on ritual immersion, 59, 173–75; Tosafist material, access to, 178
Rash *mi-Shanẓ*. *See* Samson b. Abraham of Sens
Rashba (Solomon b. Abraham ibn Adret of Barcelona): frequency of conversions and, 185; on *ḥaliẓah*, 64, 192; on money-lending at interest, 190; on *qiddushin* of apostates, 187; on ritual immersion, 6–7, 14n26, 166–69, 174, 179, 183; *Teshuvot ha-Rashba*, 166; Tosafist material, access to, 178
Rashbam (Samuel b. Meir), 9n18, 114n19, 188
Rashbash (Solomon b. Simeon Duran), 187–88
Rashi (Solomon b. Isaac): on continuous Jewishness of returning apostates, ix–x, 1–4, 7, 8, 65; on divorce, 9n18; on female apostates' sexual relations with non-Jews, 17–21, 138n1, 143; on food and wine associated with apostate, 2–3, 19n33, 22, 28n3, 38–39; on forced versus willing converts, 1, 17–21; on *ḥaliẓah*, 2, 9n18, 15–16, 68–71, 77, 90, 93, 108n12, 119, 169n9, 192–93, 206; increasing number of apostates and, 156; on inheritance by apostates, 117–18, 119, 121; on inheritance from an apostate, 115n25; Isserlein and contemporaries and, 201n11, 203, 206, 208, 219; on marriage between forced converts, witnessed by forced converts, 130–31n52; on money-lending at interest, 2, 14, 93n47, 104, 105n6, 106, 109n14, 115, 174, 179, 189; Moses *ha-Darshan* of Narbonne and, 201n11; on priestly blessing, 123; on property of apostate in hands of other Jews, 115n25, 134n59; on *qiddushin* of apostates, 3, 9n18; reasons for approach of, 23; on religious status of apostate Jews, 22, 115; on ritual immersion, 8, 9n18, 13, 60, 203; on testimony of

apostates, 19n33, 129–31, 133; Tosafists, influence on, ix–x, 1–4, 21, 161, 163, 179, 213–14
Rav Ashi, 80, 87, 88
Rav *Kohen Ẓedeq* Gaon, 95, 96n53
Rava, 80, 87, 88
religious "flip-floppers"/suspect returnees, 44, 58, 63–65, 178n29, 199, 211
religious status of apostate Jews, 21–22, 115, 158–74, 176–87, 206, 208
repentance. *See* penitential regimens
requirements for return, 7, 22, 23, 42–43
reversion. *See* rabbinic approaches to apostasy and reversion
Ri *ha-Lavan* (Isaac b. Jacob of Bohemia), 75
Ri of Dampierre (Isaac b. Samuel): Christian wine, on handling of, 159; on converts to Judaism, 145–47, 152; on female apostates' return to Jewish husband, 20, 139–40, 214; on Jews entering Christian homes, 160n39; later Tosafists influenced by, 214, 215; on money-lending at interest, 104n2, 107, 109–12, 113, 114n21, 116, 174, 189, 213–14; narrowing of lenient approach to apostasy under, 213–14; on ritual acts performed by returning apostates, 30n5, 134n59, 172; on ritual immersion, 9, 12–13, 27–40, 44, 61, 172–74, 203, 214; Solomon of Montpellier compared, 172–73; on suspect returnees/religious "flip-floppers," 63, 65; on tribunal appearance, 176; Yeḥi'el b. Joseph of Paris and, 117n26
Riba (Isaac b. Asher *ha-Levi* of Speyer), 9, 118–19, 175, 189
Ribam (Isaac b. Mordekhai of Bohemia), 20, 74, 138–39
RID (Isaiah b. Mali di Trani): on *ḥaliẓah*, 16n31, 91–92, 93n47, 102n62, 191, 216; on money-lending at interest, 109n14; Rashi, influence of, 161n42; on sexual relations between female apostate and non-Jew, 143; on testimony of apostates, 132–33
Rif (Isaac b. Jacob Alfasi), 80, 133n54, 134n58, 182
Rigaud, Eudes, 64
Rigord of St. Denis, 148n22
ritual immersion, ix–x, 4–14, 27–65; Avigdor Katz of Vienna on, 52, 68; Bernard Gui on, 5–6, 10n20, 53, 165, 167; development of, over time, 8–14, 53, 62–65, 214–16; Eleazar of Worms on, 53–56, 156; of Esther, 48, 49, 67; of *'eved kena'ani/shifḥah kena'anit* (gentile servant/slave), 59–60, 61, 147, 176–77, 183, 191, 215; evidence for popular belief in need for, 4–8; geonic period, not required in, 4, 29, 179; German Tosafists on, 45–56, 58–62, 215–16; *Ḥizzequni* Torah commentary on, 56–57, 68; Isserlein and contemporaries on, 8, 200–204, 211; Isserles and Sirkes on, 184n39; Jewish-Christian relations and, 155–57; Levites after golden calf incident and, 56–57, 200, 202; Meir of Rothenburg on, 4, 7, 57n46, 58–62, 215; as *miẓvah*, 29, 32n7, 33, 34, 44, 172, 177; northern French Tosafists on, 27–45, 56–57, 214–15

ritual immersion (*continued*)
as purification, 7, 8, 38, 45, 47–48, 49, 52, 56, 200–203; Rabiah of Cologne on, 13, 50–51, 56, 67, 68, 118–19, 215–16; Rashi on, 8, 9n18, 13, 60, 203; as repentance, 28, 32, 34, 35, 37n12, 38, 40–43, 46, 49–50, 54–55, 60–62, 67; Ri of Dampierre on, 9, 12–13, 27–40, 44, 61, 172–74, 203, 214; Riẓba on, 9–10, 12, 34, 40–45, 53, 173, 214; Samson of Sens on, 12, 29n4, 35n10, 41, 42–44, 51, 214; shaving and paring nails prior to, 5, 8, 50, 51, 57, 67–68, 200–204, 215; Simḥah of Speyer on, ix, 13, 34, 45–52, 55n43, 56, 61, 67, 156, 175, 189n55, 202, 215; in Spain/Sefardic diaspora, 165–68, 171–79, 182, 183, 184n39, 186n46, 188–89, 190–91; suspect returnees/religious "flip-floppers," 44, 58, 63–65; *Tosafot Shitah* requiring, 60–62; tribunal, appearance before, 9–10, 28–29, 32–33, 35, 37, 40–43, 50, 52, 60n54, 61, 67, 215; as un-baptism, 5, 6, 49, 56, 155, 161, 165–66, 175; as verification, 28–30, 34, 35, 38–45, 51, 61, 206
ritual murder charges (blood libel), 153
Ritva (Yom Tov b. Abraham Ishvilli), 7, 14n26, 59, 60, 166–68, 176–83, 185–87; *Ḥiddushei ha-Ritva*, 178, 183
Rivan (Judah b. Nathan), 99
Rivash (Isaac b. Sheshet), 191, 193
Riẓba of Dampierre (Isaac b. Abraham): on food and wine associated with apostate, 10, 12, 37n12; on *ḥaliẓah*, 179n30; on money-lending at interest, 179; on ritual immersion, 9–10, 12, 34, 40–45, 53, 173, 214; Spanish/Sefardic rabbis and, 173, 179, 180n31, 187; on testimony of apostates, 129; on tribunal appearance, 9; in Vercelli C1 ms., 36n11
rodef, 14n27
Rosh (Asher b. Yeḥi'el), 97n53, 142, 185n43, 188, 202
Rupert of Deutz, 157, 158–59

Sabbath observance, 30n5, 41, 43, 64–65, 191
Samson b. Abraham of Sens (Rash *mi-Shanẓ*): on formalization of apostate's return, 176; on money-lending at interest, 108n13; on priestly blessing, 128; on ritual immersion, 12, 29n4, 35n10, 41, 42–44, 51, 52n38, 214; on testimony of apostates, 134–35n59
Samson b. Joseph of Falaise, 108n13
Samuel b. Abraham *ha-Levi* of Worms (Bonfant), 47–49, 76–77, 95, 101–2, 175, 202
Samuel b. Meir (Rashbam), 9n18, 114n19, 188
Samuel b. Solomon of Falaise, 93, 106, 108n13, 111–12, 115, 215
Samuel father of Rabbenu Tam, 109n14
Schlettstadt, Samuel, 108–9nn12–13
Schwabenspiegel, 155
Second Crusade, 159
Sefardim. *See* Spain/Sefardic diaspora
Sefer Ausufot, 149–50, 152
Sefer Basar 'al Gabbei Geḥalim, 85
Sefer ha-'Ittur, 192
Sefer ha-Pardes, 17
Sefer Ḥasidim, 4, 10–12, 44, 147, 150
Sefer Miẓvot Gadol. *See* Moses b. Jacob of Coucy

Sefer Mordekhai, 17, 34, 37, 60, 70, 73, 74, 98, 139, 177, 192
Sefer Or Zarua'. *See* Isaac b. Moses *Or Zarua'* of Vienna
Semaq mi-Ẓurikh, 50, 205
servant/slave, gentile, of Jewish master, 59–60, 61, 147, 176–77, 183, 191, 215
sexual relations. *See* female apostates; marriage questions
Shabbetai b. Meir *ha-Kohen* (*Shakh*), 5
shaving and paring nails prior to ritual immersion, 5, 8, 50, 51, 57, 67–68, 200–204, 215
Shemayah (student of Rashi), 109n14
Sherira Gaon, 192
Shlomo Yitzchaki. *See* Rashi
Simḥah b. Samuel of Speyer: on divorce of Jewish wife by apostate, 76–77, 216; on *ḥaliẓah*, 17n31, 71–72, 216; on inheritance by apostates, 120–21; on money-lending at interest, 114, 216; penitential regimens required by, 49; on priestly blessing, 126, 128; RID studying with, 92; on ritual immersion, ix, 13, 34, 45–52, 55n43, 56, 61, 67, 156, 175, 189n55, 202, 215; Spanish/Sefardic rabbis and, 175, 189; on suspect returnees/religious "flip-floppers," 63n62; on testimony of apostates, 132
Sirkes, Yo'el, 5, 25, 184n39
Sirleon, Judah b. Isaac, 46, 112n17
slaughtered meat, 104, 169, 170n10, 199
slave/servant, gentile, of Jewish master, 59–60, 61, 147, 176–77, 183, 191, 215
Solomon b. Abraham ibn Adret of Barcelona. *See* Rashba
Solomon b. Abraham of Montpellier, 124n36, 129–30n50, 170–72, 175, 178, 181
Solomon b. Judah of Dreux, 112n17
Spain/Sefardic diaspora, 165–93, 218–19; *conversos*, 189–92, 219; Evreux, influence of Tosafist academy at, 177, 178, 184; frequency of apostasy and reversion in, 181, 183, 184–85, 218; geonic responsa and, 168–69, 171–75, 179, 191, 218; on *ḥaliẓah*, 174, 191–93; Jewish-Christian relations and, 163; knowledge of Tosafist/Ashkenazic materials, 179–93, 218–19; list of rabbinic scholars by geographic region, 222; money-lending at interest in, 169n9, 174–75, 179–80, 182, 187, 188n54, 189–90; priestly blessing, 171; *qiddushin* of apostates in, 174, 181–82, 187, 188n52, 188n54; religious status of returning apostate in, 168–74, 186–87; ritual immersion in, 165–68, 171–79, 182, 183, 184n39, 186n46, 188–89, 190–91; Sefardic diaspora in Northern Africa and Turkey, 187–93; sexual/marital relations of apostate, 174
spiritual enemy, view of apostate as, 160–62
suspect returnees/religious "flip-floppers," 44, 58, 63–65, 178n29, 199, 211

testimony: of apostates, 19n33, 58, 129–35, 181n33; forced converts, marriage between, witnessed by forced converts, 130–31n52; of former gamblers, 40
tevilah. *See* ritual immersion
Third Crusade, 153
Thomas Aquinas, 154n31

tiqqunei teshuvah, 49, 53–55, 156, 204, 211
Torah scroll written by apostate, 170n10
Tosafists, Rashi's influence on, ix–x, 1–4, 21, 161, 163, 179, 213–14. *See also specific Tosafists*
Tosafot Shitah, 60–62, 177–79, 182, 184, 218–19
Treves, Yo*h*anan, 209
tribunal, appearance before: ritual immersion and, 9–10, 28–29, 32–33, 35, 37, 40–43, 50, 52, 60n54, 61, 67, 215; in Spain, 172, 175, 184n39, 187–88
Tuvyah b. Elijah of Vienne, 109n13, 216

un-baptism, ritual immersion as, 5, 6, 49, 56, 155, 161, 165–66, 175

verification, ritual immersion as, 28–30, 34, 35, 38–45, 51, 61, 206

Weil, Jacob, 210
willing converts. *See* forced versus willing converts
wine: associated with apostate (*see* food and wine associated with apostate); Christian wine, Jewish handling of, 159
witnesses. *See* testimony
women. *See* female apostates
written document or certificate of reversion, 10n20, 32

Yedidyah b. Israel of Nuremberg, 96–97n53, 131
Yeḥi'el b. Joseph of Paris, 93, 115–16, 135, 142, 178, 214, 215
Yehosefyah *ha-Ger*, 146n17
Yeroḥam b. Meshullam, 185n43
yibbum, 68n2, 71, 80, 87, 90, 99, 182, 216, 218
yiḥus (lineage) and converts to Judaism, 146–48
Yom Tov b. Abraham Ishvilli. *See* Ritva
Yom Tov b. Judah, 99–100n58
Yonah b. Abraham of Gerona, 64–65, 169n9, 170, 178n29
Yosef b. Isaac *Bekhor Shor* of Orleans, 37n12
Yosef b. Samuel Tov Elem, 124n35
Yosef Ḥaviva of Barcelona, *Nimmuqei Yosef*, 4n7, 59, 60, 182–84, 186–87, 191, 218

Ẓaḥalon, Yom Tov b. Moses, 190–92
Zedekiah b. Abraham *ha-Rofe*, 46
Ẓemaḥ Gaon, 43
ziqah, 2, 15, 68, 70, 72, 77, 79–81, 86–89, 91, 109n13, 191, 192

ABOUT THE AUTHOR

Ephraim Kanarfogel is the E. Billi Ivry University Professor of Jewish History, Literature, and Law at Yeshiva University. He is also the author of the award-winning books *Jewish Education and Society in the High Middle Ages* (1992), *Peering through the Lattices: Mystical, Magical, and Pietistic Dimensions in the Tosafist Period* (2000), and *The Intellectual History and Rabbinic Culture of Medieval Ashkenaz* (2013), all published by Wayne State University Press.

www.ingramcontent.com/pod-product-compliance
Lightning Source LLC
Chambersburg PA
CBHW021943240426
43668CB00037B/688
* 9 7 8 0 8 1 4 3 4 8 2 4 6 *